Lecture Notes in Computer Science   16438

Founding Editors

Gerhard Goos
Juris Hartmanis

Editorial Board Members

Elisa Bertino, *Purdue University, West Lafayette, IN, USA*
Wen Gao, *Peking University, Beijing, China*
Bernhard Steffen, *TU Dortmund University, Dortmund, Germany*
Moti Yung, *Columbia University, New York, NY, USA*

Anna Dipace · Carla Limongelli · Mirko Marras ·
Silvio Marcello Pagliara

Editors

Artificial Intelligence with and for Learning Sciences

Past, Present, and Future Horizons

Second Workshop, WAILS 2025
Cagliari, Italy, December 10–12, 2025
Proceedings

 Springer

Editors
Anna Dipace (ID)
Pegaso Online University
Naples, Italy

Carla Limongelli (ID)
Roma Tre University
Rome, Italy

Mirko Marras (ID)
University of Cagliari
Cagliari, Italy

Silvio Marcello Pagliara (ID)
University of Cagliari
Cagliari, Italy

ISSN 0302-9743   ISSN 1611-3349 (electronic)
Lecture Notes in Computer Science
ISBN 978-3-032-17603 5   ISBN 978-3-032-17604-2 (eBook)
https://doi.org/10.1007/978-3-032-17604-2

This Springer imprint is published by the registered company Springer Nature Switzerland AG
The registered company address is: Gewerbestrasse 11, 6330 Cham, Switzerland

If disposing of this product, please recycle the paper.

Preface

This volume of the *Lecture Notes in Computer Science (LNCS)* series contains the post-workshop proceedings of the *2nd International Workshop on Artificial Intelligence with and for Learning Sciences (WAILS 2025)*, held on December 10–12, 2025, in Cagliari, Italy. Building on the success of its inaugural edition, WAILS 2025 continued to serve as a high-quality international forum at the intersection of artificial intelligence and the learning sciences. The workshop brought together researchers and practitioners from computer science, education, cognitive science, psychology, sociology, human–computer interaction, economics, and related disciplines, with the goal of fostering a productive dialogue on how artificial intelligence can support, transform, and be shaped by human learning.

The workshop received twenty submissions across the full and short papers track, all of which were accepted, and four submissions to the doctoral symposium track, three of which were accepted. Each contribution went through a single-blind review process, with on average three evaluations provided by members of the program committee. The accepted papers reflect the methodological and thematic breadth of contemporary research, spanning creativity-oriented and multimodal learning environments powered by artificial intelligence, fairness-aware and trustworthy educational technologies, teacher training, digital literacy, learning analytics, and inclusive and accessible learning ecosystems, among others. Taken together, these contributions highlight both the maturity of ongoing research and the promising new directions that are emerging.

The program featured three keynote talks, four thematic paper sessions, a doctoral symposium, and a special session. The workshop opened with a keynote talk by *Beata Klebanov* (ETS Research Institute, USA), who offered a decade-long perspective on language technologies for learner modeling. The first paper session focused on artificial-intelligence-enabled creative, personalized, and immersive learning, including studies on generative technologies, blockchain-supported metaverse ecosystems, mental-health-aware interventions, blended programming pedagogy, and translation of questions to structured queries.

The second day began with a keynote talk by *Giovanni Adorni* (University of Genoa, Italy), who examined cyber humanism as a framework for reclaiming human agency in learning environments augmented through artificial intelligence. This was followed by the doctoral consortium, featuring work on artificial intelligence literacy, retrieval-enhanced digital literacy, and interactions between students and artificial-intelligence-driven tools in mathematics classrooms. Subsequent sessions addressed responsible and trustworthy educational technologies, including confidentiality in retrieval-augmented generation, ethics literacy, calibration for fairness, self-regulated learning, and course recommendation in low-resource professional settings. The afternoon session focused on inclusion and accessibility, with contributions examining embodied frameworks for inclusion, universal design for learning, support for neurodivergent learners in virtual reality, inclusive learning ecosystems, and the experiences of female programming learners in Afghanistan. The special session finally offered an applied perspective, presenting institutional needs and real-world deployments of artificial-intelligence-supported educational solutions.

The final day featured a keynote talk by *Maria Ranieri* (University of Florence, Italy), who explored pedagogical paradoxes associated with artificial intelligence in education and outlined a framework for sustainable human–machine cooperation. The closing paper session addressed teaching innovation and professional development, examining virtual laboratories, teacher training, biopedagogical approaches, predictive technologies for bias awareness, and the preparation of prospective primary school teachers to teach artificial intelligence.

We express our sincere gratitude to all authors for their submissions, to the reviewers for their thorough and constructive feedback, and to all participants for their active engagement during the workshop. We also thank the University of Cagliari for its support. The continued success of WAILS reflects the growing international interest in bridging artificial intelligence and the learning sciences. We hope that this volume will serve as a valuable resource for researchers, practitioners, and students, and we look forward to future editions of the workshop.

December 2025

Anna Dipace
Carla Limongelli
Mirko Marras
Silvio Marcello Pagliara

Organization

General Chairs

Gianni Fenu   University of Cagliari, Italy
Antonello Mura   University of Cagliari, Italy

Program Chairs

Carla Limongelli   Roma Tre University, Italy
Mirko Marras   University of Cagliari, Italy

Doctoral Symposium Chairs

Anna Dipace   Pegaso Online University, Italy
Silvio Marcello Pagliara   University of Cagliari, Italy

Special Session Chairs

Daniela Casiraghi   Polytechnic of Milan, Italy
Giacomo Fiumara   University of Messina, Italy

Publicity Chairs

Emiliana Murgia   University of Genoa, Italy
Viviana Pentangelo   University of Salerno, Italy

Proceedings Chairs

Daniele Agostini   University of Trento, Italy
Daniela Rotelli   Sorbonne Université, France

Web Chair

Francesca Maridina Malloci   University of Cagliari, Italy

Local Organization Chairs

Gianmarco Bonavolontà   University of Cagliari, Italy
Giacomo Medda   University of Cagliari, Italy

Program Committee Members

Paola Barra   Parthenope University of Naples, Italy
Mario Luca Bernardi   University of Sannio, Italy
Geoffray Bonnin   Université de Lorraine, France
Thierry Bouwmans   La Rochelle Université, France
Antonio Bucchiarone   University of L'Aquila, Italy
Salvatore Calderaro   University of Palermo, Italy
Maria Cristina Carrisi   University of Cagliari, Italy
Maria Concetta Carruba   Pegaso Online University, Italy
Jade Mai Cock   EPFL, Switzerland
Lea Cohausz   University of Mannheim, Germany
Rossana Damiano   University of Turin, Italy
Daniele Di Mitri   DIPF, Germany
Pio Alfredo Di Tore   University of Cassino, Italy
Yannis Dimitriadis   Universidad de Valladolid, Spain
Martin Drlik   Constantine the Philosopher University in Nitra, Slovakia
Alessio Ferrato   Roma Tre University, Italy
Filomena Ferrucci   University of Salerno, Italy
David Freire-Obregón   Universidad de Las Palmas, Spain
Carmine Gravino   University of Salerno, Italy
Martin Hlosta   FFHS, Switzerland
Srecko Joksimovic   University of South Australia, Australia
Sébastien Lallé   Sorbonne University, France
Qiang Ma   Kyoto Institute of Technology, Japan
Elisa Marengo   University of Turin, Italy
Donatella Merlini   University of Florence, Italy
Alberto Montresor   University of Trento, Italy
Tanya Nazaretsky   EPFL, Switzerland
Fabio Palomba   University of Salerno, Italy

Luc Paquette	University of Illinois Urbana-Champaign, USA
Livia Petti	University of Molise, Italy
Daniela Rotelli	Sorbonne Université, France
Daniele Schicchi	CNR-ITD, Italy
Manuel Striani	University of Piemonte Orientale, Italy
Davide Taibi	CNR-ITD, Italy
Marco Temperini	Sapienza University of Rome, Italy
Michele Todino	University of Salerno, Italy
Ilaria Torre	University of Genoa, Italy
Ilaria Viola	University of Salerno, Italy
Emanuela Zappalà	University of Salerno, Italy

Keynote Talks

Cyber Humanism in Education: Reclaiming Agency through AI and Learning Sciences

Giovanni Adorni

University of Genoa, Italy

Generative Artificial Intelligence (GenAI) is rapidly reshaping how students and educators read, write, code, and collaborate, embedding AI into everyday learning workflows. This shift raises concerns about epistemic automation, cognitive offloading, intensified workload, and the de-professionalisation of teachers, while also opening opportunities for scaffolding metacognition, formative feedback, and inquiry-based learning. Existing digital and AI competence frameworks acknowledge AI literacy, but tend to frame AI as a set of tools to be used responsibly rather than as part of the cognitive and institutional infrastructures of education. In this keynote, I introduce Cyber Humanism in Education as a lens to reclaim human agency in AI-rich learning environments. Cyber Humanism views AI models, platforms, and data ecosystems as cognitive infrastructures that co-produce knowledge and shape which voices and problems become visible. Building on the Learning Sciences, we articulate three pillars: reflexive competence (knowing when and how to delegate cognitive work to AI), algorithmic citizenship (rights and responsibilities in relation to algorithmic systems), and dialogic design (treating AI as a fallible interlocutor in multi-voiced knowledge-building dialogues). I map major competence and policy frameworks (DigComp 3.0, DigCompEdu and its AI supplements, UNESCO AI competency frameworks, OECD/EC AI Literacy) onto these pillars, highlighting gaps around infrastructural participation, governance, and the role of natural language as a modelling medium. I then outline higher-education cases where a Conversational AI Educator certification pathway and Prompt-Based Learning activities make human–AI co-authorship visible, turning prompts and AI outputs into shared objects of ref lection and assessment. The keynote concludes with an agenda for the Learning Sciences that links micro-level interaction with macro questions of infrastructure, labour, and governance within the WAILS Cagliari 2025 initiative. The paper describing the work presented in this keynote is available at: arXiv:2512.16701.

Language Technology for Learner Modeling

Beata Klebanov

ETS Research Institute, USA

Language is a medium of much of human learning; as such, automated analysis of language at scale can help organize, facilitate, and assess learning. In the presentation, we will take stock of a decade of research that utilized natural language processing to aid learner modeling research, consider some examples from my research on supporting reading development with language technology, as well as look forward to new directions at the intersection of language technology and learning sciences enabled by the dramatic advances in conversational AI.

Beyond the Paradoxes of Artificial Intelligence in Education: Toward a Pedagogically Sustainable Human–Machine Cooperation

Maria Ranieri

University of Florence, Italy

The integration of Artificial Intelligence into educational processes opens promising yet complex horizons, confronting pedagogy with a series of paradoxes: automation vs autonomy, mimesis vs trust, opacity vs transparency, efficiency vs reflexivity. These tensions reveal not only technological dilemmas but also epistemological and ethical questions about the meaning of learning and the role of the human in knowledge production. This presentation examines such paradoxes through the lenses of learning theories and critical pedagogy, proposing a framework for human–machine cooperation grounded in transparency, responsibility, and participation. In this view, AI does not replace but rather augments human intelligence, supporting educational practices that foster autonomy, creativity, and critical awareness. The goal is to outline a pedagogical horizon in which AI becomes not a technology of control but a space for co-construction, reflection, and shared meaning-making in learning.

Contents

Adaptive Mental Health Interventions: Integrating VR and Generative AI in Learning Environments

Attilio Della Greca[1], Ilaria Amaro[1], and Paola Barra[2]($\boxtimes$)

[1] University of Salerno, Salerno, Italy
{adellagreca,iamaro}@unisa.it
[2] Parthenope University of Naples, Naples, Italy
paola.barra@uniparthenope.it

Abstract. This paper examines how Virtual Reality (VR) and Generative AI (GenAI) can address the growing mental health crisis among students when traditional support systems are overwhelmed. VR creates immersive therapeutic environments for exposure therapy and stress management, while GenAI enables personalized, adaptive interactions. The review covers five application areas: VR exposure therapy for anxiety, VR-based stress regulation and mindfulness, AI-driven personalization, VR social skills training, and AI-generated therapeutic content. Early evidence shows promise for scalable, engaging interventions beyond traditional clinical settings.

However, significant limitations exist: small studies, short follow-up periods, inconsistent measurements, and unresolved ethical concerns around privacy, bias, and safety. The authors propose a framework with four components—Sensing, Inference, Adaptation, and Evaluation (SIAE)—to guide ethical development and call for rigorous research, transparency, and interdisciplinary collaboration before widespread implementation.

Keywords: Virtual Reality · Generative AI · Mental Health · Learning Sciences · Human-Computer Interaction

1 Introduction

Mental health disorders represent a critical global challenge with significant implications for educational systems, as stress, anxiety, and depression have increased substantially in recent decades, particularly among students [5]. While traditional psychotherapeutic interventions such as cognitive-behavioral therapy (CBT) demonstrate efficacy, access barriers including limited counselor availability, financial constraints, and stigma prevent many individuals, especially youth, from receiving timely support [19]. This disparity between mental health needs and available resources has driven interest in scalable, technology-enhanced interventions. Two promising technologies have emerged: Virtual Reality (VR), which immerses users in controlled three-dimensional environments for

A. Dipace et al. (Eds.): WAILS 2025, LNCS 16438, pp. 1–14, 2026.
https://doi.org/10.1007/978-3-032-17604-2_1

practicing coping skills and therapeutic exercises [34], and Generative Artificial Intelligence (GenAI), which enables adaptive, human-like interactions through large language models. VR-based therapies have demonstrated therapeutic outcomes comparable to traditional in-person approaches across multiple conditions [8], while AI-driven conversational agents have produced modest yet significant reductions in anxiety and depression symptoms [13]. These systems can analyze multimodal user inputs—including text, speech, and physiological signals—to infer emotional states and deliver personalized responses [1]. The convergence of VR and GenAI offers potential for immersive, personalized interventions particularly relevant to educational contexts, where the bidirectional relationship between emotional well-being and learning capacity is well-established: mental health difficulties impair attention, memory, and motivation [40], while effective social-emotional learning interventions enhance resilience and academic performance [12]. This integration creates opportunities for simultaneously addressing mental health outcomes and educational goals within learning environments, though successful implementation requires careful consideration of methodological, technical, and ethical challenges [38].

2   Theoretical Background and Related Work

Recent years have witnessed substantial growth in research leveraging immersive and intelligent technologies for mental health support. We synthesize prior work across five interconnected domains: (1) VR for exposure therapy in anxiety-related disorders, (2) VR for stress reduction and mindfulness, (3) affective computing and AI-driven personalization, (4) VR for social and cognitive skills training, and (5) co-created learning scenarios enabled by generative AI. This review draws upon peer-reviewed empirical studies and meta-analytic evidence to highlight demonstrated benefits alongside current limitations.

2.1   VR and AI for Exposure Therapy

Virtual Reality Exposure Therapy (VRET) represents a well-established, empirically validated application of VR in mental health, wherein clients systematically confront feared stimuli within controlled virtual environments under clinician guidance. VRET enables precise manipulation of stimulus intensity while eliminating real-world risks, presenting lifelike scenarios including heights, public speaking situations, and specific phobic objects. Meta-analytic evidence demonstrates that VRET produces outcomes comparable to traditional in-person exposure therapies across diverse anxiety disorders, with Carl et al. [8] reporting large effect sizes (Hedges' g = 1.23) across 30 randomized controlled trials examining panic disorder, social anxiety disorder, and post-traumatic stress disorder (PTSD). The standardized delivery inherent in VR enhances treatment fidelity and reproducibility, while neuroimaging studies indicate that VR activates fear-extinction neurocircuitry comparably to real-world exposures, with similar amygdala and prefrontal cortex activation patterns observed via fMRI

[10]. Researchers have begun augmenting VRET with AI systems to create automated interventions, exemplified by Freeman et al. (2018), who developed an automated VR treatment for acrophobia incorporating an AI virtual coach that guided users through hierarchical height challenges without human therapist involvement; in a randomized controlled trial with 100 participants, the intervention produced an average 68% reduction in acrophobia symptoms following approximately two hours of VR therapy, with over three-quarters of participants achieving clinically significant improvements exceeding those typically observed in traditional therapies. Similar approaches have been applied to social anxiety disorder and specific phobias, incorporating animated conversational agents enabled by generative voice synthesis and motion algorithms [17], though some users express preference for human therapists and note limitations in AI responsiveness [21]. Beyond anxiety disorders, VRET has been extended to PTSD treatment through virtual recreation of traumatic contexts, producing symptom reductions comparable to traditional prolonged exposure therapy [31]. While generative AI could potentially enhance these interventions by flexibly generating contextual details—visual elements, auditory cues, or conversational components—aligned with patients' trauma narratives in real-time, its introduction into trauma-focused interventions raises critical safety considerations, including preventing AI systems from introducing unscripted traumatic content or inadequately responding to patient distress.

2.2   VR for Stress Reduction and Mindfulness

Stress regulation constitutes a critical domain with significant implications for both mental health and educational outcomes, as chronic stress and impaired emotion regulation capacities substantially compromise students' learning and overall functioning [4]. Virtual reality has demonstrated efficacy as a medium for delivering relaxation and mindfulness interventions, leveraging its immersive nature to present calming environments—including natural landscapes and meditation spaces—that enhance engagement relative to traditional relaxation techniques. Empirical evidence indicates that brief VR sessions produce measurable reductions in physiological and psychological stress indicators; Anderson et al. [3] documented in a randomized controlled trial that participants exposed to nature-based VR experiences exhibited significantly greater reductions in cortisol levels and self-reported stress compared to urban environment controls, while controlled experiments with university students have demonstrated that 10-minute VR-guided meditations acutely reduce self-reported stress and state anxiety [15]. AI augmentation can enhance stress-reduction applications through biofeedback-driven adaptation, whereby physiological sensors—including heart rate monitors, electrodermal activity sensors, and electroencephalography (EEG) devices—enable VR relaxation programs to monitor users' stress markers in real-time, with AI algorithms subsequently adjusting environmental parameters or guidance based on these data streams. Prpa et al. [30] demonstrated a prototype affective closed-loop system wherein users with anxiety engaged with VR environments paired with biofeedback devices that monitored autonomic arousal and dynamically modified virtual scenes to encourage physiological regulation, resulting in enhanced self-regulation capacity and user engagement. Generative AI can further provide virtual mindfulness coaches delivering guided meditations or cognitive reframing exercises while detecting user distress through voice or facial expression analysis and adapting guidance accordingly, creating personalized relaxation experiences according to users' current physiological states. From an educational perspective, embedding VR+AI stress regulation tools within schools and universities could address escalating student stress and burnout through accessible interventions such as brief VR mindfulness sessions with AI-guided breathing exercises, or conversational engagement with virtual counselors offering empathetic, evidence-based guidance about academic stressors. However, some users note that AI interactions may lack human warmth, suggesting that hybrid models—wherein VR+AI provides routine or on-demand support while human counselors deliver oversight and deeper therapeutic intervention—may optimally balance scalability with therapeutic depth.

2.3   Affective Personalization and Adaptive Learning

A fundamental advantage of AI integration in mental health interventions is the capacity for personalization based on users' affective and cognitive states, aligning with research on affect-aware educational technologies that detect students' emotional states—including frustration, confusion, and boredom—and adapt instruction accordingly to maintain engagement and foster positive emotional experiences [11]. Within VR-based mental health interventions, AI systems can sense users' emotions through multiple modalities—including facial expression recognition via computer vision, voice tone analysis for emotional valence detection, text-based sentiment analysis of verbalizations, and biosensor data for stress marker identification—and execute adaptive actions such as modifying relaxation scenario parameters based on heart rate feedback or triggering supportive hints when detecting user confusion during therapeutic exercises. This dynamic personalization maintains users within optimal zones for learning coping skills, conceptually analogous to Vygotsky's zone of proximal development applied to emotional regulation capacity. Generative AI substantially expands personalization possibilities by enabling real-time scenario and dialogue customization through on-demand content production; modern large language models can generate empathetic responses or therapeutic prompts tailored to users' most recent statements, potentially increasing perceived emotional support [2,33], while AI guides within VR contexts might generate personalized calming narratives or visualizations based on individual preferences, thereby enhancing comfort and sense of agency. Adaptive difficulty represents another application, wherein generative characters in social skills training scenarios could adjust conversational complexity or social cue presentation based on learner performance, maintaining appropriately challenging yet achievable interactions. However, affect-adaptive systems require careful implementation, as erroneous emotion recognition or poorly timed interventions risk adverse outcomes—such as misidentifying frustration as sadness and providing irrelevant responses—while algorithmic bias in affect detection, potentially stemming from cultural or individual differences in emotional expression, could produce inequitable or ineffective personalization [28]. Ensuring transparency regarding AI adaptation mechanisms is crucial for maintaining user trust, though initial evidence suggests users often report feeling "understood" by emotionally responsive systems, which can enhance engagement and therapeutic alliance even when interacting with virtual agents rather than human providers [20].

3   Social and Cognitive Skills Training

VR is an effective medium for simulated skills training in social and cognitive domains, offering safe, repeatable practice for challenging interpersonal and problem-solving situations—particularly for learners with autism spectrum disorder or social anxiety [18]. Empirical evidence indicates meaningful benefits: randomized VR role-play improved conversational and assertiveness skills and overall social functioning in schizophrenia [27], and VR exposures in everyday social settings reduced paranoid ideation by encouraging reality testing of interpretations [29].
GenAI amplifies these gains by enabling virtual agents to conduct open-ended, naturalistic dialogues that incorporate nuanced social cues (e.g., humor, misunderstanding, affect), thereby overcoming the constraints of scripted interactions and broadening opportunities to practice adaptive strategies across contexts [31]. For cognitive training, AI can personalize and continuously generate tasks that titrate difficulty to optimize improvements in executive functions—working memory, attention, planning—with potential applications to conditions such as depression and ADHD [22].
In education, VR+AI can power SEL experiences that foster perspective-taking and empathy (e.g., simulated bullying scenarios) and support collaborative problem-solving with AI teammates that model inclusive behaviors; critically, structured reflection and debriefing can be facilitated by AI to consolidate learning and guide targeted improvement.

4   Co-created Learning Scenarios with Generative AI

An innovative frontier in VR and GenAI integration involves co-created scenarios—experiences collaboratively shaped by users and generative systems—which empowers users as active participants in designing therapeutic or learning activities rather than passive recipients [9], aligning with user-centered approaches in psychotherapy and education where ownership and agency enhance engagement, self-efficacy, and process investment [36]. In mental health interventions, co-creation enables clients to design virtual environments reflecting their preferences, therapeutic goals, or creative expression; generative tools allow non-technical users to contribute to VR content creation, such as a student experiencing anxiety co-designing a personalized "safe space" environment by describing preferred elements—for example, "a quiet forest with gentle rain"—which AI generates for use in relaxation exercises, with the creative process itself potentially therapeutic by providing individuals with a sense of control over their healing environments. Within educational contexts, co-creation acquires additional dimensions as teachers and students collaboratively create learning scenarios addressing specific challenges such as test anxiety or peer conflict; generative AI enables educators to efficiently generate multiple scenario variations—including different virtual examination settings or playground conflict situations—with students selecting scenarios most authentic to their experiences or writing portions of scenarios and dialogues themselves, thereby providing training examples reflecting their perspectives.

Such participatory design not only increases intervention engagement but fosters metacognitive awareness as learners reflect on factors contributing to their stress and effective coping strategies. Generative AI enables on-demand co-creation through text-to-image synthesis, text-to-3D generation, and large language model story development, allowing users in VR to request environmental modifications in real-time—such as "make this room brighter and add a window overlooking a garden"—with AI immediately implementing changes to foster creative agency, while early research has explored interactive world-building systems allowing patients to select among different AI-generated nature scenes for therapy sessions, with AI adjusting environmental elements such as time of day or weather to match desired emotional tones. Co-creation raises important considerations including ensuring AI contributions align with therapeutic intent without introducing inappropriate content, addressing questions of creative authorship when AI performs substantial generative work, and maintaining transparency about human-AI collaboration.

Despite these concerns, co-creative approaches embody an empowering paradigm wherein technology becomes a collaborative tool users employ to shape their own healing and learning journeys rather than a prescriptive expert system, aligning with constructionist learning theory, which posits that individuals learn effectively by creating and personalizing artifacts—here, the therapeutic VR experience itself [26] suggesting that co-created VR scenarios powered by generative models may prove highly engaging precisely because they are collaboratively designed by and for users.

5   Methodological and Ethical Challenges

VR–GenAI interventions in mental health and education offer promise but face intertwined methodological, technical, and ethical challenges that threaten safety, efficacy, and equity. Methodologically, the evidence base remains limited: many studies are exploratory, underpowered, and short in duration, with weak controls, inadequate randomization/blinding, and an emphasis on showcasing technology rather than testing theory-driven interventions [39]. Evaluations of conversational agents similarly over-rely on self-report and seldom include longitudinal follow-up, constraining claims about sustained benefit. Progress requires rigorous randomized and implementation trials with larger, more diverse samples across ages, cultures, and school contexts; standardized outcome measures for mental-health and learning variables; and multi-site longitudinal designs to test durability and transfer (e.g., six-month maintenance of social-skills gains in classrooms).

Technically, integrating VR hardware, motion tracking, and GenAI APIs introduces reliability and latency risks that can disrupt presence and therapeutic flow, especially when large models strain real-time performance and bandwidth in resource-limited schools. Systems must include fail-safes and graceful degradation—particularly during high-stakes exposures—and adhere to VR comfort guidelines to mitigate cybersickness, which may be exacerbated by dynamic AI-driven content [35].

From a usability and measurement standpoint, interventions should be intuitive for minimally trained users, developed through human-centered, iterative testing. Beyond questionnaires, embedded digital traces (e.g., gaze, speech, physiology, in-scenario choices) could serve as assessment signals, but require validation to ensure they meaningfully index constructs such as confidence or emotion regulation and respect privacy. Current heterogeneity in reported outcomes demands cross-disciplinary frameworks that jointly assess mental-health change and educational impact (e.g., anxiety reduction alongside engagement, skill retention, and academic transfer). Developing standardized evaluation models—potentially adapted from established training frameworks—constitutes a key research priority (Fig. 1).

6 Proposed Framework: The SIAE Model for Adaptive VR+AI Interventions

To effectively integrate VR and generative AI for mental health in learning contexts, we propose an operational framework serving as a blueprint for system design and evaluation. This Sensing-Inference-Adaptation-Evaluation (SIAE) framework, inspired by prior work in affective computing and intelligent tutoring systems [7], emphasizes a closed-loop approach enabling continuous improvement. The framework comprises four iterative components:

6.1 Sensing

the system collects multimodal data regarding user state and context, including physiological signals (heart rate, electrodermal activity via wearables), behavioral cues (head movement, eye gaze, posture within VR), task performance metrics (response speed and accuracy), and explicit inputs (speech, text, menu selections). For example, during a public-speaking VR simulation, the system

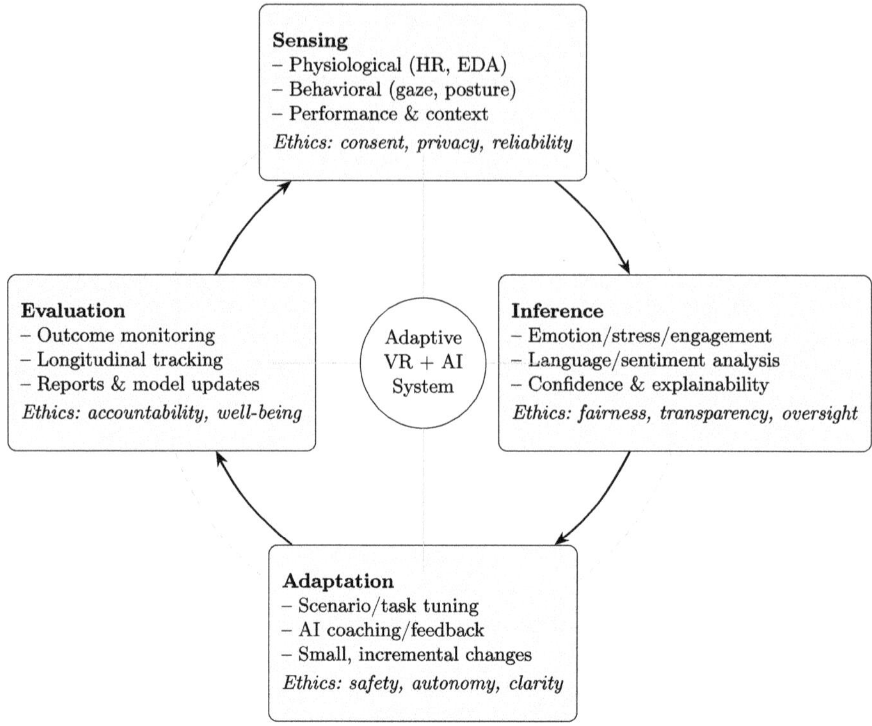

Fig. 1. The SIAE closed-loop framework for adaptive VR+AI interventions.

might detect voice tremor and predominantly downward gaze—potential anxiety indicators. Advanced configurations may incorporate electroencephalography or other biosignals when available. The guiding principle involves gathering sufficiently rich representations of users' affective and cognitive states alongside their virtual environment behaviors. Sensing also encompasses environmental context tracking—scenario difficulty levels, present stimuli, and temporal progression. This data foundation supports all subsequent processing stages, making sensor accuracy and validation through calibration procedures crucial.

6.2   Inference

AI models interpret sensed data to draw conclusions about users' psychological states or needs. This involves algorithms for emotion recognition, stress detection, engagement estimation, and skill assessment. Inference bridges raw data to actionable information—effectively answering "What is the user experiencing or requiring currently?" For instance, based on elevated heart rate and erratic head movements, the system might infer increasing anxiety; alternatively, rapid correct responses coupled with calm physiology might suggest the user could benefit from increased challenge. Generative AI, particularly large language models, can analyze linguistic content: if a user states "I cannot do this, it is too difficult," sentiment analysis might infer frustration or diminished self-efficacy. Some inferences may follow explicit rules (e.g., if heart rate exceeds threshold X, infer likely anxiety), while others employ machine learning models trained on empirical data (e.g., predicting engagement level from combined voice, posture, and performance features). Transparency is valuable—systems should ideally represent confidence in inferences and provide explanations when needed, such as displaying to facilitators that a student's estimated stress level is 8/10 based on specific indicators. Human oversight can be integrated by allowing supervisors to override or correct inferences based on additional contextual knowledge.

6.3 Adaptation

Based on inferences, systems adapt interventions in real-time to optimize outcomes. Adaptation is where generative AI particularly excels, flexibly creating new content or modifying scenarios. Adaptations may target VR environments (visual or auditory changes), task parameters, or virtual agent behaviors. For instance, if a user is inferred to experience excessive anxiety during exposure, the system might reduce difficulty—perhaps increasing virtual audience distance or providing encouraging prompts from an AI coach ("Remember to breathe deeply; you are performing well"). Conversely, if users appear under-challenged, systems might introduce novel task elements or increase difficulty levels. Adaptation can also involve strategic shifts: if students exhibit frustration with cognitive tasks, AI might transition from structured quizzes to game-like activities to restore engagement. In social skills training, adaptation might involve AI avatars adjusting conversational styles—becoming more supportive when users struggle or more challenging when ready for greater complexity. This stage represents individualized intervention delivery, with adaptations typically small and incremental rather than abrupt to maintain user trust and comfort. Systems may communicate changes ("Let's try something slightly more challenging now, given your excellent progress") to keep users informed. The goal involves maintaining users within optimal engagement zones—conceptualized as between excitement and relaxation —conducive to learning and therapeutic progress.

6.4 Evaluation

the final component closes the loop by evaluating adaptation impacts and overall intervention effectiveness, feeding back into both system knowledge and human supervision. On a micro-scale, following each adaptive action, systems can monitor new sensor inputs to assess whether desired effects occurred (e.g., after offering calming visualization, did heart rate decrease? After increasing difficulty, is performance maintained?). This continuous evaluation enables further AI adjustments as needed, analogous to thermostat iterative regulation (often implemented through reinforcement learning algorithms). On a macro-scale, evaluation involves assessing whether session goals were achieved and collecting outcome measures. For example, after sessions, systems might administer brief reflection questionnaires ("How anxious do you feel now compared to before?") or present progress summaries to users and facilitators: "Today, you practiced public speaking before a virtual audience of 20 students. You delivered a 5-minute presentation with moderate initial anxiety that decreased by session end. Eye contact maintenance improved significantly. Next session will introduce audience questions to practice interactive responses." Such feedback informs users of their progress—important for maintaining motivation—while providing data for human therapists or educators to evaluate intervention efficacy. These outcomes should be logged across sessions to track longitudinal progress and inform overall treatment or training plan adjustments. The evaluation component must connect to originally defined therapeutic or learning objectives—for instance, if the goal involved reducing public speaking anxiety, is there evidence of symptom reduction? If skill acquisition was targeted, can users demonstrate competency? This stage also enables ethical oversight application: reviewing session logs to ensure appropriate AI behavior and gathering stakeholder feedback about experiences (perceived safety, AI helpfulness, user satisfaction). In research deployments, this corresponds to collecting qualitative and quantitative data for analysis; in practical implementations, it might involve generating reports for clinicians, parents, or administrators regarding program performance (with privacy-respecting data aggregation where appropriate). During Evaluation (sharing results with stakeholders).

These four components create a closed feedback loop: Sensing → Inference → Adaptation → Evaluation → (iterating back to Sensing). Across multiple sessions, systems can refine their models—for example, personalizing inference algorithms to individual users' baseline patterns—essentially implementing ongoing machine learning personalization. The modular framework structure means improvements in any single component enhance overall system performance. For instance, more accurate emotion recognition algorithms (Inference) enable more precise adaptations; richer sensor data (Sensing) might enable entirely novel intervention types. The SIAE framework deliberately aligns with principles from both clinical intervention design and instructional design. In psychotherapy, clinicians assess patients, conceptualize their needs, deliver targeted treatments, and evaluate outcomes—our model automates and iterates this process. In education, formative assessment and differentiated instruction follow similar loops. By formalizing this approach for VR+AI contexts, we provide a blueprint ensuring developers and researchers address all critical aspects while highlighting ethical checkpoints at each stage: consent during Sensing (for data collection), fairness during Inference (ensuring unbiased models), safety during Adaptation (preventing harmful content), and transparency during Evaluation (sharing results with stakeholders).

7   Future Directions

Realizing VR and generative AI's full potential for mental health in learning sciences requires a forward-looking agenda emphasizing rigor, ethics, scalability, and interdisciplinarity. The field must transition from proof-of-concept studies to large-scale, multi-site randomized controlled trials with longitudinal follow-up assessing benefit durability [24], incorporating control conditions that isolate VR and AI contributions and developing standardized outcome metrics alongside qualitative research capturing user experiences [37]. Future systems must implement ethics-by-design through privacy safeguards, informed consent addressing AI roles, explainable AI elements, and adherence to principles of autonomy, beneficence, non-maleficence, and justice [23, 25]. Achieving scalability requires affordable hardware, cloud-based solutions with offline capabilities, training programs for non-specialist facilitators, and implementation science frameworks addressing real-world deployment barriers [14].

Interdisciplinary collaboration among computer scientists, mental health professionals, educators, and designers is essential, requiring participatory design with end-users [32], curriculum development training the next generation of researchers, data and code sharing platforms, and partnerships with policymakers and regulatory bodies [16]. Future research should explore optimal human-AI balance through hybrid care models—augmenting rather than replacing human professionals—investigating therapeutic alliance with AI agents, seamless hand-off interfaces, and trust-building mechanisms [6], ultimately envisioning integrated care models where VR+AI tools constitute one component within larger support ecosystems including peers, teachers, counselors, and families.

8   Conclusion

The integration of VR and Generative AI represents a transformative opportunity for mental health support in educational contexts, enabling immersive, scalable, and personalized interventions that address students' mental well-being alongside academic growth. Emerging evidence shows VR exposure therapies achieve efficacy comparable to traditional methods [8] and AI conversational agents produce modest but significant mental health benefits [13], though current literature exhibits fragmented approaches requiring rigorous, longitudinal research and standardized evaluation frameworks. Critical challenges include technical demands (user comfort, system reliability, real-time AI adaptation), ethical considerations (data privacy, algorithmic bias prevention, transparency, preserving human care elements), and educational context requirements including pedagogical alignment and equity [12].

The proposed Sensing-Inference-Adaptation-Evaluation (SIAE) framework provides a structured approach for developing adaptive VR+AI systems through multimodal sensing, AI-driven inference, personalized adaptation, and systematic evaluation, facilitating interdisciplinary collaboration across psychology, artificial intelligence, and human-computer interaction. Success requires a research agenda emphasizing rigorous evaluation, ethical design, scalable deployment, and interdisciplinary partnership to demonstrate clinical symptom improvement and enhanced student emotional regulation, resilience, and learning engagement, ultimately creating accessible mental health support deliverable in diverse settings and fostering learners equipped with coping skills, empathy, and self-awareness through technology-assisted experiences that are scalable, adaptive, and grounded in compassion and empirical evidence.

References

1. Abd-Alrazaq, A.A., Alajlani, M., Alalwan, A.A., Bewick, B.M., Gardner, P., Househ, M.: An overview of the features of chatbots in mental health: A scoping review. Int. J. Med. Informatics **132**, 103978 (2019). https://doi.org/10.1016/j.ijmedinf.2019.103978
2. Amaro, I., Della Greca, A., Tortora, G.: Hayt application: the use of NLP to improve the diagnosis and treatment of anxiety and depression. In: 2024 IEEE International Conference on Bioinformatics and Biomedicine (BIBM), pp. 6774–6781. IEEE (2024)
3. Anderson, A.P., Mayer, M.D., Fellows, A.M., Cowan, D.R., Hegel, M.T., Buckey, J.C.: Relaxation with immersive natural scenes presented using virtual reality. Aerospace Med. Human Perform. **88**(6), 520–526 (2017). https://doi.org/10.3357/AMHP.4747.2017
4. Arnsten, A.F.: Stress signalling pathways that impair prefrontal cortex structure and function. Nat. Rev. Neurosci. **10**(6), 410–422 (2009). https://doi.org/10.1038/nrn2648
5. Auerbach, R.P., et al.: Who world mental health surveys international college student project: prevalence and distribution of mental disorders. J. Abnorm. Psychol. **127**(7), 623–638 (2018). https://doi.org/10.1037/abn0000362
6. Bickmore, T.W., Schulman, D., Sidner, C.L.: A reusable framework for health counseling dialogue systems based on a behavioral medicine ontology. J. Biomed. Inform. **44**(2), 183–197 (2010). https://doi.org/10.1016/j.jbi.2010.12.006
7. Calvo, R.A., D'Mello, S.: Affect detection: an interdisciplinary review of models, methods, and their applications. IEEE Trans. Affect. Comput. **1**(1), 18–37 (2010). https://doi.org/10.1109/T-AFFC.2010.1
8. Carl, E., et al.: Virtual reality exposure therapy for anxiety and related disorders: a meta-analysis of randomized controlled trials. J. Anxiety Disord. **61**, 27–36 (2019). https://doi.org/10.1016/j.janxdis.2018.08.003
9. Della Greca, A., Amaro, I., Barra, P., Rosapepe, E., Tortora, G.: Enhancing therapeutic engagement in mental health through virtual reality and generative ai: a co-creation approach to trust building. In: 2024 IEEE International Conference on Bioinformatics and Biomedicine (BIBM), pp. 6805–6811. IEEE (2024)
10. Diemer, J., Alpers, G.W., Peperkorn, H.M., Shiban, Y., Mühlberger, A.: The impact of perception and presence on emotional reactions: a review of research in virtual reality. Front. Psychol. **6**, 26 (2015). https://doi.org/10.3389/fpsyg.2015.00026
11. D'Mello, S., Graesser, A.: Dynamics of affective states during complex learning. Learn. Instr. **22**(2), 145–157 (2012). https://doi.org/10.1016/j.learninstruc.2011.10.001

12. Durlak, J.A., Weissberg, R.P., Dymnicki, A.B., Taylor, R.D., Schellinger, K.B.: The impact of enhancing students' social and emotional learning: a meta-analysis of school-based universal interventions. Child Dev. **82**(1), 405–432 (2011). https://doi.org/10.1111/j.1467-8624.2010.01564.x

13. Fitzpatrick, K.K., Darcy, A., Vierhile, M.: Delivering cognitive behavior therapy to young adults with symptoms of depression and anxiety using a fully automated conversational agent (woebot): A randomized controlled trial. JMIR Mental Health **4**(2), e19 (2017). https://doi.org/10.2196/mental.7785

14. Graham, A.K., Lattie, E.G., Mohr, D.C.: Experimental therapeutics for digital mental health. JAMA Psychiat. **76**(12), 1223–1224 (2018). https://doi.org/10.1001/jamapsychiatry.2019.2075

15. Gromala, D., Tong, X., Choo, A., Karamnejad, M., Shaw, C.D.: The virtual meditative walk: Virtual reality therapy for chronic pain management. In: Proceedings of the 33rd Annual ACM Conference on Human Factors in Computing Systems, pp. 521–524 (2015). https://doi.org/10.1145/2702123.2702344

16. Huckvale, K., Torous, J., Larsen, M.E.: Assessment of the data sharing and privacy practices of smartphone apps for depression and smoking cessation. JAMA Netw. Open **2**(4), e192542 (2019). https://doi.org/10.1001/jamanetworkopen.2019.2542

17. Kampmann, I.L., Emmelkamp, P.M., Morina, N.: Meta-analysis of technology-assisted interventions for social anxiety disorder. J. Anxiety Disord. **42**, 71–84 (2016). https://doi.org/10.1016/j.janxdis.2016.06.007

18. Kandalaft, M.R., Didehbani, N., Krawczyk, D.C., Allen, T.T., Chapman, S.B.: Virtual reality social cognition training for young adults with high-functioning autism. J. Autism Dev. Disord. **43**(1), 34–44 (2013). https://doi.org/10.1007/s10803-012-1544-6

19. Kazdin, A.E., Blase, S.L.: Rebooting psychotherapy research and practice to reduce the burden of mental illness. Perspect. Psychol. Sci. **6**(1), 21–37 (2011). https://doi.org/10.1177/1745691610393527

20. Lucas, G.M., Gratch, J., King, A., Morency, L.P.: It's only a computer: Virtual humans increase willingness to disclose. Comput. Hum. Behav. **37**, 94–100 (2014). https://doi.org/10.1016/j.chb.2014.04.043

21. Lucas, G.M., Rizzo, A., Gratch, J., Scherer, S., Stratou, G., Boberg, J., Morency, L.P.: Reporting mental health symptoms: Breaking down barriers to care with virtual human interviewers. Front. Robot. AI **4**, 51 (2017). https://doi.org/10.3389/frobt.2017.00051

22. Lumsden, J., Edwards, E.A., Lawrence, N.S., Coyle, D., Munafò, M.R.: Gamification of cognitive assessment and cognitive training: a systematic review of applications and efficacy. JMIR Serious Games **4**(2), e11 (2016). https://doi.org/10.2196/games.5888

23. Mittelstadt, B.: Principles alone cannot guarantee ethical ai. Nature Mach. Intell. **1**(11), 501–507 (2019). https://doi.org/10.1038/s42256-019-0114-4

24. Mohr, D.C., Riper, H., Schueller, S.M.: A solution-focused research approach to achieve an implementable revolution in digital mental health. JAMA Psychiat. **75**(2), 113–114 (2017). https://doi.org/10.1001/jamapsychiatry.2017.3838

25. Nebeker, C., Torous, J., Bartlett Ellis, R.J.: Building the case for actionable ethics in digital health research supported by artificial intelligence. BMC Med. **17**(1), 137 (2019). https://doi.org/10.1186/s12916-019-1377-7

26. Papert, S., Harel, I.: Situating constructionism. In: Constructionism, pp. 1–11. Ablex Publishing (1991)

27. Park, K.M., et al.: A virtual reality application in role-plays of social skills training for schizophrenia: a randomized, controlled trial. Psych. Res. **189**(2), 166–172 (2011). https://doi.org/10.1016/j.psychres.2011.04.003
28. Picard, R.W.: Future affective technology for autism and emotion communication. Philosoph. Trans. Royal Society B: Biol. Sci. **364**(1535), 3575–3584 (2009). https://doi.org/10.1098/rstb.2009.0143
29. Pot-Kolder, R.M., et al.: Virtual-reality-based cognitive behavioural therapy versus waiting list control for paranoid ideation and social avoidance in patients with psychotic disorders: A single-blind randomised controlled trial. Lancet Psych. **5**(3), 217–226 (2018). https://doi.org/10.1016/S2215-0366(18)30053-1
30. Prpa, M., Tatar, K., Françoise, J., Riecke, B., Schiphorst, T., Pasquier, P.: Attending to breath: exploring how the cues in a virtual environment guide the attention to breath and shape the quality of experience to support mindfulness. In: Proceedings of the 2018 Designing Interactive Systems Conference, pp. 71–84 (2018). https://doi.org/10.1145/3196709.3196765
31. Rizzo, A., Shilling, R.: Clinical virtual reality tools to advance the prevention, assessment, and treatment of PTSD. Eur. J. Psychotraumatol. **8**(sup5), 1414560 (2017). https://doi.org/10.1080/20008198.2017.1414560
32. Sanders, E.B.N., Stappers, P.J.: Co-creation and the new landscapes of design. CoDesign **4**(1), 5–18 (2008). https://doi.org/10.1080/15710880701875068
33. Sharma, A., Lin, I.W., Miner, A.S., Atkins, D.C., Althoff, T.: Towards facilitating empathic conversations in online mental health support: a reinforcement learning approach. In: Proceedings of The Web Conference 2020, pp. 194–205 (2020). https://doi.org/10.1145/3366423.3380097
34. Slater, M., Sanchez-Vives, M.V.: Enhancing our lives with immersive virtual reality. Front. Robot. AI **3**, 74 (2016). https://doi.org/10.3389/frobt.2016.00074
35. Stanney, K.M., Lawson, B.D., Rokers, B., Dennison, M., Fidopiastis, C., Stoffregen, T., Fulvio, J.M., et al.: Identifying causes of and solutions for cybersickness in immersive technology: Reformulation of a research and development agenda. Int. J. Human-Comput. Interact **36**(19), 1783–1803 (2020). https://doi.org/10.1080/10447318.2020.1828535
36. Steen, M.: Co-design as a process of joint inquiry and imagination. Design Issues **29**(2), 16–28 (2013). https://doi.org/10.1162/DESI_a_00207
37. Torous, J., Lipschitz, J., Ng, M., Firth, J.: Dropout rates in clinical trials of smartphone apps for depressive symptoms: a systematic review and meta-analysis. J. Affect. Disord. **263**, 413–419 (2020). https://doi.org/10.1016/j.jad.2019.11.167
38. Tortora, A., Amaro, I., Della Greca, A., Barra, P.: Exploring the role of generative artificial intelligence in virtual reality: Opportunities and future perspectives. In: International Conference on Human-Computer Interaction, pp. 125–142. Springer (2025)
39. Valmaggia, L.R., Latif, L., Kempton, M.J., Rus-Calafell, M.: Virtual reality in the psychological treatment for mental health problems: a systematic review of recent evidence. Psych. Res. **236**, 189–195 (2016). https://doi.org/10.1016/j.psychres.2016.01.015
40. Vogel, S., Schwabe, L.: Learning and memory under stress: implications for the classroom. npj Sci. Learn. **1**(1), 16011 (2016). https://doi.org/10.1038/npjscilearn.2016.11

AI and Ethics Literacy in Secondary School: A Pilot Study

Aldo Pisano[✉] [iD], Ines Crispini [iD], and Rossana Adele Rossi [iD]

University of Calabria, Via Pietro Bucci, 87036 Rende, CS, Italy
aldo.pisano@unifg.it, {ines.crispini,
rossana_adele.rossi}@unical.it

Abstract. This paper presents the findings of a pilot study on AI & Ethics Literacy conducted in Italian secondary schools during the academic years 2023–2025. The project sought to investigate whether specific training on AI ethics is needed alongside technical AI education. The study involved 193 students from technical institutes and high schools in southern Italy. The intervention, lasting eight hours per class, was based on a dialogical Philosophical Enquiry (PhiE) methodology, fostering critical thinking, cooperative dialogue, and ethical awareness. Data were collected through entry and exit questionnaires and a content knowledge test. Results demonstrate significant improvements in students' ethical awareness, knowledge of AI concepts, and recognition of algorithmic biases. Higher engagement and receptivity were observed particularly among third-year technical students and first-year high school students. These findings underscore the importance of integrating AI ethics into the curriculum (e.g. within civic education) as a way to prepare students for an AI-driven society in a critically informed manner.

Keywords: AIED · Ethics · Philosophical Enquiry

1 Introduction

The rapid advancement of Artificial Intelligence (AI) raises profound educational and ethical challenges [4]. Beyond technical knowledge, students must be prepared to critically reflect on the societal implications of AI and to develop an ethical mindset towards technology [7]. As highlighted by Holmes et al. [12] and Cuomo et al. [5], AI education in secondary schools requires not only technical literacy but also a structured ethical reflection, in line with international guidelines [15]. Recent works on AI literacy highlights the need for equipping learners with the competencies to understand and evaluate AI's impact on society [5, 13, 22, 24, 25, 31]. In response to this need, our study builds upon the Large Ethics Model (LEM) framework and the PAIA model [28] of ethical risks to contextualize AI ethics education in secondary schools. The LEM is a broad theoretical-ethical framework that integrates the *PAIA* dimensions of AI risk – Pervasiveness [36], Autonomy [26], Invisibility, Adaptivity [31] – with a comprehensive educational approach to AI ethics. In LEM, education is seen as a critical bottom-up

A. Dipace et al. (Eds.): WAILS 2025, LNCS 16438, pp. 15–28, 2026.
https://doi.org/10.1007/978-3-032-17604-2_2

process preparing individuals to live in a world of human–machine coexistence [25, 31]. The model emphasizes the shared responsibility of key stakeholders – Policymakers, Funders, Programmers, and Users [3, 6, 16, 31] – in ensuring ethical AI development and use. It also accounts for common pitfalls such as *ethical bias* (viewing "ethics" as merely restrictive) and *automation bias* (overestimating AI infallibility) [29]. Within this framework, "AI & Ethics Literacy" programs in schools serve as a vital component, aiming to foster critical and responsible understanding of AI from an early age. In practical terms, our pilot project was designed to integrate ethical inquiry into AI education for secondary students. The central research questions were:

- Do secondary students exhibit a demand for structured AI ethics education alongside technical learning? and
- Can such education be effectively integrated into existing curricula (e.g. civic education) without overburdening teachers or students?

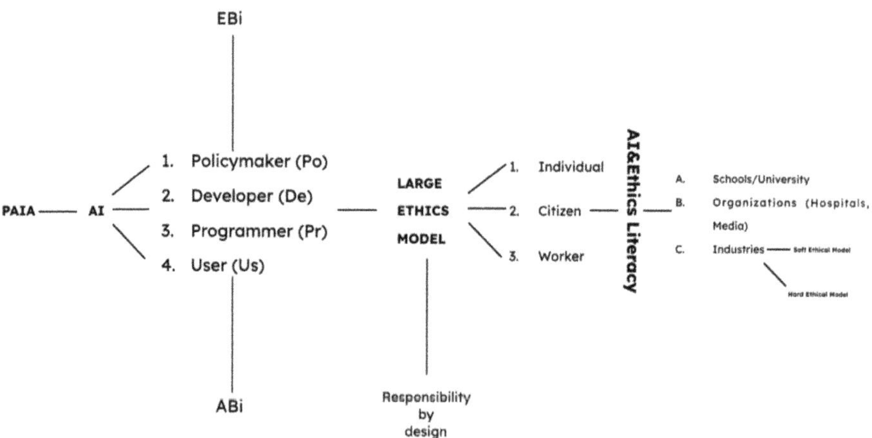

Fig. 1. The Large Ethics Model (LEM) – The LEM conceptual framework connects the PAIA risk dimensions of AI (Pervasiveness, Autonomy, Invisibility, Adaptivity) to an AI & Ethics Literacy program. It emphasizes education and ethical awareness across all stakeholders involved in AI systems – from policymakers (Po), Funders (Fu) and Developers (De) to end-users (Us) – in order to promote responsible AI coexistence. *Ethical bias* (misperceiving ethics as an obstacle) and *automation bias* (over-reliance on AI) are identified as key challenges to be addressed through education.

To address these questions, we combined ethical theory, critical pedagogy, and hands-on dialogue-based teaching methods. We hypothesized that students would not only improve their factual knowledge of AI and ethics, but also increase their awareness of ethical issues (such as bias and accountability) and express support for including these topics in their curriculum. Figure 1 below illustrates the *Large Ethics Model (LEM)* that guided our approach, bridging the PAIA risk categories with an AI ethics education program. The diagram situates our AI&Ethics Literacy intervention within a broader ethical ecosystem, linking educational content on AI risks to the roles of stakeholders and highlighting the need to overcome ethical bias and automation bias through literacy and critical thinking. This framework aligns with international proposals that emphasize not only algorithmic transparency but also ethical literacy in AI education [5, 7, 24].

With this framework in mind, the following sections describe our methodology, present quantitative and qualitative results of the pilot, and discuss the implications for integrating AI ethics into secondary education.

2 Methodology

2.1 Research Design

We followed a mixed-method research design to evaluate the pilot program. Quantitative data were collected via pre- and post-intervention questionnaires (with Likert-scale items) and a post-intervention knowledge test. Qualitative data were obtained from open-ended questionnaire responses. The intervention consisted of four sessions (each ~ 2 h) conducted in regular class time (total ~ 8 h per class). The four sessions covered:

- Session 1 – Introduction to Ethics: Basic ethical theories (deontology, consequentialism, virtue ethics) and key concepts such as autonomy, responsibility, and moral agency [1, 9].
- Session 2 – Introduction to AI: Fundamental AI concepts (types of AI agents – analytical, executive, interactive; Narrow vs. General AI) and discussions on what "intelligence" means in humans and machines [6, 10, 24].
- Session 3 – Ethics of AI, Part 1: Social and ethical issues of AI, focusing on biases (e.g. automation bias, discrimination in algorithms) and the importance of fact-checking and fairness [3, 10, 22];
- Session 4 – Ethics of AI, Part 2: Strategies for trustworthy AI (the European pillars of trustworthy AI – e.g. transparency, accountability) and an overview of forthcoming regulations (the EU AI Act). This session concluded with a hands-on group activity: students worked in teams to ethically design an autonomous vehicle scenario (using a digital polling tool for decision-making), applying the principles learned.

Throughout the course, the teaching approach was grounded in the Philosophical Enquiry (PhiE) methodology [2, 19, 33]. In this student-centered approach, the teacher acted as a facilitator rather than a lecturer. Each session began with a stimulus (e.g. a short story, thought experiment, or real-world scenario) to spark discussion. Students were then guided to form a "community of inquiry," collaboratively exploring questions such as "What would you do?" and eventually "What is the right thing to do?" in the given context. The facilitator intervened with probing questions – "Why do you think that?", "Can we clarify this idea?" – to deepen reflection and keep the discussion focused. This method encouraged critical thinking, respectful dialogue, and the co-construction of knowledge among peers [2, 33].

2.2 Participants and Context

The pilot was implemented across two public schools in Calabria, Italy: a technical-institute and a university-oriented high school (liceo). Within these schools, we involved both first- year (grade 9) and third-year (grade 11) classes to compare effects across different ages (approximately 14-year-olds vs 16–17-year-olds). Initially, 193 students participated in the entry (pre- test) phase, and 163 students completed the exit (post-test) phase, reflecting some natural attrition. The sample included a mix of academic tracks: from technical/vocational curricula (with a science/ technology focus) to traditional academic curricula (science-oriented and humanities-oriented tracks). This diverse context allowed us to explore how student background might influence engagement with AI ethics. All student participation was voluntary and integrated into normal class activities with school approval.

2.3   Instruments and Data Collection

Three custom instruments were developed in collaboration with the University of Calabria's education department:

- Entry Questionnaire (Pre-test): 15 Likert-scale items plus demographic questions. This questionnaire, given before the first session, assessed baseline student perceptions and knowledge. It included sections on students' initial interest in AI and ethics, prior knowledge of AI and ethical issues, and their attitudes toward school teaching methods.
- Exit Questionnaire (Post-test): 26 Likert-scale items (parallel in structure to the entry questionnaire) plus one open-ended question. This was administered after the last session. The quantitative items measured students' appreciation of the teaching methodologies used (e.g. opinion on the dialogical and cooperative format), their appreciation of the content learned (ethics, AI, AI ethics topics), their perceived usefulness of the course, and their interest in seeing AI ethics integrated into the regular curriculum. The open-ended questions invited students to comment on what they liked or disliked about the course and to suggest improvements.
- Content Knowledge Test: A 15-item multiple-choice test, created to objectively measure what students learned. It covered key concepts from the course: (~5 questions on general ethics, ~ 4 on AI, ~ 5 on AI ethics). Example items included definitions of bias, identifying an AI ethics principle, or recognizing implications of AI in society. Students completed this test immediately after the final session.

All Likert-scale items were scored 1–5 (1 = "Not at all", 5 = "Very much") and were treated as interval data for analysis. To ensure honest responses, the questionnaires were anonymous (students used codes known only to themselves to match pre/post responses). Teachers were not present during questionnaire administration, reducing social pressure. The data collection was conducted G-forms.

2.4   Data Analysis

We used IBM SPSS and Python for data analysis and visualization. First, we performed descriptive statistics to summarize students' feedback and test performance. We computed mean scores and standard deviations for each questionnaire item and for aggregate indices (e.g. overall content appreciation). We also examined differences in these scores across subgroups: by school type (technical vs. university-oriented) and by year (first vs. third). Secondly, we conducted inferential statistical tests. For learning outcomes, we used paired t-tests to compare pre- vs. post-intervention responses on matched items (e.g. ethical awareness self-rating before and after) and to assess the significance of knowledge gains (comparing pre-test vs. post-test scores on comparable questions). Effect sizes (Cohen's d) were calculated for significant gains to gauge their magnitude. Additionally, we ran Pearson correlations to explore relationships between certain variables of interest – for example, the correlation between a student's interest in AI ethics and their support for including it in the curriculum, and how this might differ by class type or age. Qualitative responses from the open-ended questions were analyzed thematically. This analysis provided context and depth to the quantitative findings, illustrating why students responded as they did. All analyses were conducted according to ethical research standards. The pilot was low-risk; however, we obtained informed consent via the schools, and we explained to students that their feedback was for research purposes and would be anonymized.

3 Results

3.1 Descriptive Findings

Overall, students evaluated the experimental course very positively. On a 1–5 scale, the mean appreciation for the new content areas – Ethics, AI, and AI Ethics – ranged roughly between 3.9 and 4.0 (Fig. 2).

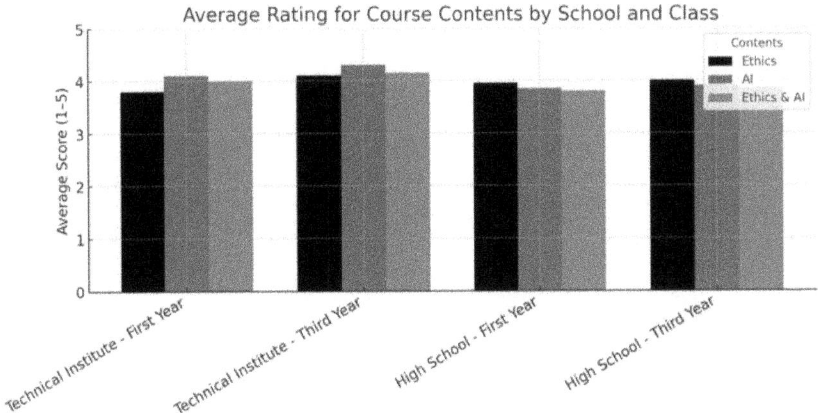

Fig. 2. Average ratings (scale 1–5) of course contents on Ethics, Artificial Intelligence, and Ethics & AI, compared across school types and class levels.

This indicates that students found the AI ethics topics more engaging than their usual curriculum. An in-depth breakdown revealed some noteworthy patterns. Students from the technical institute expressed slightly higher appreciation (on average) for the content than those from the high school, across all topics. For instance, discussions of AI and its ethical issues resonated strongly in technical classes – likely reflecting those students' greater familiarity with technology and its applications. Similarly, third-year students reported higher enjoyment and interest than first-year students (e.g. older students often gave content ratings a few tenths of a point higher on the 5-point scale). The highest content appreciation was observed in the subgroup of third- year technical students, which achieved the top mean scores for all content areas. In contrast, the first-year university oriented- high school (liceo) students tended to give the most reserved ratings – though even in this subgroup, the average ratings were well above neutral (above 3 on the scale). These differences suggest that student maturity and the relevance of content to their study track influenced how much they valued the course. In summary, while all groups found the AI ethics content beneficial, the perceived value was greatest among older students in a technology-focused track.

In terms of teaching methods, the feedback was also positive overall. Students appreciated the departure from traditional lecturing in favor of interactive and reflective learning. Among the various methodological aspects, two stood out as particularly appreciated: (1) the collaborative "knowledge co-construction" activities – working in groups to discuss and solve problems – and (2) the emphasis on respectful, open dialogue where every student could voice their thoughts (Fig. 3). These two aspects received the highest average ratings (for example, students rated the statement "I enjoyed working together to build answers as a group" with a mean around 3.6/5, and "I appreciated that we could openly discuss and debate ideas" around 3.5/5). Many students commented that they felt more actively involved in the learning process than usual, which made the sessions "interesting" and "stimulating" rather than "boring". On the other hand, a few students found the philosophical discussions challenging – noting that they were not used to open-ended questions – highlighting a potential area to scaffold younger participants' discussion skills.

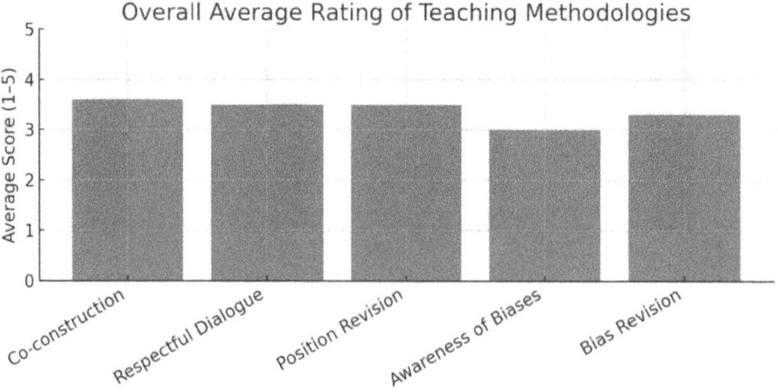

Fig. 3. Average ratings (scale 1–5) of the teaching methodologies employed during the course. Results show that co-construction, respectful dialogue, and position revision received the highest evaluations, while awareness of biases and bias revision were rated slightly lower. These findings suggest that participatory and dialogical approaches were perceived as more engaging by the students.

Student performance on the content test further corroborated the questionnaire feedback. Overall, students answered a majority of the 15 multiple-choice questions correctly, with an average score of 11.3 out of 15 (75%). Third-year classes performed slightly better (mean ~ 12/15) than first-year classes (mean ~ 10/15). Similarly, technical institute students had marginally higher scores on factual AI questions (e.g. identifying examples of AI or understanding terms like "machine learning"), whereas high school students excelled on ethical scenario questions that involved reasoning. These differences, while present, were not extremely large; they suggest that prior exposure and cognitive maturity played a role in how much content was absorbed. Importantly, even students who didn't score highly on the test often still reported positive experiences – indicating that enjoyment and perceived utility did not always align with measurable knowledge gains (we explore this in the Discussion).

3.2 Pre-Post Comparisons

To evaluate the effectiveness of the intervention, we compared relevant measures from the pre- and post-study questionnaires. The paired-sample t-tests revealed statistically significant improvements on several key dimensions. Notably:

- Ethical Awareness: Students' self-reported awareness of ethical issues in technology showed a clear increase. For example, in the pre-survey many students admitted they had rarely thought about AI's impact on society; by the post-survey, most indicated a heightened awareness. The improvement in the composite "ethical awareness" score was significant ($p < 0.001$). The effect size was large (Cohen's d $\approx$ 0.8), suggesting a substantial educational impact. Qualitatively, students moved from vague notions of "ethics is about good/bad in general" to being able to articulate specific concerns like bias or privacy in AI.
- AI Knowledge: We observed a significant gain in factual knowledge about AI concepts and terminology. This was evident both in self-assessments and objectively (the content test scores improved compared to a subset of similar questions asked before the course). For instance, before the course less than half the students knew what an algorithmic bias was, whereas after the course a strong majority answered these correctly. The average improvement in the knowledge test for matched items corresponded to a moderate effect size (d $\approx$ 0.6). This indicates the intervention succeeded in conveying core concepts despite its short duration.
- Bias Recognition: One focus of the pilot was teaching students to recognize biases in AI (such as automation bias and data bias). After the course, we noted a significant shift: students were more skeptical of AI's objectivity and more aware that AI can reflect human biases. This shift was significant ($p < 0.01$) with an effect size in the medium-to-large range (d $\approx$ 0.7). While not all misconceptions were eliminated, students showed greater critical thinking – for example, in open responses some mentioned that "AI is only as fair as the data you feed it" or pointed out that algorithms can discriminate.

In summary, the pre/post comparisons confirm that the pilot achieved its educational aims: it measurably increased students' knowledge about AI and ethics and broadened their ethical perspective. We acknowledge that an 8-h intervention can only do so much; yet, within these limits, the gains were meaningful. All reported improvements were confirmed with statistical significance, reinforcing our confidence that these changes were due to the intervention rather than chance.

3.3 Correlation Analysis

We examined Pearson correlations (Fig. 4) to explore how different aspects of student feedback interrelated, especially regarding engagement and willingness to see AI ethics in school programs.

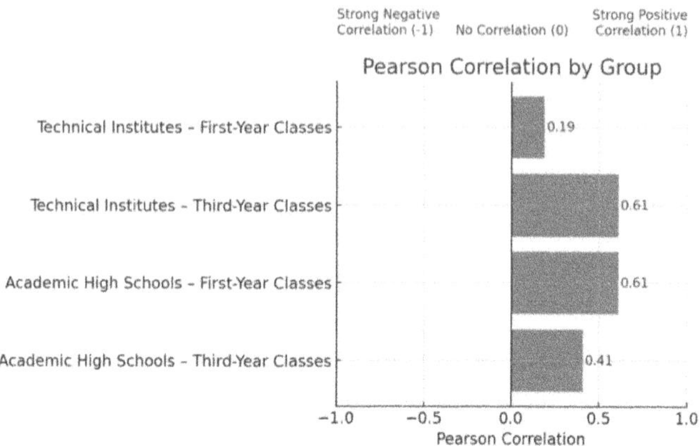

Fig. 4. Pearson correlation coefficients by group, comparing Academic High Schools and Technical Institutes across first- and third-year classes.

One key finding was that these correlations varied across class types and ages, indicating that the pilot resonated differently with different groups:

- In the third-year technical classes, there was a strong positive correlation ($r \approx 0.61$) between students' interest in learning more about AI ethics and their support for integrating such content into regular civic education.
- Similarly, in the first-year high school classes, we found an almost identical correlation ($r \approx 0.60$) between interest and curricular willingness. This was interesting because, as noted, first- year high schoolers had given somewhat lower absolute ratings to the course content; however, those who did find it interesting clearly made the connection that it should be part of the curriculum.
- Among third-year high school students, the correlation was moderate ($r \approx 0.41$). Many of these students were positive about the course, but some viewed it as a one-off enrichment rather than something to formally integrate. This could be due to their already heavy curriculum or a focus on upcoming final years of school.
- In first-year technical students, interestingly, we observed only a weak correlation ($r \approx 0.19$) between interest and desire for curricular integration. This might indicate that the younger technical students, while they enjoyed the hands-on aspects of the course, didn't yet connect it to a need for systemic curricular change – possibly because at age 14 they have less perspective on curriculum decisions or because they are still adjusting to high school itself.

These patterns suggest that maturity and context influence how students perceive the role of AI ethics education. Older and more tech-focused learners not only enjoyed the content but also became advocates for it, whereas younger or more academically traditional learners might need more exposure or support to see it as a necessary part of their formal education. For our research questions, this provides insight into where AI ethics modules might gain the most traction (for example, third-year technical classes emerged as prime candidates for further implementation, combining high engagement with a strong call for curricular inclusion).

3.4 Qualitative Insights

The open-ended responses from students enriched our understanding of the above results. A dominant theme was appreciation for dialogical and interactive learning. Many students wrote that they found the discussions "interesting" or "fun," and enjoyed being able to express their opinions on ethical dilemmas. Some example comments: "It was really stimulating to debate these questions with classmates", "I liked that there wasn't a single correct answer, we had to think for ourselves". This feedback reinforces the quantitative finding that the PhiE methodology was well-received.

Another common theme was a desire for more such lessons. Students frequently suggested extending the duration of the project or integrating it as a regular class: "It would be useful to have a weekly hour about current technology and ethics". This indicates a latent demand among students for contemporary and critical topics that connect school learning to real-world issues.

Students also pointed out concerns and insights they gained: many mentioned biases, discrimination, and ethical risks of AI as important things they learned. For instance, one student noted "I didn't know algorithms could be biased; now I understand why AI needs to be monitored". Others brought up privacy or the prospect of AI making decisions in serious contexts (like self-driving car dilemmas), often expressing that this made them realize the importance of human oversight and ethics. Such reflections show that even a short intervention can seed important critical awareness.

A few responses provided constructive criticism or ambivalence. A small number of students found the discussions "a bit chaotic" or said they would have liked more concrete answers: "Sometimes I was confused about what the conclusion was". This suggests that some students might benefit from clearer summaries or take-home points after each discussion. Additionally, a handful of students were already very tech-savvy and commented that some explanatory parts (like AI definitions) were too basic for them, whereas others needed those parts. This underlines the diversity in prior knowledge and the need to balance the material.

Finally, regarding the current education system, an entry-questionnaire prompt asked what students would improve about school in general. The responses (collected before the intervention) overwhelmingly called for "more interactive lessons", "more dialogue between teachers and students", "learning things useful for life", and "using more technology in class". In essence, students themselves – prior to experiencing the pilot – were voicing exactly the kind of changes that this project attempted to offer (dialogue, relevance, tech integration). This congruence likely contributed to the positive reception:

the pilot was meeting a demand students had already articulated. It also signals that initiatives like AI & Ethics Literacy can align with broader student desires for educational reform, beyond just the topic of AI.

4 Discussion

Our pilot project demonstrates that introducing AI ethics through an interactive, philosophy-driven approach is both feasible and beneficial in secondary education. The findings confirm that AI & Ethics Literacy addresses a genuine educational need: students are not only lacking this content in their standard curricula, but they are also curious and motivated to engage with it when given the opportunity. Several important points emerge from the results:

- Enhanced Engagement through Dialogue: Consistent with our expectations, students showed higher engagement with interactive and dialogical methods compared to traditional teaching. The PhiE methodology [33], in which students actively discuss and debate, clearly resonated. This aligns with educational research suggesting that students learn better when they are co-creators in the learning process rather than passive listeners [8]. In our study, the high appreciation scores for collaborative and respectful discussion indicate that even topics perceived as "abstract" (like ethics) can be made approachable and exciting through the right pedagogy [5, 17]. For educators and curriculum designers, this is a valuable insight: integrating AI ethics need not be a dry addition to the syllabus – it can leverage student participation and thereby enhance overall engagement in the classroom.
- Influence of Age and School Type: The receptivity to AI ethics education was not uniform across all student groups. Our data suggest that maturity (school year) and educational track significantly affect outcomes. Third-year students (regardless of school type) derived more benefit and showed more enthusiasm than first-year students. This could be due to cognitive development – older teens can better grasp complex, abstract issues – as well as due to having more prior knowledge to connect with the new material. Similarly, students in the technical institute, whose everyday studies relate more to technology, found the AI ethics content especially pertinent (their interest possibly reinforced by seeing direct connections to their field). From a practical standpoint, these differences imply that curriculum integration might be most impactful in certain grades or contexts.
- Challenges in Bias Recognition: One area that emerged as challenging was the recognition and understanding of bias in AI. While students improved in awareness, the discussion and qualitative feedback show that fully internalizing concepts like algorithmic bias or fairness is not immediate. This finding suggests that targeted pedagogical strategies are needed to reinforce understanding of AI biases – possibly through more concrete demonstrations or hands-on activities. It's an important lesson for future implementations: topics like bias and ethics, which involve unlearning assumptions, might need extended treatment beyond a single short module. Nonetheless, the willingness of students to engage on these topics is an encouraging sign for eventually achieving deeper understanding.

- Alignment with Curriculum and Civic Education: The strong interest students showed in integrating AI ethics into their regular curriculum supports the case for formally including such content in education standards. Students themselves see it as relevant to their lives – a point that curriculum planners should heed, since relevance often drives educational success. By framing AI ethics within civic education (which in many countries, including Italy, covers digital citizenship, media literacy, etc.), schools can address the societal implications of technology in a structured way. This aligns well with broader educational goals: democratic participation (understanding AI's role in democracy), critical digital citizenship (being able to navigate an AI-pervaded information landscape responsibly), and ethical awareness in science and technology. Our pilot thus provides a timely empirical nod to the calls from scholars and policymakers to include ethics in STEM education. It shows that not only is it possible to do so, but it is also welcomed by students.
- Feasibility and Adaptability: On a practical note, the pilot's success across two different school environments indicates that such a program is feasible to implement without excessive burden. We deliberately kept the intervention short (8 h) and slotted it into existing civic education hours, making it a realistic addition rather than a competing subject. We did encounter some logistical challenges, like coordinating with school schedules and handling a large number of questionnaire responses, but these are surmountable with planning.

4.1 Limitations

It is essential to acknowledge the study's limitations when interpreting the results. First, the sample, while diverse in some respects, was geographically limited to one region and involved a modest number of classes (and those who volunteered for the pilot). Thus, there may be selection bias – these schools and teachers might have been particularly open to innovative pedagogy, and students might have been influenced by that context. Future studies should include a broader range of schools (urban/rural, different socioeconomic contexts) to ensure generalizability. Second, the short-term nature of the evaluation means we captured immediate learning and reactions, but not long-term retention or behavioral change. We do not know, for instance, if students will retain their knowledge of AI ethics or their critical perspective a year later. Longitudinal research is needed to see if a one-off module has lasting impact or if regular reinforcement is required. Third, our data relied partly on self- report (e.g. students rating their awareness), which can introduce response biases (some might give favorable answers to please the researchers or due to enthusiasm). We mitigated this with anonymity and by triangulating with objective test results and qualitative data, but it remains a consideration. Lastly, the absence of a formal control group (we did not have classes that continued with "business as usual" for direct comparison) means we cannot completely rule out other factors influencing the improvements (though the magnitude and specificity of changes strongly suggest the intervention's effect). Despite these limitations, the study provides valuable preliminary evidence and a foundation for more rigorous future experimentation.

5 Conclusions and Future Research

This study provides empirical evidence of the feasibility and benefits of introducing AI ethics education in secondary schools. In an eight-hour pilot intervention, we observed enhanced student knowledge, heightened ethical sensitivity, and enthusiastic engagement across a variety of classroom settings. Students not only learned about AI and ethics, but also enjoyed the process, as reflected in their feedback and active participation. The approach bridged technical content with ethical inquiry, showing that even complex issues like algorithmic bias or the moral implications of AI can be tackled successfully with teens when using an interactive, discussion-based pedagogy.

Looking ahead, there are several avenues to expand and refine this work:

- Wider Scope [5, 22]: Future research should implement the AI & Ethics Literacy program in a broader range of schools and regions, including different countries, if possible, to evaluate its effectiveness across diverse cultural and educational contexts.
- Longitudinal Studies [10]: To assess long-term impact, it would be valuable to follow up with students, months or even years after the intervention. A longitudinal design could include refresher sessions and measure outcomes like students' course choices or their behavior online (e.g. fact-checking information, awareness of privacy)
- Curriculum Integration and Teacher Training [7, 12, 13]: As we move from pilot to practice, it will be important to develop structured curriculum materials and teacher training modules. By creating a teacher's guide, lesson plans, and perhaps a repository of case studies or dilemmas, we can make it easier for any teacher to adopt the program. Training teachers in the PhiE method and basic AI concepts is crucial for scaling – this could be done through workshops or online courses.
- Enhancing Bias Education [20, 22]: Based on our findings that bias recognition is challenging, we suggest incorporating more interactive demonstrations of bias into the program.
- Evaluating Impact on Attitudes and Choices [34, 36]: Beyond knowledge tests, future work could examine if AI ethics education influences students' attitudes toward technology and their personal values. These broader impacts can substantiate the argument that AI ethics literacy is not just academically enriching but also life-shaping.

In closing, our pilot study underscores the importance and timeliness of integrating AI ethics into secondary education. As AI systems become ever more prevalent in society, from social media algorithms to smart devices, tomorrow's citizens must be equipped not only with technical understanding but with ethical discernment. Education is the key to this preparation. By aligning with frameworks like the LEM and addressing risks identified by models like PAIA, educational programs can ensure that the next generation is ready to navigate an AI-driven future responsibly. We have shown that students and teachers are ready for this innovation in the classroom. It is our hope that curriculum developers and policymakers take note of these findings and work to embed AI and ethics literacy into school programs worldwide, thereby fostering a more informed, critical, and ethical society.

Aknowledgments. This study received financial and scientific support from the Italian Society for the Ethics of Artificial Intelligence (SIpEIA). It also received scientific support from the Department of Culture, Education and Society, University of Calabria (UNICAL); Consulta di Bioetica Onlus; and the Istituto Italiano di Bioetica. The study was approved by the University Ethics Committee of the University of Calabria (UNICAL). We gratefully acknowledge Prof. Tiziana Catarci (President of SIpEIA; Sapienza University of Rome and CNR), Prof. Maurizio Mori (Consulta Nazionale di Bioetica), Prof. Luisella Battaglia (Istituto Italiano di Bioetica), and Prof. Colin de la Higuera (University of Nantes, UNESCO Chair RELIA) for their valuable contributions. We also thank School Principals Rosita Paradiso and Annina Carnevale, as well as the teacher coordinators who oversaw the project in their schools, Prof. Anna Ziviello and Prof. Francesca Pizzuti.

References

1. Beauchamp, T.L., Childress, J.F.: Principles of Biomedical Ethics. Oxford University Press, New York (1979)
2. Birch, D.: Provocations: Philosophy for Secondary School. Crown House Publishing, Carmarthen, UK (2014)
3. Cath, C., Wachter, S., Mittelstadt, B., et al.: Artificial Intelligence and the 'Good Society': The US, EU, and UK approach. Sci. Eng. Ethics **24**, 505–528 (2018)
4. Coeckelbergh, M.: AI Ethics. The MIT Press, Cambridge (2020)
5. Cuomo, S., Ranieri, M., Biagini, G.: Scuola e Intelligenza Artificiale. Percorsi di alfabetizzazione critica. Carocci, Roma (2024)
6. Damiano, L., Dumouchel, P.: Vivre avec les robots. Essai sur l'empathie artificielle. Éditions du Seuil, Paris (2016)
7. De la Higuera, C.: A Report about Education, Training Teachers and Learning Artificial Intelligence: Overview of Key Issues. Université de Nantes, pp. 1–12 (2018)
8. Dewey, J.,: Come pensiamo. Una riformulazione del rapporto fra il pensiero riflessivo e l'educazione. Raffaello Cortina, Milano (2019)
9. Donatelli, P.: Etica. I classici, le teorie, le linee evolutive. Einaudi, Torino (2015)
10. Floridi, L.: Etica dell'Intelligenza Artificiale. Sviluppi, opportunità, sfide. Raffaello Cortina, Milano (2022)
11. High-Level Expert Group on AI: Ethics Guidelines for Trustworthy AI. European Commission, Brussels (2019)
12. Holmes, W., Porayska-Pomsta, K. (eds.): The Ethics of Artificial Intelligence in Education: Practices, Challenges, and Debates. Routledge, London (2023)
13. Holmes, W., Porayska-Pomsta, K., Holstein, K., et al.: Ethics of AI in education: towards a community-wide framework. Int. J. Artif. Intell. Educ. **32**, 504–526 (2022)
14. Jaeger, W.: Paideia. The Ideals of Greek Culture: Volume I: Archaic Greece: The Mind of Athens. Oxford University Press, Oxford (1986)
15. Jobin, A., Ienca, M., Vayena, E.: The global landscape of AI ethics guidelines. Nat. Mach. Intell. **1**, 389–399 (2019)
16. Jonas, H.: The imperative of responsibility. In: Search of an Ethics for the Technological Age. University of Chicago Press, Chicago (1984)
17. Kimmons, R., Allman, B., Rosenberg, J., et al.: Trends and Topics in Educational Technology, 2023 Edition. TechTrends **67**, 583–591 (2023)
18. Lem, S.: Summa Technologiae. LUISS, Roma (2024)
19. Lipman, M.: Thinking in Education, 2nd edn. Cambridge University Press, Cambridge (2003)

20. Liu, C., Cui, J., Shang, R., Xiao, Y., Jia, Q., Gehringer, E.: Improving problem detection in peer assessment through pseudo-labeling using semi-supervised learning. In: Proceedings of the 15th International Conference on Educational Data Mining, pp. 391–397. International Educational Data Mining Society, Durham, United Kingdom (2022)
21. Long, D., Magerko, B.: What is AI literacy? Competencies and design considerations. In: Proceedings of the 2020 CHI Conference on Human Factors in Computing Systems, pp. 1c16 (2020)
22. Luckin, R., Cukurova, M.: Designing educational technologies in the age of AI: a learning sciences-driven approach. Br. J. Educ. Technol. **50**, 2824–2838 (2019)
23. McFarlane, D.C., Latorella, K.A.: The scope and importance of human interruption in human-computer interaction design. Hum.-Comput. Interact. **17**, 1–61 (2002)
24. Panciroli, C., Rivoltella, P.C.: Pedagogia algoritmica. Morcelliana, Brescia (2023)
25. Pisano, A.: Supervisionare per educare. L'etica come valutazione del rischio del caso AIED. Educrazia. Rivista di riflessioni pedagogiche e didattiche **1**(2), 136–148 (2023)
26. Pisano, A.: Enkrateia e Dopamina: per un'etica degli algoritmi contro il riduzionismo neurobiologico e comportamentista. Bioetica. Rivista Interdisciplinare **32**(1), 153–172 (2023)
27. Pisano, A.: Facing artificial tyranny. How to save democracy through education in the AI era and rethinking argumentation skills. In: Democratica, S. (ed.) Proceedings of the Third International Conference of the journal Scuola Democratica. Education and/for Social Justice. Vol. 1: Inequality, Inclusion, and Governance, pp. 72–84. Associazione "Per Scuola Democratica", Rome (2025)
28. Pisano, A.: Does the AI Need a Genealogy? The 'PAIA' Model and the Question Concerning Technology for the AI Regulation. Mimesis Journal – Mechané **9** (1) (2025)
29. Saranya, A., Subhashini, R.: A systematic review of explainable artificial intelligence models and applications: recent developments and future trends. Dec. Analyt. J. **3**, 1–14 (2023)
30. Selwyn, N., Jandric, P.: Postdigital living in the age of Covid-19: unsettling what we see as possible. Postdigit. Sci. Educ. **2**, 989–1005 (2020)
31. Tiribelli, S.: Identità personale e algoritmi. Carocci, Roma (2023)
32. Weinberger, D.: The rise of particulars: AI and the ethics of care. Philosophies **8**, 1–10 (2024)
33. Worley, P.: The If Machine: Philosophical Enquiry in the Classroom. Bloomsbury Academic, London (2010)
34. Zawacki-Richter, O., Marín, V.I., Bond, M., Gouverneur, F.: Systematic review of research on artificial intelligence applications in higher education: Where are the educators? Int. J. Educ. Technol. High. Educ. **16**(1), 1–27 (2019)
35. Zuboff, S.: The Age of Surveillance Capitalism: The Fight for the Human Future at the New Frontier of Power. Public Affairs, New York (2018)
36. Zhang, L., Fu, K., Liu, X.: Artificial intelligence in education: ethical issues and its regulations. In: Proceedings of the 5th International Conference on Big Data and Education (ICBDE 2022), pp. 1–6 (2022)

AI and Universal Design for Learning: Perspectives for Accessible and Multimodal Teaching

Giulia Angeloni[✉]

University "G. D'Annunzio" Chieti-Pescara, University of Macerata, Pescara, Italy
g.angeloni5@unimc.it

Abstract. This paper investigates the intersection of Universal Design for Learning (UDL) and artificial intelligence (AI) as a framework for inclusive education. Rather than being conceived solely as a technical tool, AI is approached here as both a means and an object of learning. When embedded in UDL, intelligent technologies can enhance accessibility, diversify modes of participation, and stimulate reflection on their algorithmic implications.

To exemplify this potential, we present Art Detective – Seeing with IA, an interdisciplinary activity for lower secondary school inspired by the national programme Innovamenti – Intelligenza Artificiale (Ministry of Education, Italy). The activity was redesigned through UDL principles to ensure flexibility and engagement. Students collaboratively built a small dataset of artworks, trained a simple classification model using accessible tools, and critically analysed the outputs. Alongside technical exploration, students engaged in discussions on accuracy, bias, and limitations, thus linking AI literacy with creativity and critical thinking.

Observations highlight that multimodal resources, adaptive tools, and collaborative tasks supported diverse learners, including those with special educational needs and linguistic barriers. The teacher's role emerged as crucial in scaffolding technical challenges and facilitating ethical discussions. The case illustrates how the combination of UDL and AI literacy can foster inclusive and equitable learning environments, while also indicating future directions for empirical research and teacher professional development.

Keywords: Universal Design for Learning (UDL) · AI Literacy · Inclusive Education

1 Introduction

Artificial intelligence is taking on an ever-increasing role in educational contexts, opening up new scenarios of innovation and challenges. Tools such as machine translation systems, text-to-speech and virtual tutors promise to reduce barriers to entry and personalize learning (Togni, 2025), but questions remain regarding bias, transparency and the evolution of the role of teachers (van Toorn, 2024; Popenici & Kerr, 2017).

© The Author(s), under exclusive license to Springer Nature Switzerland AG 2026
A. Dipace et al. (Eds.): WAILS 2025, LNCS 16438, pp. 29–42, 2026.
https://doi.org/10.1007/978-3-032-17604-2_3

In recent years, international initiatives such as AI4K12 (Artificial Intelligence for K-12)[1] in the United States and UNESCO reports[2] have underlined the urgency of promoting widespread AI literacy as early as primary school, both as a learning content and as a tool to support educational processes (Yim, 2024; Song et al., 2024).

At the same time, European policies (European Commission, 2022) insist on the need for an ethical and responsible adoption of AI in education, linking it to the goals of inclusion and social justice set out in the United Nations 2030 Agenda.

In this approach, Universal Design for Learning (UDL) offers a robust pedagogical approach to guide the use of AI toward inclusion and equity, thanks to its principles of representation, engagement, and action/expression (CAST, 2018; Meyer, Rose & Gordon, 2014).

Recent studies have shown how the integration of UDL and AI can not only improve accessibility and participation but also strengthen the sense of digital citizenship and technological agency (Guatelli, 2023; Moscato & Pedone, 2024; Moriña, Carballo & Doménech, 2025).

The aim of this contribution is therefore to explore the potential of the integration between AI and UDL for the design of inclusive and adaptive educational environments.

---

[1] This is an initiative launched in 2018 by the Association for the Advancement of Artificial Intelligence (AAAI) and the Computer Science Teachers Association (CSTA), with the support of the National Science Foundation (NSF) in the United States. The aim is to define national guidelines for the teaching of artificial intelligence in kindergarten, primary and secondary school (K-12). The project identified the "Five Big Ideas in AI", which constitute the fundamental conceptual nuclei for AI education:

- Perception – computers perceive the world using sensors.

- Representation & Reasoning – intelligent agents maintain representations of the world and use them to reason.

- Learning – agents can learn from data.

- Natural Interaction – agents interact naturally with humans.

- Societal Impact – AI affects society in both positive and negative ways.

   These five ideas are not only a technical curriculum, but also intend to provide a foundation for developing critical and ethical skills, connecting AI to digital citizenship and inclusion (Touretzky et al., 2019).

[2] UNESCO (2021), *AI and Education: Guidance for Policy-Makers.* https://www.unesco.org/en/articles/ai-and-education-guidance-policy-makers?hub=32618.UNESCO (2022), *K-12 AI Curricula: A Mapping of Government-Endorsed AI Curricula.* https://unesdoc.unesco.org/ark:/48223/pf0000386693.UNESCO (2023), *Guidance for Generative AI in Education and Research.* https://unesdoc.unesco.org/ark:/48223/pf0000391105.UNESCO (2024), *AI Competency Framework for Students and Teachers.* https://unesdoc.unesco.org/ark:/48223/pf0000395236.

To this end, after a review of the theoretical model, we present an application case (Art Detective – Seeing with AI), aimed at stimulating critical thinking and creativity in secondary school students, and discuss the results in terms of accessibility, participation and equity.

2 Theoretical Framework

This section outlines the theoretical structure integrating Universal Design for Learning (UDL) and artificial intelligence (AI) for inclusive instructional design. After recalling the UDL principles (representation, action/expression, engagement), we discuss how AI tools can expand multimodality, accessibility and personalization, highlighting the mediative role of the teacher in managing risks, bias and transparency. Section 2.1 summarises the key concepts, while the following ones delve into literature, international models and educational impacts.

2.1 Universal Design for Learning

Universal Design for Learning is a pedagogical framework that was created with the aim of designing accessible and flexible educational environments from the outset, overcoming the traditional compensatory approach. The central idea is that variability is not an exception, but a physiological feature of human functioning: each student carries with him cognitive, cultural, linguistic and motivational differences that must be considered as a starting point in instructional design (CAST, 2018; Meyer, Rose & Gordon, 2014).

The model is based on three key principles, also called *multiple means*: engagement (why you learn), representation (what you learn) and action and expression (how you learn). These principles correspond to different neural networks in the human brain and allow for motivation, accessibility, and the possibility of expression for a wide variety of students. As pointed out in the Italian ministerial document on digital civic education, the UDL represents a transition from a logic "for the few" to a logic "for all", in which strategies created for students with special educational needs become a common heritage (Guatelli, 2023).

From a pedagogical point of view, a proactive and universal design is proposed: instead of retroactively adapting materials for individual cases, a flexible learning environment is built that reduces the need for individual accommodations (Moscato & Pedone, 2024). This vision is also reflected in the concept of inclusive digital citizenship, which implies accessibility and distributive justice for all citizens, regardless of personal or socio-economic conditions (Sánchez Corrales, 2024).

Research conducted in universities confirms the effectiveness of UDL: teacher training on this model increases the quality of teaching practices and student engagement (Moriña, Carballo & Doménech, 2025). In addition, the connection with other frameworks, such as DigCompEdu, strengthens their operational potential, providing teachers with concrete tools to integrate digital skills and inclusion into their practices (European Commission, 2022).

We can therefore consider it as a paradigm shift: from the idea of a standardized curriculum and only then adapted to the needs and abilities of individuals, to the idea of a curriculum designed from the beginning to be flexible, accessible and fair. It is in this perspective that the encounter with AI is placed, which, if integrated according to UDL principles, can further expand the possibilities of representation, expression and engagement.

2.2 AI for Educational Inclusion

Artificial intelligence is currently one of the emerging technologies with the greatest potential for transforming the education system. If inserted within intentional pedagogical models inspired by values of equity, it can become not only a support for traditional teaching, but a real tool for the construction of inclusive learning environments.

The inclusion perspective, in fact, cannot be understood only as a subsequent *adaptation* for the benefit of students with specific educational needs, but must be considered as a structural principle of instructional design (CAST, 2024; Meyer, Rose & Gordon, 2014).

With this in mind, AI can expand educational opportunities for all, reduce barriers to entry and encourage the participation of individuals with different characteristics, backgrounds and cognitive styles.

The most widespread applications currently highlight the concreteness of this potential: text-to-speech and speech-to-text tools support students with visual, auditory or motor disabilities; machine translation systems facilitate the learning of non-Italian-speaking students, reducing linguistic barriers to inclusion; adaptive learning platforms tailor content and activities based on skill level, progress and learning styles; immersive augmented and virtual reality environments allow educational experiences otherwise unattainable (Togni, 2025; Hwang, 2014).

These solutions, if properly integrated, concretize the three principles of Universal Design for Learning—representation, engagement and action/expression—making effective the flexible and accessible design evoked by the approach (Moscato & Pedone, 2024).

A further area in which AI shows significant potential is that of formative and inclusive assessment. Machine learning algorithms can analyze the data generated during teaching activity to provide personalized feedback, monitor student progress and adapt verification tests in real time. This reduces the risk that standardized measurement tools penalize students with divergent cognitive styles or special educational needs, favoring instead self-assessment and self-regulation paths (Wang et al., 2024).

Alongside these positive prospects, however, the literature warns against some potentially problematic drifts. Educational AI, if not regulated by ethical principles and participatory processes, can introduce new forms of systemic exclusion. Algorithmic biases, generated by incomplete or culturally unbalanced datasets, risk reproducing pre-existing stereotypes and inequalities (Popenici & Kerr, 2017; Rudin, Wang & Coker, 2019).

In addition, the increasing opacity of many automated systems poses serious questions in terms of transparency and accountability, reducing the possibility of control by teachers and students.

The example of the Nadia project[3]—a virtual assistant developed with the collaboration of people with disabilities but then discontinued due to lack of sustainability—shows how the absence of clear governance and genuine user engagement can result in failures that undermine trust and accentuate exclusion (van Toorn, 2024).

To avoid such risks, it is necessary to place the use of AI within an inclusive pedagogy, understood as a practice aimed at expanding participation, ensuring equal learning opportunities and strengthening student motivation. It is not a question of indiscriminately introducing digital tools, but of integrating them into coherent educational projects, capable of enhancing diversity and supporting the development of transversal skills.

A relevant contribution in this direction is represented by the model proposed by Song and colleagues (2024), which integrates the principles of UDL with the Five Big Ideas of the AI4K12 initiative (Touretzky et al., 2019).

In fact, it starts from the need to design learning experiences on AI that are not only effective from a disciplinary point of view, but also inclusive and fair.

In particular, the framework organizes the fundamental contents of AI education – perception, representation and reasoning, learning, natural interaction and social impact – within the three UDL dimensions: the why (engagement), the what (representation) and the how (action & expression).

These conceptual axes are flanked by six "praxes", i.e. pedagogical practices exemplified with concrete educational activities, which aim to make AI understandable, accessible and motivating for students with different backgrounds, abilities and needs.

This model not only facilitates access and personalization, but transforms artificial intelligence itself into an object of learning, stimulating the understanding of its functions, its limits and its ethical and social implications (Table 1).

AI-mediated educational inclusion must also be understood as a co-design process. Technology, in fact, becomes truly transformative only if the subjects involved in the school context—students, teachers and families—actively participate in its definition, implementation and evaluation.

A co-design logic makes it possible to adapt solutions to the real needs of contexts, reducing the risk of technocratic impositions while promoting forms of algorithmic representation and distributive justice in the data economy (Sánchez Corrales, 2024).

In this scenario, the role of the teacher is confirmed as central.

The teacher cannot be replaced by artificial intelligence, but becomes its critical and pedagogical mediator. It is the teacher who transforms an adaptive platform into an opportunity for meaningful learning, a chatbot into a tool for critical reflection, an automatic evaluation system into a resource for the student's self-regulation.

---

[3] Nadia was a virtual assistant promoted in 2017 by Australia's National Disability Insurance Scheme (NDIS), with the aim of facilitating access to services for people with disabilities. The voice of the system was voiced by actress Cate Blanchett and the design was developed in co-design with end users. Despite expectations, the project was halted in 2019 due to high costs, difficulty in updating content, and accuracy limitations. This failure is often cited in the literature as a warning against the risks of inclusive initiatives not accompanied by sustainable governance and continuous user involvement.

Table 1. The framework proposed by Song et al. 2024.

UDL Principles	Engagement (Why)	Representation (What)	Action and Expression (How)
5 Big Ideas of AI4K12	**Perception**	**Representation & Reasoning**	**Learning**
6 Praxes	**Natural Interaction**	**Societal Impact**	
	Scaffolded engagement with AI	*Contextualized learning of AI*	*Multiple means of representation of AI concepts*
	Critical and ethical reflection	*Collaborative and inclusive practices*	*Opportunities for diverse action and expression*

In the absence of this mediation, AI risks reducing educational complexity to a set of mechanical procedures, depriving learning of its relational, creative and social dimension (Moscato & Pedone, 2024; Moriña, Carballo & Doménech, 2025).

Using AI for educational inclusion is not simply about adding a technological layer to traditional teaching, but requires a structural rethinking of instructional design. Only an approach based on accessibility, flexibility and participation can make technology an ally in the construction of truly inclusive educational environments, capable of responding to the challenges of a complex and digitally mediated society.

2.3 AI Literacy and Inclusive Education

Alongside the use of AI as a tool to support accessibility and personalization, there is a strong need to develop artificial intelligence literacy (AI literacy), understood as a set of cognitive, practical and critical skills necessary to understand, use and evaluate intelligent technologies (Stolpe & Hallström, 2024; Sperling et al., 2024).

It is not just a matter of acquiring technical familiarity with tools based on machine learning or natural language processing, but of ensuring that all students, regardless of their personal conditions or socio-cultural background, have the opportunity to become active participants in educational and social processes in which artificial intelligence is increasingly pervasive.

The literature identifies at least three dimensions of AI literacy (Long & Magerko, 2020; Yim, 2024):

Conceptual and technical knowledge, i.e. understanding what AI is, how it works, and recognizing systems based on algorithms and machine learning.

Practical skills, i.e. the ability to use tools appropriately and productively to support learning and problem-solving.

Critical and ethical awareness, which involves reflecting on social impacts, risks of bias, transparency of systems and implications for educational equity.

Recent studies underline how a reductive approach to AI literacy—centered solely on technical mastery—risks generating new inequalities: some students can become expert users of intelligent tools without developing critical analysis skills, while others risk being excluded from access to such resources (Popenici & Kerr, 2017; Gentile et al., 2023).

To steer AI literacy towards inclusive purposes, several authors suggest adopting a multiliteracy vision, in which AI is integrated as part of broader *technological literacy*, connected to scientific knowledge, socio-technical skills and ethical skills (Stolpe & Hallström, 2024).

This perspective is particularly relevant in the field of primary and secondary education, where technological literacy should be introduced not only as a disciplinary content, but as a transversal practice capable of supporting the participation of students with different backgrounds (Song et al., 2024).

In this scenario, Universal Design for Learning represents an essential point of reference. If AI literacy is to be inclusive, it is necessary to design paths that recognize the variability of students and offer multiple ways of access and participation (CAST, 2024). The UDL provides the methodological framework for declining concepts through different languages and tools: visual simulations for those who learn best with graphic stimuli; unplugged activities and role-playing games for those who prefer practical experience; guided narratives or chatbot interactions for auditory learners (Meyer, Rose & Gordon, 2014; Moscato & Pedone, 2024).

Building inclusive AI literacy also involves teacher training. Recent research has shown that many teachers say they are poorly prepared for the pedagogical integration of AI, despite recognizing its potential (Sperling et al., 2024; Pitrella et al., 2023). It is therefore necessary to promote professional development paths that, in addition to transmitting technical knowledge, help teachers reflect on the pedagogical and ethical implications (Ding et al., 2024). Training that integrates UDL and AI literacy allows teachers to become critical mediators, capable of introducing intelligent technologies into their practices without losing the human and inclusive dimension of education.

This link is therefore bidirectional: on the one hand, UDL makes AI literacy accessible to different students, preventing conceptual complexities from becoming barriers. On the other hand, AI literacy reinforces the mission of UDL, since equipping all students with the necessary skills to understand and critically interrogate artificial intelligence means ensuring its full participation in school and social life. In this perspective, AI literacy is not just a new discipline, but an inclusive practice that contributes to training citizens capable of using technology to build equity and educational justice (Song et al., 2024).

2.4   Connecting UDL, Inclusive AI, and AI Literacy

The theoretical framework discussed shows how the integration between Universal Design for Learning, artificial intelligence for educational inclusion and AI literacy constitutes a coherent model to address the challenges of contemporary schooling. UDL provides pedagogical principles for flexible and accessible design, AI offers tools that expand learning opportunities, and AI literacy ensures that these tools are understood and used critically.

The convergence of these three axes prepares the ground for innovative teaching experiences, such as the Art Detective – Seeing with AI application case, presented in the next section.

3   Classroom Implementation: *Art Detective – Seeing with AI*

This section describes the Art Detective activity, conceived as part of a teacher training course and subsequently applied in the classroom with inclusive and experimental purposes. Objectives, context, participants, operational phases and tools used are presented, along with the role of the teacher as a facilitator and critical mediator in the integration of AI. The experience was conceived as an exploratory educational intervention, aimed at testing the feasibility and adaptability of the AI-supported UDL approach in a real-world context.

Figure 1 provides a schematic representation of the design structure adopted for this activity.

	Teacher mediation: Choice of tools and prompts, verifications, de-biasing, privacy & ethics, transparency			
Instructional input	**UDL Principles**	**AI Components**	**Task sequence**	**Expected outcomes**
Objectives Contents Student needs, Context constraints.	Representation Action and Expression Engagement.	Content generation (text/images) Text/speech synthesis Visual aids Adaptivity.	1. Exploration 2. Activation 3. Construction 4. Reworking 5. Sharing & Evaluation.	Accessibility Participation Motivation Inclusion

Fig. 1. UDL × AI framework for "Art Detective": UDL principles guide design; AI tools enable multimodality and adaptivity; teacher mediation steers choices, verification, and ethics; the five-step sequence leads to accessibility, participation, motivation, and inclusion.

3.1   Context and Purpose

In classroom implementation, *Art Detective – Seeing with AI,* art, due to its exploratory and interpretive nature, was chosen as a privileged context to stimulate critical observation, aesthetic reflection and creativity, while AI was used as a tool to make these processes more accessible and inclusive.

The operational sheet is inspired by an activity developed within the national training course "Innovations – Artificial Intelligence", available on the ministerial platform Scuola Futura.

This initiative, promoted by the Ministry of Education and Merit, offers laboratory experiences in which artificial intelligence is explored both as a learning object and as a teaching support tool.

The Art Detective – Seeing with AI experience has been adapted and reformulated according to the principles of Universal Design for Learning with the aim of offering a concrete example of integration between intelligent technologies and school inclusion.

The aims of the course were mainly two: on the one hand, to promote the active and motivated participation of all students, including those with special educational needs or language and cultural barriers; on the other hand, to develop a form of applied AI literacy, encouraging students to reflect not only on the content of the works analyzed but also on the functioning, limits and impact of the digital tools used (Song et al., 2024; Stolpe & Hallström, 2024).

The activity is therefore situated within the UDL framework, adopted as a model to ensure flexibility, accessibility and plurality of expression. In particular, the path has been designed to decline the three fundamental principles—multiple means of representation, multiple modes of engagement and multiple forms of action/expression (CAST, 2024; Meyer, Rose & Gordon, 2014)—offering all students differentiated opportunities for fruition, participation and production.

3.2 Description of the Activity

The *Art Detective – Seeing with AI* activity invites students to explore AI functionality through an authentic task: the training of an automatic classification system capable of recognizing different types of artistic images, such as portraits, landscapes or still lifes. The course is developed in a laboratory and collaborative form: participants contribute to the construction of a small dataset, use accessible digital tools to implement a simple machine learning model and are guided to critically reflect on the results obtained. The activity is therefore proposed not only as a technical experience to approach the functioning of artificial intelligence, but also as an opportunity to stimulate critical thinking, creative expression and educational inclusion, discussing with students the potential and limits of technologies in the educational context (Table 2).

Table 2. Sheet inspired by experiences carried out in the MOOC "Innovations – Artificial Intelligence" (INDIRE, 2025), adapted in an operational key for the school integration of AI and UDL.

Unit Title	Art Detective – Seeing with AI
School Grade	Lower secondary school
Subjects	Art & Image, Digital Civics, Technology
Duration	6–8 h (divided into 4–5 meetings)
Learning objectives	Understand how AI works; develop critical thinking and multimodal modes of expression; collaborate on the production of accessible content
Activated skills	Digital (DigComp), citizenship, creativity, collaboration, communication
Tools used	eachable Machine or MIT App Inventor; visual datasets; audio/text-to-speech apps; mind maps

(continued)

Table 2. (continued)

Unit Title	Art Detective – Seeing with AI
Phases of the unit	1. Exploration 2. Activation 3. Construction 4. Reworking 5. Sharing and Evaluation
Applied UDL principles	Multiple representation (visual, textual, audio); differentiated expression (text, oral, graphic); active engagement and authentic tasks
Evaluation	Rubric + self-assessment + logbook + multi-format final paper
Points of attention	Lead critical reflection on AI biases and limitations; ensure accessibility and inclusiveness

3.3 Tools and Resources

A combination of digital tools and technologies based on artificial intelligence was adopted for the implementation of the activity, selected with the aim of ensuring accessibility, diversification of learning methods and active participation.

Key tools include:

Text-to-Speech (TTS) and Speech-to-Text, implemented to ensure accessibility for students with visual, auditory or motor difficulties, and to promote multi-channel use of content. These tools support the UDL principle of *representation*, offering multiple ways of accessing information (visual, auditory and textual).

Machine translation systems, used to make the activity accessible even to non-Italian-speaking students. The integration of translation has made it possible to expand opportunities for participation and to build a multilingual and intercultural context. This aspect embodies both *representation*, offering information in different languages, and *action & expression*, allowing students to express themselves in the language in which they feel most competent.

Adaptive quizzes and dynamic assessment environments, proposed at the end of the activity to verify comprehension and stimulate self-assessment. Through machine learning-based systems, the questions were adapted according to the students' answers, modulating the level of difficulty. This tool is linked to the principle of *action & expression*, as it allows students to demonstrate their knowledge in personalized and progressively more complex forms.

Multimodal support materials, such as high-definition images of the works, simplified text descriptions and audio-narrative resources. This plurality of materials, in line with the logic of *design for all*, has guaranteed each student the possibility of accessing the content according to their preferences or needs.

Overall, the integration of these tools has made it possible to articulate the three UDL principles in a coherent way: *representation* through multimodality and linguistic accessibility, *engagement* thanks to investigative dynamics and the use of chatbots, and *action & expression* through adaptive quizzes and multilingual productions.

3.4 Application of UDL Principles

The *Art Detective – Seeing with AI* activity was structured with the intention of translating the three key principles of UDL into practice, so as to ensure accessibility and participation for all students, regardless of background, cognitive styles or any special educational needs.

The principle of *representation* has been implemented through a plurality of languages and formats, which have combined the high-definition images of the works of art with simplified textual descriptions, explanatory videos, audio-narratives and multimodal materials. This choice has made it possible for students with different needs to access the content, reducing barriers to learning and offering personalized opportunities for use.

The principle of *engagement* guided the construction of the investigative dynamic of the "art detective", which made the activity authentic, motivating and stimulating. The automatic classification activities strengthened the students' curiosity, while the collaborative dimension of the path—from the construction of the dataset to the collective discussion of the results—promoted a sense of belonging, cooperation and shared responsibility.

Finally, the principle of *action & expression* was realized by offering students the opportunity to demonstrate what they have learned through different products and channels. Some chose to develop descriptive texts or digital concept maps, others preferred multimedia presentations, oral narratives or multilingual contributions. Adaptive quizzes and dynamic assessment tools have further enhanced this dimension, allowing everyone to express their skills in differentiated and progressively more complex ways.

In this way, the framework did not remain an abstract theoretical reference, but oriented the entire design and management of the laboratory in an operational way, transforming the introduction of AI from a possible source of new barriers to leverage for the construction of truly inclusive and equitable experiences.

3.5 Observations and First Results

The observations collected during the experimentation show a high degree of curiosity and engagement on the part of the students, favored by the authentic nature of the task and the investigative dynamics that made them protagonists of the learning process. The possibility of training a machine learning model and verifying its results has stimulated spontaneous discussions on the accuracy of classifications, the limitations of datasets and possible algorithmic biases, opening up critical reflections in line with the purposes of AI literacy (Song et al., 2024; Popenici & Kerr, 2017).

The use of multimodal and accessible tools also encouraged the participation of students with language difficulties or special educational needs, who were able to interact with the content through different channels. Machine translation and text-to-speech have expanded the possibilities of use, helping to reduce communication barriers.

Some points of attention also emerged. Some students initially expressed difficulties in approaching the more technical aspects of the activity, such as the construction of the dataset or the use of classification tools. These critical issues have been mitigated thanks to the mediation role of the teacher, who has been confirmed as crucial in providing personalized support and guiding collective reflection on the results (Moscato & Pedone, 2024; Moriña, Carballo & Doménech, 2025).

In addition, the experience showed the need for more relaxed teaching times to allow a deep understanding of the basic concepts of this technology.

Overall, the experience made it possible to combine the development of disciplinary and basic skills on AI with the promotion of collaboration, creativity and critical thinking, demonstrating that the principles of UDL, if applied systematically, can make intelligent technologies extremely effective tools for building inclusive learning environments.

3.6 Critical Issues and Limitations

The intervention described has some methodological limitations that circumscribe its interpretative scope and transferability. Firstly, it is a qualitative and small-scale experience, carried out in a single school context and characterized by a predominantly observational and descriptive design. In the absence of control groups and systematic quantitative measures, the results are not generalizable and do not allow for precise isolation of the effect of the UDL framework from possible concomitant factors, such as the novelty effect or the intrinsic motivation of the participants. In addition, the lack of longitudinal surveys limits the possibility of assessing the durability of the observed outcomes, in particular with regard to the inclusion and motivation dimensions.

From a technological and content point of view, the use of pre-trained AI tools determines a form of technological dependence and introduces potential cultural and linguistic biases in the generated materials. This issue is particularly relevant when AI is used not only as a support tool, but also as a learning object, since in the absence of critical mediation it could contribute to conveying partial or distorted representations.

In terms of instructional design, another limitation concerns the role of teachers: although participating teachers received targeted training as part of the course, this is not yet embedded in a structured and transferable model. The effective implementation of the activity has in fact required specific pedagogical, digital and ethical skills, which are not necessarily spread homogeneously among all teachers. This represents a potential obstacle to the scalability and replicability of the intervention in less experienced contexts.

Finally, the issues of ethics, privacy and transparency have been addressed in a preliminary manner and not yet integrated into a systematic procedural model, leaving open relevant issues regarding data management and the communication of the intrinsic limits of the AI tools adopted.

4 Conclusions and Future Prospects

The analysis conducted showed that the encounter between UDL and artificial intelligence does not only represent a methodological innovation, but a possible conceptual turning point for educational design. AI, if guided by solid pedagogical frameworks, does not limit itself to removing technical barriers, but becomes an epistemic device capable of redefining access to knowledge, multiplying forms of expression and strengthening the critical dimension of learning.

The case presented demonstrates that AI can be both a means and an object of inclusive education: an operational tool to personalize and make content accessible, but also educational content through which students experiment, understand and problematize algorithmic logics, biases and ethical implications. This dual level opens up unprecedented scenarios for education, in which technology is not an accessory but an integral part of an equity-oriented curriculum.

The role of the teacher remains crucial not merely as a technical facilitator, but as a critical mediator capable of transforming the use of intelligent tools into opportunities for shared reflection. In this perspective, teacher training takes on a strategic value: without specific AI literacy skills and without the ability to decline them in the principles of UDL, innovation risks translating into new forms of exclusion.

The future prospects are articulated on several levels. On the research side, longitudinal studies will need to be launched to assess the real impact of AI and UDL-based activities in terms of learning, equity and motivation. In terms of educational practice, it is necessary to develop repertoires of activities that can be replicated and adapted to different school contexts, supported by open source platforms and accessible tools. In terms of teacher training, the priority emerges for specific paths that combine AI literacy and UDL principles, so that teachers can take on the role of critical mediators and not mere users of technological tools. Finally, in terms of policies, there is an urgent need to define institutional guidelines that guarantee the responsible, transparent and fair adoption of AI in schools, in line with the objectives of inclusion and digital citizenship promoted at European level.

In the near future, the integration between AI and UDL can undoubtedly become the ground on which to build a new paradigm of inclusive education in the algorithmic era, capable of training citizens who are not only competent in the use of intelligent technologies, but also aware of their social and cultural implications.

References

CAST: Universal Design for Learning Guidelines version 2.2. CAST, Wakefield (2018)

Meyer, A., Rose, D.H., Gordon, D.: Universal Design for Learning: Theory and Practice. CAST Publishing, Wakefield (2014)

Guatelli, N.: Education Policies and Inclusion of Diversity: The Perspective of Universal Design for Learning (UDL). University of Insubria, Varese (2023)

Moriña, A., Carballo, R., Doménech, A.: Transforming higher education: a systematic review of faculty training in UDL and its benefits. Teach. High. Educ. (2025). https://doi.org/10.1080/13562517.2025.2465994

Moscato, M., Pedone, F.: Enhancing inclusive teaching. A teacher professional development research grounded in UDL principles. Pedagogical Perspective, TSTT Special Issue, 110–125 (2024). https://doi.org/10.29329/pedper.2024.37

Bray, A., Brown, M., Kershner, R.: What next for Universal Design for Learning? A systematic literature review of UDL research in higher education. Br. J. Edu. Technol. **54**(6), 1202–1224 (2023). https://doi.org/10.1111/bjet.13364

Song, Y., Weisberg, L.R., Zhang, S., Tian, X., Boyer, K.E., Israel, M.: A framework for inclusive AI learning design for diverse learners. Comput. Educ. Artif. Intell. **6**, 100212 (2024). https://doi.org/10.1016/j.caeai.2024.100212

Yim, I.H.Y.: A critical review of teaching and learning AI literacy: developing an intelligence-based AI literacy framework for primary school education. Comput. Educ. Artif. Intell. **7**, 100319 (2024). https://doi.org/10.1016/j.caeai.2024.100319

Stolpe, M., Hallström, J.: Artificial intelligence literacy for technology education. Comput. Educ. **206**, 104903 (2024). https://doi.org/10.1016/j.compedu.2023.104903

Sperling, E., Arnold, N., Laanpere, M., Luckin, R.: In search of artificial intelligence (AI) literacy in K-12 education: a systematic review. Comput. Educ. **205**, 104886 (2024). https://doi.org/10.1016/j.compedu.2023.104886

Ding, A.-C.E., Shi, L., Yang, H., Choi, I.: Enhancing teacher AI literacy and integration through different types of cases in teacher professional development. Comput. Educ. Open **6**, 100178 (2024). https://doi.org/10.1016/j.caeo.2024.100178

Popenici, S.A.D., Kerr, S.: Exploring the impact of artificial intelligence on teaching and learning in higher education. Res. Pract. Technol. Enhanc. Learn. **12**, 22 (2017). https://doi.org/10.1186/s41039-017-0062-8

van Toorn, G.: Inclusion interrupted: lessons from the making of a digital assistant by and for people with disability. Gov. Inf. Q. **41**, 101900 (2024). https://doi.org/10.1016/j.giq.2023.101900

Togni, J.: Development of an Inclusive Educational Platform Using Open Technologies and Machine Learning: A Case Study on Accessibility Enhancement. arXiv preprint arXiv:2503.15501 (2025)

Hwang, G.J.: Definition, framework and research issues of smart learning environments: a context-aware ubiquitous learning perspective. Smart Learn. Environ. **1**(4), 1–14 (2014)

Commission, E.: Digital Education Action Plan 2021–2027: Resetting Education and Training for the Digital Age. Publications Office of the European Union, Luxembourg (2022)

Touretzky, D.S., Gardner-McCune, C., Martin, F., Seehorn, D.: Envisioning AI for K-12: what should every child know about AI? In: Proceedings of the AAAI Conference on Artificial Intelligence, vol. 33, pp. 9795–9799. AAAI Press, Palo Alto (2019)

Sánchez Corrales, V.: Designing for inclusion in AI-driven learning: towards algorithmic justice in education. Comput. Educ. Artif. Intell. **5**, 100201 (2024). https://doi.org/10.1016/j.caeai.2024.100201

Artificial Intelligence and Virtual Labs.
A Controlled Study of a Teaching Experience
in an ITS Academy Course

Agostino Sorbara[1,2]($\boxtimes$)

[1] Università di Macerata, Macerata, Italia
`agostinosorbara@libero.it`
[2] Università MagnaGræcia di Catanzaro, Catanzaro, Italia

Abstract. The integration of Artificial Intelligence in Higher Technical Education represents both a challenge and an opportunity to innovate educational processes. This study presents an experimental teaching model applied to an ITS Academy course, in which students simulated an experiment using a Virtual Labs platform, supported by integrative Artificial Intelligence tools. The experience was evaluated through rubrics, observational reports, and a questionnaire on the use of Artificial Intelligence, actively involving students and teachers. The results highlight how the informed use of Artificial Intelligence technologies can strengthen technical and scientific skills, promoting a Learning-by-Doing approach and fostering personalized learning. The research proposes a replicable teaching model and reflects on the methodological limitations and future prospects of systematically integrating Artificial Intelligence into Higher Technical Education curricula, highlighting the potential and critical aspects of this new educational approach. The results suggest that Artificial Intelligence, if used appropriately, can provide powerful cognitive and operational support in Higher Technical Education contexts.

Keywords: ITS Academy · Artificial Intelligence · Virtual Labs

1 Introduction

Artificial Intelligence (AI) is transforming the educational structure of the Higher Technical Education sector, offering new opportunities for personalized learning, data analysis and scientific communication.

In recent years, Artificial Intelligence has assumed an increasingly important role in educational processes, particularly in Higher Technical Education. Its ability to process information, generate content, support decisions, and even more so the ability for students to learn through the "Learning by Doing" methodology, which is well suited to generation Alpha students and ITS Academy students, has opened up new perspectives for personalized learning, the simulation of complex scenarios, and the assessment of skills.

This study arose from the need to document and analyze the educational experience of ITS Academy students, with the aim of evaluating the effectiveness of integrating

A. Dipace et al. (Eds.): WAILS 2025, LNCS 16438, pp. 43–47, 2026.
https://doi.org/10.1007/978-3-032-17604-2_4

Virtual Labs and Artificial Intelligence tools in promoting scientific learning and the development of transversal skills.

2 Literature Review

In recent years, the convergence of virtual environments and Artificial Intelligence has brought about a major shift in educational practices, shaping a coherent framework for educational innovation. Several studies have highlighted how these technologies, despite their different approaches, synergistically contribute to making learning more interactive, personalized, and effective.

On the one hand, virtual environments have emerged as useful tools with high potential for conceptual exploration. Studies by Avila-Garzon et al. (2021) and Cao & Yu (2023) have demonstrated that virtual environments allow students to explore complex concepts through visual simulations and hands-on interactions. The practical interactions offered by these environments allow students to overcome the limitations of traditional teaching, promoting a deeper and more concrete understanding of content.

At the same time, Artificial Intelligence has introduced new ways to support learning. According to Berardinetti et al. (2024), in the educational context, Artificial Intelligence manifests itself through a wide range of tools and applications, including Intelligent Tutoring Systems and automatic exercise correction. These tools not only automate processes but also offer adaptive learning experiences.

In particular, Intelligent Tutoring Systems represent a point of convergence between Artificial Intelligence and personalized learning. Gentile et al. (2023) and Gulbay et al. (2025) highlight their transformative impact, highlighting how these systems are among the most significant innovations in educational Artificial Intelligence, capable of shaping tailored learning paths for each student.

This technological transformation has also had repercussions on pedagogical methodologies. O'Donell et al. (2024) observed that the introduction of Artificial Intelligence in Higher Education has brought about a radical change in teaching practices, paving the way for more dynamic models.

A concrete example of this evolution is the laboratory model proposed by Carraro LAB at the Didacta 2024 conference. The concept of Techno-Methodologies integrates immersive environments and Artificial Intelligence, demonstrating the effectiveness of simulation as a teaching tool and outlining a systemic approach to educational innovation.

3 Methodology

The study was conducted during an ITS Academy course in the "Chemistry and New Life Technologies" area.

The students used:

- A 3D platform for simulating the experiment;
- Artificial Intelligence tools (ChatGPT, Copilot, Gemini, Others) to support theoretical understanding and technical reporting;
- Digital tools for data analysis.

The teaching protocol was divided into seven phases:

1) Theoretical introduction: presentation of the key concepts and Artificial Intelligence tools;
2) Theoretical concepts;
3) Presentation of the Virtual Labs: Use of simulated environments for bio-technological experiments;
4) Simulation with the Virtual Lab: execution of the virtual experiment with data collection;
5) Data analysis: interpretation of results with the support of integrative Artificial Intelligence tools;
6) Drafting the technical report: writing the technical report with the support of integrative Artificial Intelligence tools;
7) Evaluation and reflection: students self-assessment and completion of the evaluation questionnaire on the use of Artificial Intelligence, the teacher compile the report of observation.

The virtual platform integrated Artificial Intelligence features to personalize learning paths.

The evaluation was carried out using a grid structured on six dimensions:

- Scientific understanding of contents;
- Conscious use of Artificial Intelligence;
- Decision-making autonomy;
- Ability to data analysis;
- Communication with appropriate technical language;
- Critical reflection).

Each area rated in tenths (score from 1 to 10).
The research methods used were of the following type:

- Semi-experimental;
- Mixed;
- Evidence-Based Results (EBR).

4 Results

The analysis of the data collected anonymously through observation reports, the evaluation rubrics drawn up by the teachers, and the evaluation questionnaire on the use of Artificial Intelligence administered to the students, highlight significant aspects of the teaching experience.

Overall, the average course grade was 7.8, with 68% of students achieving a passing grade in all areas. 24% of students achieved an average grade between 9 and 10, which is considered excellent; 44% achieved an average grade between 7 and below 9, which is considered good; 24% achieved a grade between 6 and below 7, which is considered sufficient; 4% achieved an average grade between 5 and below 6, which is considered insufficient, and another 4% achieved an average grade below 5, which is considered seriously insufficient.

Grouping the data by area, we obtain that the average rating for the area "scientific understanding" is 8.16, for the area "conscious use of AI" it is 7.44, for the area "decision-making autonomy" it is 7.76, for the area "scientific communication" it is 7.92, and for the area "critical reflection" it is 7.84.

All students used at least one AI integration tool. ChatGPT was the most used (80% of students), followed by Copilot (72% of students), and Gemini (60% of students), while other AI integration tools were used by 48% of students.

Seventy-six percent of students used AI integration tools for content generation, 32% for organizing ideas, 24% for reviewing writing, and 60% for finding sources.

Regarding the ease of use of Artificial Intelligence integrative tools, 60% of students stated that they found using Artificial Intelligence integrative tools quite easy, 16% very easy, 4% extremely easy, 12% difficult, and 8% very difficult.

Overall, all students were satisfied with their experience with Artificial Intelligence. Specifically, 24% were fairly satisfied, 44% were very satisfied, and 32% were extremely satisfied.

5 Discussion

The integration of Artificial Intelligence in Higher Technical Education is a growing interest in the international scientific community. The study's results showed that this integration has improved the quality of learning, fostering the development of transversal skills (analysis, communication, autonomy, critical thinking, problem solving, etc.) and technical-scientific skills, essential for educational success. Furthermore, it creates a dynamic, experiential, meaningful, adaptive, and engaging learning environment, where students have the opportunity to explore even complex content.

The results emerging from the teaching experience confirm the potential of Artificial Intelligence as a support tool in Higher Technical Education paths, where the use of Artificial Intelligence can promote better training, greater inclusion and greater autonomy of students. However, the need to train students in a critical and conscious use of tools with Artificial Intelligence technologies is highlighted. Access to Artificial Intelligence tools, while offering new learning opportunities, also requires assessing the quality, reliability, and impartiality of the information received. This awareness is echoed in the survey published by Di Fazio (2025), which reveals that 8 out of 10 Italian students aged 14 to 19 explicitly request that Artificial Intelligence be taught in schools. The same survey highlights their recognition of not yet being able to use these technologies critically and consciously, calling for specific training in this area.

As also stated by Giannoli F. (2025), Artificial Intelligence can be a valuable ally in teaching, but only if introduced with awareness and gradually. It is not a question of replacing traditional methods, but of integrating them with new possibilities.

Educating students to use Artificial Intelligence critically and consciously represents one of the most pressing challenges facing the school system today.

Access to Artificial Intelligence tools, while offering new learning opportunities, also requires assessing the quality, reliability, and impartiality of the information received.

6 Conclusions

The research shows that the use of Artificial Intelligence, if integrated in a structured way, can improve the quality of learning in the ITS Academy courses in the area of "chemistry and new life technologies", also representing an innovative and suitable system for the students of the Alpha generation, these students grow up with Virtual Reality, Augmented Reality and Artificial Intelligence, and for them it is natural to find them in their study paths.

The modular design of the activity based on progressive phases and evaluation rubrics allowed us to monitor learning in a structured way.

References

Avila-Garzon et al.: Augmented reality in education: an overview of twenty-five years of research. Contemp. Educ. Technol. **13**(3) (2021)

Berardinetti, V., Santangelo, F.A., Traetta, L.: Innovazioni in classe: come l'IA sta trasformando l'insegnamento e l'apprendimento. Educ. Sci. Soc. **2**, 386–399 (2024)

Cao, W., Yu, Z.: The impact of augmented reality on student attitudes, motivation and learning achivements-a meta-analysis (2016–2023). Hum. Soc. Sci. Commun. **10**(1), 1–12 (2023)

Di Fazio, M.: Insegnateci l'IA anche a scuola. L'Espresso, 9 giugno 2025 (2025)

Gentile, M., et al.: Do we still need teachers? Navigating the paradigm shift of the teacher's role in the AI era. Front. Educ. **8** (2023)

Giannoli, F.: Case Study: Introduzione dell'Intelligenza Artificiale nello Studio. Bricks **5**, 176–181 (2025)

Gulbay, E., et al.: Integrazione dell'Intelligenza Artificiale e della Realtà Aumentata nel corso di Laurea in Scienze della Formazione Primaria: prospettive e applicazioni. Quaderni del GLIA, N° 4, pp. 181–200

O'Donnel, F., Porter, M., Fitzgerald, S.: The role of artificial intelligence in higher education: higher education students use of AI in academic assignments. Irish J. Technol. Enhanced Learn. **8**(1) (2024)

Carraro Lab. https://www.carraro-lab.com/home. Accessed 31 Aug 2025

Better Now: Bridging Theory and Practice in Blockchain-Enabled Educational Metaverse

Dario Di Dario(✉)[iD], Pier Paolo Pastore[iD], Fabio Palomba[iD], and Carmine Gravino[iD]

University of Salerno, Fisciano, Italy
{ddidario,fpalomba,gravino}@unisa.it, p.pastore13@studenti.unisa.it

Abstract. This work implements a blockchain-based framework for educational metaverses within *SENEM*, an immersive learning environment. Ethereum and IPFS were integrated to support decentralized uploading, storage, and retrieval of lecture materials. The resulting prototype formalizes requirements for secure content management and possibly improve integrity, traceability, and privacy. Overall, this work offers a first step toward transparent immersive learning systems and a proof-of-concept for future usability research.

Keywords: Educational Metaverse · Blockchain · Software Engineering

1 Introduction

Advances in Artificial Intelligence (AI), extended reality (XR), and distributed technologies are transforming education. Their convergence has given rise to the *metaverse*—a persistent, shared, and immersive environment for interaction among users and digital objects [5,7]. In education, it fosters collaborative and experiential learning, enhancing engagement and accessibility through 3D spaces and avatars [11]. Yet, these benefits introduce challenges of trust, data integrity, and privacy—core to both learning sciences and ethical AI [6]. *Blockchain* offers a foundation for secure and decentralized learning ecosystems. Through immutability and transparency, it supports credentialing, assessment, and privacy-preserving record management [1,2,13], and can operate as *public*, *private*, or *consortium* networks—differing in access control and governance—supporting persistent ownership and accountability in educational metaverse systems.

Recent studies highlight decentralized identity, verifiable credentials, and transparency as core principles, driving advances in blockchain-based learning and accreditation frameworks [8–10,12]. However, most work remains conceptual, lacking systematic integration within operational immersive environments.

To advance this field, our prior study [3] introduced a theoretical blockchain framework for the educational metaverse, outlining architectural principles to

A. Dipace et al. (Eds.): WAILS 2025, LNCS 16438, pp. 48–53, 2026.
https://doi.org/10.1007/978-3-032-17604-2_5

address privacy, security, and interoperability. While conceptual, it required a realistic platform for implementation. SENEM (Software Engineering-eNabled Educational Metaverse) fulfills this need [11]. Developed with educators and students' needs, *SENEM* combines immersive classrooms, avatars, and multimedia tools, providing an effective environment for implementing and evaluating blockchain-based learning services. This paper contributes by: (1) implementing our blockchain framework within an immersive educational metaverse, bridging theory and practice; (2) engineering decentralized lecture-management functionality; and (3) provide feasibility through use-case scenarios and execution flows.

Our results show that the proposed blockchain framework can be concretely implemented within an educational metaverse. Integrated into *SENEM* through practical use case scenarios, we show how educational resources can be securely and transparently managed in a decentralized way. This work advances metaverse engineering by bridging theory and practice and supporting the development of future AI-enabled learning environments.

2 Related Work

Most studies on blockchain in education frame its core properties—*immutability, transparency, decentralization*, and *smart contracts*—as direct benefits for learning environments. Nizamuddin et al. [10] use Ethereum smart contracts for courses and certifications. Mozumder et al. [9] propose a blockchain roadmap for decentralized and private metaverse education, Mourtzis et al. [8] employ blockchain to enable trusted accreditation in University 5.0. Most studies adopt blockchain's technical features without addressing their systematic integration into education. The practical implementation of these capabilities within educational metaverses remains largely unexplored. Grounded in *Metaverse Engineering* [4], our work views the metaverse as a socio-technical system where privacy and security are key concerns. In prior work [3], we proposed a blockchain-based framework to address these issues, though it lacked validation in a concrete implementation. This paper extends that work by integrating the framework into *SENEM* [11], an engineered educational metaverse.

3 From Theoretical Framework to Implementation

3.1 Blockchain Framework for Educational Metaverses

The framework is structured around two pillars: (1) the *goals* that blockchain aims to achieve in educational metaverses, and (2) the *design strategies* guiding its integration. Its main objective is to enable secure, transparent, and decentralized management of educational data, addressing the trust and ownership issues common in centralized systems. Blockchain supports this goal through guarantees of privacy, authenticity, and verifiability of learning assets.

Three deployment models are considered: *public, private,* and *consortium* blockchains. The consortium model provides the most balanced governance structure for academic collaborations, allowing fine-grained control over openness and access. The framework is organized into four layers: (1) **Application Layer**, which hosts the metaverse interface and user interactions; (2) **Learning Layer**, responsible for handling academic progress, grades, and multimedia data; (3) **Cross-Chain Layer**, ensuring interoperability and security across multiple blockchains (which is not implemented within the scope of this study); and (4) **Blockchain Storage Layer**, which guarantees persistence through blockchain, IPFS, and smart contracts. While prior work defined the framework, no educational environment had yet implemented it. This study fills that gap by integrating the framework into SENEM and linking the metaverse front end with the underlying blockchain layers, as shown in Fig. 1.

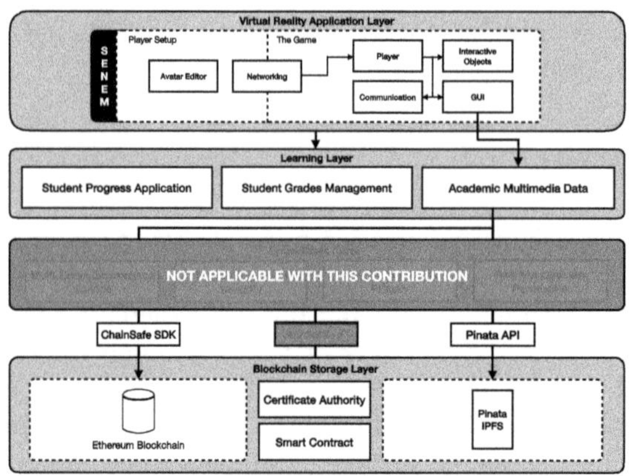

Fig. 1. Framework evolution with SENEM.

3.2 Implementation

Following metaverse engineering principles [4], the implementation focused on lecture slides as academic resources for blockchain integration in immersive learning. We identified four key functional requirements: **FR1.** *uploading*, **FR2.** *storing*, **FR3.** *modifying*, and **FR4.** *retrieving* lecture materials within SENEM.

Application Layer. *SENEM* [11] serves as the 3D virtual classroom where users interact through customizable avatars and multiple communication modes (voice, text, and gestures). The environment includes features such as a virtual projector and a collaborative whiteboard for multimedia presentations. To enable blockchain-based lecture management, two new interfaces were developed: an *Upload Panel*—i.e., Fig. 2a—for storing materials on-chain and a *Download Panel*—i.e., Fig. 2b—for retrieving them. Interface design followed four principles: immersive consistency, operational simplicity, clear system-state feedback, and restricted teacher-only control for blockchain operations.

Learning and Storage Layers. The learning layer manages multimedia content, while the storage layer integrates Ethereum and IPFS through **ChainSafeSDK** and **Pinata APIs**. Each user creates a **MetaMask** wallet to authenticate and establish content ownership. Smart contracts written in **Solidity** handle validation and on-chain recording, ensuring transparency and immutability. IPFS supports decentralized file storage and retrieval directly from SENEM's Unity interface, where successful uploads are visually confirmed within the classroom environment. Combined, these technologies enable secure ownership, transparent verification, and persistent storage of educational materials.

The resulting system bridges theory and practice by linking *SENEM* to Ethereum and IPFS, demonstrating the framework's practical instantiation. It enhances integrity, transparency, and privacy in immersive learning while laying the groundwork for future empirical evaluation.

In the following section, we defined a set of use case scenarios to illustrate the flow of events and errors when using the new functionalities.

4   Use Case Scenarios

UC-FR.1 Lecture Upload with IPFS. (Main Scenario)

Flow of Events: The environment provides a panel for IPFS-based content management Fig. 2. Users can *upload* an entire lecture or *update* an existing file (see UC-FR.3); here, we focus on the former. Users select a file (.JPG/.JPEG) from their local device, which is then processed by creating a new Pinata IPFS group acting as a lecture folder. During the operation, feedback indicates the upload progress. Once completed, the system asks whether the lecture should also be stored on the blockchain; if confirmed, the process continues with UC-FR.2.

Error Handled: The system handles *empty folders*, *invalid files*, and *network interruptions*, notifying the user and restoring the environment. Pinata naming conflicts are resolved by replacing or renaming files.

UC-FR.2 Ethereum Blockchain Storage

Pre-Condition: At least UC-FR.1 has been successfully executed once.

Flow of Events: After the lecture is uploaded to IPFS, the system enables blockchain storage. This action triggers a transaction via the connected wallet. Users can verify transaction details within the wallet. Once confirmed, a smart contract records the lecture hash on the blockchain. Upon completion, the system provides confirmation of successful on-chain storage.

Error Handled: The system handles cases where *no wallet is detected* or the user *declines registration*, leaving the lecture stored only on IPFS. *Network or transaction failures* interrupt the process and generate an error notification.

UC-FR.3 Update Existing Lecture

Pre-condition: The user update an existing lecture from UC-FR.1.

Flow of Events: The user chooses the lecture to modify and uploads new slides. The system retrieves the existing lecture from IPFS and provides its details, allowing the user to replace the full lecture or add/remove slides. Throughout the update, the system displays progress and feedback messages. Once the operation is completed, the lecture can also be stored on the blockchain following the procedure in UC-FR.2.

Error Handled: The system handles *missing lectures, invalid files*, and *network failures*, notifying the user and preventing changes to the stored lecture.

UC-FR.4 Visualize or Download Lecture

Pre-Condition: UC-FR.1 and UC-FR.2 must have been executed at least once.

Flow of Events: Users access stored lectures through a dedicated panel (Fig. 2b), which displays lectures stored on IPFS and those also registered on the blockchain, indicated by a green marker. The user selects a lecture to visualize or download, and the system displays a progress bar during retrieval. After completion, the slides load into the virtual projector for delivery.

Error Handled: The system handles *network issues* and *rate-limit errors*; in the latter, a retry mechanism automatically resumes downloads without data loss. Users are notified of all issues with corresponding corrective actions.

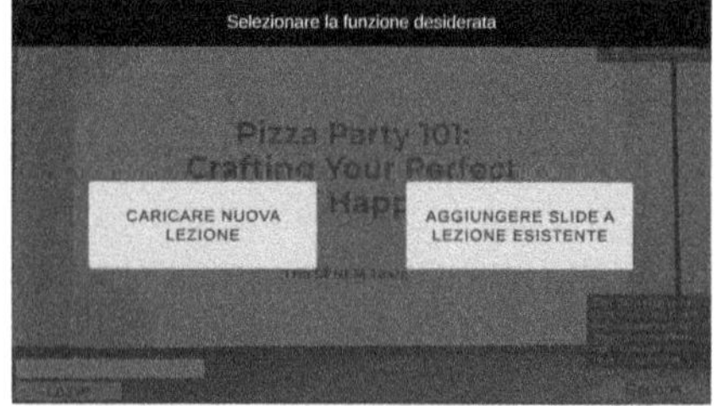

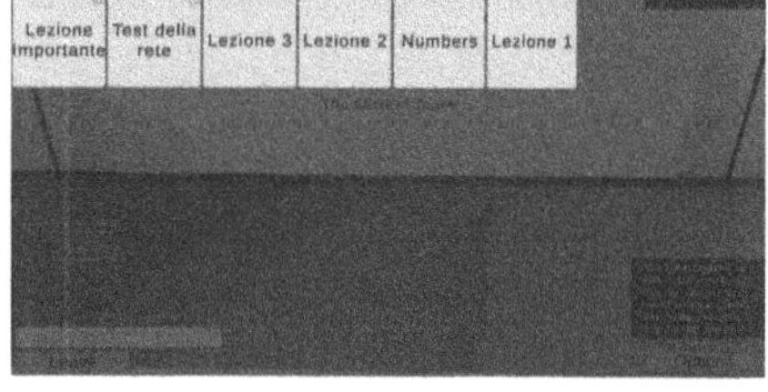

(a) UC-FR.1 Upload a new lecture or add new slides to an existing one.

(b) UC-FR.4 Visualize or download a lecture.

Fig. 2. Panel for managing educational resources with Blockchain.

5 Conclusion

This study applies a theoretical blockchain framework within an educational metaverse by implementing *SENEM* using the ChainSafe SDK and Pinata. The system integrates Ethereum and IPFS to enable decentralized content management in a 3D learning environment. However, we believe that higher-level tools can simplify development and improve maintainability. The current implementation is limited by its dependence on Unity and by the lack of empirical evaluation. Future work will extend the framework to other platforms and include user studies with educators and learners to assess usability, usefulness, and educational value. Overall, the results highlight the need for more accessible, scalable, and user-validated blockchain solutions for immersive education.

References

1. Alammary, A., Alhazmi, S., Almasri, M., Gillani, S.: Blockchain-based applications in education: a systematic review. Appl. Sci. **9**(12), 2400 (2019)
2. Chen, G., Xu, B., Lu, M., Chen, N.-S.: Exploring blockchain technology and its potential applications for education. Smart Learn. Environ. **5**(1), 1–10 (2018). https://doi.org/10.1186/s40561-017-0050-x
3. Di Dario, D., Bilott, U., Sibilio, M., Gravino, C., Palomba, F.: Toward a secure educational metaverse: a tale of blockchain design for educational environments. In: 2023 49th Euromicro Conference on Software Engineering and Advanced Applications (SEAA), pp. 159–166. IEEE (2023)
4. Di Dario, D., Palomba, F., Gravino, C.: Another brick in the wall: a systematic mapping study toward defining metaverse engineering through socio-technical issues. ACM Comput. Surv. **37**, 777 (2024)
5. Dionisio, J.D.N., Iii, W.G.B., Gilbert, R.: 3d virtual worlds and the metaverse: current status and future possibilities. ACM Comput. Surv. (CSUR) **45**(3), 1–38 (2013)
6. Holmes, W., et al.: Ethics of AI in education: towards a community-wide framework. Int. J. Artif. Intell. Educ. **32**(3), 504–526 (2022)
7. Lin, H., Wan, S., Gan, W., Chen, J., Chao, H.C.: Metaverse in education: Vision, opportunities, and challenges. In: 2022 IEEE International Conference on Big Data (Big Data), pp. 2857–2866. IEEE (2022)
8. Mourtzis, D., Angelopoulos, J., Panopoulos, N.: Metaverse and blockchain in education for collaborative product-service system (PSS) design towards university 5.0. Procedia CIRP **119**, 456–461 (2023)
9. Mozumder, M.A.I., Athar, A., Armand, T.P.T., Sheeraz, M.M., Uddin, S.M.I., Kim, H.C.: Technological roadmap of the future trend of metaverse based on IoT, blockchain, and AI techniques in metaverse education. In: 2023 25th International Conference on Advanced Communication Technology (ICACT), pp. 1414–1423. IEEE (2023)
10. Nizamuddin, N., Shuhaiber, A.: Blockchain and the metaverse: personalized learning for a digital future. In: 2024 6th International Conference on Blockchain Computing and Applications (BCCA), pp. 271–278. IEEE (2024)
11. Pentangelo, V., Di Dario, D., Lambiase, S., Ferrucci, F., Gravino, C., Palomba, F.: SENEM: a software engineering-enabled educational metaverse. Inf. Softw. Technol. **174**, 107512 (2024)
12. Rani, P., Sachan, R.K., Kukreja, S.: A systematic study on blockchain technology in education: initiatives, products, applications, benefits, challenges and research direction. Computing **106**(2), 405–447 (2024)
13. Sharples, M., Domingue, J.: The blockchain and kudos: a distributed system for educational record, reputation and reward. In: Verbert, K., Sharples, M., Klobučar, T. (eds.) EC-TEL 2016. LNCS, vol. 9891, pp. 490–496. Springer, Cham (2016). https://doi.org/10.1007/978-3-319-45153-4_48

Biopedagogy, Artificial Intelligence, and Enactivism: Findings from a Mixed-Methods Study on 540 Education Professionals

Sara Pellegrini[1], Antonio Cuccaro[2], Chiara Gentilozzi[3], and Riccardo Sebastiani[1(✉)]

[1] Link Campus University, Rome, Italy
r.sebastiani@unilink.it
[2] Nicolò Cusano, Telematic University, Rome, Italy
[3] University of Macerata, Macerata, Italy

Abstract. The research presented here explores the intersection between biopedagogy, artificial intelligence and enactivism, outlining a new theoretical and operational space in which education is once again conceived as a living system, capable of combining the organic dimension of life with the artificial dimension of intelligence. The contribution is rooted in the European medical-pedagogical tradition and, through an empirical mixed-methods survey conducted on 540 education professionals, attempts to answer a crucial question for contemporary pedagogy: can the integration of physicality, technology and care generate more inclusive, personalised and sustainable educational models?

The analysis of the data shows that artificial intelligence, if accompanied by ethical and reflective principles, can be considered a valuable aid to biopedagogy and, with it, to the embodied paradigm, favouring the genesis of a "surgical pedagogy" that does not replace the human part but echoes it, putting relationships, presence and experience back at the centre of educational action.

Keywords: Biopedagogy · Enactivism · Embodiment

1 Research Rationale

Education has always been at the centre of pedagogical debate because it balances the desire to understand life and every historical transformation of education stems from a tension between the desire to understand life and the need to guide it. Contemporary society, characterised by speed and algorithmic logos, tends to redefine the task of pedagogy by seeking to maintain education as the cornerstone of humanisation, whose ultimate bulwark is not to delegate thought to a binary code.

Considering this trend, the task of biopedagogy is to try to restore depth to the educational relationship. Thanks to the encounter with the sciences of complexity [1] and the neurosciences of consciousness [2], biopedagogy is indispensable for understanding

A. Dipace et al. (Eds.): WAILS 2025, LNCS 16438, pp. 54–59, 2026.
https://doi.org/10.1007/978-3-032-17604-2_6

and interpreting education as a living system, within which the act of teaching is not simply transmission but a real relationship. In this way, the introduction of artificial intelligence into schools has a dual impact: on the one hand, it promises precision, adaptability, personalisation of pathways and predictive tools for functional diagnosis; on the other, it raises ethical and relational issues, threatening the dialogical substance of teaching.

Enactivism, which sees knowledge as a way of inhabiting the world through the body [3], seeks to bring harmony to this contrast because it reminds us that knowledge arises from gesture, encounter and relationship, rather than from calculation or abstraction.

This study therefore stems from the question: *how can the convergence of biopedagogy, artificial intelligence and the enactive approach promote the construction of inclusive, personalised and sustainable* educational models?

2 Methodology

The research, conducted between May 2024 and August 2025, adopts an exploratory design with a mixed methodology, consistent with the idea of education as a living system [4] and with the complex and interconnected vision of knowledge proposed by Morin [5].

What gives depth to the research framework is the fact that knowledge does not run along a straight line but is constructed in the interaction between the body, the environment and consciousness in an embodied practice [6].

Observation and participation are not separate from the methodology but are intertwined in an enactive perspective, where empirical data is always an expression of meaning. The questionnaire was designed to try to understand how teachers perceive the encounter between Bio-pedagogy, Artificial Intelligence (AI) and Enactivism within learning contexts. The questionnaire, consisting of nine questions, included a cognitive-perceptual area focused on knowledge of biopedagogy, trust and use of AI, areas of application and ethical or educational challenges, and a socio-demographic area with essential data on gender, age and educational qualifications: at the end of the questionnaire, an open question prompted individual reflection on the relationship between body, technology and learning, and the questionnaire was sent via SurveyMonkey. It is available in Appendix A, to ensure transparency and replicability.

The questionnaire participants were 540 teachers, educators and trainers enrolled in TFA specialisation courses and 30 CFU qualifying courses at Link Campus University.

Under Italian law, these courses are reserved for teachers already in service, which means that the entire sample can be defined as professional and teaching. Participants completed the questionnaire voluntarily and in accordance with anonymity, ethical standards and informed consent.

The quantitative data were analysed using SPSS v.29 through descriptive statistics (frequencies and percentages). The qualitative data were analysed according to the approach of Braun and Clarke [7] with independent coding by two researchers and subsequent construction of a shared codebook ($\kappa = 0.82$), including categories such as educational care, cognitive corporeality, algorithmic transparency and critical trust. The triangulation between the two levels of analysis made it possible to integrate the dimensions of the data and to return a reading consistent with the biopedagogical and enactive framework of the research.

The sample, which was self-selected and non-probabilistic, limits the generalisability of the results, just as the online administration may have introduced differences related to access and digital skills. The cross-sectional design does not allow for causal inferences, but the presence of trainee teachers nevertheless provides a realistic and dynamic portrait of the Italian education system in transition.

3 Results

The quantitative analysis provides a heterogeneous picture, but one that is consistent with the hypothesis of a transition towards a pedagogical culture that is more aware of the relationships between the body, technology and knowledge [8]. When asked about their familiarity with biopedagogy, 44.2% of the sample said they were "not very familiar" and 29.8% said they were "moderately familiar", while only 25.7% said they were "very" or "extremely familiar". This distribution shows that knowledge is still limited but growing, especially among younger teachers [9]. Regarding the use of artificial intelligence in special education, 39.6% of participants responded affirmatively, indicating practices that are still in the minority but are gradually expanding. The areas perceived as most promising concern the personalisation of educational pathways (71.5%), continuous monitoring of learning (67.4%) and support for the diagnosis of special educational needs (33.9%). As shown in Fig. 1, teachers recognise personalisation and learning monitoring as the main areas of application of AI in a biopedagogical context, highlighting a pragmatic and relational rather than a substitutionist approach.

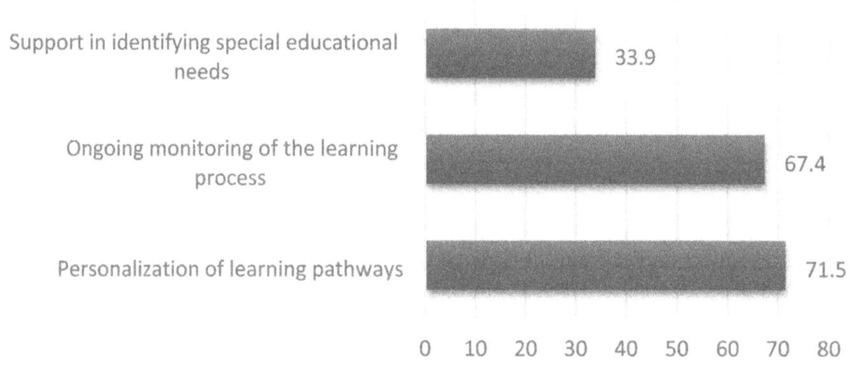

Fig. 1. Perceived areas of application of Artificial Intelligence in special education (n = 540).

Among the main challenges, the lack of specific training (47.0%) and ethical and privacy concerns (14.3%) stand out, confirming the need for an integrated educational approach that combines technological innovation and relational sensitivity [10].

The qualitative analysis identified three recurring themes:

1. The centrality of personalisation, described as "the possibility of tailoring learning to each student";
2. The idea of an alliance between teachers and AI, understood as support for monitoring and inclusive design;
3. The ethical and educational dimension, linked to the need to "educate on the cultural use of AI".

The results converge towards a biopedagogical and enactive vision of education, in which digital technology does not replace the body but extends its possibilities for relationship and educational care. Overall, the data confirm that biopedagogy, artificial intelligence and the enactive approach do not operate as distinct fields, but as complementary components of the same learning ecology, capable of integrating data analysis, corporeality and reflexivity [11].

4 Discussion and Conclusion

The results confirm that the convergence of biopedagogy, artificial intelligence and enactivism constitutes a common horizon of epistemological renewal. The integration of these paradigms allows us to view education as a relational ecosystem, where the physical and digital dimensions intertwine in the construction of shared meanings [12]. The limited but growing awareness of biopedagogy, together with the positive perception of AI as a tool for personalisation and inclusion, suggests an ongoing process of professional transition: teachers are beginning to recognise the body and relationships as the true mediators of innovation, overcoming the opposition between human and artificial [13]. The data collected shows that the real educational challenge posed by AI is not its technical use, but the integration of technology into pedagogical practice. The lack of specific training, which affected almost half of the participants, highlights the urgent need for a new professional literacy that combines digital skills and sensitivity.

Qualitative data show that participants see technology not as a substitute tool, but as a collaborator in terms of both the affective profile and the educational gesture that improves care conditions [14]. Education is therefore confirmed as a living and dialogical process, where knowledge arises from the interaction between mind, body and environment. If we consider AI through the enactive paradigm, it does not simplify the complexity of learning but reveals its subtle fabric: that of an intelligence that is situated, ethical and attentive to human contexts. The conclusions of the study, although not generalisable, indicate that biopedagogy can offer the conceptual language to guide the educational use of AI towards the goals of personalisation, inclusion and sustainability.

The encounter between biopedagogy, enactive theory and technology pave the way for a reformulation of the role of the teacher as a mediator of meaning, capable of integrating data, emotions and relationships into a single horizon of educational care [15].

Disclosure of Interests. The authors declare no competing interests.

Appendix: Original questionnaire used in the study

The following questionnaire was administered to 540 teachers, educators, and trainers enrolled in teacher specialization and qualification courses at Link Campus University between May 2024 and August 2025. It is reproduced here in its original English version, in order to ensure transparency, replicability, and methodological consistency. No personal or identifying data were collected from participants.

1. How Familiar Are You with the Concept of Biopedagogy?

Not at all familiar; Slightly familiar; Moderately familiar; Very familiar; Extremely familiar.

2. Have You Ever Used Artificial Intelligence as a Support in Special Education?

Yes; No.

3. Which Aspects of Artificial Intelligence Do You Consider Most Useful for Precision Pedagogy? Select All that Apply

Personalization of the learning path; Predictive analysis of student performance; Support in diagnosing special educational needs; Creation of inclusive teaching materials; Continuous monitoring of progress.

4. In Your Opinion, What Are the Main Challenges in Integrating AI into Special Education?

Lack of financial resources; Resistance to change among teachers; Lack of specific training; Ethical and privacy concerns; Technological limitations.

5. How do you think Artificial Intelligence can improve Precision Pedagogy practices?

6. How useful do you think the integration between Biopedagogy and Artificial Intelligence is for enhancing inclusion and the personalization of educational pathways?

1; 2; 3; 4; 5; 6; 7; 8; 9; 10 (1 = Not at all likely—10 = Extremely likely).

7. In which year did you obtain your degree?

8. What is your gender?

Male; Female; Non-binary; Prefer not to answer

9. What is Your Age?

References

1. Morin, E.: Introduzione al pensiero complesso. Sperling & Kupfer, Milano (1993)
2. Damasio, A.: Self Comes to Mind: Constructing the Conscious Brain. Pantheon Books, New York, NY (2010)
3. Varela, F.J., Thompson, E., Rosch, E.: The Embodied Mind: Cognitive Science and Human Experience. MIT Press, Cambridge, MA (1991)
4. Damasio, A.: Self Comes to Mind. Pantheon Books, New York, NY (2010)
5. Morin, E.: La via. Per l'avvenire dell'umanità. Raffaello Cortina, Milano (2012)
6. LeDoux, J.E., Brown, R.: A higher-order theory of emotional consciousness. Proc. Natl. Acad. Sci. **114**(10), E2016–E2025 (2017)
7. Braun, V., Clarke, V.: Successful Qualitative Research: A Practical Guide for Beginners. SAGE Publications, London (2013)
8. Damiani, P., Gomez Paloma, F.: Embodiment e DAD nella prospettiva inclusiva. Italian Journal of Health Education, Sports and Inclusive Didactics 4(4, Suppl. 2) (2020)

9. Pellegrini, S.: Biopedagogy and Artificial Intelligence. QTimes XVI(3), 773–780 (2024)
10. Gomez Paloma, F.: Embodied Cognitive Science. Atti incarnati della didattica. Edizioni Nuova Cultura, Roma (2013)
11. Vanacore, R., Gomez Paloma, F.: Progettare gli spazi educativi. Un approccio interdisciplinare tra architettura e pedagogia. Anicia, Roma (2020)
12. Rosati, A., Sebastiani, R.: Intelligenza artificiale e nuove prospettive di ricerca pedagogica. QTimes – webmagazine (2021)
13. Lau, H., Michel, M., Fleming, S.M.: The philosophical significance of metacognition. Trends Cogn. Sci. **26**(7), 555–567 (2022). https://doi.org/10.1016/j.tics.2022.04.006
14. Rivoltella, P.C.: Neurodidattica. Insegnare al cervello che apprende. Raffaello Cortina, Milano (2012)
15. Gamelli, I. (a cura di): Ma di che corpo parliamo? I saperi incorporati nell'educazione e nella cura. FrancoAngeli, Milano (2012)

Combining Qualitative and Quantitative Insights Within a Python Programming Blended Course

Daniela Rotelli[✉][iD], Yves Noël[iD], and Paola Costa Cornejo[iD]

Sorbonne Université, Paris, France
{daniela.rotelli,yves.noel}@lip6.fr,
paola.costa-cornejo@sorbonne-universite.fr

Abstract. This study explores the integration of qualitative and quantitative data within a blended Python programming course for second-year bachelor's students. By combining student questionnaire responses with Moodle interaction logs, we investigate the alignment between students' self-reported behaviours and their actual learning activities. We identify distinct learning and self-regulation patterns such as cumulative review, retrieval practice, precrastination, procrastination, and well-organised study habits. The findings offer insights into student autonomy and time management in remote learning contexts, highlighting the potential of mixed methods to improve the design and evaluation of the pedagogical curriculum in educational technologies.

Keywords: Mixed Methods Triangulation · Self-Regulated Learning · Blended Learning Analytics

1 Introduction and Related Work

The increasing adoption of blended learning formats requires innovative approaches to effectively assess and support student learning behaviours. Learning Management Systems (LMS) generate rich quantitative data that can reveal patterns in student interaction and engagement. However, these data alone lack insight into the underlying motivations, perceptions, and self-regulation strategies of learners. Incorporating qualitative data through questionnaires or interviews complements quantitative logs by providing a deeper understanding of student experiences.

This empirical study aims to investigate the alignment between students' self-reported learning behaviours and their actual online interactions within a second-year bachelor's degree blended Python programming course. By combining qualitative questionnaire responses with quantitative Moodle interaction logs, the objective is to explore how students perceive and enact self-regulated learning strategies such as time management in a remote learning context. Understanding these relationships is critical for informing pedagogical design and improving evaluation practices in educational technologies.

A. Dipace et al. (Eds.): WAILS 2025, LNCS 16438, pp. 60–74, 2026.
https://doi.org/10.1007/978-3-032-17604-2_7

Previous research underscores the complementary strengths of mixed methods in educational data analysis [2]. Log data analysis from learning management systems (LMS) has been used to uncover learning patterns and assess engagement [9], while questionnaires provide subjective insights into motivation, autonomy, and learning strategies [12]. Triangulation of these data sources can support a richer and more nuanced understanding of learning behaviours in blended and online environments.

Drawing on these established frameworks, this empirical study contributes to the growing body of research that examines the triangulation of qualitative and quantitative data to better understand self-regulated learning in technology-enhanced education. It specifically addresses two research questions: *RQ1)* Do students' perceptions about their learning behaviours match their logged interactions? *RQ2)* Are students capable of self-regulation in remote working? The insights gained can inform the design of blended courses that support student autonomy and pedagogical effectiveness.

2 Educational Context and Dataset

The study was carried out as part of the NLSU (Nouvelles Licences à Sorbonne Université) project at the Faculty of Science of Sorbonne Université, Paris, France[1]. The NLSU project aims to offer innovative and multidisciplinary bachelor's degree programmes in the fields of science and engineering. Among its goals, it aims to create blended courses to ensure good logistics and consolidate support mechanisms. Sorbonne Université provides teachers with a pedagogical service, CAPSULE, for the creation and structuring of courses to support teaching activities, as well as the co-design and implementation of teaching training plans[2].

This paper presents an Informatics course for second-year bachelor students awarding 3 ECTS (*European Credit Transfer and Accumulation System*) credits, whose teachers agreed to participate in the NLSU project. The users consented to the analytical use of their activity data.

In the initial phase, an educational engineer worked with the course teachers to develop and deliver the course in a blended format, while performing an educational engineering process ranging from the development of the targeted learning outcomes to the development of educational activities and assessments. The course took place in the 1st semester of 2023/2024 and includes 32 students and 2 teachers. In-person classes were organised between zero and three hours per week of theory and hands-on practice, spanning 13 weeks. This means that during certain weeks, students were required to learn independently. The learning management system Moodle was used to complement lectures and laboratories. Moodle courses were organised with various resources (files, pages) and activities (quizzes, assignment) according to the requirements of the teachers[3].

---

[1] https://anr.fr/ProjetIA-17-NCUN-0005.

[2] https://capsule.sorbonne-universite.fr/le-centre/.

[3] MoodleDocs - Resources: https://docs.moodle.org/405/en/Resources; Activities: https://docs.moodle.org/405/en/Activities.

The second phase addressed analysing the results of this pedagogical transformation along with continuously improving the pedagogical practices put in place. This approach is part of a collaborative and interdisciplinary reflection process (teacher-researcher, educational engineer, and research engineer) specific to the Scholarship of Teaching and Learning (SoTL) model [3,4]. The pedagogical service was asked to evaluate the effectiveness of the blended design of this course. To perform this evaluation, the pedagogical service's educational engineers prepared a questionnaire aimed at assessing student self-regulation and, more generally, the suitability of the learning design for students. Twenty-four students responded to the questionnaire. For this reason, of the initial 32 students, the eight who did not participate were not considered in the analysis.

The questionnaire was submitted in French, necessitating translation. For gender conversion, we used the gender used in a survey investigating the UK population in terms of gender [8]. For questions based on Likert scales, we used the Dictionary of Statistics and Methodology [7] to translate the scales.

Table 1 gives an overview of the dataset that provides the bachelor's degree year, the subject, the semester, the ECTS, the number of students and teachers, the number of student actions (#St. actions), and the number of actions for one student (#A:s). Based on the answers given in the Profile section of the questionnaire (Sect. 3.1), most of the students identify as male (33%) or female (42%), while 25% did not provide an answer or did not find their gender listed. The majority of the respondents (92%) are between the ages of 19 and 21. Two students indicated that they were 22 years or older. There are several reasons for this age difference. Some students did not choose this field at the beginning of their higher education and, either by choice or necessity, changed direction (after one or two years of preparatory classes, medicine, etc.). Others repeated a year or had professional experience but chose to continue their studies and advance their higher education. Based on their self-assessment, most of the students did not have strong prior knowledge of the Python language. More than half (14 out of 24) are at low or very low levels (7) or even have no prior knowledge (7). Four students are at an average level and only six have a good or very good level.

We did not observe a significant correlation between the variables 'gender' and 'age' with prior Python skills. Nevertheless, there is a tendency for women to position themselves at a low or very low prior level (7 out of 10).

3   Methodology

This study uses a mixed-methods approach, combining qualitative data collected through a questionnaire with quantitative data from interaction logs, to obtain a more comprehensive and triangulated understanding of student behaviour.

3.1   Data Collection

We collected two types of data: quantitative data, which corresponds to student logs recorded from interactions with the Moodle platform, and qualitative data, which refer to responses to the questionnaire administered to students.

Table 1. Dataset overview

year	subject	semester	ECTS	#students	#teachers	#St. actions	#A:s
2nd	Informatics	S1	3	24	2	28,110	1,171

Gender				Age			
Female	Male	Prefer not to say	Not listed	19	20	21	22+
10	8	4	2	8	9	5	2

Python Prior Knowledge						
	No knowledge	Minimal	Basic	Average	Good	Very good
	7	5	2	4	4	2

Quantitative Data Collection: Log Data. Moodle logs were collected using the Logstore xAPI plugin [16] installed in the Sorbonne Université Moodle platform that allows the conversion of logs into xAPI statements[4]. The Logstore xAPI plugin enables the complete pseudonymisation of personal information to protect data privacy. It prevents unwanted information breaches by hashing the user's full name, email address, and user ID using a secret key, thus allowing the protection of user privacy and data sharing among the researchers involved in the NLSU project. Pseudonymised data were extracted in JSON format. A sample record of the JSON file normalised through the Python json library (https://docs.python.org/3/library/json.html) to be visualised as a table, is shown in *Table* 2.

Table 2. Example of a JSON record extracted then normalised.

Timestamp	User	Object_id	Context
2023-09-11T18:44:20	d01c53814276c0116335ed140077	'https://[anonym]/mod/page/view.php?id=22711'	Course questions on variables

Description	Path	RelatedActivities[a]
Consider the following instruction: >> a==b; Tick the statement(s) that are TRUE.	\mod_quiz\event\attempt_submitted	'https://mymoodle/course/view.php?id=153', 'https://mymoodle/mod/quiz/view.php?id=22957, 'https://mymoodle/mod/quiz/attempt.php?attempt=39993&cmid=22957'

[a]The RelatedActivities field is more complex. For reasons of space and alignment, we have only included information relevant to the current example.

Qualitative Data Collection: Questionnaire Answers. The questionnaire, which takes about 15 min to complete, was distributed online using Moodle's "Questionnaire" tool[5]. Before being sent to researchers, the Moodle platform admin team of Sorbonne Université fully pseudonymised the questionnaire usernames using the same secret key used for the Moodle xAPI statements. The

---

[4] Experience API specification - https://github.com/adlnet/xAPI-Spec/blob/master/xAPI-Data.md#parttwo.

[5] Moodle Questionnaire - https://moodle.org/plugins/mod_questionnaire.

questionnaire consists of 23 questions (20 closed or Likert scale questions covering many points to be assessed and 3 open-ended questions) and is organised around four major areas:

- **Profile**: 6 questions about gender, age, Python prior knowledge, level of autonomy for remote work, organisation of work time, workspace;
- **Participation in the course**: 4 questions focusing on the importance of the course for the academic path, the cooperative atmosphere, the feedback from teachers, consultation of resources;
- **Perception of the course**: 11 questions focusing on the understanding of the skills to be developed, the flexibility of the course, the estimated time required for the activities, the perceived difficulty, the support from teachers;
- **Approach to learning**: 2 questions focusing on how students studied the course, the perceived satisfaction, the time spent learning, the behaviour towards the activities offered, the behaviour in class, the attitude towards the exam;

3.2   Data Integration

Since the questionnaire and the dataset were hashed using the same secret key (Sect. 3.1), we were able to correlate the interaction data obtained from the platform with the responses to the questionnaire.

For the purposes of this empirical study, we selected the questions that allowed us to compare students' responses with their online behaviour. For RQ1, we selected the question: *Did you read the lesson content before answering the quiz?*, which is part of the "Participation in the course" area. For RQ2, we selected two questions: *1) How would you rate your level of autonomy for remote working? 2) How confident are you in your ability to structure and organise your time for remote working?* which are both part of the "Profile" area.

To identify which indicators would allow us to infer the behaviours stated in the questionnaire from the logs (in the form of xAPI statements), we first looked at the organisation of the course. The course is organised into 10 chapters, each consisting of two subchapters: *course* and *TP/TD*. The *course* subchapter usually contains a Page[6], with the lesson content for that chapter, and a Quiz[7] to evaluate the comprehension/acquisition of the content. *TP* (Travaux pratiques) refers to teaching sessions in which students carry out practical work to apply theoretical knowledge in a practical way and develop practical skills; *TD* (Travaux dirigés) refers to small group classes in which students apply theoretical knowledge, work on exercises, ask questions, and interact with the teacher to deepen their understanding. The activities to be carried out within the subchapter *TP/TD* may include a Quiz, an Assignment[8], or a Forum[9].

The structure representing the organisation of the course is shown in Fig. 1 (click the image to download for enhanced visualisation).

---

[6] Moodle Page - https://docs.moodle.org/401/en/Page_resource.
[7] Moodle Quiz - https://docs.moodle.org/401/en/Quiz_activity.
[8] Moodle Assignment - https://docs.moodle.org/401/en/Assignment_activity.
[9] Moodle Forum -https://docs.moodle.org/401/en/Forum_activity.

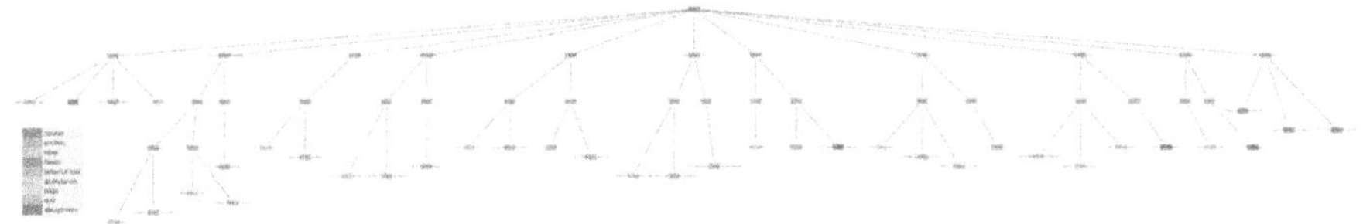

Fig. 1. The organisation of the course in chapters and subchapters.

3.3 Sequence of Actions

To answer the question "Did you read the lesson content before answering the quiz?" students used the Likert scale: *never, occasionally, sometimes, almost always*, and *always* [7]. Most of the students (19 out of 24) answered that they always (14) or almost always (5) read the course before answering the questions, 1 student sometimes, 1 student occasionally, and 3 students stated that they had never read the lesson before answering the quiz.

To compare students' perception about their learning behaviours with their logged interactions, thus answering RQ1, we need to analyse the sequence of their actions in their activity logs. Information about activity module type can be extracted from the *Path* field of the xAPI statement (Table 2) where mod\page represents a page, mod\quiz a quiz, mod\forum a forum, etc. Additionally, the *Path* contains information about the action performed on a module. For example, a student can read a page, submit an assignment, and post some content in a forum. Also, since a quiz can be taken multiple times, for each attempt taken, a different attemptID is recorded in the *Object_id* field.

To know whether students first read the course content and then answered the related questions, we considered only actions related to the modules Page (for course content) and Quiz (for questions). It is important to note that a page can only be read, and when a student accesses a page, the event "course module viewed" is recorded. At the same time, when a student accesses a quiz, the "course module viewed" event indicates that the user viewed the quiz description, rather than answering any quiz questions [15]. Since our focus is exclusively on actions related to quiz answers and the review of responses ('Quiz attempt started', 'Quiz attempt viewed', 'Quiz attempt summary viewed', 'Quiz attempt reviewed', 'Quiz attempt submitted'), we removed all events "course module viewed" for the quiz. Moreover, for each quiz attempt, we can have multiple actions (a student starts a new attempt, then answers some questions, submits, and reviews the attempt). Thus, we merged all subsequent actions related to the same attempt. Finally, not all chapters have both a Page and a Quiz. In Chap. 6 (Fig. 1), the course subchapter lacks a quiz. As a result, since we need to explore the Page-Quiz sequence, we examined 7 of the 10 chapters.

For each student, we were therefore able to extract the sequence of actions performed on pages and quizzes. An example of a sequence can be: Page 1, Quiz 1.1, Quiz 1.2, Page 2, Quiz 2.1, Quiz 1.3, Page 1, Page 3, Quiz 3.1, Quiz 3.2, Page 2, Quiz 1.1, Quiz 1.2, where Page 1 corresponds to the page of Chap. 1 and Quiz 3.2 corresponds to the quiz of Chap. 3, attempt 2.

Because students receive feedback on their answers, being able to access attempts again ('Quiz attempt reviewed') is very useful for learning purposes because it allows students to learn from their mistakes [13]. In fact, in the example above, the student accessed Quiz 1.1 and 1.2 after completing Page 2 and 3. This could indicate that, when faced with similar situations, they wanted to review the answers they had given and the feedback they had received in previous exercises. It is important to note that the feedback includes a comment explaining why the student's answer is wrong or suggesting that certain topics be reviewed depending on the type of mistake.

Thereafter, for each quiz, we checked if students had first read the corresponding course: Page1 before Quiz1, Page2 before Quiz2, and so on. Although a student can access Page 4 before reading Page 3, Quiz 4 must be taken after reading Page 4 to respect the order Page-Quiz as asked in the questionnaire question.

To compare these perceptions with the sequence, for each student, whenever, for each chapter, the activities had been performed in reverse order (the quiz before the page) or one of the two activities had not been completed (only quiz or only page), we considered that the page-quiz sequence had not been respected for that chapter. We then calculated how many times out of 7 chapters students had followed the sequence and assigned a percentage to the results. The percentage was then converted to the Likert scale based on the following thresholds: 100: always, 80: almost always, 50: sometimes, 20: occasionally, and 0: never. For example, if a student followed the page-quiz sequence 6 times out of 7, in 86% of cases (almost always), they read the course before answering the quiz questions.

3.4   Self-regulation in Remote Working

To answer the question "How would you rate your level of autonomy for remote working" students used the Likert scale: *very poor, poor, average, good,* and *excellent* [7]. Most of the students (16 out of 24) answered that they have a good (15) or excellent (1) level of autonomy to work remotely, 6 consider themselves to have an average level of autonomy and only 2 report having a low (1) or very low (1) level. Although the majority of the students feel they have a good level of autonomy to work remotely, when asked if they feel able of structuring and organising their remote working time ("How confident are you in your ability to structure and organise your time for remote working?"), the answers reveal a disparity between students' overall perception of autonomy and their ability to manage and structure their time while working remotely: 13 students consider themselves extremely able (1) or very able (12), 9 consider themselves as fairly able to organise their time and two consider themselves not very able.

To compare these perceptions with their actions, thus answering RQ2, we examined students' actions across all ten chapters. To classify the activities, we followed the same procedure as for the analysis of the sequence of actions (Sect. 3.3). However, we did not restrict the data solely to pages and quizzes; instead, we took into account all activities conducted in each chapter (Fig. 1) to identify the temporal density of actions for each subchapter. For each subchapter, we have therefore grouped all activities, classifying them as C (all course content-type activities), Q (all quiz-type activities), and TP/TD (all TP/TP-type activities). For example, Chap. 1 contains two course contents, two quizzes, and one TP/TD. All activities performed on course contents are classified as C1, on quizzes as Q1, and on TP/TD as TP1. On the other hand, Chap. 8 contains three course contents, no quizzes, and one TP/TD resulting in C8 and TP8. Subsequently, for each student, we grouped the density of daily actions by type of activity. This allowed us to observe that, for example, student Z, during the first week, worked on C1 and C2 on Monday, again on C1 and C2 on Tuesday, and on Q1 on Wednesday. The rest of the week, no work was performed.

As already mentioned, the course is organised into chapters, each of which contains a series of activities to be completed. One of the elements that affects the final assessment is participation in course activities, for which specific deadlines are communicated to students at the beginning of the academic year. Deadlines provide essential structure within blended learning environments, encouraging students to divide tasks into small parts and progress steadily through course material. Without set due dates, students are more likely to postpone tasks, which can result in a stressful last-minute rush and poorer learning outcomes [19]. Deadlines and structured pace also reinforce the benefit of having students keep pace with course lessons for effective teaching and progression [5]. Teachers can confidently proceed with the explanation, as long as a substantial proportion of students are following along.

However, it is important to note that these activities are not compulsory for participating in the final exam, which means that students can decide not to complete them and manage their own learning time independently. Each course (C1, C2, etc.) is structured with a series of examples, and notebooks are used to make examples and to test what has been explained. Quizzes are therefore used as a self-assessment tool, and the ability to review feedback for each attempt allows students to learn from their mistakes. Students have one or two weeks, considering class suspension periods, to complete a Course-Quiz task or a TP/TD task. For example, within two weeks after the start of the academic year, students were required to have finalised the tasks C1-Q1 and C2-Q2. During the next two weeks, the emphasis will be on C3-Q3 and TP1. After the deadline, the courses (C1, C2, etc.) remain accessible; however, Quizzes and TP/TDs are no longer available for testing, just for review purposes.

4 Results and Discussion

To showcase the value of the proposed methodology, we applied it to the course described in Sect. 2. We first report on the comparison between student perceptions and actual actions (Sect. 4); then we inspect students' capability of self-regulation (Sect. 4).

RQ1: Do students' perceptions about their learning behaviours match their logged interactions? Table 3 shows the results of the comparison.

Table 3. Perception vs results.

Perception	Users	Result	Users
(100%) always	14	always	11
		sometimes	3
(80%) almost always	5	always	3
		almost always	2
(50%) sometimes	1	sometimes	1
(20%) occasionally	1	almost always	1
(0%) never	3	always	3

In the questionnaire, 14 students answered that they always read the course before answering the questions. Upon examining the results, it is evident that 11 students consistently adhered to the Page-Quiz sequence; however, 3 of these students did so only nearly consistently. Similarly, three of the students who believed that they had consistently adhered to the sequence did so on every occasion. This may indicate a level of uncertainty regarding their own actions or perhaps that they do not recall if they adhered to the sequence or not. The student who responded with "sometimes" did, in fact, adhere to the order sometimes. What most impressed us was the student who claimed to "occasionally" follow the order, despite actually adhering to it practically consistently; even more notable were the three students who, according to their perception, "never" followed the Page-Quiz sequence, but in reality they did so consistently. Our experience suggests that these students may not have understood this question. We do not believe that it was a matter of lack of attention or fatigue, given that the question was the second to arise. Conducting interviews with the students would yield more insight; but due to the pseudonymisation of the results, their names remain untraceable.

The representation of the sequences (Fig. 2) allowed us to compare the behaviour of the students. The y-axis represents the seven chapters in which both courses (Pages) and quizzes are present. The x-axis represents the sequence of actions where the light, almost white base indicates that no actions were taken (NE = non expedit); the light pink colour indicates access to the page; the pink colour, which increases in intensity with the number of attempts (QA), indicates activities carried out on a quiz depending on the attempt. Analysis of the representations led us to identify three rather different behaviours.

Student A accesses the course for each chapter and then makes a series of quiz attempts (numerous in Chaps. 1 and 2 and Chap. 6). This activity may seem typical for studying, but the student continuously consults prior courses. Since the course is organised by chapters, necessitating a solid understanding of previous chapters to address subsequent topics, when we analysed this sequence at

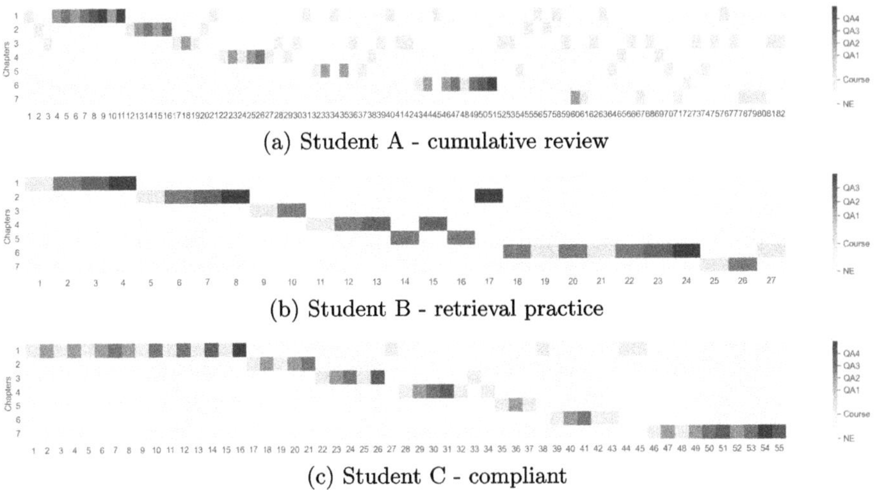

(a) Student A - cumulative review

(b) Student B - retrieval practice

(c) Student C - compliant

Fig. 2. Page-Quiz sequence representation.

first, we attributed this behaviour to uncertainty or an inability to fully understand the content. According to the literature [6,10,21,24], this behavious is identified as 'cumulative review' or 'spaced repetition'. It consists of systematically rereading and reviewing chapters already studied each time a new one is studied, starting with the one being studied and gradually going back to the first one. This strategy helps to better consolidate information and connect new concepts to those already learnt, allowing greater integration and memorisation. We have classified students with this sequence behaviour as *cumulative review*.

Student B exhibits a completely different behaviour. At the beginning (Chaps. 1 to 4), this student never reviews the quiz attempts to understand and correct their mistakes. Neither do they consult the course material between attempts or for Chap. 5. They simply keep trying illustrating a learning pattern based on trial and error [20] and also known as 'retrieval practice' where self-testing (taking the quiz) is significantly superior to other strategies for the long-term retention of information. The test is not just a measure of learning; it is a powerful learning tool in itself [11]. We have classified students with this sequence behaviour as *retrieval practice*.

Student C exhibits the behaviour expected by the teacher. The teachers informed the students that, according to them, the optimal approach was to address the content lectures initially before progressing to the quizzes. Student C initially read the lesson, then completes a quiz, reviews the course, retakes the quiz, and revisits the course again if uncertainties arise. This alternation persists in all chapters, illustrating a learning pattern based on learning from one's mistakes [17] and a combination between retrieval practice and cumulative review. We have classified students with this sequence behaviour as *compliant*, since they follow the instructions provided by the teacher.

We observed the behaviour of the other students and we classified 7 students as "A" (although one student always started from lesson 1 to get to the most recent lesson), 3 students as "B", and 5 students as "C". For 5 students, we identified a behaviour between "A" and "C", and for 3 students a behaviour between "B" and "C".

RQ2: Are students capable of self-regulation while working remotely? To evaluate the student's ability to self-regulate in remote work, we examined the heatmaps of the density of student participation over weeks with course materials and deadlines (Fig. 3). The y-axis illustrates the course activities grouped in blocks (limited by dotted lines) according to the specified deadline indicated in red. The x-axis denotes the timeline over weeks, marked by weekdays. Since the level of student actions can vary depending on the types of activities, we used the normalize function of the sklearn.preprocessing library[10] to normalise the data per row.

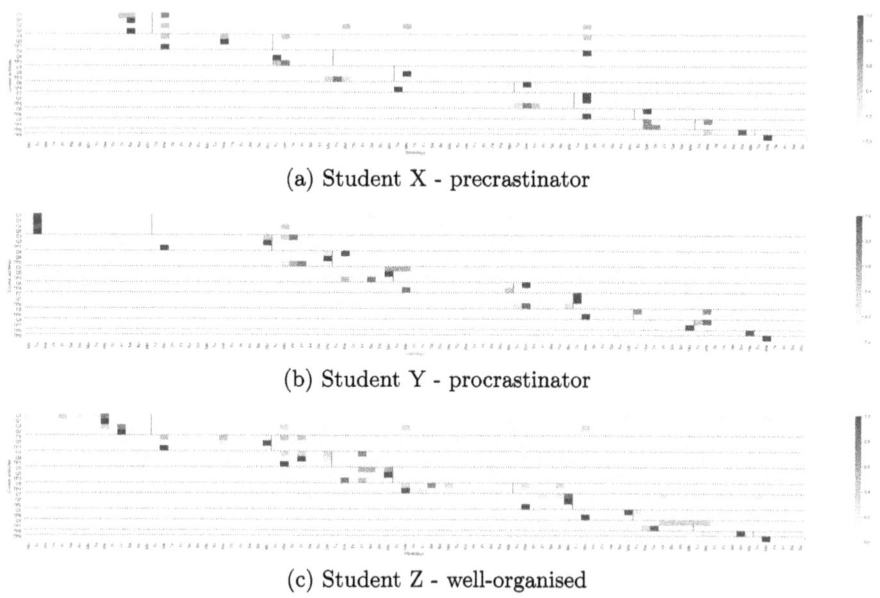

(a) Student X - precrastinator

(b) Student Y - procrastinator

(c) Student Z - well-organised

Fig. 3. Density of actions over weeks according to deadlines.

Student X, excluding the first deadline, completes all activities at the beginning of the week, typically between Tuesday and Wednesday, and then no longer accesses the course materials. We have classified this type of student as a *precrastinator*. A precrastinator is an individual who tends to complete tasks as soon

---

[10] https://scikit-learn.org/stable/modules/generated/sklearn.preprocessing.
normalize.html.

as possible, often at the expense of extra effort or reduced efficiency, motivated by the desire to reduce mental workload and avoid the stress associated with pending tasks [14]. In academic contexts, a precrastinator could be described as someone who actively seeks to finish academic tasks early or before deadlines, possibly to reduce future cognitive load or anxiety [18].

Student Y has a completely opposite behaviour. Excluding the first deadline, activities occur predominantly on Mondays, the designated deadline day. We have classified this type of student as a *procrastinator*. A procrastinator is an individual who consistently delays or postpones necessary academic tasks despite knowing that this delay will likely result in negative consequences. Academic procrastination is strongly associated with personality traits such as fear of failure, which often leads to poor academic performance, increased stress, and emotional distress [22,23].

Student Z completes the required tasks several days prior to the deadline (deadline 1) or near the deadline (deadline 6). It is important to note that, unlike students X and Y, student Z engages with the activities consistently throughout the week, accessing the content continuously. We have classified this type of student as *well-organised*. A well-organised student systematically manages their academic materials, time, and tasks through structured strategies and routines. This includes skills such as tracking assignments, organising study materials, managing time effectively, and planning tasks in manageable steps. Such skills help reduce confusion and stress, improve task completion, and promote better academic performance by promoting self-monitoring and systematic study habits [1].

We examined the behaviour of the other students and classified 7 as precrastinators, 2 as procrastinators, 13 as well-organised, and 2 who initially exhibited precrastination, but subsequently switched their behaviour to procrastination after the first half of the course. Numerous factors may explain this change, and conducting interviews with students may be beneficial. However, to protect the privacy of the students involved in the investigation, this is not possible.

In Table 4, we compare the results of this observation with the responses to the two questions of the questionnaire (Sect. 3.4), to answer RQ2.

Table 4. Self-regulation comparison

Autonomy in Remote Work	Time Organisation	Results
1 excellent	1 extremely able	7 precrastinator
15 good	12 very able	13 well-organised
6 average	9 fairly able	2 procrastinator
1 low	2 not very able	2 pre&procrastinator
1 very low	0 not able at all	

We can group the well-organised with the precrastinators, thereby confirming their perception about having a good/excellent level of time management and autonomy. Similarly, we include pre&procrastinators among those who have average autonomy and adequate time management skills. This comparison is closely aligned with the responses to the questionnaire, especially considering that two students, who described themselves as unable to organise their time and with limited autonomy, can be identified as the two procrastinators.

5   Conclusion and Future Work

This empirical study explores the value of integrating qualitative questionnaire data with quantitative LMS logs to gain a comprehensive understanding of student learning behaviours. The results revealed diverse learning patterns, including cumulative review, retrieval practice, and varying degrees of self-regulation, also characterised by precrastination, procrastination, and well-organised study habits. Combining questionnaire responses, LMS logs, and qualitative interviews helped us to deepen our understanding to support targeted pedagogical interventions. Specifically, these findings highlight the critical role of supporting student' time management and autonomy, especially in remote learning contexts. Identifying students who may be struggling with time management or self-regulation can be fundamental before problems become critical. Teachers could offer personalised and timely interventions, encouraging autonomy while also providing the necessary support.

However, although this approach offers a promising framework for enhancing blended and remote learning environments by monitoring and fostering student self-regulation skills, several limitations must be acknowledged. The relatively small sample size (24 respondents out of 32 students) restricts the generalisability of the findings. The findings are particularly revealing for this cohort; however, they should be regarded as an exploratory study that requires validation through larger and more varied cohorts. Future implementations will include larger cohorts and diverse disciplines, with integration of additional data sources such as academic performance. Additionally, the absence of interview data due to pseudonymisation limited the ability to explore deeper insights into student behaviours. In a forthcoming research endeavour, we intend to integrate comprehensive qualitative data (such as responses from open-ended questions or interviews) to enhance the explanatory depth of the underlying reasons for the behaviours. Since this work is based on the Scholarship of Teaching and Learning (SoTL) model, we also intend to investigate the potential downsides of precrastinators with respect to well-organised and procrastinators, to provide a more nuanced picture of self-regulation strategies, since the former could not always be efficient.

Acknowledgments. Work supported by the NLSU (Nouvelles Licences à Sorbonne Université) project (ANR-17-NCUN-0005) funded by the ANR during the NCU call for proposals.

References

1. Anderson, D.H., Munk, J.A.H., Young, K.R., Conley, L., Caldarella, P.: Teaching organizational skills to promote academic achievement in behaviorally challenged students. Teach. Except. Child. **40**(4), 6–13 (2008)
2. Asogwa, V.C., Hamisu, M., Ede, M.O.: Methodological triangulation in educational research: pros and cons. Propellers J. Educ. **2**(1), 79–87 (2023)
3. Biémar, S., Daele, A., Malengrez, D., Oger, L.: Le «scholarship of teaching and learning»(sotl). proposition d'un cadre pour l'accompagnement des enseignants par les conseillers pédagogiques. Revue internationale de pédagogie de l'enseignement supérieur **31**(31 (2)) (2015)
4. Boyer, E.L.: Scholarship reconsidered: Priorities of the professoriate. ERIC (1990)
5. Capinding, A.T.: Online teaching effectiveness and teacher's readiness: Impact on student's satisfaction and academic performance. Int. J. Instr. **17**(2), 383–400 (2024)
6. Carpenter, S.K., Pan, S.C., Butler, A.C.: The science of effective learning with spacing and retrieval practice. Nature Rev. Psychol. **1**(9), 496–511 (2022)
7. Cleary, R.: Dictionary of statistics and methodology. J. Am. Stat. Assoc. **94**(446), 657 (1999)
8. English, K.K.: How should UK population surveys represent differences in terms of sex and gender? Ph.D. thesis, University of Glasgow (2025)
9. Henrie, C.R., Bodily, R., Larsen, R., Graham, C.R.: Exploring the potential of LMS log data as a proxy measure of student engagement. J. Comput. High. Educ. **30**(2), 344–362 (2018)
10. Karpicke, J.D., Roediger, H.L., III.: Repeated retrieval during learning is the key to long-term retention. J. Mem. Lang. **57**(2), 151–162 (2007)
11. Karpicke, J.D., Roediger III, H.L.: The critical importance of retrieval for learning. Science **319**(5865), 966–968 (2008)
12. Okumus Ceylan, N.: The relationship between learner autonomy and motivation. Turkish Online J. Educ. Technol.-TOJET **20**(4), 150–158 (2021)
13. Race, P.: Using feedback to help students to learn. The Higher Education Academy (2001)
14. Rosenbaum, D.A., Gong, L., Potts, C.A.: Pre-crastination: Hastening subgoal completion at the expense of extra physical effort. Psychol. Sci. **25**(7), 1487–1496 (2014)
15. Rotelli, D., Monreale, A.: Processing and understanding moodle log data and their temporal dimension. J. Learn. Anal. **10**(2), 126–141 (2023)
16. Rotelli, D., Noël, Y., Lallé, S., Luengo, V., Pesce, D.: A moodle plugin for rich xapi data logging. In: European Conference on Technology Enhanced Learning, pp. 748–754. Springer (2023)
17. Ruthig, J.C., Jones, K., Vanderzanden, K., Gamblin, B.W., Kehn, A.: Learning from one's mistakes. Social Psychol. (2017)
18. Sauerberger, K.: When doing things later is the best choice: precrastination as an individual difference. University of California, Riverside (2019)
19. Smith, C.: The impact of homework deadline times on college student performance and stress: a quasi-experiment in business statistics. J. Stat. Data Sci. Educ. 1–10 (2025)
20. Starch, D.: A demonstration of the trial and error method of learning. Psychol. Bull. **7**(1), 20 (1910)
21. Thomas, L., et al.: The cumulative method as a central approach in the mathematics classroom. Ph.D. thesis, Lethbridge, Alta.: University of Lethbridge, Faculty of Education, 1997 (1997)

22. Tibbett, T.P., Ferrari, J.R.: The portrait of the procrastinator: risk factors and results of an indecisive personality. Personality Individ. Differ. **82**, 175–184 (2015)
23. Tibbett, T.P., Ferrari, J.R.: Return to the origin: what creates a procrastination identity? Curr. Issues Pers. Psychol. **7**(1), 1–7 (2019)
24. Yawn, C., Van Ravenswaay, L., Marcello, K., Nisly, S.: Cumulative cognition: strengthening learning with progressive content delivery. J. CME **14**(1), 2532247 (2025)

Confidential Retrieval-Augmented Generation in Educational Contexts

Ludovico Boratto[1], Francesco Congiu[1,2]($\boxtimes$), Gianni Fenu[1], Giacomo Medda[1], and Antonello Pau[1]

[1] University of Cagliari, 09124 Cagliari, Italy
`{ludovico.boratto,fenu,giacomo.medda,antonello.pau}@unica.it`
[2] University of Macerata, 62100 Macerata, Italy
`f.congiu@unimc.it`

Abstract. In recent years, the Retrieval-Augmented Generation (RAG) paradigm has become central to improving the reliability of systems based on Large Language Models (LLMs), as it grounds generation in evidence from external knowledge sources. However, much of the literature focuses almost exclusively on retrieval effectiveness, overlooking a crucial requirement in educational and professional settings: content confidentiality. The absence of mechanisms ensuring that only authorized documents are returned to the user risks limiting adoption in real scenarios. We present RetrievEM, a confidentiality-aware RAG framework validated on the BEIR/FiQA benchmark. Our approach pursues a dual objective: (i) improving retrieval by combining heterogeneous signals from different components, and (ii) ensuring that returned content complies with user-specific access constraints. RetrievEM integrates dense retrieval, reranking with cross-encoders, score-level fusion, and access-aware persona generation. Experimental results show that fusion yields substantial gains over individual components. Considering the limited accessible documents and RAG-related selection bias, we introduce Backfill, a post-processing algorithm that increases the search depth by exploring beyond the initial top-k results, preserving confidentiality without sacrificing retrieval utility. Overall, our RAG system can deliver pedagogically useful content while respecting access policies, demonstrating that effectiveness and confidentiality can coexist.

Keywords: Retrieval-Augmented Generation · Confidential Artificial Intelligence · Educational Technology

1 Introduction

Within modern information systems [2,3,6,7,11], Information Retrieval (IR) plays a key role in enabling users to access documents relevant to their queries. However, IR typically requires the formulation of precise, keyword-based queries, which can be challenging for non-technical users. Conversely, Large Language Models (LLMs) - a class of Transformer-based models capable of understanding

A. Dipace et al. (Eds.): WAILS 2025, LNCS 16438, pp. 75–86, 2026.
https://doi.org/10.1007/978-3-032-17604-2_8

and generating natural language - make information access more intuitive; yet their responses are non-deterministic and not always predictable or verifiable.

The combination of these two paradigms has given rise to Retrieval-Augmented Generation (RAG), which combines the retrieval precision with the generative fluency of LLMs. RAG systems enhance factual grounding and reduce hallucinations by incorporating evidence retrieved from external sources.

A major challenge in applying RAG to *educational contexts* concerns confidentiality: ensuring that information retrieval and generation processes comply with access-control and privacy requirements, preventing the exposure of sensitive materials to unauthorized users. For instance, a lecturer may use the system to retrieve access confidential assessment rubrics or internal teaching notes, whereas a student should only access publicly available learning materials. Similarly, academic administrators might retrieve aggregated analytics on student performance, while individual-level data should remain inaccessible. In financial literacy education (the domain of our experiments) these confidentiality issues become even more relevant, as educational resources may include proprietary datasets, students' financial scenarios, or graded assignments.

Developing a RAG system that is genuinely useful for education therefore requires careful *data governance*: managing access to different knowledge sources, protecting queries and responses in transit, and enforcing policies that prevent information leaks across roles (e.g., teacher, student, tutor). These safeguards ensure that the benefits of assistance do not come at the cost of data protection.

Despite the growing popularity of RAG in education, most studies have prioritized retrieval accuracy or generative fluency over privacy-aware design. Early works such as REALM [8] and RAG [10] established the paradigm of integrating retrieval with generation, while more recent methods like EXSEARCH [13] explored adaptive retrieval mechanisms. However, none of them natively address document confidentiality or access control, both crucial in learning environments.

Recent research has begun to address these limitations by proposing privacy-preserving retrieval and secure RAG architectures. For example, Zeng et al. [18] mitigate privacy risks using fully synthetic data in RAG pipelines, showing that such corpora can preserve retrieval utility while preventing sensitive information leakage. Chakraborty et al. [4] investigate Federated RAG, demonstrating how decentralized retrieval allows collaboration across institutions without sharing private data. Similarly, Cheng et al. [5] introduce RemoteRAG, a privacy-preserving cloud service ensuring secure query handling and access-controlled retrieval. Nonetheless, these privacy-oriented strategies have seldom been applied to *educational systems*, leaving open the question of how to design RAG pipelines that are both effective and confidentiality-preserving.

To explore this issue within a realistic domain, we focus on financial education—an area where both content and learner data are sensitive. Financial learning involves interpreting data-rich materials (e.g., market analyses, budget simulations) while ensuring that student queries, learning progress, and personal examples remain protected. As our reference dataset, we adopt the Financial Question Answering (FiQA) corpus from the BEIR framework [17], which

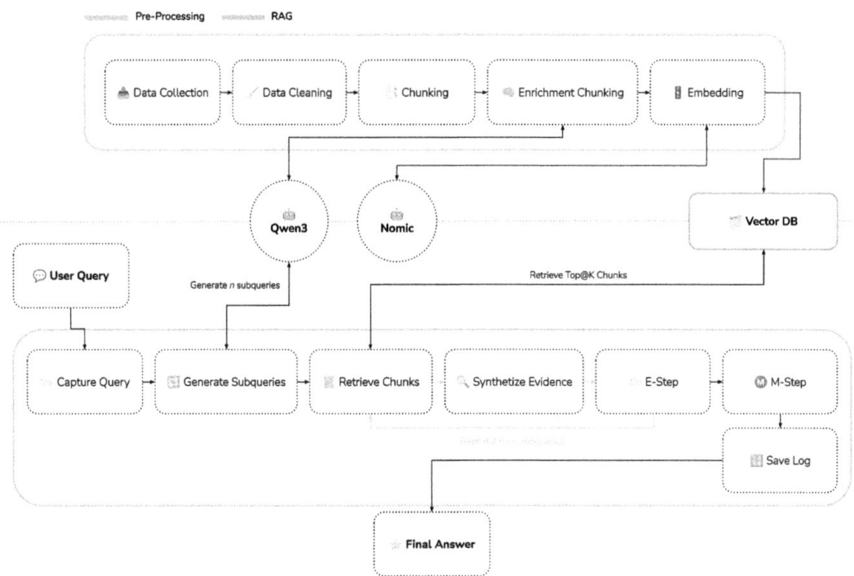

Fig. 1. RetrievEM architecture: high-level overview of core functional modules.

enables controlled experimentation in a domain that mirrors authentic financial reasoning tasks.

In this work, we make three main contributions: (i) we examine the role of confidentiality in the design of RAG pipelines for educational support; (ii) we demonstrate how FiQA can serve as a secure yet realistic corpus for exploring confidentiality-aware RAG; and (iii) we outline learning scenarios and evaluation strategies showing how such systems can enhance financial information literacy while ensuring compliance with data protection requirements.

2   Methodology

In this section, we present the *Confidentiality-aware* architecture of RetrievEM and the design choices that guide the subsequent modules. Our goal is to maximize retrieval and generation effectiveness while managing the trade-offs and respecting access constraints, without resorting to fine-tuning base models (Fig. 1).

2.1   Data Preparation

RAG systems aid the generation of reliable content through the retrieval of external knowledge. It is then crucial for such knowledge to be prepared before being fed into our architecture. Datasets for question answering typically consist of passages (documents to be retrieved), queries (user questions), and relevance judgments (qrels) indicating which documents are relevant. We follow common practices in the educational domain [15] and design a clear and reliable pipeline to ensure content is appropriate, coherent, and confidentiality-compliant:

- Cleaning: we apply a textual cleaning step by removing redundant headers, markup, extra spacing, and unwanted metadata.
- Chunking: we split passages into fixed-size segments with a 20% overlap between windows, ensuring better context coverage during retrieval.
- Chunk Enrichment: we augment each textual chunk through additional metadata to enable more accurate and less noisy retrieval. Specifically, metadata, such as title and summary, was generated with a compact LLM (*Qwen3-0.6B* [16]) in zero-shot mode to keep the process lightweight. Metadata also include the confidentiality levels associated with each document in the dataset.
- Embedding: we employ text encoders to embed chunks and their respective metadata into a latent representation. As the embedding process is crucial for the retrieval pipeline, we explore different solutions and assess their performance, focusing on state-of-the-art approaches.
- Ingestion: we use a vector database that supports large-scale approximate nearest neighbor search (ANN) to enable the document retrieval through a query. In particular, we relied on Qdrant[1], but RetrievEM can be easily adapted to any vector database. Embeddings are stored along with their respective confidentiality level to enable runtime filtering and ensure results respect access constraints and confidentiality policies.

2.2   Retrieval-Augmented Generation

RetrievEM builds on the steps of data preprocessing and ingestion in Qdrant, and it can operate in two main modes. The first is the *interactive mode*, in which the framework answers queries from students or lecturers with relevant content that complies with confidentiality constraints. In this scenario, the pipeline is designed to assign an access level to the user at runtime and manage the access policy dynamically. This component is currently under development and represents the natural evolution towards real-world system deployment.

The second is the *validation mode*, which enables systematic offline testing on benchmark queries. It is not common for corpora to provide confidentiality metadata at the query level. In light of this, RetrieveEM integrates an additional step of query enrichment that dynamically generates synthetic personas [14]. The process generates personas with an associated access level L_q linked to a query q. Specifically, n_p queries from the corpus are sampled according to a uniform distribution and fed into an LLM (*Qwen3-0.6B* [16]) to generate n_p personas. The remaining queries are randomly assigned to these personas, simulating a set of queries performed by distinct users. This strategy enables confidentiality-aware analyses in setups lacking access-levels information.

---

[1] https://qdrant.tech/.

Retrieval Stage. Independently of the mode, RetrievEM integrates a query decomposition process to increase the semantic coverage of input queries. Each query q is converted into a set of sub-queries $\{q_i\}_{i=1}^{n_q}$, representing trajectories aimed at exploring sub-aspects of the search space [9]. We leverage the in-context learning ability of LLMs to perform this task by relying on the lightweight and fast *Qwen3-0.6*. Each generated sub-query q_i is then transferred to the vector database, which retrieves k candidate documents via approximate nearest neighbor (ANN) search. Although each retrieved document is associated with a similarity score, such a score is conditioned by the respective sub-query used for retrieval. Therefore, we employ reranking strategies to address the non-trivial task of selecting the k candidate documents that maximize the relevance for the initial query q.

Reranking Stage. After dense retrieval, documents and queries are processed through a Cross-Encoder Reranker (CE) that reassess the relevance of retrieved documents. Unlike embedding-based similarity, the reranker jointly encodes the pair (q, d) (e.g., [CLS] q [SEP] d [SEP]), allowing it to capture more fine-grained semantic distitions. For example, two documents on compound interest may appear equivalent to the dense retriever, but the CE can recognize that one contains only a generic definition while the other provides a step-by-step explanation, resulting in more useful outputs in educational contexts. Although computationally more expensive, this step yields rankings where the most relevant and pedagogically rich documents receive more visibility and importance.

To integrate retriever and reranker signals, we adopt two strategies, namely Linear Fusion (LF) and Reciprocal Rank Fusion (RRF). LF combines normalized scores through a weighted average:

$$s_{\mathrm{LF}}(d \mid q; \alpha) = (1 - \alpha)\, s_{\mathrm{dense}}(d \mid q) + \alpha\, s_{\mathrm{CE}}(d \mid q), \quad \alpha \in [0, 1] \tag{1}$$

α is a factor that balances the retriever's and reranker's impact, with $\alpha = 0$ relying solely on the retriever and $\alpha = 1$ solely on the reranker. $\alpha \approx 0.5$ combines breadth (maximized by the retriever) and precision (maximized by CE).

On the other hand, RRF merges rankings by positions rather than scores:

$$s_{\mathrm{RRF}}(d \mid q) = \sum_{m \,\in\, \mathrm{Dense,\ CE}} \frac{1}{\gamma + r_m(d)} \tag{2}$$

where *Dense* denotes the ANN retrieval, $r_m(d)$ is the position of document d in method m's ranking, and γ is a smoothing constant (typically $\gamma = 60$ [1]) that prevents the top ranks from excessively dominating the result. This approach boosts documents ranked highly by both models and provides a robust compromise, even under different scoring scales. For instance, a document placed 2nd by the retriever and 3rd by the CE scores higher than one ranked 1st by one model but 50th by the other.

Post-processing Stage. After dense retrieval and reranking, the system applies a post-processing stage to ensure that the final response is accurate, confidentiality-aware, and pedagogically useful. The process unfolds in three steps.

First, a confidentiality filter ensures that retrieved documents comply with user access policies. Each document has a confidentiality level A_d and each user/persona associated with the respective queries has an access level L_u, with the policy requiring $L_u \geq A_d$. Hence, any document that is not compliant with the confidentiality policy is filtered out and ignored in later steps. Second, the authorized evidence chunks are synthesized into a coherent summary through an LLM (*Qwen3-0.6*). For each sub-query q_i, evidence chunks are aggregated into a summarized evidence v_i. In other words, the system combines and reorganizes relevant fragments, avoiding redundancy and linking related concepts. From an educational standpoint, this is equivalent to taking notes from multiple sources and rephrasing them into a clear, linear explanation.

Third, the synthesized candidates undergo a re-scoring and selection process. Each trajectory is defined as a (sub-query, evidence) pair $\tau_i = [q_i; v_i]$, with $[\cdot; \cdot]$ the concatenation operator. This concatenated structure is used to compute a new score by comparison with the query q, and, in validation scenarios, also to a reference answer g. Formally, the score is defined as:

$$s(\tau_i \mid q, g; \lambda) = \lambda \cdot \cos\big(\mathbf{e}(\tau_i), \mathbf{e}(q)\big) + (1 - \lambda) \cdot \cos\big(\mathbf{e}(\tau_i), \mathbf{e}(g)\big), \qquad (3)$$

where cos denotes cosine similarity, $\mathbf{e}$ the embedding operator, and λ the trade-off parameter. In evaluation and interactive settings without g, the score reduces to $s(\tau_i) = \cos(\mathbf{e}(\tau_i), \mathbf{e}(q))$. The trajectory with the highest score is selected as the basis for the answer, ensuring both relevance and didactic adequacy.

Finally, the selected evidence is passed to an LLM (*Qwen3-0.6*) in a structured prompt. At this stage, the model does not hallucinate content but generates a fluent explanation grounded in verified material. The resulting output integrates accuracy (through retrieval and scoring), confidentiality (through access control), and clarity (through synthesis and structured generation).

3 Experimental Results

In this section, we present and discuss the experimental results obtained with RetrievEM, with the aim of validating the architectural choices and analysing the extent to which the framework can improve retrieval quality while simultaneously enforcing confidentiality constraints. Accordingly, this section is structured as follows: we first describe the *Experimental Setup*, detailing the adopted dataset, the procedure for enriching it with confidentiality metadata and personas, and the evaluation metrics. We then report the results of our experiments, discussing key findings and aiming to answer the following research questions:

RQ1. How effective are fusion strategies compared to standard retrieval?
RQ2. What is the impact of the backfill safe-Aware mechanism?

3.1   Experimental Setup

Dataset. To evaluate the performance of RetrievEM, we adopted the `FiQA` dataset, which is part of the BEIR benchmark [17] and widely used in the literature for *Financial Question Answering*. `FiQA` is characterized by its highly specialized domain (finance and economics), and provides not only a large document corpus but also a set of queries and corresponding relevance judgments (*qrels*). In particular, the collection consists of 57,638 documents and 6,648 queries, making it well-suited for evaluating IR systems. However, `FiQA` does not include confidentiality levels for documents and users (i.e., queries). Therefore, we estimate a confidentiality level A_d in a zero-shot setting using a pre-trained entailment recognition classifier[2] to assess the logical relationship between premises and hypotheses. Specifically, the model processes the passage text and assigns an integer value from 1 to J representing the confidentiality level, we set $J = 5$ to reflect a five-point Likert scale. In educational contexts, this allows us to distinguish between public content intended for students (levels 1–2) and specialized or sensitive materials aimed at teachers or domain experts (levels 4–5).

RAG Setup. A key design choice is the selection of the textual encoder for the retrieval stage. Specifically, the selection process involved testing several state-of-the-art encoders, and *Nomic* [12] emerged as the most effective model for the financial domain. We set $n_p = 10$ for persona generation, $n_q = 3$ for query decomposition (each input query is expanded into three sub-queries generated by *Qwen3*), and $\gamma = 60$ for RRF smoothing. Unless otherwise indicated, we set the number of retrieved documents to 100.

Metrics. For the performance analysis, we adopted a set of classical IR and more recent dimensions related to confidentiality. The former include Precision@k (P@k), which measures the proportion of relevant documents among the top k results; MAP@k, which computes the mean of the cumulative precision values at the ranks where relevant documents occur; and nDCG@k, which assesses the overall ranking quality by penalizing relevant documents retrieved at lower ranks; Hit@k, which represents the probability of finding at least one relevant document within the top k positions.

3.2   RQ1 - Fusion Strategies Effectiveness

The first Research Question investigates the impact of different fusion strategies within the RetrievEM framework. The underlying intuition behind this analysis is that heterogeneous signals, such as the scores produced by the dense retriever and the cross-encoder, may be *complementary*: the former provides coverage, while the latter offers higher ranking precision. The question, therefore, is whether a weighted combination of these signals can overcome the limitations of the individual models, and to what extent simpler methods (e.g., RRF) can compete with more sophisticated approaches.

---

[2] https://huggingface.co/facebook/bart-large-mnli

Table 1. RQ1: Performance comparison among *Dense*, *CE*, *LF*, and *RRF*. Best results are highlighted in bold.

Metric	Dense	CE	LF	RRF
P@1	0.2169	0.2884	0.2991	0.2169
MAP@10	0.2730	0.3397	0.3506	0.2730
NDCG@10	0.2250	0.2808	0.2929	0.2250
HIT@10	0.4498	0.5878	0.5247	0.4498

Table 2. RQ1: Ablation study on *Linear Fusion* across different α values. Best results are highlighted in bold.

Metric	$\alpha = 0.10$	$\alpha = 0.30$	$\alpha = 0.50$	$\alpha = 0.70$	$\alpha = 0.90$
P@1	0.2918	0.2924	0.2931	0.2951	0.2991
MAP@10	0.3448	0.3452	0.3457	0.3471	0.3506
NDCG@10	0.2888	0.2891	0.2896	0.2905	0.2929
HIT@10	0.5200	0.5202	0.5205	0.5213	0.5247

The analysis begins by comparing the proposed technique against the main baselines. As shown in Table 1, *LF* outperforms both *Dense* and *CE* on *P@1*, *MAP@10*, and *nDCG@10*. In particular, *P@1* increases from 0.2884 (CE) to 0.2991 and *MAP@10* from 0.3397 to 0.3506, highlighting the benefits of a weighted combination: the retriever contributes coverage, while the re-ranker improves precision in the top ranks. For *HIT@10*, CE achieves the highest value (0.5878), while fusion remains competitive (0.5247), suggesting that the method prioritizes quality in the top positions over broad coverage.

A relevant comparison is with *RRF*, a simple but widely adopted method for combining heterogeneous models. In our setting, *RRF* exhibits clearly inferior performance compared to *LF* across all metrics, essentially matching the dense retriever. This behavior suggests that the reranker's contribution is diluted in the *RRF* combination, likely because the dense retriever dominates the ranking. These findings are consistent with previous observations that *RRF* tends to be competitive only when sources provide partially complementary signals.

The performance of *LF* in Table 1 refers to the configuration with the fusion weight yielding best results, according to an ablation study conducted on a validation set by varying α. Table 2 shows the effect of this study on the test set, with a clear monotonic improvement across all metrics as the contribution of the re-ranker increases and $\alpha = 0.90$ consistently emerging as the best configuration.

3.3   RQ2 - Confidentiality Preservation

The second RQ examines the effectiveness of the Backfill mechanism in mitigating key structural limitations that arise in retrieval scenarios subject to confidentiality constraints, without excessively compromising performance.

Two main factors motivate this analysis: (i) Reduction of the accessible catalog—when strict access policies are enforced, the set of documents actually available to each user is drastically reduced. This increases the risk of failing to retrieve relevant content simply because it is not authorized. (ii) Selection bias introduced by top-k—in RAG systems, the choice of the parameter k (i.e., the number of documents retrieved in the initial stage) determines which candidates are passed to the reranker. A fixed k value introduces a structural bias: if relevant documents do not appear in the initial top-k, they will never be considered, even if potentially important.

The Backfill mechanism directly addresses these two issues. After applying *confidentiality filtering* (which ensures full compliance with access policies $L \geq A$), Backfill increases the search depth by exploring beyond the initial top-k results and re-ranking these additional candidates using the reranker. This deeper exploration reaches documents that may be difficult to surface directly through the user's query, but which are both relevant and authorized as well.

Figure 2 clearly illustrates the impact of this strategy on retrieval metrics. The use of Backfill leads to an increase in HIT@10, indicating that a larger number of queries are able to retrieve at least one relevant document. At the same time, an improvement in NDCG@10 can be observed, as relevant documents are promoted to higher and therefore more visible positions in the final ranking. Conversely, P@10 tends to decrease, since deeper exploration also introduces fewer relevant documents, reducing the average number of relevant results per query. Overall, these findings show that Backfill introduces a controlled trade-off between precision and coverage: by extending the search depth, the system can satisfy more queries and improve the visibility of relevant documents, at the cost of a moderate reduction in precision. This behavior reflects realistic

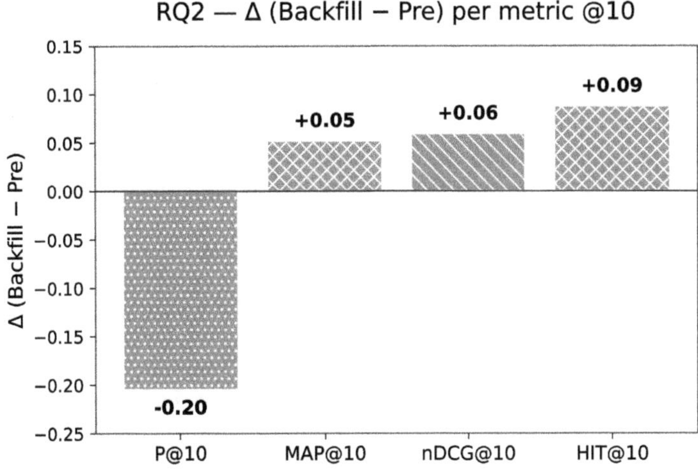

Fig. 2. RQ2. Change in performance after applying the *Backfill* mechanism with respect to the *Pre*-filtering step (corresponding to LF with $\alpha = 0.9$).

educational scenarios in which confidentiality constraints significantly restrict the space of accessible documents, and deeper search becomes essential to preserve the pedagogical utility of the system.

4   Conclusions and Future Work

This work introduced RetrievEM, a *Confidentiality-Aware* RAG framework designed for educational contexts and validated on the `BEIR/FiQA` benchmark. The system demonstrates that it is possible to combine retrieval effectiveness with strict access-control constraints, providing accurate and pedagogically useful responses while preserving confidentiality.

In terms of effectiveness, fusion strategies proved superior to individual components: Linear Fusion with $\alpha = 0.9$ achieved the best performance, outperforming both dense retriever and cross-encoder taken individually, and surpassing that achieved by reciprocal rank fusion. On the confidentiality side, enforcing access policies inevitably reduces the pool of accessible documents while amplifying the bias introduced by top-k retrieval. To mitigate this, we proposed the Backfill strategy, which extends the search depth beyond the initial top-k results and re-ranks additional candidates. This approach improves *Hit* and *NDCG*, ensuring higher coverage and better visibility of relevant documents, but it reduces P@10 due to broader inclusion. In short, Backfill trades precision for coverage, providing a practical balance between strict access enforcement and utility of the retrieved results.

The study also highlights several limitations. First, performance depends heavily on the embedding space, with results and rankings sensitive to the choice of model. Moreover, gains from reranking and query decomposition are not uniform across all queries, exposing variability across queries. Computational costs also increase substantially when incorporating multiple strategies after the retrieval stage, such as fusion-based scoring and the Backfill mechanism.

Looking ahead, future work will focus on adaptive policies that dynamically select retrieval, fusion, and backfill depth based on query characteristics, developing cost-aware mechanisms that optimize efficiency. We also plan to extend the evaluation to educational datasets with real confidentiality constraints and to conduct user studies assessing the framework's pedagogical value and usability.

Acknowledgments. We acknowledge financial support from the National Recovery and Resilience Plan (NRRP), Mission 4 Component 2 Investment 1.1 - Call for tender No. 3277, published on December 30, 2021, by the Italian Ministry of University and Research (MUR), funded by the European Union – Next Generation EU. Project Code ECS0000038 – Project Title eINS Ecosystem of Innovation for Next Generation Sardinia – Grant Assignment Decree No. 1056 adopted on June 23, 2022, by the MUR (CUP F53C22000430001).

References

1. Benham, R., Culpepper, J.S.: Risk-reward trade-offs in rank fusion. In: Proceedings of the 22nd Australasian Document Computing Symposium, ADCS 2017. Association for Computing Machinery, New York, NY, USA (2017). https://doi.org/10.1145/3166072.3166084
2. Boratto, L., Fabbri, F., Fenu, G., Marras, M., Medda, G.: Counterfactual graph augmentation for consumer unfairness mitigation in recommender systems. In: Frommholz, I., et al. (eds.) Proceedings of the 32nd ACM International Conference on Information and Knowledge Management, CIKM 2023, Birmingham, United Kingdom, 21–25 October 2023, pp. 3753–3757. ACM (2023). https://doi.org/10.1145/3583780.3615165
3. Boratto, L., Fenu, G., Marras, M., Medda, G.: Practical perspectives of consumer fairness in recommendation. Inf. Process. Manag. **60**(2), 103208 (2023)
4. Chakraborty, A., Dahal, S., Gupta, H.: Federated retrieval-augmented generation: a systematic mapping study. In: Findings of the Association for Computational Linguistics: EMNLP 2025, pp. 4521–4535 (2025). https://aclanthology.org/2025.findings-emnlp.388
5. Cheng, Z., Zhang, Z., Wang, Y., Yuan, C., Yao, J.: RemoteRAG: a privacy-preserving LLM cloud RAG service. In: Findings of the Association for Computational Linguistics: ACL 2025, pp. 2341–2355 (2025). https://aclanthology.org/2025.findings-acl.197
6. Dessí, D., Dragoni, M., Fenu, G., Marras, M., Reforgiato Recupero, D.: Deep learning adaptation with word embeddings for sentiment analysis on online course reviews. In: Deep Learning-Based Approaches for Sentiment Analysis, pp. 57–83. Springer (2020)
7. Fenu, G., Galici, R., Marras, M., Recupero, D.R.: Exploring student interactions with AI in programming training. In: Adjunct Proceedings of the 32nd ACM Conference on User Modeling, Adaptation and Personalization, UMAP Adjunct 2024, Cagliari, Italy, 1–4 July 2024. ACM (2024). https://doi.org/10.1145/3631700.3665227
8. Guu, K., Lee, K., Tung, Z., Pasupat, P., Chang, M.: Retrieval augmented language model pre-training. In: Proceedings of the 37th International Conference on Machine Learning, ICML 2020, 13–18 July 2020, Virtual Event. Proceedings of Machine Learning Research, vol. 119, pp. 3929–3938. PMLR (2020). http://proceedings.mlr.press/v119/guu20a.html
9. Huang, J., et al.: Layered query retrieval: an adaptive framework for retrieval-augmented generation in complex question answering for large language models. Appl. Sci. **14**(23) (2024). https://www.mdpi.com/2076-3417/14/23/11014
10. Lewis, P., et al.: Retrieval-augmented generation for knowledge-intensive NLP tasks. In: Larochelle, H., Ranzato, M., Hadsell, R., Balcan, M., Lin, H. (eds.) Advances in Neural Information Processing Systems 33: Annual Conference on Neural Information Processing Systems 2020, NeurIPS 2020, 6–12 December 2020, virtual (2020). https://proceedings.neurips.cc/paper/2020/hash/6b493230205f780e1bc26945df7481e5-Abstract.html
11. Medda, G., Fabbri, F., Marras, M., Boratto, L., Fenu, G.: GNNUERS: fairness explanation in GNNs for recommendation via counterfactual reasoning. ACM Trans. Intell. Syst. Technol. **16**(1), 6:1–6:26 (2025). https://doi.org/10.1145/3655631

12. Nussbaum, Z., Morris, J.X., Duderstadt, B., Mulyar, A.: Nomic embed: training a reproducible long context text embedder (2024)
13. Shi, Z., Yan, L., Yin, D., Verberne, S., de Rijke, M., Ren, Z.: Iterative self-incentivization empowers large language models as agentic searchers. CoRR abs/2505.20128 (2025). https://doi.org/10.48550/arXiv.2505.20128
14. Shin, J., Hedderich, M.A., Rey, B.J., Lucero, A., Oulasvirta, A.: Understanding human-AI workflows for generating personas. In: Proceedings of the 2024 ACM Designing Interactive Systems Conference, DIS 2024, pp. 757–781. Association for Computing Machinery, New York, NY, USA (2024). https://doi.org/10.1145/3643834.3660729
15. Takagi, S., Yamauchi, R., Kumagai, W.: Towards autonomous hypothesis verification via language models with minimal guidance (2023). https://arxiv.org/abs/2311.09706
16. Qwen Team: Qwen3 technical report (2025). https://arxiv.org/abs/2505.09388
17. Thakur, N., Reimers, N., Rücklé, A., Srivastava, A., Gurevych, I.: BEIR: a heterogeneous benchmark for zero-shot evaluation of information retrieval models. In: Thirty-Fifth Conference on Neural Information Processing Systems Datasets and Benchmarks Track (Round 2) (2021). https://openreview.net/forum?id=wCu6T5xFjeJ
18. Zeng, J., Zhang, Z., Li, Y., Li, W., Zhang, J.: Mitigating the privacy issues in retrieval-augmented generation (RAG) via pure synthetic data. arXiv preprint arXiv:2406.14773 (2024). https://arxiv.org/abs/2406.14773

Enhancing Teacher Education: AI Potential in Anticipating Teacher Implicit Biases Through Realistic Simulations

Giulia Giacometti[(✉)]

Department of Education, University of Genova, Genoa, Italy
gg.giacomettigiulia@gmail.com

Abstract. Inclusive education is a growing challenge, linked to the complexity of classroom management and student diversity. This complexity can accentuate implicit biases among teachers, particularly towards minorities, and contribute to burnout and attrition. Artificial intelligence (AI) has already shown the potential to improve and accelerate training, offering more tools to reach the goal of inclusion. However, there is still a lack of applications that directly address teachers' implicit bias awareness and encourage genuine personal reflection within an impactful training program. Here is presented a theoretical framework proposing the use of AI, trained on standardised implicit bias tests, to create hyper-realistic, teacher-tailored simulations that provide new learning opportunities and allow teachers to self-assess their implicit biases.

Keywords: Predictive AI · Implicit bias · Teacher education · Inclusion

1 Introduction

1.1 Obstacles to Scholastic Inclusion

The growing complexity and heterogeneity of classrooms have made the implementation of inclusive pedagogical practices increasingly challenging.

In recent years, Italian classrooms have become progressively diverse, with a significant increase in minority groups: both students with disabilities and foreign minors, including those unaccompanied. In 2023, over 900,000 students were non-Italian citizens, mostly from non-European countries [1]. At the same time, the number of pupils with disabilities has also grown, along with the consequent demand for support teachers [2]. However, many educational institutions and teachers are not yet fully prepared to deal with this complexity.

Teachers' Challenges in Managing Diversity. Teachers face increasing pressure due to insufficient resources, growing class sizes, rising social expectations and declining public recognition of their role. These difficulties have contributed to a gradual abandonment of the profession, often within the first five years of their career [3].

A. Dipace et al. (Eds.): WAILS 2025, LNCS 16438, pp. 87–93, 2026.
https://doi.org/10.1007/978-3-032-17604-2_9

The processes of reception and inclusion require specific skills and coordinated work between teachers, reception centres and educational communities, but prejudice, language barriers and relational closures make it difficult to create truly inclusive and participatory environments, also putting the well-being and motivation of teachers at risk.

In the Italian context, the guidelines of the Ministry of Education and Merit (MIM) promote a model of inclusion based on a holistic approach, with constant and coordinated collaboration between teachers, professionals and institutions, so that every educational intervention integrates didactic, social and relational aspects. However, relational difficulties between new entrants, class groups and school staff can hinder the building of bonds and make inclusion pathways more difficult [4].

Many teachers say they believe deeply in the values of inclusion, but at the same time report emotional and operational fatigue in translating these principles into everyday practice. If not recognised and managed, these attitudes can influence judgements and behaviors, hindering the goal of inclusion [5].

Implicit Biases and Risk Factors for Inclusion. Inclusion also requires teachers to critically reflect on their own stereotypes and prejudices to foster respectful environments and impart social and interpersonal skills to students. The concept of bias refers to systematic distortions in cognitive processes that lead to judgements that are not entirely rational and objective. In the educational context, these biases are linked to stereotypes and prejudices, unfavourable attitudes based solely on membership of a group, which influence teaching and learning [6].

There is a difference between explicit (conscious) and implicit (automatic) attitudes, with the latter forming the basis of academic prejudice [7], influencing teachers' expectations even when they claim to be impartial [8–10]. The discrepancy between implicit and explicit attitudes can generate cognitive dissonance [11] a psychological tension that can lead to stress and burnout. Furthermore, implicit attitudes are linked to the Pygmalion effect [5], which can be understood as a self-fulfilling prophecy where teachers' unconscious expectations influence students' behavior, compromising their performance [12]. The literature confirms that the persistence of teachers' automatic biases particularly disadvantages ethnic minorities [13], widening the achievement gap between students.

Risks of Failure in Managing Implicit Biases. According to the general burnout model [14], social and emotional skills, together with awareness of implicit attitudes, are crucial factors in increasing teachers' self-efficacy and reducing the risk of burnout. The discrepancy between educational ideals and behaviors influenced by implicit biases can generate stress and, in severe cases, burnout [11].

Although schools with many minority students can show higher teacher burnout when staff feel unprepared [15], sustained, well-supported exposure to multicultural classrooms and effective teaching strategies can increase self-efficacy and reduce burnout [16, 17], consistent with intergroup contact theory [18]. Besides, a high level of self-efficacy is closely related to teachers' well-being and contributes to reduce stress and burnout [19]. Hence, against stress correlated risks, it is essential to develop continuous education programmes for school staff, aimed not only at improving teaching skills, but also at recognising and managing implicit biases. This would also help to prevent cognitive dissonance, improve relationships with students and lighten the psychological burden on teachers [20].

1.2   Teacher Training for Inclusion

Teacher education programmes should follow OECD and UNESCO guidelines emphasising the need for continuous, interdisciplinary training based on social-emotional skills, aimed at increasing awareness, empathy and social-emotional skills, for example through Social Emotional Learning (SEL), to address the growing complexity of classrooms [21]. However, they point out that many education systems still implement fragmented training programmes that are poorly linked to real-world practice, limiting their effectiveness [22, 23]. Numerous SEL training programmes launched, both in universities' courses and in service, have shown significant results [21]. Similarly, structured journeys that include self-reflection, role-playing and guided discussions can effectively reduce implicit biases and increase intercultural awareness [24] However, the training system for teachers in Italy is procedure-based and not always sufficiently practised through continuative, laboratory-based, reflective training courses integrated with everyday school life, often neglecting a more relational approach [25]. Accordingly, to face teachers' implicit biases, it is essential to promote highly engaging training programs that integrate meaningful experiences of awareness, direct contact, and interaction with minorities, as well as opportunities to understand and manage personal fears and preconceptions (Fiorucci, 2019). Such programs achieve their greatest impact when they are institutionalized and systematically implemented across the entire teaching workforce. In contrast, constrained resources and high staff turnover often hinder the continuity of professional development and the consistent transmission of inclusive competences [3, 22]. Standardized training accessible to all schools would enable teachers not only to be better prepared to deal with complex classes, but also to develop greater awareness of their own socio-emotional skills and implicit biases. It is essential to develop systematised training courses that are easily accessible and ensure a high fit with their situation, so that they have the necessary tools and skills regardless of structural limitations.

AI Solutions for Teacher Education and Class Management.   To implement the standardisation of these programs, schools have already begun to experiment with artificial intelligence (AI) based solutions and machine learning (ML) systems. AI based high-fidelity simulations appear to increase awareness of implicit biases among teachers, demonstrating how immersive practical experiences can improve the ability to recognise and manage bias in daily interactions with students [26–28]. The experience of virtual embodiment has been explored for its potential to positively influence attitudes and behaviors. This immersive experience significantly increases perspective taking, empathy and prosocial practices towards culturally different groups, more so than simple non-immersive reflective activities [29]. However, without a proper fit with personal preconceptions and the realistic context of the class, the result can be less impactful. The challenge is ensuring that algorithms are developed with fairness-aware approaches and adapted to local cultural and linguistic contexts [30], avoiding "garbage in-garbage out" effects. Teachers' implicit biases risk being transferred, replicated and amplified, into educational datasets used to train ML systems [31].

Implicit Measures. Even individuals who perceive themselves as open-minded and unbiased may, in fact, exhibit negative attitudes at unconscious level [13]. Implicit tests provide a more authentic assessment of unconscious associations, overcoming the limitations of questionnaires that are subject to social desirability bias [9, 20]. Among the most widely used procedures are priming tests and the Implicit Association Test (IAT)[1] [32]. Hence, implicit attitudes can be detected through spontaneous responses to both verbal and visual stimuli, without the need for conscious cognitive processing [33, 34]. An alternative tool for measuring implicit attitudes is the Relational Responding Task (RRT) [35]. A recent study applied RRT to the educational context for the first time, showing that even in the absence of explicit bias, teachers may harbour implicit negative expectations towards students belonging to ethnic minorities [8]. This opens new perspectives for better understanding the ethnic gap and self-fulfilling prophecies that can influence the academic performance of minority students. These measures aim to capture implicit associations that often escape individual awareness.

Few theoretical studies have developed interventions aimed at addressing teachers' implicit biases, combining data-driven tools with implicit measures. However, these studies were not fitted to individual teachers, did not propose immersive simulations capable of enhancing the realism and coherence with actual classroom contexts, were not built as a self-assessment tool and some were prescriptive potentially hindering training efficacy [30].

2   Concept and Methods

The conceptual hypothesis proposed in this article is whether predictive artificial intelligence trained using current implicit measures (IAT and RRT), applied to the analysis of teachers' biases, can be integrated as a self-assessment tool in teacher education. A systematic approach is proposed that uses validated tools to assess areas that are potentially critical for inclusive teaching and the difficulties encountered in specific classroom contexts. The output of the self-assessment will be employed to construct a simulated training environment using realistic scenarios that reproduce the characteristics of these critical issues. Since every output will be tailored to each individual teacher, it may be possible to help them face their implicit biases in a precise and specific manner. Feasible ways of using this approach and their possible outcomes are outlined below, while referring to future stages of design and experimentation in real school contexts.

Proposed Method. The proposed deployment envisions the use of a familiar system for teachers, such as a centralised web platform for courses and materials that links to external tools (i.e. assessment based on IAT/RRT). To facilitate access, it can be used a module or extension that integrates directly into the scholastic electronic register, using existing and protected logins and data, with anonymisation of results and informed consent prior to training.

After the login, the teacher would have access to a platform that evaluates through IAT or RRT unrecognised implicit biases, analyses potential areas of difficulty and the

---

[1] A concrete and accessible example is provided by Harvard's Project Implicit, available online (https://implicit.harvard.edu/implicit/selectatest.html).

possible outcome that these biases may have on classroom dynamics. For the training of ML systems, the integration of information on class composition, historical data on teacher experience and teacher perceptions of the classroom climate can represent a resource for defining output, together with the analysis of implicit measurement results. It would then be possible to estimate the probability of recurring implicit biases, such as the implicit automatic associations "gender → mathematics" or "ethnicity → discipline" [8].

Once completed, the system would generate a personalised report and suggest educational contents that would help raise awareness and reduce behavioral errors. A crucial point is that the output must not be prescriptive: in fact, the aim should not be to issue individual judgements, but to provide feedback on any risk profiles, which should be used to guide tailored training courses. Thanks to the capabilities of generative AI, it would also be possible to develop vignettes, scenarios or simulations of realistic classroom and school environments. These simulations could be amplified through virtual reality (VR) or augmented reality (AR). These outputs could also be integrated into customised teacher training programs, for instance, within a class group, using role play and guided self-reflection through a self-assessment process. This material would have the potential to offer tailored courses based on the specific needs of teachers and the priorities of individual institutions, making training more flexible, accessible and adaptable to different school environments. It would also be possible to track the evolution of implicit biases over time, showing progress and critical issues, thus promoting continuous and targeted training.

3 Conclusion and Future Works

This paper proposes a theoretical framework for exploring how AI systems could help teachers recognise and reduce their implicit biases, with benefits for educational inclusion. Such tools could offer teachers the opportunity to reflect on how their behaviors influence classroom interactions and to identify areas for improvement, while respecting their autonomy. Designed as a non-prescriptive self-assessment, the feedback could significantly complement existing debiasing activities in teacher training.

A key constraint relates to biases in the data sets or inadequate representation of teachers and students, which could affect the reliability of the predictions. In the future, this approach could enable teachers to monitor their own implicit attitudes themselves and receive tailored feedback without external supervision. Targeted practices and guided frameworks could help translate these insights into concrete strategies for self-regulation, empathy, and critical thinking. Co-designing such practices with all parties involved in the school could enrich professional development by integrating technical, pedagogical, and personal growth. Experimental studies and classroom trials will be needed to validate the efficacy of these tools and support their wider adoption.

References

1. Ministero dell'Istruzione e del Merito: Gli alunni con cittadinanza non italiana a.a. 2022/2023 (2024)

2. ISTAT: L'inclusione scolastica degli alunni con disabilità. Anno 2022–2023 (2024)
3. Global report on teachers: addressing teacher shortages and transforming the profession. Global report on teachers: addressing teacher shortages and transforming the profession (2024). https://doi.org/10.54675/FIGU8035
4. Santagati, M., Barzaghi, A.: Studio conoscitivo sui minori stranieri non accompagnati in Italia e l'accesso all'istruzione (2021)
5. Rosenthal, R., Jacobson, L.: Pygmalion in the classroom. Urban Rev. **3**, 16–20 (1968). https://doi.org/10.1007/BF02322211
6. Dovidio, J.F., Glick, P., Hewstone, M.: The SAGE Handbook of Prejudice, Stereotyping and Discrimination, pp. 1–672 (2010)
7. Eagly, A.H., Chaiken, S.: The Psychology of Attitudes. Harcourt Brace Jovanovich College Publishers (1993)
8. Costa, S., Pirchio, S., Glock, S.: Teachers' and preservice teachers' implicit attitudes toward ethnic minority students and implicit expectations of their academic performance. Int. J. Intercult. Relat. **89**, 56–62 (2022). https://doi.org/10.1016/j.ijintrel.2022.05.006
9. Denessen, E., Hornstra, L., van den Bergh, L., Bijlstra, G.: Implicit measures of teachers' attitudes and stereotypes, and their effects on teacher practice and student outcomes: a review. Learn. Instr. **78**, 101437 (2022). https://doi.org/10.1016/J.LEARNINSTRUC.2020.101437
10. Costa, S., Langher, V., Pirchio, S.: Teachers' implicit attitudes toward ethnic minority students: a systematic review. Front. Psychol. **12**, 712356 (2021). https://doi.org/10.3389/fpsyg.2021.712356
11. Costa, S., Pirchio, S., Shevchuk, A., Glock, S.: Does teachers' ethnic bias stress them out? The role of teachers' implicit attitudes toward and expectations of ethnic minority students in teachers' burnout. Int. J. Intercult. Relat. **93**, 101757 (2023). https://doi.org/10.1016/J.IJINTREL.2023.101757
12. Lorenz, G.: Subtle discrimination: do stereotypes among teachers trigger bias in their expectations and widen ethnic achievement gaps? Soc. Psychol. Educ. **24**, 537–571 (2021). https://doi.org/10.1007/s11218-021-09615-0
13. Pit-ten Cate, I.M., Glock, S.: Teachers' implicit attitudes toward students from different social groups: a meta-analysis. Front. Psychol. **10**, 491099 (2019). https://doi.org/10.3389/fpsyg.2019.02832/xml
14. Pikić Jugović, I., Marušić, I., Matić Bojić, J.: Early career teachers' social and emotional competencies, self-efficacy and burnout: a mediation model. BMC Psychol. **13**, 1–14 (2025). https://doi.org/10.1186/S40359-024-02323-2/FIGURES/6
15. Bottiani, J.H., Duran, C.A.K., Pas, E.T., Bradshaw, C.P.: Teacher stress and burnout in urban middle schools: associations with job demands, resources, and effective classroom practices. J. Sch. Psychol. **77**, 36–51 (2019). https://doi.org/10.1016/J.JSP.2019.10.002
16. Lazarides, R., Watt, H.M.G., Richardson, P.W.: Teachers' classroom management self-efficacy, perceived classroom management and teaching contexts from beginning until mid-career. Learn. Instr. **69**, 101346 (2020). https://doi.org/10.1016/J.LEARNINSTRUC.2020.101346
17. Ulbricht, J., Schachner, M.K., Civitillo, S., Noack, P.: Teachers' acculturation in culturally diverse schools - how is the perceived diversity climate linked to intercultural self-efficacy? Front. Psychol. **13**, 953068 (2022). https://doi.org/10.3389/FPSYG.2022.953068/XML
18. Pettigrew, T.F., Tropp, L.R., Wagner, U., Christ, O.: Recent advances in intergroup contact theory. Int. J. Intercult. Relat. **35**, 271–280 (2011). https://doi.org/10.1016/J.IJINTREL.2011.03.001
19. Ortan, F., Simut, C., Simut, R.: Self-efficacy, job satisfaction and teacher well-being in the K-12 educational system. Int. J. Environ. Res. Public Health **18**, 12763 (2021). https://doi.org/10.3390/IJERPH182312763

20. Ayala, M.C., Webb, A., Maldonado, L., et al.: Teacher's social desirability bias and Migrant students: a study on explicit and implicit prejudices with a list experiment. Soc. Sci. Res. **119**, 102990 (2024). https://doi.org/10.1016/J.SSRESEARCH.2024.102990

21. Marchi, V., Sacchetti, M.C., Cavallini, F., Vascelli, L.: Promoting social and emotional learning in primary schools: a scoping review of intervention programs. J. Clin. Dev. Psychol. **6**, 88–113 (2024). https://doi.org/10.13129/2612-4033/0110-4528

22. UNESCO: Inclusive teaching: preparing all teachers to teach all students (2020)

23. Brussino, O.: Mapping policy approaches and practices for the inclusion of students with special education needs. In: OECD Education Working Papers, OECD Publishing No. 227 (2020). https://doi.org/10.1787/600fbad5-en

24. Gabrielli, S., Szpunar, G., Livi, S.: Ridurre il pregiudizio implicito in classe per favorire l'inclusione: un percorso di formazione con gli insegnanti pre-servizio. Educ. Sci. Soc. **1**, 140–158 (2020). https://doi.org/10.3280/ESS1-2020OA9476

25. Ianes, D., Demo, H., Dell'Anna, S.: Inclusive education in Italy: historical steps, positive developments, and challenges. PROSPECTS **49**(3), 249–263 (2020). https://doi.org/10.1007/S11125-020-09509-7

26. Higgins, S., Alcock, S., De, A.B., et al.: Perspective matters: a systematic review of immersive virtual reality to reduce racial prejudice. Virtual Real. **28**, 1–21 (2024). https://doi.org/10.1007/s10055-024-01024-w/figures/3

27. Christensen, R., Knezek, G., Kruse, S.: Reducing Bias and Promoting Equity through a Simulated Teaching Environment (2024)

28. Shekell, C., Mikeska, J.N., Kaur Bharaj, P.: Using simulation experiences to address bias in teaching practices. Int. Soc. Technol. Educ. (ISTE) **35**, 796–820 (2023). https://doi.org/10.1080/1046560X.2024.2350148

29. Lucifora, C., Schembri, M., Poggi, F., et al.: Virtual reality supports perspective taking in cultural heritage interpretation. Comput. Hum. Behav. **148**, 107911 (2023). https://doi.org/10.1016/J.CHB.2023.107911

30. Gauthier, A., Rizvi, S., Cukurova, M., Mavrikis, M.: Is it time we get real? A systematic review of the potential of data-driven technologies to address teachers' implicit biases. Front. Artif. Intell. **5**, 994967 (2022). https://doi.org/10.3389/FRAI.2022.994967/BIBTEX

31. Eckhardt, S., Knaeble, M., Bucher, A., et al.: "Garbage In, Garbage Out": mitigating human biases in data entry by means of artificial intelligence. In: Lecture Notes in Computer Science (LNAILNB), vol. 14144, pp. 27–48 (2023). https://doi.org/10.1007/978-3-031-42286-7_2/TABLES/2

32. Fazio, R.H., Olson, M.A.: Implicit measures in social cognition research: their meaning and use. Annu. Rev. Psychol. **54**, 297–327 (2003). https://doi.org/10.1146/annurev.psych.54.101601.145225

33. Greenwald, A.G., Cvencek, D., Dovidio, J.F., et al.: The implicit association test at age 20: what is known and what is not known about implicit bias (2023). https://doi.org/10.31234/osf.io/bf97c

34. Nosek, B.A., Hawkins, C.B., Frazier, R.S.: Implicit social cognition: from measures to mechanisms. Trends Cogn. Sci. **15**, 152–159 (2011). https://doi.org/10.1016/j.tics.2011.01.005

35. De Houwer, J., Heider, N., Spruyt, A., et al.: The relational responding task: toward a new implicit measure of beliefs. Front. Psychol. **6**, 132367 (2015). https://doi.org/10.3389/fpsyg.2015.00319

Experimenting with Generative AI in Screenwriting for Film Schools

Angelica Lo Duca[1] and Daniela Rotelli[2(✉)]

[1] IIT-CNR, Pisa, Italy
`angelica.loduca@iit.cnr.it`
[2] Sorbonne Université, Paris, France
`daniela.rotelli@lip6.fr`

Abstract. This paper presents an experimental study on the integration of generative artificial intelligence (GenAI) into film education, focussing on the collaborative creation of a short screenplay. Using GenAI tools, we developed a multistage workflow combining AI-generated outputs, knowledge bases in history and psychology, and human-in-the-loop revisions. The process produced a narrative structure and screenplay, which were subsequently evaluated for narrative coherence, originality, and feasibility. Beyond the artistic result, the experiment highlights the pedagogical potential of GenAI as a creative partner in film schools. We argue that GenAI can foster creativity, critical reflection, and AI literacy when embedded in a structured, human-centred learning framework. At the same time, we discuss limitations such as historical inaccuracies, narrative inconsistencies, and ethical sensitivities to the portrayal of traumatic contexts. Our findings suggest that GenAI, when carefully integrated, can serve as both a creative tool and an educational resource for training future filmmakers.

Keywords: Generative Artificial Intelligence · Screenwriting · Education · AI Literacy

1 Introduction

The advent of Generative Artificial Intelligence (GenAI) is fundamentally reshaping creative and educational practices, providing novel opportunities for learning, collaboration, and critical reflection [25]. In film education, emerging technologies present opportunities to enhance creativity, promote critical thinking, and develop AI literacy while also posing methodological, ethical, and pedagogical issues. Despite growing interest in the integration of GenAI into creative processes, there is still a lack of systematic investigation of the responsible and critical integration of these technologies [12].

This study addresses this gap by presenting an exploratory investigation of GenAI for co-designing an original screenplay within an educational context.

A. Dipace et al. (Eds.): WAILS 2025, LNCS 16438, pp. 94–109, 2026.
https://doi.org/10.1007/978-3-032-17604-2_10

Originating from the Cort-IA3[1] contest for film writers, the experiment adopts the perspective of film school students engaged in collaborative human-machine creativity. The proposed workflow combines generative output, curated historical and psychological/behavioural knowledge bases, and human-in-the-loop revisions throughout all key phases of screenwriting. Using and comparing GenAI tools to write, evaluate, and subsequently produce a fictional short film, the aim was to produce a creative artefact and examine how such a process could serve as an educational model for integrating GenAI into film schools.

Guided by the RQ: "How can GenAI enhance creativity and critical reflection in film education?", the contribution of this article lies in presenting a replicable human-centred methodology that combines AI-assisted generation with disciplinary knowledge and participatory revision, illustrating how students can engage with AI critically rather than passively. Our findings suggest that GenAI, when carefully integrated, can act as both a stimulus for creativity and a scaffold for reflective practice, offering valuable insights into the development of AI literacy among students in film education.

2   Related Work

Recent studies have explored how GenAI can act as a co-designer in creative processes, supporting both narrative construction and critical engagement [27]. Cake [5] examines the collaborative application of GenAI in the development of screenplays, demonstrating that AI can serve as a collaborative partner in screenwriting and narrative design. Monserrat and Srnec [18] view GenAI as a transformative presence in film schools, redefining expressive possibilities while raising new questions about authorship and interpretation. On the other hand, Doshi and Hauser [9] observed that GenAI can enhance individual creativity, though it may lead to reduced collective diversity in creative outcomes, suggesting a trade-off between generative support and originality. At the same time, Chen et al. [7] underscore that passive reliance on GenAI can reduce cognitive engagement and lead to shallow narrative results; thus, responsible human intervention remains essential.

In the field of education, recent investigations report on the impacts on student engagement and learning perceptions when AI tools are introduced into classroom activities [31]. Xia et al. [32] delineate the rapid advancement of GenAI adoption in higher education, identifying both opportunities and open questions about methodological rigour and domain-specific applications. Early implementation studies confirm the potential benefits of GenAI deployment in higher education settings, but also emphasise the need for careful instructional design and responsible integration [3]. Giannakos et al. [12] emphasise the importance of carefully designed workflows that combine GenAI with disciplinary knowledge, curated data, and continuous human oversight. Authors such as Al-kfairy et al. [1] map the ethical imperatives involved in using GenAI, particularly when

---

[1] https://www.sophia.vision/cort-ia/.

narratives interact with traumatic historical contexts. Here, the risk of perpetuating inaccuracies or insensitive representations is significant, and embedding critical human review within AI-assisted workflows is pedagogically crucial. Islam and Greenwood [15] further caution against the loss of student agency, recommending that learners retain responsibility and creative ownership even as AI becomes a more substantive partner. Finally, the use of AI as both creator and evaluator of creative work introduces an additional layer of complexity and potential over-reliance, which need to be balanced by transparent, critical assessment processes.

These insights show that the implementation of GenAI in educational and creative contexts serves not only as an accelerator for creative output but also as a scaffold for developing AI literacy and critical reflection, provided that educational frameworks remain human-centred and ethically informed.

3   Methodology

We operationalise the research question through the following four objectives: *(i)* practising narrative construction, *(ii)* fostering critical engagement with GenAI, *(iii)* integrating disciplinary knowledge, and *(iv)* enhancing AI literacy. Each stage of the process is aligned with one or more of these objectives, ensuring that innovative experimentation with GenAI is integrated into a comprehensive educational framework.

Practicing Narrative Construction. The workflow mirrors the traditional stages of screenwriting (controlling idea, subject, characters, dramatic structure, and dialogue) while enriching them with GenAI intervention. At each stage, students practice the core principles of narrative design, such as defining themes, building characters with motivations and conflicts, and structuring the narrative using the three-act arc [10]. This structure divides the narrative into three parts: setup, conflict, and resolution. Other narrative models exist, like the hero's journey [6] but for simplicity, we consider only the three-act structure. However, our methodology can be extended to these other models as well.

Fostering Critical Engagement with GenAI. Students are encouraged to evaluate, adapt, or reject GenAI suggestions. For example, GenAI produces multiple narrative options that students compare with their initial intentions, reshaping them to preserve coherence and originality. In this way, GenAI serves as both a creative partner and a reflective stimulus, while students maintain control over the creative direction.

Integrating Disciplinary Knowledge. To guarantee trustworthiness and contextual depth, the workflow requires that students complement AI-generated content with selected sources. Historical and psychological-behavioural knowledge bases will serve as input before the development of characters and plot. This integration enables students to anchor their narratives in specific historical contexts and realistic psychological dynamics, connecting creative writing with disciplinary learning.

Enhancing AI Literacy. By alternating AI-assisted generation and AI-supported evaluation, students are exposed to the strengths and limitations of GenAI models. This dual dynamic fosters awareness of issues such as narrative quality, ethical sensitivity, and the risks of over-reliance on automated feedback [33].

3.1   Workflow

Figure 1 illustrates the process undertaken by students to collaboratively design a screenplay through GenAI. The co-design process unfolds in successive phases that mirror the traditional stages of screenwriting but are enriched by GenAI intervention. Once the *controlling idea* and the *subject* are defined by students, they explore AI-generated variations to broaden and test their starting point. To improve character reliability and plot creation and to ensure that students gain knowledge about the subject they want to develop, they are asked to augment GenAI tools with two additional inputs: a *historical* knowledge base (KB), containing historical documents related to the specific subject, and a *psychological and behavioural* KB, containing documents associated with character specific psychology. As *characters* are introduced according to the controlling idea, the subject, and the KBs, GenAI provides possible archetypes, motivations, and conflicts, which students subsequently refine to ensure psychological plausibility and narrative coherence. This phase is followed by the construction of a *plot*, where GenAI suggests alternative three-act frameworks along with turning points and climactic developments. Students use these proposals to experiment with narrative pacing and tension while learning to apply classical *screenplay* writing principles. In the drafting stage, AI-generated dialogues and scene descriptions offer preliminary material that students can adapt stylistically to achieve consistency and authorial voice. Finally, in the *evaluation* step, the script is assessed using a different GenAI tool, which provides feedback on coherence, originality, and feasibility. This evaluation step is combined with human reflection and peer critique, ensuring that the process is both technologically supported and pedagogically grounded. The outcome of the co-design process is the *final story*.

The alternation of AI-assisted generation and AI-supported evaluation promotes the perception of AI as a dialogic partner that enriches creative exploration and reflective learning. Moreover, the proposed methodology fosters technical proficiency in screenwriting and AI literacy, defined as the capacity to recognise the advantages, constraints, and ethical considerations of GenAI tools.

4   Experiment

To evaluate the feasibility of our methodology, we acted as students and conducted an experiment aimed at creating a screenplay for a 20-minute short film, a process made more effective by the fact that one of the authors also has professional experience in fiction writing. Firstly, we conducted a comprehensive analysis to identify the most appropriate GenAI technology to implement the proposed methodology [19, 26]. We selected OpenAI ChatGPT 5, Gemini 2.5

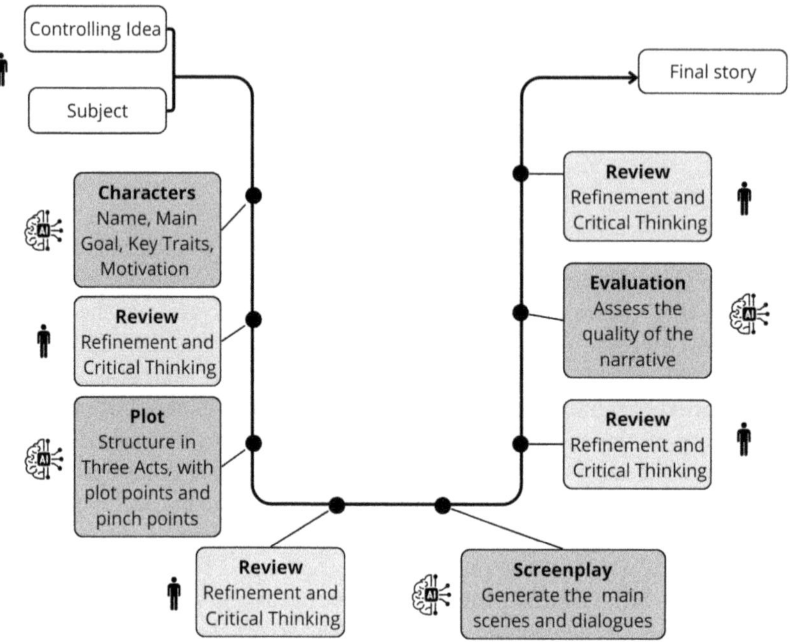

Fig. 1. The steps undertaken by students to co-design a screenplay using GenAI.

Flash, Copilot Smart GPT-5, DeepSeek-V3.2, and Claude Sonnet 4.5 to compare their performance on narrative creation [16,21]. For each GenAI tool, we generated three stories, which were then compared and rated using a questionnaire submitted to people recruited through Mechanical Turk. The comprehensive details of this evaluation are delineated in a separate publication which is currently under review. Since Copilot received the highest rating, we selected Copilot as the GenAI tool for our experiments. The workflow depicted in Fig. 1 was executed within a single conversation on the Copilot interface. This approach enabled us to leverage Copilot's memory functionality, which preserves the results of previous interactions inside the same chat session.

4.1   Initial Setup

The process begins with the articulation of a *controlling idea*: *Only by reconciling with one's past can one find peace.* The *subject*, defined in the box, is then developed according to the author's personal interest in the topic. This step is not only functional for screenplay generation, but also aims to guide us, as students, in the acquisition of fundamental skills in narrative design: identifying a core theme, defining it within a historical and cultural context, and translating it into a concrete subject to develop [2].

> **Subject**
>
> Mechelen (Belgium), April 19, 1943. Marie and Anne, two twin sisters aged three, were travelling with their parents and their older brother Pierre in convoy number 20 headed to the Auschwitz concentration camp. During the journey, the train was attacked by three young members of the Belgian resistance. The girls were saved by Youra 'Georges' Livchitz, who managed to take them with him to Kiev. Pierre also survived and was placed with a Belgian family. Both their parents died during the attack. In June 1943, Livchitz was arrested. The two sisters were hidden by his fiancée's family, but on the way down to the basement, Anne tripped and suffered a cut across the palm of her hand. The wound was stitched up but left a deep scar on the palm, which greatly shocked Marie, who witnessed both the fall and the stitching. Following Livchitz's arrest, the two sisters were separated. Marie was taken in by a peasant family in Odessa (USSR). Anne was taken in by a very wealthy Jewish family in Los Angeles (USA). October 18-22, 1964. Tokyo Olympics Artistic Gymnastics. Marie and Anne, despite their separation, share the same passion. They meet on the competition field and meet for the first time. Historical context: it is the height of the Cold War, with the conflict between the USSR and the USA. During the vault, Marie performs after Anne. Anne prepares for the test and covers her hands with chalk to ensure a firmer grip. At that moment, Marie, who is waiting behind Anne, sees the scar. The lid of the box of her memories opens.

The activity of defining the subject represents a *design scaffold* that allows students to explore how historical and psychological dimensions can be translated into narrative structures. To facilitate this, two supplementary knowledge bases (KB): a *historical* KB, containing documents related to the selected historical period [4, 8, 24, 28–30], and a *psychological and behavioural* KB, are implemented to ground the plausibility of the reactions and motivations of the characters [13, 23].

These resources serve a dual function. On the one hand, they enrich the generative models with reliable contextual data, mitigating the risks of historical inaccuracies or stereotypes; on the other hand, they require students to participate in preparatory research, thus fostering both domain-specific learning (history, psychology) and *AI literacy*. This enable the interplay between curated human knowledge and AI-generated content, developing awareness of the advantages and limitations of GenAI when applied to sensitive or complex subjects.

4.2 Characters

In the second phase, the focus shifts to character creation. This step represents a crucial opportunity for students to understand how abstract narrative principles (e.g., conflict, motivation, arc of transformation) can be concretised into structured character profiles [22]. The activity is structured sequentially, starting with the introduction of the protagonist, followed by the antagonist, and then the supporting characters.

The Protagonist. While the protagonist could have been selected manually, this task is delegated to Copilot (see the prompt below) to explore its potential as a co-designer in the educational process. In doing so, students are not only exposed to AI-generated creative content, but are also required to critically evaluate its adequacy, coherence, and alignment with the original controlling idea and subject. This promotes *AI literacy*, as students must recognise when GenAI output is useful and when it requires refinement or rejection.

> **Prompt for Protagonist Generation**
>
> Based on the following controlling idea [...] and subject [...], create a main protagonist. Provide: name, role, key traits, central motivation, and main goal.

Copilot generated a structured profile of a protagonist centred on Marie Livchitz, a Soviet gymnast competing at the 1964 Tokyo Olympics. Copilot described the character through key traits such as resilience, discipline, and introversion, while her central motivation was defined as the search for identity and reconciliation with suppressed memories. Importantly, GenAI reframed the protagonist's goal from athletic victory to emotional healing through reconnection with her sister, Anne, demonstrating how generative models can suggest alternative narrative directions that students must critically evaluate.

To increase plausibility and avoid generic or stereotypical representations, acting as students, the AI-generated profile is refined using curated knowledge bases: historical (HKB) and psychological and behavioural (PBKB). This step embodies a human-centred and participatory design practice, as students actively mediate between AI output and authoritative human sources. The integration of these resources produced a more nuanced protagonist. Maria Livchits, portrayed as a Soviet gymnast shaped by wartime trauma, displacement, and ideological indoctrination. The HKB grounded her in post-war Soviet society, while the PBKB enriched her with specific values, fears, strengths, and behavioural tendencies.

This process trains students to combine AI generation with evidence-based revision, fostering both narrative competence and responsible use of GenAI. It illustrates how students can move beyond passive consumption of machine output, developing instead a reflective practice that balances creativity with critical inquiry and socio-ethical sensitivity.

The Antagonist. In the initial attempt to define the antagonist, Copilot was instructed to identify this character autonomously. However, the system produced peripheral figures such as Maria's gymnastics coach or other secondary roles. This outcome provides an educational opportunity: it reveals to students both the creative potential and the limitations of GenAI when left unguided. Students can thus observe how GenAI tends to generate conventional or surface-level suggestions, underscoring the importance of human intervention in shaping meaningful narrative conflict.

For this reason, the antagonist is defined manually: Anne, that is Maria's twin sister, who grew up in the United States. This choice illustrates a principle of participatory and human-centred design: while GenAI can contribute to the generative process, critical human agency remains essential for narrative depth and educational value [14].

Once Anne was created, we tasked Copilot with refining her profile, using the same historical and psychological/behavioural knowledge bases applied to the protagonist. This step enriched Anne's characterisation and demonstrated to students how structured prompts and curated resources can guide GenAI systems to more coherent and contextually grounded results.

Copilot's output defined Anne Rosenfeld as a symbolic counterpoint to Maria. Rather than embodying malice, Anne represents Western values of freedom, openness, and emotional expression, standing in tension with Maria's repression and Soviet upbringing. Traits such as charisma, idealism, empathy, and stubbornness positioned her as simultaneously supportive and disruptive. Her central motivation is to restore the broken bond with her sister and to honour Youra Livchitz's legacy through remembrance and testimony. Consequently, her primary goal is not athletic success, but encouraging Maria to confront their shared trauma, thus acting as a catalyst for reconciliation and transformation.

This process illustrates how antagonists in narrative design can be reconceptualised as narrative foils—characters who challenge the protagonist's worldview and foster development [20]. By engaging with GenAI outputs critically and contextually, students develop both narrative competence and AI literacy, learning to identify when generative systems' suggestions align with human educational goals and when they require reinterpretation.

The Supporting Characters. To extend the narrative beyond the central conflict, we, as students, are asked to co-design supporting characters with the assistance of Copilot (see the prompt below). Since students must decide which characters contribute meaningfully to the story and which risk dispersing the narrative focus, this activity highlights how GenAI can be used to provide creative input and stimulate critical evaluation and selection.

> **Prompt for Supporting Character Generation**
>
> Propose 2–3 supporting characters who interact with the protagonist and antagonist. For each, describe: name, role, key trait, and how they influence the protagonist's journey or the antagonist's plans.

Copilot generated three character profiles, each designed to act as a catalyst in the trajectories of both the protagonist and antagonist. *Irina Volkova*, Maria's Soviet coach and surrogate mother figure, is characterised as embodying ideological discipline and emotional restraint: she initially reinforces Maria's silence but later models the possibility of release. *David Rosenfeld*, Anne's adoptive father and Holocaust survivor, symbolises the moral imperative of remembrance and testimony, indirectly influencing Maria by bridging memory between the sisters. *Lev Petrov*, Maria's Soviet teammate, is presented as an emotionally perceptive but politically cautious ally, offering Maria a space for vulnerability and growth.

This phase illustrates the importance of iterative design choices. Students are encouraged to evaluate GenAI proposals according to both narrative principles (coherence, relevance, dramatic economy) and ethical considerations (representation of trauma, historical accuracy). Given the short-film format, we integrated only two supporting characters (Irina Volkova and Lev Petrov) into the screenplay. This deliberate reduction provided us with a practical exercise in prioritisation, teaching how to balance narrative richness with thematic coherence and production feasibility.

Therefore, the process reinforced two educational outcomes: first, the ability to critically engage with AI-generated options rather than accepting them uncritically; and second, the development of narrative awareness, as students learn to recognise the structural role of supporting figures in enabling the transformation of the protagonist. In this way, the integration of GenAI into character design becomes an educational tool to foster both creative decision-making and responsible use of generative technologies.

4.3 Plot

In the next phase, the focus was on the generation of the overall plot for which we used the following prompt:

> **Prompt for Plot Generation**
>
> Using the controlling idea, the subject and the characters defined with their arcs, generate a high-level three-act story outline supported by the HKB.

This stage enables to see how abstract narrative principles, such as the three-act structure, inciting incidents, and dramatic turning points, can be operationalised through collaboration with generative AI [17]. Importantly, the activity was conceived as a critical and iterative process in which students can evaluate, refine, and sometimes reject GenAI suggestions to align them with both narrative goals and ethical considerations.

Copilot produced a structured three-act outline that integrates the controlling idea, historical subject, and character arcs. Act I (*"The Vault of Memory"*) established the Olympic setting and introduced the scar as the catalyst for Maria's suppressed trauma. Act II (*"The Scar Between Us"*) developed the central conflict through flashbacks to the Holocaust and interactions in the Olympic Village, where supporting characters such as Lev and Irina acted as enablers or challengers of Maria's confrontation with her past. Act III (*"The Quiet Reunion"*) resolved the narrative through reconciliation between the sisters, achieved through recognition and shared memory. The scar thus became both a literal and a metaphorical motif of survival and healing.

To encourage students to engage more actively, Copilot was asked to refine the plot by adding an inciting incident, three major plot points, pinch points (that is, a demonstration of the nature, power, and essence of the antagonist force), and a MacGuffin (i.e., an object or device that serves as a trigger for the plot) [17]. Copilot proposed the Olympic gold medal as a symbolic external objective, embodying national pride, personal ambition, and Cold War rivalry. The refined narrative included increasing political pressure, resurfacing trauma, and personal choice between ideology and truth. Significantly, the medal ultimately lost relevance, as reconciliation and remembrance prevailed over external achievement.

This exercise demonstrates how GenAI can be used to rehearse storytelling techniques while also exposing students to the limits of generative systems. Students can then be encouraged to discuss questions such as: *Does the AI-proposed MacGuffin add narrative depth or distract from the central theme? How should politically and historically sensitive contexts be represented? When should symbolic resolution replace literal outcomes?*. In this way, the plot-design phase functioned both as a creative activity and as a training ground for *AI literacy*, teaching to balance algorithmic suggestions with human judgment, ethical awareness, and narrative intentionality.

4.4 Screenplay

The final step of the workflow consists of translating the narrative outline into a full screenplay. This stage exemplifies how GenAI can be integrated into the creative writing process as a drafting partner that requires critical engagement and continuous refinement. A dedicated workflow is then implemented on three sequential prompts, each corresponding to a different act of the short film. To reinforce principles of *AI literacy*, the screenplay is generated in a new conversation with Copilot, which required reframing the instructions and reflecting on how prompt design shapes the quality and style of the output. The first prompt instructs the system to draft the opening act of a 10 to 15 min short film, embedding key narrative elements (historical context, Cold War rivalry, Holocaust memory, inciting incident, MacGuffin, and plot points) together with technical requirements of professional screenwriting (uppercase scene headings, concise visual descriptions, centred dialogue, and minimal acting directions). Copilot was explicitly asked to adopt a cinematic rhythm, favoured by image-driven sentences typical of dramatic storytelling.

Two further prompts extend the script to Acts II and III. This stepwise process helps to provide students with a model of how complex creative tasks can be decomposed into manageable phases when collaborating with GenAI. At the same time, it emphasises the need for participatory, human-centred design. GenAI provides raw narrative material, while students retain the ability to evaluate coherence, correct inconsistencies, and adapt tone and style.

Beyond the production of a draft screenplay (approximately 8âĂŞ12 pages), the educational value of this stage lies in teaching students how to balance the benefits and limitations of GenAI systems. Students are exposed to both the creative potential of generative models and the ethical challenges of representing historically sensitive contexts. This dual perspective fosters technical competence in screenwriting and critical reflection and responsible authorship in working with generative technologies.

4.5   Evaluation

The evaluation phase is conceived as a way to test the quality of the screenplay and as an educational exercise in critical reflection. We compare human judgment with GenAI-based feedback, thus learning how generative systems can act as evaluators as well as creators. This dual role of GenAI supports the development of *AI literacy*, as students are trained to interpret automated assessments critically rather than accept them as authoritative.

Two distinct GenAI systems were used: Perplexity PRO and ChatGPT 5. Both were provided with the complete script and asked to evaluate it in terms of narrative quality, originality, character development, and feasibility within the short film format.

Perplexity Evaluation. Perplexity highlighted the general strength of the narrative structure and praised the originality of combining Olympic competition with Holocaust memory and Cold War rivalry. The evaluation commended the symbolic use of recurring motifs, such as the scar and the train whistle, and noted the emotional intensity of the reunion scene. At the same time, it identified areas for improvement: the need to strengthen external conflict (e.g., through political or media pressure), to differentiate secondary roles (Irina versus Soviet officials), to condense certain dialogue sequences, and to enhance the symbolic dimension of the title by reinforcing the motif of "dust." Interestingly, the system suggested a revised ending based on visual imagery rather than dialogue, opening a discussion on multimodal forms of storytelling.

This evaluation provides students with concrete, actionable feedback that they could debate and selectively adopt. It also exposes them to the limitations of automated critique, such as the risk of privileging stylistic suggestions over deeper ethical or cultural concerns.

ChatGPT Evaluation. ChatGPT offered a complementary perspective, focussing on narrative quality, originality, and feasibility. The system confirmed the coherence and emotional impact of the story, praising the credible transformation of the protagonist from repression to reconciliation. At the same time, it recommended balancing psychological depth with external action to maintain dramatic rhythm. In terms of feasibility, ChatGPT positively assessed the limited cast and locations but highlighted the cost and complexity of flashbacks, suggesting symbolic rather than literal staging.

The educational value lies in prompting students to weigh different forms of automated critique and to reflect on how these align with human judgment. Rather than providing definitive answers, GenAI evaluations can serve as a prompt for classroom discussion on narrative design, production constraints, and the ethics of representation.

5   Results and Discussion

The experiment presented so far led to the development of a complete draft screenplay for a short film, produced through a structured workflow that combined GenAI outputs, curated historical and psychological/behavioural knowledge bases, and continuous human-in-the-loop revisions. The resulting script demonstrated narrative coherence, originality, and feasibility, as confirmed by GenAI-based evaluations and human feedback.

Beyond the creative artefact, the study achieved several educational outcomes. First, the staged co-design workflow (controlling idea, subject, characters, plot, screenplay, and evaluation) showed that AI systems can be positioned as dialogic partners rather than as replacements for human creativity. Second, the integration of historical and psychological sources enriched the GenAI-generated material, mitigating inaccuracies and fostering deeper contextual learning. Third, the process encouraged students to critically evaluate the reliability, coherence, and ethical implications of AI outputs, thus contributing to the development of AI literacy. Finally, by employing GenAI both as a generator and as an evaluator, the experiment highlighted the potential of automated feedback to stimulate reflection if combined with human judgment.

The results suggest that generative systems can be used as a creative catalyst, a reflective partner, and a vehicle for teaching responsible authorship. The screenplay itself represents a tangible output, but the most significant contribution lies in defining a replicable, pedagogically grounded methodology for engaging with GenAI in creative learning contexts.

Table 1 aligns the intended educational goals with the achieved outcomes. By achieving each objective, we showed that the answer to our research question is positive and that the path we followed is promising.

Table 1. "Summary of main results

Educational Objective	Outcome Achieved
Design of educational GenAI workflows	Structured co-design process used across all phases (idea, subject, characters, plot, script, evaluation).
Integration of disciplinary knowledge	Historical and psychological KB enriched GenAI outputs, improving accuracy and contextual depth.
Promotion of AI literacy	Critical engagement with GenAI suggestions, fostering awareness of affordances, limitations, and ethical concerns.
Evaluation practices	Dual use of GenAI as generator and evaluator stimulated reflection through comparison of automated and human feedback.

5.1 Limitations

Although this study offers promising insights on the integration of AI tools in film education, several aspects call for further investigation. First, the experiment was conceived as a proof of concept, with the authors simulating the role of students. This approach allowed us to gain a close, reflective perspective on the design of the workflow, but it also means that the results should be interpreted as exploratory rather than conclusive. A natural next step will be to extend the study to real classroom settings, where diverse learners and educators can provide richer evidence of effectiveness and impact. Second, the evaluation of our methodology was primarily qualitative and focused on narrative coherence, originality, and feasibility. While this lens highlighted the creative affordances of GenAI, it leaves open questions about broader educational outcomes, such as enhancing creativity, critical thinking, or the development of AI literacy. Future work could incorporate longitudinal studies and mixed-method approaches to capture these dimensions more comprehensively. Third, the workflow relied on specific GenAI tools. This dependency provided a concrete testbed, but also suggests that the findings may evolve with new models and platforms. Comparative studies across tools and versions would further clarify the robustness and adaptability of the approach. Additionally, using AI systems not only as generators but also as evaluators of creative work introduces the danger of over-reliance on automated judgments. Although such tools can provide valuable feedback, their limitations, particularly in recognising cultural nuance or ethical sensitivity, must be explicitly acknowledged. For this reason, our study frames AI evaluation as a stimulus for human reflection rather than as a final arbiter. This caution is particularly relevant in creative domains such as cinema, where authenticity and expressive intention remain central [18].

5.2 Ethical Consideration

The integration of GenAI into film education raises several ethical considerations that go beyond the technical design of workflows or the creative quality of the outputs. A central issue concerns authorship and agency. Although GenAI systems can generate substantial narrative content, our study emphasises that students must remain the primary agents of creative and intellectual decisions. Considering AI as a co-designer rather than an autonomous author helps protect human creativity and ensures that learners develop the capacity to critically evaluate, adapt, and sometimes reject machine suggestions [15]. Another key dimension involves historical responsibility and representation. In our experiment, the screenplay engaged with contexts marked by trauma, such as the Holocaust and the Cold War. However, GenAI systems are prone to inaccuracies, simplifications, or even insensitive portrayals of such events. This raises the ethical imperative of embedding critical human oversight and curated KB into educational workflows so that learners can confront and correct these shortcomings [1]. Far from being a mere technical issue, this process offers an educational opportunity: students are trained to recognise the ethical weight of storytelling and to approach sensitive content with responsibility and respect. A further consideration relates to equity and access. Not all students or institutions may have the same opportunities to use advanced GenAI tools. This raises the risk of reinforcing a digital divide within creative education. Therefore, designing methodologies that remain adaptable across different resources and contexts is an important ethical goal for future research [11].

6   Conclusion and Future Work

This paper presented an exploratory study on integrating GenAI into film education through a structured co-design workflow for screenwriting. Our preliminary findings indicate that generative systems can serve as both creative partners and educational tools, supporting critical engagement, disciplinary integration, and the development of AI literacy. Although the study remains a proof-of-concept, its methodological contributions provide a replicable framework for embedding GenAI into creative learning contexts. Future work will extend this approach to classroom settings, allowing for more robust evidence of its educational impact and informing the responsible design of AI-supported curricula in the arts. Since the use of generative tools could imply biases in the data, inherited from the tools used and from the specific versions of the tools, future implementations will include the creation of a comparative benchmark between models, with common evaluation criteria and an analysis of the model's narrative biases (such as gender roles, cultural clichés, and emotional tones). Furthermore, to evaluate the impact of the framework used, we plan to add a triangulated evaluation with questionnaires, quality ratings by external experts, as well as coherence and originality analysis using NLP models.

References

1. Al-kfairy, M., Mustafa, D., Kshetri, N., Insiew, M., Alfandi, O.: Ethical challenges and solutions of generative ai: an interdisciplinary perspective. Informatics (2024)
2. Bach, B., et al.: Narrative design patterns for data-driven storytelling. In: Data-driven storytelling. AK Peters/CRC Press (2018)
3. Belkina, M., et al.: Implementing generative ai (genai) in higher education: a systematic review of case studies. Comput. Educ.: Artif. Intell. (2025)
4. Bensimon, A.: Belgium, 19 april 1943: the attack on the 20th convoy. https://k-larevue.com/en/belgium-19-april-1943-the-attack-on-the-20th-convoy/ (Jan 2024), k-LaRevue
5. Cake, S.: Artificial intelligence as a collaborative tool for script development. Media Practice and Education (2025)
6. Campbell, J.: The hero with a thousand faces, vol. 17. New World Library (2008)
7. Chen, Y., et al.: Effects of generative artificial intelligence on cognitive effort and task performance: study protocol for a randomized controlled experiment among college students. Trials **26**(1), 244 (2025)
8. Daria Gridiaeva: Youra livchitz. https://www.gw2ru.com/history/236952-20th-convoy-attack-save-jews-auschwitz-youra-livchitz (2025)

9. Doshi, A., Hauser, O.: Generative ai enhances individual creativity but reduces the collective diversity of novel content. Science Advances (2024)
10. Field, S.: Screenplay: The foundations of screenwriting. Delta (2005)
11. Fu, Y., Weng, Z.: Navigating the ethical terrain of ai in education: A systematic review on framing responsible human-centered ai practices. Computers and Education: Artificial Intelligence (2024)
12. Giannakos, M., et al.: The promise and challenges of generative ai in education. Behaviour & Information Technology
13. Grime, J.J.: The educational effect of forced separation on twins. Ph.D. thesis, University of Toledo (2008)
14. Harrell, D.F., Zhu, J.: Agency play: Dimensions of agency for interactive narrative design. In: AAAI spring symposium: Intelligent narrative technologies II (2009)
15. Islam, G., Greenwood, M.: Generative artificial intelligence as hypercommons: Ethics of authorship and ownership. J. Business Ethics (2024)
16. Ivančo, J.: Evaluation of modern tools for data scientists (2025)
17. Lo Duca, A.: Become a Great Data Storyteller: Learn how you can drive change with data. John Wiley & Sons (2025)
18. Monserrat, A.L., Srnec, N.M.: Reflection-ai: artificial intelligence as a redefining force for expressive filmmaking in film schools. Front. Commun. (2025)
19. Ni, M.: Study on large language models in story generation: Unveil the narrative potential of large language models (2024)
20. Porteous, J., Lindsay, A.: Protagonist vs antagonist provant: narrative generation as counter planning. In: Proceedings of the 18th International Conference on Autonomous Agents and MultiAgent Systems, pp. 1069–1077 (2019)
21. Rahman, A., et al.: Comparative analysis based on deepseek, chatgpt, and google gemini: Features, techniques, performance, future prospects. arXiv preprint arXiv:2503.04783 (2025)
22. Ryan, M.L.: Cheap plot tricks, plot holes, and narrative design. Narrative **17**(1), 56–75 (2009)
23. Shields, J.: Twins brought up apart. Eugenics Review **50**(2), 115–123 (1958)
24. Thomas, R.: Convoy 20 — escaping auschwitz. https://www.ronthomasauthor.com/snippets-of-history/convoy-20-escaping-auschwitz (2025). Accessed 01 Oct 25
25. Wang, S., Wang, F., Zhu, Z., Wang, J., Tran, T., Du, Z.: Artificial intelligence in education: a systematic literature review. Expert Syst. Appl. (2024)
26. Wang, Y., Kreminski, M.: Can LLMs generate good stories? insights and challenges from a narrative planning perspective. arXiv preprint arXiv:2506.10161 (2025)
27. Wang, Y.: Becoming a co-designer: the change in participants' perceived self-efficacy during a co-design process. CoDesign **21**(1), 52–73 (2025)
28. Wikipedia contributors: Attack on the twentieth convoy. https://en.wikipedia.org/wiki/Attack_on_the_twentieth_convoy (nd). Accessed 01 Oct 25
29. Wikipedia contributors: Youra livchitz. https://en.wikipedia.org/wiki/Youra_Livchitz (nd). Accessed 01 Oct 25
30. Williams, A., Ehrlich, S.: Escaping the train to auschwitz. https://www.bbc.com/news/magazine-22188075 (Apr 2013), bBC News
31. Wood, D., Moss, S.H.: Evaluating the impact of students' generative ai use in educational contexts. J. Res. Innov. Teach. Learn. (2024)

32. Xia, Q., Weng, X., Ouyang, F., et al.: A scoping review on how generative artificial intelligence transforms assessment in higher education. Int. J. Educ. Technol. High. Educ. (2024)
33. Zhai, C., Wibowo, S., Li, L.D.: The effects of over-reliance on ai dialogue systems on students' cognitive abilities: a systematic review. Smart Learning Environments (2024)

Exploring the Role of Professional Development in Fostering AI Competence Among Teachers in Southern Switzerland

Lucio Negrini[1]([⊠]) [iD], Marika Lamacchia[2] [iD], Maria Concetta Carruba[3] [iD], Emanuele Delucchi[1] [iD], Masiar Babazadeh[1] [iD], Francesca Mangili[1] [iD], and Alberto Termine[1] [iD]

[1] University of Applied Sciences and Arts of Southern Switzerland, Manno, Switzerland
lucio.negrini@supsi.ch
[2] University of Macerata, Macerata, Italy
[3] Università Telematica Pegaso, Naples, Italy

Abstract. Artificial Intelligence (AI) has the potential to reshape educational practices through, for example adaptive platforms, generative models, or predictive systems, offering opportunities for personalization, inclusivity, and efficiency. However, the mere exposure of teachers to such tools does not ensure the development of critical competences, highlighting the importance of AI Literacy defined as the set of knowledge, skills, and attitudes required to critically understand, evaluate, and use AI responsibly. Little empirical evidence exists on how professional training shapes its development. This study addresses this gap by investigating the relationship between teachers' participation in AI-related training and their perceived levels of AI Literacy. Data were collected using a descriptive-correlational survey design ($N \approx 701$). The analysis plan includes descriptive statistics, Welch's t-tests, linear regression, and cluster analysis. The analyses identified three different teacher profiles suggesting the need for differentiated training for fostering operational and ethical AI competences. The findings aim to inform both teachers' professional development and policy frameworks, bridging the gap between technological innovation and educational practice.

Keywords: AI Literacy · Teacher Professional Development · Ethical and Pedagogical AI Competences

1 Introduction

1.1 Context and Significance

Artificial Intelligence (AI) is increasingly regarded by some researchers as one of the most disruptive innovations in contemporary education systems and could have the potential to reshape teaching, assessment, and organizational practices [1, 2]. Educational applications include for example adaptive platforms, conversational chatbots, predictive systems, and generative models for automated content production [2–4]. In schools, such technologies enable for example personalized learning or real-time feedback, offering also inclusive and transformative benefits [5, 6].

© The Author(s), under exclusive license to Springer Nature Switzerland AG 2026
A. Dipace et al. (Eds.): WAILS 2025, LNCS 16438, pp. 110–120, 2026.
https://doi.org/10.1007/978-3-032-17604-2_11

At the same time, pedagogical and ethical concerns arise regarding privacy, algorithmic bias, decision-making transparency, and the redefinition of teachers' roles [7, 8]. To address these challenges, the concept of AI Literacy has emerged, defined as the set of knowledge, skills, and attitudes required to critically understand, evaluate, and responsibly use AI [10, 11]. According to Southworth and Migliaccio [12], AI Literacy can be therefore divided into four components: understand, use, evaluate, and ethically navigate AI. To be AI literate, each citizen needs both operational knowledge, understanding what AI is and how to use it, and ethical knowledge, enabling them to reflect on the limitations, biases, and broader ethical implications of AI systems.

The development of AI Literacy among teachers is a strategic priority, as it enables the effective integration of AI in the classroom and prepares students for future challenges. Research shows that mere exposure to technological tools does not guarantee the acquisition of critical competences: intentional, reflective learning mediated by structured training pathways is necessary [13]. In Switzerland, the Swiss Federal Council [14] highlights the need to strengthen AI competences in all educational levels, therefore also teachers need specific training.

1.2 Research Gap and Objectives

Despite the growing interest in AI Literacy, the role of teacher professional development in fostering it has only recently begun to receive systematic attention. Emerging evidence suggests that participation in structured training can positively influence teachers' knowledge, attitudes, and self-efficacy regarding AI. For instance, Ding et al. [16] showed that professional development programs combining direct instruction with case-based discussions, improved AI Literacy levels among middle school teachers. Similarly, Riggs [17] reported that a professional development (PD) initiative enhanced teachers' confidence in using AI tools and their intention to adopt them in the classroom, particularly among participants with initially limited expertise. In the German context, an online training course for in-service teachers also demonstrated significant gains in literacy, attitudes, and perceived self-efficacy. In that case the integration of knowledge transfer, practical application, and critical reflection was particularly effective in developing AI literacy, confirming the importance of targeted professional development for successful AI integration [18]. Nevertheless, these findings remain limited to small-scale interventions, often relying on heterogeneous measures, which constrain the generalizability of results and highlights the need for further investigation into the sustained impact of formal training on educators' AI Literacy.

This study seeks to contribute by examining the relationship between prior training experiences and teachers' perceived AI Literacy levels in Southern Switzerland.

1.3 Research Questions

RQ1: To what extent are teachers' perceived AI Literacy levels associated with their prior training experiences?

RQ2: Which AI Literacy profiles emerge among teachers?

RQ3: How are these profiles related to their training experiences?

2 Methods and Materials

2.1 Research Design

The study is part of the national project Bridging the Gap: Empowering Teachers about AI Education, funded by the Swiss National Science Foundation (SNSF) and promoted by IDSIA (USI-SUPSI) and the Department of Education and Learning (DFA/ASP SUPSI).

A descriptive-correlational quantitative design was adopted to explore the relationship between professional development and teachers' perceptions of their AI literacy. Data were collected via an online questionnaire administered through the Qualtrics platform.

The research design comprised four analytical phases: sample description, group comparison, predictive modelling, and profile identification.

Given the heterogeneity of previous training experiences, the "training" variable was operationalized as self-reported participation in one or more AI-related initiatives, regardless of format, duration, or content. This approach allowed for a broad initial investigation of the phenomenon, while recognizing the need for more detailed measures in future studies.

2.2 Participants

A convenience sample of lower-secondary (approx. ages 11–14) and upper-secondary (approx. ages 15–18) school teachers in Southern Switzerland was recruited through institutional mailing lists, professional networks, and school channels. The sample consists of 701 teachers and is heterogeneous in terms of gender, age, experience, and school level (see Table 1). Women were the majority (59.6%), with a balanced distribution of age groups. Most teachers are from lower secondary schools (67.6%) and have more than 10 years of experience (66.3%).

Table 1. Demographic and professional characteristics of the sample.

Category	Group	Count	Percentage
Gender	Female	418	59.6%
	Male	274	39.1%
	Not reported	9	1.3%
School level	Lower secondary	474	67.6%
	Upper secondary	199	28.4%
	Not reported	28	4.0%
Teaching experience	Less than 5 years	100	14.3%
	5–10 years	136	19.4%
	More than 10 years	465	66.3%
Age group	Under 30	63	9.0%

(continued)

Table 1. (*continued*)

Category	Group	Count	Percentage
	30–40	162	23.2%
	40–50	249	35.5%
	50–60	195	27.8%
	Over 60	32	4.6%

2.3 Instruments

The questionnaire was adapted for the SNSF project from an instrument developed by the SUPSI research group involved in the BEST4Ethical AI initiative, it required about 10 min to complete. Participation was voluntary and anonymous.

It included different sections on topics such as the experience with AI and trust in it, attitudes towards the use of AI in education, the criteria in the choice of AI tools for the classroom that they apply and open ended questions. In this paper we focus on the following sections:

1. Socio-demographic and professional background: gender, age, and seniority of the teachers
2. AI-related training: assessed with a multiple-choice item (training during university studies vs. continuing education), recoded as a binary variable ($0 =$ no prior AI training; $1 =$ at least one prior training).
3. AI Literacy scale (Wang, Rau, & Yuan [9]): 12 Likert items (1–7) translated into Italian and reorganized into the two dimensions investigated in this study: operational AI Literacy and ethical AI Literacy:
   - Operational AI Literacy (9 items: awareness, usage, evaluation of AI tools)
   - Ethical AI Literacy (3 items: privacy, bias, responsible use) (Table 2)

Table 2. AI Literacy scale by Wang, Rau & Yuan [9]

Item	Description	Construct	Loading
AW_1	I can distinguish between smart devices and non-smart devices.	Awareness	.72
AW_8	I do not know how AI technology can help me. [R]	Awareness	.64
AW_9	I can identify the AI technology employed in the applications and products I use.	Awareness	.70
US_1	I can skilfully use AI applications or products to help me with my daily work.	Usage	.72
US_3	It is usually hard for me to learn to use a new AI application or product. [R]	Usage	.66
US_5	I can use AI applications or products to improve my work efficiency.	Usage	.72
EV_2	I can evaluate the capabilities and limitations of an AI application or product after using it for a while.	Evaluation	.71
EV_3	I can choose a proper solution from various solutions provided by a smart agent.	Evaluation	.72
EV_6	I can choose the most appropriate AI application or product from a variety for a particular task.	Evaluation	.78
ET_1	I always comply with ethical principles when using AI applications or products.	Ethics	.76
ET_2	I am never alert to privacy and information security issues when using AI applications or products. [R]	Ethics	.60
ET_5	I am always alert to the abuse of AI technology.	Ethics	.73

[R]indicates that item is in reverse form.

Internal consistency was high for operational literacy (Cronbach's $\alpha = .89$), whereas the ethical literacy subscale showed lower reliability (Cronbach's $\alpha = .57$), which is expected for shorter scales assessing conceptually broad constructs. The ethical dimension was nevertheless retained given its theoretical relevance for characterizing teachers' ability to critically navigate AI systems, and future studies will consider scale refinement and expansion. The other three dimensions were united since they all analyze some aspects of operational competencies. For the purpose of this study, it was not necessary to analyze them separately.

2.4 Procedure and Ethics

The survey was administered online via the Qualtrics platform. Data was collected and processed in compliance with the new Swiss Federal Data Protection Act (nLPD). Participation was anonymous, and responses were not linked to any personal identifiers.

2.5 Data Analysis

Data analysis was performed using Jamovi[1], with the following steps:

- Descriptive statistics were used to characterize the sample and the two AI Literacy dimensions.

---

[1] Jamovi. Open-source statistical software. Available at: https://www.jamovi.org.

- Independent-samples Welch's t-tests examined group differences based on prior training, and effect sizes (Cohen's d) were reported.
- Linear regression models estimated the predictive contribution of prior training and demographic variables to perceived operational and ethical AI Literacy.
- TwoStep cluster analysis was applied to identify teacher profiles. The method was chosen due to its ability to manage continuous variables and to compute model-fit indicators (e.g., silhouette coefficient) to support solution quality.

Statistical significance was evaluated at conventional thresholds, and assumptions relevant to each procedure were checked where applicable.

3 Results

3.1 Descriptive Statistics

Descriptive analysis showed medium–high levels of perceived AI Literacy among participants, considering both ethical and operational dimensions. Means were around 5.0 (SD $\approx$ 1.2) for ethical literacy and 4.0 (SD $\approx$ 1.2) for operational literacy on a 7-point Likert scale. Distributions were balanced, without particular clustering at the minimum or maximum values. Shapiro–Wilk tests indicated deviations from normality ($p = .007$ and $p < .001$), a common outcome in attitudinal measures based on ordinal items. 54.6% of the participants' teachers claimed to have never had specific training on AI, while the other 45.4% participated in one or more training in the past, most of them during continuing education.

3.2 Group Comparisons

Independent-samples Welch's t-tests were conducted to examine differences in ethical and operational AI Literacy between teachers who had received prior training and those who had not. In addition to statistical significance, effect sizes were reported using Cohen's d, in order to assess the magnitude of the observed differences.

Trained teachers obtained a mean score of 4.95 (SD = 1.24) in the ethical literacy construct, while untrained teachers scored a mean of 4.99 (SD = 1.13). According to Welch's t-test the difference was not statistically significant ($t\_484 = .386$, $p = .700$, Cohen's d = .035).

For operational literacy, the effect was stronger: trained teachers reported significantly higher scores (M = 4.26, SD = 1.13) compared to their untrained colleagues (M = 3.68, SD = 1.18), Welch's t-test indicated a statistically significant difference ($t\_493 = -5.66$, $p < .001$), with a moderate effect size (Cohen's d = -0.519).

3.3 Regression Model

Despite deviations from normality indicated by the Shapiro–Wilk test, the linear regression remains appropriate, as OLS estimation is generally robust in large samples [15]. The linear regression model including "Prior Training", "Gender", "Experience", and "Age" explained about 8% of the variance in perceived operational AI Literacy ($R2 =$

0.085). Training emerged as a significant predictor ($\beta = 0.54$, $p < .001$), as well as gender ($\beta = 0.21$, $p < .001$), while experience, and age had no significant effects. The regression model for the perceived ethical literacy explained only 3% of the variance ($R2 = 0.035$). In this case only gender emerged as a significant predictor ($\beta = -0.28$, $p = .007$).

3.4 Cluster Analysis

A TwoStep cluster analysis was conducted on perceived ethical and operational AI Literacy composite scores. The solution yielded a satisfactory silhouette index (0.5) and automatically identified three distinct teacher profiles:

- High AI Literacy profile ($N = 170$): high scores in both dimensions (Operational M = 5.17; Ethical M = 5.37).
- Reflective profile ($N = 105$): moderate perceived operational competences (M = 3.40) and high perceived ethical awareness (M = 6.19).
- Low-confidence profile ($N = 215$): medium perceived operational (M = 3.30) and ethical literacy (M = 4.06).

The profiles highlight heterogeneous patterns of perceived AI competences among teachers. The coexistence of strong ethical awareness with moderated perceived operational skills in the Reflective profile suggests that ethical sensitivity does not necessarily translate into confidence in classroom implementation. Conversely, the Low-confidence profile indicates a need for broader foundational support across both dimensions.

Overall, the identified profiles provide a descriptive overview of different competence configurations, supporting the idea that differentiated approaches may be needed to develop both perceived operational and ethical AI Literacy in the teaching population.

4 Discussion

This exploratory study investigates to what extent prior training experiences correlate with teachers' perceived AI Literacy levels, distinguishing between operational and ethical dimensions, and seeks to identify distinct teacher profiles.

4.1 Group Differences and Regression Model

The comparison between trained and untrained teachers revealed no significant differences in self-assessed perceived ethical literacy, but trained teachers scored significantly higher on operational aspects. This finding suggests that prior training mainly enhanced teachers' perceived operational competences with AI tools, but doesn't appear to be associated with the development of ethical competences. This is also in line with the urgency of delivering training to teachers after the launch of ChatGPT in November 2022. Most of the initial training initiatives focused on how ChatGPT works, paying less attention to its ethical implications.

The results also confirm the centrality of professional development while reducing the role of socio-demographic variables such as age or teaching experience often assumed to predict operational digital competences. Gender appears correlated with perceived operational and ethical AI competences, albeit in opposite directions. Male teachers tend to report higher perceived operational competences, whereas female teachers show stronger perceived ethical competences. This last assumption will be further analyzed in future studies.

4.2   AI Literacy Profiles (Cluster Analysis)

The TwoStep cluster analysis, based on perceived ethical and operational AI Literacy, identified three distinct teacher profiles:

- High AI Literacy profile: teachers with consistently high scores in both dimensions. These teachers show advanced knowledge and confident use of AI systems, combined with strong awareness of ethical implications. They may act as early adopters or peer mentors in capacity-building initiatives.
- Reflective profile: teachers with high ethical awareness but moderate operational competences. This profile suggests a high sensitivity to responsible and critical AI use, yet limited familiarity with hands-on integration in practice. Targeted professional development focusing on concrete use cases and classroom applications may particularly benefit these teachers.
- Low-confidence profile: teachers with medium scores in both dimensions and lower perceived mastery. This may reflect uncertainty around both technical and ethical aspects of AI. For this group, scaffolded, introductory training combining basic knowledge, guided exploration, and practical examples could be a key first step.

This three-profile structure confirms the heterogeneity of teachers' perceived AI competences and suggests that a one-size-fits-all approach to professional development would likely be ineffective. Training initiatives may be more impactful if differentiated according to profile-specific characteristics, e.g., targeted workshops for reflective teachers, foundational pathways for low-confidence teachers, and advanced roles or learning communities for highly competent teachers.

These results can therefore inform the design of adaptive professional development programs, where teachers' initial perceived literacy serves as a starting point to customize learning trajectories and foster both operational and ethical AI competences in schools.

4.3   Methodological Reflections and Limitations

Three main limitations must be acknowledged:

- First, the cross-sectional design does not allow us to infer causal relationships between training and teachers' perceived AI competences.
- Second, the study relies exclusively on self-reported perceptions of competences. Such measures may not fully mirror actual performance and are susceptible to social-desirability and over-/underestimation biases. Therefore, results should be interpreted in terms of perceived AI Literacy, rather than objective mastery.

- Third, prior AI-related training was operationalized as a binary variable, without accounting for differences in duration, delivery mode, or content focus. This simplification may lead to an underestimation of the contribution of targeted or high-quality professional development initiatives.

In addition, although the sample size strengthens statistical robustness, the use of convenience sampling may limit generalizability to other educational contexts.

Future studies should integrate performance-based measures (e.g., authentic tasks or observational rubrics) to triangulate self-reports, and adopt a more fine-grained characterization of professional development experiences. Despite these limitations, the combination of descriptive statistics, group comparisons, regression models, and cluster analysis supports the robustness of the findings and provides a replicable analytical framework for further investigations.

5 Conclusions and Future Directions

5.1 Summary of Results

This study examined teachers' perceived AI Literacy in Southern Switzerland, focusing on the role of prior professional development. The findings indicate that participation in AI-related training is the strongest predictor of perceived operational AI Literacy among the analyzed variables, while perceived ethical AI Literacy appears more widespread and less sensitive to training exposure. Gender also emerged as a significant predictor in opposite directions for the two dimensions, suggesting that perceptions of AI competences may be influenced by different professional or personal experiences.

The identification of three distinct profiles, High AI Literacy, Reflective, and Low-confidence, confirms the heterogeneity of teachers' perceived competences. This diversity suggests that differentiated professional development pathways may better support teachers' readiness to critically adopt AI in educational settings, integrating both operational and ethical aspects.

5.2 Implications for Practice and Policy

The results point to the need for scalable and customizable training strategies, aligned with teachers' starting profiles. Initiatives may include:

- Introductory and scaffolded approaches for Low-confidence teachers;
- Hands-on workshops to support Reflective teachers in translating ethical awareness into confident use;
- Advanced and leadership-oriented learning opportunities for High AI Literacy teachers, including mentoring or learning-community roles.

Education authorities and decision-makers could leverage these profiles to design targeted teacher development policies, optimizing resources and fostering a more balanced integration of operational and ethical competencies across the teaching population.

5.3 Future Research Directions

Future studies should:

- Adopt longitudinal or quasi-experimental designs to assess changes after training;
- Include performance-based measures to complement self-reports;
- Refine the categorization of professional development experiences (e.g., duration, format, content focus);
- Conduct comparative analyses across Swiss cantons and international contexts to assess the transferability of results.

Overall, this exploratory study provides an evidence-based framework to inform the design of adaptive professional development in the field of AI in education, while highlighting the importance of advancing both operational and ethical dimensions of teachers' AI Literacy.

Acknowledgments. This research was funded in whole or in part by the Swiss National Science Foundation (SNSF), grant number LAAGP0_223920. For the purpose of open access, a CC BY public copyright licence is applied to any author accepted manuscript (AAM) version arising from this submission.

Disclosure of Interests. The authors have no competing interests to declare that are relevant to the content of this article.

References

1. Holmes, W., Bialik, M., Fadel, C.: Artificial Intelligence in Education. Center for Curriculum Redesign, Boston (2019). https://doi.org/10.58863/20.500.12424/4276068
2. Zawacki-Richter, O., Marín, V.I., Bond, M., Gouverneur, F.: Systematic review of research on artificial intelligence applications in higher education – where are the educators? Int. J. Educ. Technol. High. Educ. **16**(1), 39 (2019). https://doi.org/10.1186/s41239-019-0171-0
3. Ait Baha, T., El Hajji, M., Es-Saady, Y., Fadili, H.: The impact of educational chatbot on student learning experience. Educ. Inf. Technol. **29**, 10153–10176 (2024). https://doi.org/10.1007/s10639-023-12166-w
4. Göksel, N., Bozkurt, A.: Artificial intelligence in education: current insights and future perspectives. In: Sisman-Ugur, S., Kurubacak, G. (eds.) Handbook of Research on Learning in the Age of Transhumanism, pp. 224–236. IGI Global, Hershey (2019). https://doi.org/10.4018/978-1-5225-8431-5.ch014
5. Pellegrini, S., Sebastiani, R.: L'integrazione di IA e tecnologia assistiva nella didattica speciale: un cambio di paradigma nella formazione degli insegnanti e nel supporto agli studenti. Ital. J. Spec. Educ. Inclusion **12**(2), 1–17 (2024). https://doi.org/10.7346/sipes-02-2024-13
6. Pagliara, S.M., et al.: The integration of artificial intelligence in inclusive education: a scoping review. Information **15**, 774 (2024). https://doi.org/10.3390/info15120774
7. Mittelstadt, B.D., Allo, P., Taddeo, M., Wachter, S., Floridi, L.: The ethics of algorithms: mapping the debate. Big Data Soc. **3**(2), 1–21 (2016). https://doi.org/10.1177/2053951716679679
8. Gouseti, A., James, F., Fallin, L., Burden, K.: The ethics of using AI in K-12 education: a systematic literature review. Technol. Pedagog. Educ. (2025). https://doi.org/10.1080/1475939X.2024.2428601

9. Wang, B., Rau, P.L.P., Yuan, T.: Measuring user competence in using artificial intelligence: validity and reliability of artificial intelligence literacy scale. Behav. Inf. Technol. **42**(9), 1324–1337 (2022). https://doi.org/10.1080/0144929X.2022.2072768

10. Ng, D.T.K., Leung, J.K.L., Chu, S.K.W., Qiao, M.S.: Conceptualizing Ai literacy: an exploratory review. Comput. Educ. Artif. Intell. **2**, 100041 (2021). https://doi.org/10.1016/j.caeai.2021.100041

11. Long, D. Magerko, B.: What is AI literacy? Competencies and design considerations. In: Proceedings of the 2020 CHI Conference on Human Factors in Computing Systems (CHI 2020), pp. 1–16. Association for Computing Machinery, New York, NY, USA (2020). https://doi.org/10.1145/3313831.3376727

12. Southworth, J., et al.: Developing a model for AI across the curriculum: transforming the higher education landscape via innovation in AI literacy. Comput. Educ. Artif. Intell. **4**, 100127 (2023). https://doi.org/10.1016/j.caeai.2023.100127

13. Brandão, L., Pedro, L., Zagalo, N.: Teachers' professional development for AI in education: challenges and opportunities. Dig. Educ. Rev. **45**, 151–157 (2024). https://doi.org/10.1344/der.2024.45.151-157

14. Swiss Confederation, Interdepartmental Working Group on Artificial Intelligence (IDAG AI): Challenges of Artificial Intelligence. Report to the Federal Council. Federal Department of Economic Affairs, Education and Research (EAER), State Secretariat for Education, Research and Innovation (SERI), Bern (2019)

15. Lumley, T., Diehr, P., Emerson, S., Chen, L.: The importance of the normality assumption in large public health data sets. Annu. Rev. Public Health **23**, 151–169 (2002). https://doi.org/10.1146/annurev.publhealth.23.100901.140546

16. Ding, A.C.E., Shi, L., Yang, H., Choi, I.: Enhancing teacher AI Literacy and integration through different types of cases in teacher professional development. Comput. Educ. Open **5**, 100178 (2024). https://doi.org/10.1016/j.caeo.2024.100178

17. Riggs, V.: Impact of AI literacy professional development on teaching: evaluating changes in perceptions and classroom practices. Am. J. STEM Educ. **7**, 37–50 (2025). https://doi.org/10.32674/rbajg012

18. Lademann, J., Henze, J., Honke, N., Wollny, C., Becker-Genschow, S.: Teacher training in the age of AI: impact on AI Literacy and teachers' attitudes. Preprint, ResearchGate (2024). https://www.researchgate.net/publication/393476812

Facilitating Information Extraction in Education by Translating Questions from Students, Instructors, and Managers Into Knowledge Graph Queries Through Large Language Models

Ludovico Boratto[ID], Gianni Fenu[ID], Theo Floris[ID],
Francesca Maridina Malloci[ID], Andrea Giovanni Martis[✉][ID], Marco Sau[ID],
and Marco Tocco[ID]

University of Cagliari, Cagliari, Italy
ludovico.boratto@acm.org, {fenu,francescam.malloci,marco.tocco}@unica.it,
{t.floris16,a.martis12,m.sau11}@studenti.unica.it

Abstract. Educational organizations increasingly rely on digital technologies, which produce large amounts of data about learners, courses, and learning activities. Despite having the potential to support several educational downstream tasks, this wealth of information often remains inaccessible to non-technical stakeholders due to its complexity and fragmentation. Recent advances in large language models (LLMs) provide a solution to this limitation by enabling access to complex and heterogeneous data through natural language (NL). In this work, we explore how LLMs can empower information extraction from educational knowledge graphs by translating NL questions into graph database queries. To address the lack of resources in this area, we propose a pipeline for generating synthetic natural language questions grounded in realistic educational scenarios, reflecting the needs of students, instructors, and administrators. We then benchmark several state-of-the-art LLMs on the task of translating natural language questions into graph database queries. The results indicate substantial room for improvement: the best-performing model, Mistral-small, achieved a Return Results score of 62%, followed by a finetuned Llama 3 at just under 54%. These findings highlight the current limitations of LLMs in reliably querying KGs via NL and point to the need for more robust, domain-specific solutions. **Repository**: https://github.com/tail-unica/eduquestions-to-cypher.

Keywords: Educational extraction · Conversational interface · Learning data management

1 Introduction

Modern education strongly relies upon digital technologies. Learning platforms, course repositories, assessment tools, and collaboration environments

A. Dipace et al. (Eds.): WAILS 2025, LNCS 16438, pp. 121–132, 2026.
https://doi.org/10.1007/978-3-032-17604-2_12

continuously record interactions between learners, instructors, and educational resources. These data hold enormous potential for improving teaching and learning, from enabling personalized course recommendations to supporting institutional decision-making. Yet, their volume, diversity, and fragmentation make it difficult for stakeholders, such as students seeking guidance, instructors designing curricula, or administrators evaluating programs, to extract meaningful insights.

To facilitate its fruition, researchers and practitioners are adopting Knowledge Graphs (KGs) to represent educational data as structured and interconnected forms [13]. KGs, semantic data structures that model real-world entities and relationships, can capture not only facts, such as which student is enrolled in which course, but also relationships among concepts, prerequisites, and learning outcomes. In doing so, they offer a foundation for more transparent, explainable, and holistic approaches to educational data analysis [3].

Although KGs open opportunities to enhance adaptive learning, evidence-based pedagogy, and cross-institutional research, interacting with these data models is far from straightforward. Accessing their information typically requires specialized query languages, such as Cypher or SPARQL, which are well beyond the expertise of most educators, learners, or policy actors [18]. This creates a critical accessibility gap, as the ones who could benefit most from educational data often cannot use it directly [15].

Recent advances in Large Language Models (LLMs) offer a promising way to face this limitation. By translating everyday questions posed in natural language into executable queries, LLMs can provide intuitive access to complex data sources [7]. While such techniques have been explored in domains like e-commerce, geography, or entertainment, education has remained largely under-explored, also due to the lack of publicly available datasets and benchmarks tailored to its needs. This leaves open important questions about how well current language models can support information extraction for teaching, learning, and institutional governance purposes.

In this work, we address this problem by developing a pipeline for the automatic generation of natural language question collections, grounded in realistic educational scenarios, reflecting the needs of several educational roles such as students, instructors, and learning platform managers. We then employed multiple LLMs for translating the generated questions into Cypher, a specialized language to query graph databases. Finally, we assess the ability of the selected LLMs in the Text-to-Cypher task along several metrics. The obtained results highlight both the opportunities and limitations of current models, with implications for the design of future systems of this class in education.

2   Related Works

2.1   Natural Language to Query Languages

Research on translating natural language (NL) into structured queries has a long history, spanning relational databases, knowledge bases, and, more recently, property graphs. Early work focused on rule-based or statistical approaches to map NL questions into SQL, supported by datasets such as GeoQuery [21]. With deep learning, larger datasets enabled systems capable of handling compositional queries across different domains [20,22].

Parallel efforts emerged for KGs, with benchmarks for the translation of NL questions into graph queries [5,14,17]. More recently, the growing adoption of property graph databases such as Neo4j[1], coupled with the rise of LLMs, has led to research on NL-to-Cypher translation. However, datasets remain scarce and often specific to a narrow set of fields [16]. This has limited progress in educational applications, despite their need for accessible query interfaces. Recent work has shown that LLMs can generate executable Cypher queries over complex graph structures, highlighting their potential for query translation tasks [11]. Specialised fine-tuning often yields better accuracy, especially for graph-oriented languages such as Cypher [12]. Still, education remains underexplored: to date, there is a lack of resources such as datasets, models, and benchmarks for NL-to-Cypher tailored to educational data.

2.2   Information Management and Extraction in Education

Alongside advances in query translation, the learning sciences have long emphasized the challenge of making educational data accessible to diverse stakeholders. Modern systems, ranging from learning management platforms to MOOCs and online repositories, generate massive amounts of interaction logs, resource metadata, and learner performance records. Turning this wealth of information into meaningful insights is essential for applications such as personalized learning, curriculum analytics, institutional decision-making, and teaching support.

To address the fragmentation of educational datasets, researchers have proposed integrating them into KGs, which offer a unified and semantically rich representation [13]. KGs support advanced applications such as semantic search, prerequisite mapping, and intelligent tutoring. Yet, as highlighted in recent reviews [9], the benefits of KGs remain limited to technically skilled users, since interacting with these complex frameworks still requires specialized knowledge.

Beyond knowledge representation, information extraction methods have also been explored to make educational data more usable. For instance, researchers in [1] introduce a chatbot that leverages KGs and LLMs to provide transparent, mentoring-style recommendations tailored to the needs of learners. Similarly, EDGE [2] demonstrates how natural language interfaces can allow students and instructors to query and navigate complex educational graphs without requiring technical expertise. These studies illustrate the growing role of automated extraction techniques in converting end-user needs into actionable insights.

This line of work highlights a broader issue in the AI and learning sciences community: ensuring that data-driven systems are not only technically powerful but also accessible, transparent, and aligned with pedagogical needs [4]. To this end, our work leverages existing resources, spanning from publicly available educational graphs to general-purpose LLMs, to examine the ability of the latter

---

[1] **Neo4j**: https://neo4j.com/.

in interpreting the needs of the educational actors, and translating them into structured data query commands, hence acting as a bridge between educational stakeholders and the intricate data stores.

3   Methodology

Following the provisioning of the educational KGs, the main workflow is organized in three phases Fig. 1: in the initial phase, we generated four synthetic collections of NL questions grounded to realistic data, one for each of the different educational KGs we employed. The second phase implements the generation of golden test sets of Cypher queries trough the automatic translation of the synthetic question collections. In the final phase, we execute the obtained Cypher queries against the four educational graphs, evaluating the performance of each employed model along several qualitative and quantitative metrics.

3.1   Educational Knowledge Graphs Selection

KGs organise data by highlighting relationships between entities. In education, these entities can be students, instructors, courses, topics, or resources, with edges capturing links such as enrollments or prerequisites. Unlike traditional tables, KGs let users navigate information through connections, similarly to concept maps. In the context of this study, we identified four publicly accessible educational datasets and subsequently organized them into KGs [3]. The selected datasets contain essential information about learners, courses, and other key entities relevant to the educational domain. The inclusion of these entities was driven by their central role in the learning scenarios envisioned in this study.

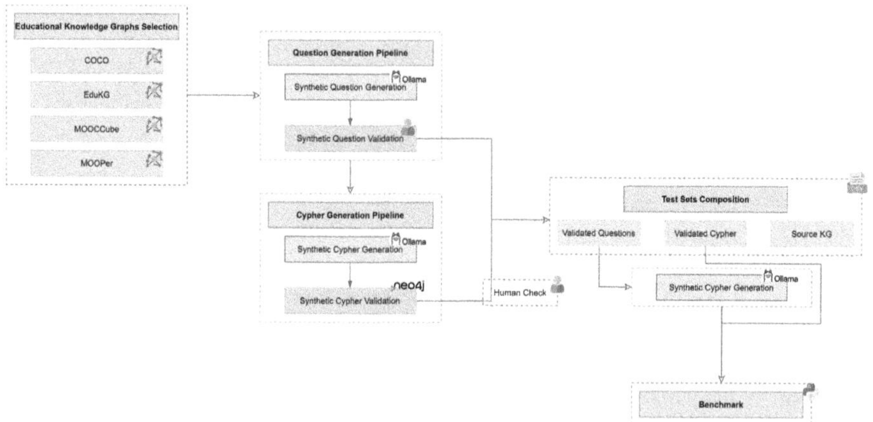

Fig. 1. Our experimental workflow includes the generation and validation of NL questions and the respective Cypher queries, statistical data analysis, and benchmarking of LLMs for text-to-Cypher generation.

Table 1 summarizes the number of nodes, relationships, and unique properties for each KG. This table helps quantify the structural complexity that the models had to deal with when interpreting queries.

3.2   Synthetic Question Generation

For the synthetic generation (1) of the educational questions, through a collective brainstorming, we manually sampled a set of the available LLMs from the public providers Ollama[2] and Hugging Face[3], aiming to encompass models from different organizations and of different sizes (Table 2). Concurrently, we designed a tailored prompt for the generation of realistic educational questions, incorporating information such as the KG schema, user roles (Student, Instructor, Educational Manager), and the number of questions per role to ensure credibility, balance, and diversity. After collectively evaluating the selected models, we opted for Mistral-Small 3.1 (24B) for question generation, as it best captured the KG structure and produced coherent educational queries.

At the end of this process, we obtained a total of 120 questions per dataset, amounting to 480 questions overall. The validation of these questions will be discussed in the next section.

3.3   Synthetic Question Validation

A careful analysis of the various sets of questions led us to uncover multiple repeated or unrealistic questions. Therefore, through a voting approach held within our research group, we deliberately selected the 70 questions with the highest quality in terms of credibility and applicability among the 120, resulting in a total collection of 280 questions. This process allowed us to create four test sets, less affected by bias induced by repetition of equivalent questions or even unreasonable requests, aligned with our objective of studying the applicability of LLMs to extract insights from educational KGs in realistic scenarios.

Table 1. The main statistics of the four knowledge graphs employed in our study.

Dataset	#Nodes	#Relationships	#Properties
COCO [6]	4,356,990	3,333,124	16
EduKG [8]	4,327	29,143	8
MOOCCube [19]	354,605	10,403,863	8
MOOPer [10]	55,990	275,287	15

Table 2. Overview of the open-source LLMs employed for generating synthetic natural language questions, detailing their main attributes such as publisher, parameter count (in billions), and model size.

Model	Publisher	Parameters	Size
Mistral-small	Mistral AI	24B	14 GB
Gemma3	Google DeepMind	12B	8.1 GB
Llama3.2	Meta	3B	2.0 GB
Llama3.1	Meta	8B	4.9 GB
Magistral	Mistral AI	24B	14.0 GB
DeepSeek-R1	DeepSeek	32B	20 GB

3.4   Synthetic Cypher Generation

The goal of the Synthetic Cypher Generation step (1) is to define the base for golden sets of NL questions and Cypher queries pairs, essential for the subsequent benchmark task. Leveraging the Mistral-Small 3.1 model and a tailored prompt, the 280 validated questions obtained from the question validation step were translated into 280 Cypher queries. Due to prompt size limits and privacy concerns, generated queries included fictitious entities and relationships not present in the employed KGs, serving as structural blueprints. Though not directly executable, they established patterns later refined with real entities and validated against the KGs, ensuring scalable and privacy-aware query generation.

3.5   Synthetic Cypher Validation

The query validation was performed in two steps: first, we verified the relevance of the NL questions with respect to the obtained Cypher query, and second, we refined the Cypher queries to remove sporadic errors. Corrections were applied particularly in relationships and pattern-matching clauses. Golden test sets of Cypher queries were built with 70 question–query pairs per KG, substituting the placeholders in the generated queries with real data from the KGs. This step ensured that the synthetic cypher queries were executable and aligned with the intended semantics. The golden sets served as a reliable ground truth for evaluating the LLM-generated queries, ensuring that the subsequent benchmarking phase is both accurate and practically relevant.

3.6   Benchmarking LLMs on Text-to-Cypher

The evaluation benchmark is performed against the four selected KGs employing seven open-source LLMs, listed in Table 3. We selected the language models to include both fine-tuned and general-purpose versions, considering also diversity in terms of numbers of parameters, spanning from 2.8 billion to 24 billion parameters for the biggest model. Using a refined prompt, we iterated the generation of the Cypher query collections based on the validated questions for each

Table 3. Overview of the open-source LLMs employed for translating natural language questions into Cypher queries, detailing their main attributes such as publisher, parameter count (in billions), and model size.

Model Name	Fine-tuned	Parameters
Stable-Cypher-Instruct	Yes	2.8B
Mistral-Small	No	24.0B
Llama 3 Text-to-Cypher-Demo	Yes	8.0B
Magistral	No	24.0B
Gemma3	No	12.0B
Llama 3.2	No	3.2B
Qwen3	No	14.0B

Table 4. Benchmark results on Cypher query generation across models. Values in bold indicate the best performance for each metric, whereas underlined values represent the second-best.

Model	Fine-Tuned	Timeout %	Returns Res %	Cosine Mean	Std	Jaccard Mean	Std	Levenshtein Mean	Std	Jaro-Winkler Mean	Std
stable-cypher-instruct	Yes	70.72	11.07	0.8191	0.1102	0.2209	0.1541	0.3771	0.1930	0.7355	0.1344
mistral-small	No	9.64	**62.14**	**0.9607**	0.0438	**0.6063**	0.2629	**0.7727**	0.2086	**0.9093**	0.05225
t.onjo-llama3_demo	Yes	**6.07**	53.92	0.9233	0.0505	0.3711	0.1806	0.5860	0.1937	0.8676	0.0638
magistral	No	20.72	48.22	0.9095	0.0519	0.3515	0.1576	0.5649	0.1910	0.8556	0.0650
gemma3	No	72.86	15.00	0.8772	0.0562	0.3453	0.1917	0.5671	0.1926	0.7717	0.0844
llama3.2	No	39.64	30.36	0.8750	0.0622	0.2564	0.1363	0.4453	0.1651	0.8061	0.0850
qwen3	No	100.00	0.00	0.6132	0.0745	0.0292	0.0124	0.0419	0.0177	0.5040	0.0214

of the seven LLMs. We employed several evaluation metrics to assess the performance of the selected LLMs in generating Cypher queries: Timeout, Return Results, Cosine similarity, Jaccard similarity, Levenshtein distance, and Jaro-Winkler similarity. While Timeout and Return Results quantify the outcome of the generated queries execution, the remaining similarity metrics detail how semantically and syntactically similar is the synthetic query set compared to the ground truth set defined in the second phase of the workflow Fig. 1.

4 Experimental Results

In our evaluation we benchmarked seven LLMs across four educational KGs. These KGs varied in size and complexity, ranging from smaller, specialized collections (EduKG [8]) to large, heterogeneous ones (COCO [6]). See Table 4.

4.1 Comparison Across LLMs

Quantitatively, general-purpose models with strong reasoning abilities performed best. For instance, *Mistral-Small* achieved the highest execution success rate, returning correct results in more than 60% of cases, and showed the strongest semantic similarity to gold-standard queries. In contrast, the fine-tuned *Stable-Cypher-Instruct* model underperformed, suggesting the limitations of narrow-domain fine-tuning. While this behavior might be biased by the usage of Mistrall-Small for the question generation, the question validation process held by our research group members aimed at mitigate this through the selection of the most human-like and educational viable question.

We also observed systematic failure cases. *Qwen3* produced queries that consistently timed out, yielding a 0% success rate across all datasets. Larger models did not guarantee stronger performance: in several cases, smaller models such as *Llama3.2* outperformed larger counterparts, highlighting that efficiency and adaptability are not strictly correlated with scale.

Our analysis revealed a consistent gap between linguistic similarity metrics and functional metrics. Models often generated queries that appeared similar to the respective golden queries but failed at execution, underscoring the need to investigate beyond individual similarity or utility metrics.

4.2   Impact of the Graph Characteristics

Performance patterns align with graph characteristics (see Fig. 2). The **COCO** [6] KG, the largest and most complex in our study, proved especially challenging for all models. Its size and structural diversity—covering millions of nodes and multiple entity types—led to frequent execution failures. Even the best-performing model, *Mistral-Small*, managed to return valid results for only about 44% of queries. Simpler models, such as *Llama3.2*, surprisingly outperformed more specialized systems like *Stable-Cypher-Instruct*, suggesting that sheer scale or fine-tuning alone is not enough when managing highly heterogeneous educational datasets. For educational stakeholders, this highlights how large institutional datasets can overwhelm current LLMs, leading to incomplete insights.

In contrast, the smaller **EduKG** [8] dataset yielded considerably better results. Here, Mistral-Small reached nearly 69% success, while the fine-tuned *Llama3 Text-to-Cypher* achieved similar levels of performance. The relative simplicity of EduKG's structure—fewer nodes, clearer relationships—allowed multiple models to generate valid queries more consistently. Even models that struggled on COCO [6] improved significantly. This indicates that LLMs may be reliable mediators in more narrowly scoped educational settings, such as high school-to-university curriculum planning, where datasets are less fragmented.

MOOCCube [19] presented an interesting contrast: despite containing over 10 million relationships, some models improved their performance on this dataset. *Mistral-Small* recorded its best performance overall, successfully executing around 70% of queries, while *Magistral* also performed better than in other contexts. Yet for most other models, performance dropped, likely due to the graph's high relational density, which complicates query generation. This divergence suggests that certain architectures are better at navigating dense relational structures. For practitioners, it underscores the need to carefully select and test models against the specific complexity profile of the data.

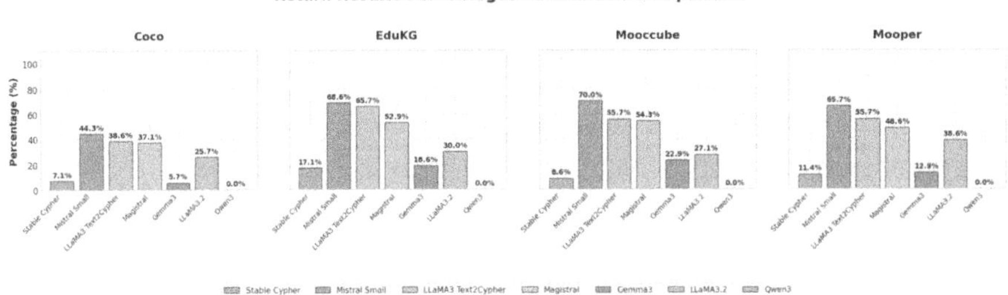

Fig. 2. Percentage of queries that successfully returned results upon execution across different test sets.

Finally, the **MOOPer** [10] KG, though smaller in scale than COCO [6] or MOOCCube [19], posed unique challenges because of its richer property structures and multi-hop relationships. Here, performance declined again, even for previously strong models like Mistral-Small. The added complexity of multi-step paths and diverse property types led to more frequent errors. This result indicates that data complexity is not only about size: the richness of properties and depth of relationships are equally important barriers. For the learning sciences, this signals that AI systems need to be evaluated not just on scale but on how well they cope with different structural characteristics of educational data.

4.3   Implication for Learning Sciences

The findings from our benchmark carry important implications for the adoption of AI in educational contexts, particularly regarding inclusivity and data accessibility. Historically, educational actors accessed complex data through static and limited interfaces, such as rule-based generated reports or predefined web pages. Personalized information extraction required technical expertise in query languages and created a barrier for the people who could benefit most from the insights. The successes in our results highlight that LLMs can lower barriers to complex data, acting as a bridge between humans and data. A well-posed NL question can be automatically translated into a structured query, enabling intuitive access to information that would otherwise require technical expertise. Possible scenarios in this context may include instructors and academic advisors seeking to understand student learning pathways or identify resource gaps, learners trying to navigate complex curricula or find resources related to their interests intuitively, administrators and curriculum planners needing to analyze enrollment patterns or assess program effectiveness.

The samples of Table 5 show how *Mistral-Small* successfully translated the NL question into a Cypher query that correctly connected subjects hierarchically and subsequently with courses. The query executed without errors and returned valid results, demonstrating the ability of the model to navigate multi-hop relationships in the graph. By contrast, the query produced by *Llama3.2* introduced

Table 5. Example Cypher queries generated by different models.

Question	Which Subjects are parent subjects of '`Programming Fundamentals`' and are covered in Courses with an objective of '`Make smart investment choices on cryptocurrency.`'?
`mistral- small`	MATCH (s1:Subject name: 'Programming Fundamentals')<-[r:subjectIsParentOf]-(parentSubject:Subject) WITH parentSubject MATCH (c:Course)-[:courseCovers]->(parentSubject) WHERE c.objective = 'Make smart investment choices on cryptocurrency.' RETURN DISTINCT parentSubject
`llama3.2`	MATCH (s:Subject)-[r:subjectIsParentOf originalPredicate: 'Programming Fundamentals']-(p:Subject) OPTIONAL MATCH (c:Course)-[:courseCovers]->(s) WHERE c.name = 'Make smart investment choices on cryptocurrency' RETURN s.name AS ParentSubject

an incorrect relationship type, and failed to execute properly. This contrast highlights the dual nature of current systems: they can generate accurate and useful queries in some cases, but even small deviations in graph structure can quickly lead to unusable or misleading outputs. In the education domain, a preliminary benchmark of the AI systems before deployment can help to assess their capabilities and identify failure points before they provide unreliable results.

5   Conclusions and Future Work

This paper introduced new test collections of educationally grounded natural language questions and used them to benchmark LLMs for query generation over educational KGs. Our results show that while general-purpose LLMs can lower barriers to accessing complex educational data, their reliability remains inconsistent, especially on more complex datasets. For the learning sciences, this highlights both the potential and the risks of deploying LLM-based systems in practice. They offer a pathway toward more inclusive and data-driven education, but only if paired with rigorous evaluation and safeguards. Looking ahead, we plan to fine-tune the most promising models to see if domain-specific training can narrow the gap between generated and gold queries. This will also let us test their potential for practical applications, such as chatbots that help users run complex queries without knowing query languages. In conclusion, our long-term objective is to make KGs accessible to everyone by using LLMs in user-friendly platforms, enabling natural language queries and supporting accessible educational tools.

Acknowledgements. We acknowledge financial support from the National Recovery and Resilience Plan (NRRP), Mission 4 Component 2 Investment 1.1 - Call for tender No. 3277, published on December 30, 2021, by the Italian Ministry of University and Research (MUR), funded by the European Union – Next Generation EU. Project

Code ECS0000038 – Project Title eINS Ecosystem of Innovation for Next Generation Sardinia – Grant Assignment Decree No. 1056 adopted on June 23, 2022, by the MUR (CUP F53C22000430001).

References

1. Abu-Rasheed, H., Abdulsalam, M.H., Weber, C., Fathi, M.: Supporting student decisions on learning recommendations: an LLM-based chatbot with knowledge graph contextualization for conversational explainability and mentoring. arXiv preprint arXiv:2401.08517 (2024)
2. Afreen, N., et al.: Edge: a conversational interface driven by large language models for educational knowledge graphs exploration. In: Proceedings of the 33rd ACM International Conference on Information and Knowledge Management, CIKM 2024, pp. 5159–5163. Association for Computing Machinery, New York, NY, USA (2024). https://doi.org/10.1145/3627673.3679231
3. Afreen, N., et al.: Learner-centered ontology for explainable educational recommendation. In: Adjunct Proceedings of the 32nd ACM Conference on User Modeling, Adaptation and Personalization, UMAP Adjunct 2024, pp. 567–575. Association for Computing Machinery, New York, NY, USA (2024). https://doi.org/10.1145/3631700.3665226
4. Alfredo, R., et al.: Human-centred learning analytics and AI in education: a systematic literature review. Comput. Educ. Artif. Intell. 6, 100215 (2024). https://doi.org/10.1016/j.caeai.2024.100215
5. Bordes, A., Usunier, N., Chopra, S., Weston, J.: Large-scale simple question answering with memory networks. arXiv preprint arXiv:1506.02075 (2015)
6. Dessì, D., Fenu, G., Marras, M., Reforgiato Recupero, D.: COCO: semantic-enriched collection of online courses at scale with experimental use cases. In: Rocha, Á., Adeli, H., Reis, L.P., Costanzo, S. (eds.) WorldCIST 2018. AISC, vol. 746, pp. 1386–1396. Springer, Cham (2018). https://doi.org/10.1007/978-3-319-77712-2_133
7. Hong, Z., et al.: Next-generation database interfaces: a survey of LLM-based text-to-SQL. IEEE Trans. Knowl. Data Eng., 1–20 (2025). https://doi.org/10.1109/TKDE.2025.3609486
8. Hubert, N., Brun, A., Monticolo, D.: New ontology and knowledge graph for university curriculum recommendation. In: ISWC 2022 - The 21st International Semantic Web Conference. Hangzhou / Virtual, China, October 2022. https://hal.science/hal-03768154
9. Li, H., Appleby, G., Brumar, C.D., Chang, R., Suh, A.: Knowledge graphs in practice: characterizing their users, challenges, and visualization opportunities. IEEE Trans. Visual Comput. Graphics 30(1), 584–594 (2024). https://doi.org/10.1109/TVCG.2023.3326904
10. Liu, K., et al.: MOOPer: a large-scale dataset of practice-oriented online learning. In: Qin, B., Jin, Z., Wang, H., Pan, J., Liu, Y., An, B. (eds.) CCKS 2021. CCIS, vol. 1466, pp. 281–287. Springer, Singapore (2021). https://doi.org/10.1007/978-981-16-6471-7_22
11. Mandilara, I., Androna, C.M., Fotopoulou, E., Zafeiropoulos, A., Papavassiliou, S.: Decoding the mystery: how can LLMs turn text into cypher in complex knowledge graphs? IEEE Access 13, 80981–81001 (2025). https://doi.org/10.1109/ACCESS.2025.3567759

12. Ozsoy, M.G., Messallem, L., Besga, J., Minneci, G.: Text2Cypher: bridging natural language and graph databases (2024). https://arxiv.org/abs/2412.10064
13. Qu, K., Li, K.C., Wong, B.T.M., Wu, M.M.F., Liu, M.: A survey of knowledge graph approaches and applications in education. Electronics **13**(13) (2024). https://doi.org/10.3390/electronics13132537
14. Saleem, M., Nazari Dastjerdi, S., Usbeck, R., Ngonga Ngomo, A.C.: Question answering over linked data: what is difficult to answer? What affects the f scores? (2017)
15. Samala, A.D., et al.: Unveiling the landscape of generative artificial intelligence in education: a comprehensive taxonomy of applications, challenges, and future prospects. Educ. Inf. Technol. **30**(3), 3239–3278 (2025)
16. Tiwari, A., Malay, S.K.R., Yadav, V., Hashemi, M., Madhusudhan, S.T.: Autocypher: improving LLMs on cypher generation via LLM-supervised generation-verification framework. In: Proceedings of the 2025 Conference of the Nations of the Americas Chapter of the Association for Computational Linguistics: Human Language Technologies (Volume 2: Short Papers), pp. 623–640. Association for Computational Linguistics, Albuquerque, New Mexico, April 2025. https://doi.org/10.18653/v1/2025.naacl-short.53
17. Trivedi, P., Maheshwari, G., Dubey, M., Lehmann, J.: LC-QuAD: a corpus for complex question answering over knowledge graphs. In: d'Amato, C., et al. (eds.) ISWC 2017. LNCS, vol. 10588, pp. 210–218. Springer, Cham (2017). https://doi.org/10.1007/978-3-319-68204-4_22
18. Tsampos, I., Marakakis, E.: Domain- and language-adaptable natural language interface for property graphs. Computers **14**(5) (2025). https://doi.org/10.3390/computers14050183
19. Yu, J., et al.: MOOCCube: a large-scale data repository for NLP applications in MOOCs. In: Proceedings of the 58th Annual Meeting of the Association for Computational Linguistics, pp. 3135–3142. Association for Computational Linguistics, Online, July 2020. https://doi.org/10.18653/v1/2020.acl-main.285
20. Yu, T., et al.: Spider: a large-scale human-labeled dataset for complex and cross-domain semantic parsing and Text-to-SQL task. arXiv preprint arXiv:1809.08887 (2018)
21. Zelle, J.M., Mooney, R.J.: Learning to parse database queries using inductive logic programming. In: Proceedings of the National Conference on Artificial Intelligence, pp. 1050–1055 (1996)
22. Zhong, V., Xiong, C., Socher, R.: Seq2SQL: generating structured queries from natural language using reinforcement learning. arXiv preprint arXiv:1709.00103 (2017)

From Functions to Indicators: A Framework to Assess the Impact of AI on Self-regulated Learning

Marika Lamacchia[1] , Francesco Facciorusso[1(✉)] , and Maria Concetta Carruba[2]

[1] University of Macerata, Macerata, Italy
{m.lamacchia2,f.facciorusso}@unimc.it
[2] Pegaso Telematics University, Naples, Italy

Abstract. Self-Regulated Learning (SRL) is a core construct in educational sciences, describing students' ability to activate cognitive, metacognitive, motivational, and behavioral processes aimed at achieving learning goals. SRL is articulated in phases of forethought, performance, and self-reflection, and is tightly connected with executive functions such as planning, inhibition, and working memory. While students with Special Educational Needs often experience difficulties in developing SRL competences, recent advances in Artificial Intelligence (AI) in education, adaptive systems, automated feedback, learning analytics, and intelligent tutoring systems, offer new opportunities for personalized scaffolding. However, research still lacks systematic instruments to evaluate whether and how AI functionalities effectively foster SRL. This paper addresses this gap by proposing a conceptual evaluation framework that integrates Zimmerman's cyclical model, Pintrich's multidimensional approach, and the Winne-Hadwin process-oriented model of SRL with updated taxonomies of AI in education that include GenAI and conversational agents. The framework operationalizes the relationship between AI functionalities and SRL phases/areas through observable indicators, concrete examples (e.g., ALEKS, ASSISTments, AutoTutor), and measurement tools that combine self-report instruments (MSLQ, MAI, LASSI) with trace-based, microanalytic protocols recommended by contemporary SRL analytics research. As an initial conceptual proposal, the framework requires empirical validation through controlled studies that assess construct validity, temporal stability, and cross-context generalizability. Despite these limitations, it contributes to theory and practice by systematizing analysis of AI's impact on SRL, guiding researchers in designing validation studies, and offering educators and developers a structured guide for responsible AI adoption in inclusive educational contexts.

Keywords: Self-Regulated Learning · Artificial Intelligence in Education · Evaluation Framework

1 Introduction

1.1 Context and Significance

The development of Self-Regulated Learning (SRL) is recognized as a key competence for academic achievement and the construction of student autonomy, particularly in inclusive and complex educational settings. SRL is defined as the ability of learners to activate cognitive, metacognitive, motivational, and behavioral processes in order to attain learning goals [1, 2]. Contemporary research emphasizes that SRL is not a static trait but a dynamic, cyclical set of processes—forethought, performance, and self-reflection—that are closely associated with executive functions such as planning, inhibition, and working memory [5, 6]. These neurocognitive mechanisms are fundamental predictors of academic success and adaptability to demanding tasks, especially for students with Special Educational Needs who often experience difficulties in self-regulatory processes [7].

1.2 Scientific and Pedagogical Rationale

From a psychopedagogical perspective, SRL is not only a desirable educational outcome but also a precondition for meaningful learning, as it enables students to monitor strategies, regulate motivation, and transfer skills across contexts [3, 4]. Recent years have witnessed significant advances in Artificial Intelligence (AI) technologies applied to education, including adaptive systems, intelligent tutors, predictive analytics, automated feedback, and, most recently, Generative AI (GenAI) and Large Language Models (LLMs) [11, 12]. These technologies introduce new opportunities to scaffold SRL through personalized, real-time support, adaptive pacing, metacognitive prompts and dialogic interactions that can foster reflection and strategic planning [2–4, 11].

1.3 State of Research and Identified Gap

Despite the proliferation of AI-based educational tools, a critical methodological gap persists: the literature does not provide systematic, validated frameworks to assess whether, and in which ways, different AI functionalities, including emerging GenAI applications, effectively foster the various phases and dimensions of SRL [18, 19]. Contemporary SRL analytics research increasingly emphasizes trace-based, microanalytic measurement protocols that capture temporal sequences of learner actions, enabling more valid inferences about monitoring and control processes [19, 20]. Recent work demonstrates that Large Language Models (LLMs) can support automated coding of SRL in think-aloud protocols, opening new methodological possibilities. The integration of these advances, such as GenAI affordances, trace-based measurement into a coherent evaluative framework remains underexplored. This gap hampers both rigorous empirical evaluation and the design of AI systems aligned with pedagogical principles and responsible AI guidelines [18, 19].

1.4 Contribution and Paper Structure

This paper addresses the identified gap by proposing a conceptual evaluation framework that integrates three complementary SRL models: Zimmerman's cyclical model [1], Pintrich's multidimensional approach [2], and Winne and Hadwin's process-oriented, information-processing model [18, 22], which explicitly emphasizes fine-grained monitoring, control, and recursive adaptation within and across SRL phases. The framework maps these models onto an updated taxonomy of AI functions in education that includes not only traditional ITS, adaptive systems, and learning analytics, but also Generative AI and conversational agents. It aims to provide researchers, educators, and developers with a theoretically grounded and operationally applicable tool to evaluate AI's impact on SRL and, more broadly, on the development of executive functions, while also supporting equity and inclusion in education [15].

The remainder of the paper is structured as follows: Sect. 2 reviews the theoretical foundations of SRL and the main AI functions in education; Sect. 3 outlines the methodological approach adopted to build the framework; Sect. 4 presents the resulting evaluation matrix and its use; Sect. 5 discusses implications and limitations; and Sect. 6 concludes by outlining future research directions.

2 Background

2.1 Theoretical Foundations of SRL

Among the most influential frameworks, Zimmerman conceptualized SRL as a cyclical process with three phases: forethought, including goal setting and strategic planning; performance, involving self-monitoring and task control; and self-reflection, where learners evaluate outcomes and generate causal attributions [1]. This model highlights the dynamic and recursive nature of self-regulation, in which strategies are continuously adapted in response to feedback.

Pintrich extended this perspective by introducing a multidimensional approach. Rather than focusing solely on temporal phases, his framework distinguishes four domains of regulation, cognitive, motivational/affective, behavioral, and contextual, through which self-regulatory processes can operate simultaneously [2]. For example, learners not only plan cognitive strategies but also regulate emotions, sustain motivation, and adapt behaviors to the learning environment. Furthermore, the Winne-Hadwin model has emphasized the process-oriented and information-processing nature of SRL. It focuses on the fine-grained monitoring and control loops, where learners gather and interpret information about task conditions and their learning operations, adapting strategies based on ongoing feedback. This model is especially relevant for trace-based analytics, as it maps well onto datasets capturing detailed temporal sequences of learner actions [23, 24].

These complementary models provide a comprehensive theoretical foundation: Zimmerman's cyclical phases capture the sequential progression of SRL, Pintrich's framework accounts for its multidimensional and context-sensitive character, and Winne-Hadwin offers a detailed process-level lens suited for real-time measurement and learning analytics.

Table 1. Integrated framework of Self-Regulated Learning based on Zimmerman's cyclical phases and Pintrich's multidimensional areas (adapted from Zimmerman, [1]; Pintrich, [2]).

SRL Phases (Zimmerman)	Cognitive	Motivational / Affective	Behavioral	Contextual
Forethought / Planning	Setting cognitive goals; planning study strategies	Task value; activating intrinsic motivation; self-efficacy	Initial organization; time management before starting	Assessing learning context; selecting resources
Performance / Monitoring & Control	Monitoring comprehension; applying metacognitive strategies	Regulating emotions; sustaining motivation during tasks	Managing time and effort; seeking help when needed	Adapting to environmental and social demands
Self-reflection / Evaluation	Analyzing outcomes; self-evaluating strategies	Causal attributions of success/failure; reflecting on effort	Revising behaviors; redefining goals	Evaluating adequacy of resources and conditions

2.2 Neuroscientific Basis and Executive Functions

While educational models describe how students regulate learning, neuroscience explains which brain mechanisms underpin these processes. SRL is strongly associated with executive functions, primarily located in the prefrontal cortex, which orchestrate goal-directed behavior and adaptation to complex tasks [5].

- Working memory supports the maintenance and manipulation of relevant information, enabling planning and real-time monitoring.
- Inhibitory control allows suppression of impulsive responses or ineffective strategies, sustaining persistence toward goals.
- Cognitive flexibility enables shifting between strategies and adapting to changing task demands.

Diamond showed that executive functions not only predict academic performance but also resilience and emotional regulation [6]. Neuroimaging studies have further highlighted the role of the dorsolateral prefrontal cortex and its connections with the hippocampus, implicated in metacognitive regulation and memory consolidation.

Accordingly, SRL can be understood as the behavioral and pedagogical manifestation of neurocognitive processes: when learners plan, monitor, and reflect, they enact underlying executive functions that become observable through metacognitive and regulatory strategies. This interpretation reinforces the importance of designing educational interventions, including AI-based ones, that explicitly target these neural circuits to foster self-regulation.

2.3 AI Functions in Education

Parallel to these theoretical and neuroscientific advances, research on Artificial Intelligence in education has delineated several functional areas. Four consolidated categories are frequently cited [11, 12]:

- Adaptive systems & personalisation, tailoring content and sequencing to learner profiles;
- Assessment & feedback, providing immediate automated evaluation and formative guidance;
- Profiling & prediction (Learning Analytics/EDM), leveraging data to forecast trajectories and risks;
- Intelligent Tutoring Systems (ITS), offering interactive scaffolding and metacognitive prompts.

The rapid development of Generative AI and conversational agents has introduced innovative possibilities to dynamically scaffold higher-order SRL processes such as reflection, motivation regulation, and strategic planning [12, 15]. These systems can engage learners in dialogic interactions, generate personalized prompts, and assist in coding SRL processes. Recent research and policy increasingly acknowledge a methodological gap in the systematic development and validation of comprehensive frameworks capable of assessing how diverse AI functionalities distinctly and integratively support the multiple phases and domains of self-regulated learning, particularly at fine-grained process and event levels, through multilayered temporal data analysis [25, 26].

While emerging tools like conversational agents and Generative AI show promise for fostering reflection and adaptation [15], both research [4, 16] and policy [14] highlight the urgent need for systematic and responsible frameworks to guide their educational use.

3 Methods and Materials

3.1 Methodological Approach

The framework was developed within the tradition of framework building, which involves the construction of conceptual models grounded in a critical and comparative review of the literature. This approach was selected because it enables the integration of consolidated theoretical perspectives with applied cases, thereby producing a tool that is both academically rigorous and transferable to educational practice.

3.2 Procedure

The procedure consisted of a three-step procedure:

1. Identification of AI functionalities in education, drawing on key reviews and institutional reports [11–14]. Four macro-categories were identified: adaptive systems & personalisation, assessment & feedback, profiling & prediction (Learning Analytics/EDM), and Intelligent Tutoring Systems (ITS). This selection was updated to explicitly include emerging Generative AI and conversational agents, reflecting recent advances not covered in earlier taxonomies

2. Mapping of SRL dimensions, an integrated approach combining Zimmerman's cyclical model, Pintrich's multidimensional framework and the process-oriented Winne-Hadwin model, which distinguishes between cognitive, motivational/affective, behavioral, and contextual areas. This composite model accounts for the complexity of SRL phases, multidimensional regulation domains, and fine-grained process mechanisms [4, 6].
3. Definition of observable indicators: for each cell in the intersection of AI functions and SRL phases/domains, we developed operational indicators based on validated measurement tools (e.g., MSLQ, LASSI, SRLIS, and MAI), complemented by recent microanalytic and trace-based protocols documented in contemporary SRL analytics research [16, 24].

3.3 Validated Measurement Tools

To bridge theoretical constructs and observable indicators, the framework relies on validated instruments widely used in SRL research:

- MSLQ (Motivated Strategies for Learning Questionnaire): measures goal orientation, self-regulation, and time management.
- SRLIS (Self-Regulated Learning Interview Schedule): semi-structured interview identifying SRL strategies.
- MAI (Metacognitive Awareness Inventory): assesses metacognitive knowledge and regulation.
- LASSI (Learning and Study Strategies Inventory): evaluates study strategies and motivational components.
- SRL microanalysis protocols: event-specific tools to monitor SRL processes in real time.

This integration ensures that the framework is not only theoretically robust but also empirically verifiable [16]. To overcome the limitations of self-report tools, especially their inability to capture fine-grained, temporal dynamics of SRL, the framework also includes microanalytic protocols and trace-based analytics: event-specific assessment tools designed to monitor SRL processes as they occur in context, enabling temporal segmentation and coding of strategic behaviors, often supported by automated or LLM-based coding methods [15, 16].

4 Results

4.1 Presentation of the Matrix

The main outcome of this study is the development of a conceptual evaluation matrix (Table 1), which integrates Zimmerman's cyclical model of SRL [1] and Pintrich's multidimensional framework [2] with the main categories of artificial intelligence functionalities in education, as identified by consolidated reviews [11, 12].

The following table presents an updated, detailed framework that maps key AI functionalities onto the multidimensional phases and areas of Self-Regulated Learning (SRL), as conceptualized by Zimmerman's cyclical model and Pintrich's taxonomy, further enriched by Winne-Hadwin's process-oriented perspective. Operational indicators are explicitly defined with concrete, measurable criteria. The table additionally outlines robust measurement and validation strategies, emphasizing the combination of established psychometric instruments, trace-based analytics, and microanalytic protocols (Table 2).

Table 2. Framework for Assessing the impact of AI functionalities on Self-Regulated Learning (SRL).

AI Function Category	SRL Phase/Area	Observable Indicators	Example AI Tools / Systems	Measurement & Validation Strategies	Winne-Hadwin Mechanisms Mapped
Adaptive Systems & Personalisation	Forethought / Cognitive & Motivational	Goal-setting prompts (frequency, content specificity); Personalized learning path adjustments; Pre-task scaffolds via LLMs	ALEKS; GenAI planning assistants	Log analysis of goal updates; Coding of LLM scaffold dialogs; Construct validity via think-aloud protocols	Monitoring of task conditions, plan formulation
	Performance / Monitoring & Control	Real-time pacing adaptations; Hints proportional to learner errors; Self-monitoring prompts with time stamps	ALEKS adaptive sequencing; GenAI real-time tutors	Trace-based event coding; Reliability checks; Temporal stability tests	Recursive control loops, conditional strategy execution
	Self-reflection / Evaluation & Regulation	Automated mastery reports; Reflective prompts personalized by conversational agents	ALEKS mastery reports; GenAI reflective agents	Convergent validity with self-report scales; Cross-context consistency checks	Adaptive revision and strategy deployment
Assessment & Feedback	Forethought / Cognitive & Motivational	Task success criteria/rubrics; Pre-task feedback on strategy selection	ASSISTments pre-task guidance	Rubric-based scoring validation; Pre/post intervention performance comparison	Monitoring and anticipation of task demands
	Performance / Monitoring & Control	Immediate formative feedback; Automated error detection with tailored hints	AES; ASSISTments	Event-level error coding; Inter-rater reliability; Learning analytics trace validation	Continuous error monitoring and correction

(continued)

Table 2. (*continued*)

AI Function Category	SRL Phase/Area	Observable Indicators	Example AI Tools / Systems	Measurement & Validation Strategies	Winne-Hadwin Mechanisms Mapped
	Self-reflection / Evaluation & Regulation	Metacognitive feedback; Self-explanation justification prompts	ASSISTments reflection scripts	Latent construct validation; Sentiment analysis; Longitudinal outcome tracking	Ongoing evaluation and causal attribution
Profiling & Prediction (LA/EDM)	All phases / Multidimensional	Risk state alerts; Learner profiling; Predictive adaptive recommendations	Predictive dashboards; GenAI prediction models	Algorithmic validation; Reliability of predictive accuracy; Consequential validity	Monitoring control loops and conditional adjustments
Intelligent Tutoring Systems (ITS)	Forethought / Planning & Cognitive Control	Explicit goal articulation; Strategy planning support via dialogic exchanges	AutoTutor; Cognitive Tutor	Dialogue analysis with coding schemes; Validated microanalytic protocols	Fine-grained monitoring and control through interaction
	Performance / Monitoring & Control	Self-explanation prompts; Gradual scaffolding fading	AutoTutor; ITS scaffolding	Temporal coding of scaffold usage; Interobserver agreement; Trace data convergence	Feedback loops for adaptive strategy deployment
	Self-reflection / Evaluation & Regulation	Reflection dialogues; Attribution prompts; Facilitation of transfer	AutoTutor reflection dialogues	Narrative coding reliability; Longitudinal reflection analysis; Generalizability testing	Recursive evaluation and adaptive learning strategy
	Profiling & prediction (LA/EDM)	Historical reports vs. targets; corrective strategies	Predictive analytics dashboards	LA metrics; post-unit questionnaires	
	Intelligent Tutoring Systems (ITS)	Functional attributions; plan revision; transfer prompts	AutoTutor reflection dialogues	SRL microanalysis (post-task)	

4.2 How to Use the Matrix

The matrix serves a dual function:

- Analytical function: the matrix enables a precise classification of diverse AI functionalities in relation to the phases (forethought, performance, self-reflection) and multidimensional areas (cognitive, motivational/affective, behavioral, contextual) of Self-Regulated Learning (SRL). This avoids generic or superficial descriptions and allows identifying which specific AI capabilities target particular mechanisms and processes within SRL.
- Operational function: the matrix directly connects observable, operationalized indicators of learner behavior and AI interaction with validated measurement tools, including both traditional self-report instruments and modern trace-based, microanalytic protocols. This facilitates transparent, replicable data collection and analysis, supporting rigorous evaluation of AI impacts on SRL both quantitatively and qualitatively.

The application examples included illustrate how the framework can be implemented in real educational contexts, offering practical support for both empirical research and instructional design. The matrix thus represents a methodological device that enables comparable and replicable empirical observations, addressing the current methodological gap in evaluating AI's impact on SRL processes.

5 Discussion

5.1 Neurocognitive Grounding of Self-regulated Learning (SRL)

Neuroscientific research has clarified that self-regulated learning processes are associated with the activity of specific executive functions. The dorsolateral prefrontal cortex is involved in planning and updating working memory; the anterior cingulate cortex plays a crucial role in error monitoring and strategy adjustment; and prefrontal–hippocampal connections support the re-elaboration and consolidation of outcomes [5, 6]. These findings show that self-regulatory difficulties are observable at a neurocognitive level, underscoring the importance of developing tools that can strengthen them.

5.2 AI Technologies as Regulatory Co-agents

Artificial intelligence technologies can be understood as external scaffolds that help activate and strengthen the executive circuits underlying self-regulation. Adaptive systems modulate task difficulty and pacing, reducing cognitive overload and supporting working memory; automated feedback and self-assessment prompts stimulate metacognitive monitoring and error control; predictive dashboards enhance the ability to maintain direction towards goals; and intelligent tutoring systems, through reflective prompts and guided explanations, foster reflection and strategic flexibility. Within this framework, AI does not replace students' cognitive processes; rather, it functions as a pedagogical co-agent, providing regulatory stimuli that can progressively be internalized by the learner.

5.3 Implications for Students with Self-regulation Difficulties

Many students with special educational needs present executive function fragilities that directly compromise self-regulation. In ADHD, deficits in inhibition and sustained attention lead to difficulties in maintaining stable goals and continuously monitoring progress [8]. In specific learning disorders (SLD), such as dyslexia and dyscalculia, challenges related to working memory and self-monitoring, with consequences for planning and the effectiveness of study strategies [9]. In autism spectrum conditions, even in non-severe forms, impairments in cognitive flexibility and planning result in strategic rigidity and difficulties in transferring learning across contexts [10].

The proposed framework addresses these challenges in two main ways:

1. By enabling the identification of sensitive observable indicators of these difficulties (e.g., time management, strategy switching, frequency of goal revision, reflection on errors);
2. By linking these indicators to validated measurement tools and relevant AI functionalities, such as adaptive systems to support working memory, intelligent tutors with metacognitive prompts to stimulate self-monitoring, and predictive dashboards to assist planning.

In this way, the matrix is not limited to describing difficulties but becomes an operational device for designing tailored educational and habilitative interventions that can strengthen self-regulatory processes and improve school participation, while also mitigating the cognitive and emotional difficulties associated with such conditions.

5.4 Professional and Research Implications

The proposed matrix operates at multiple levels:

- For teachers, it provides a practical guide to critically evaluate AI technologies in terms of their contribution to self-regulatory processes;
- For educationalists and psychologists, it offers a tool to integrate cognitive, metacognitive, and emotional objectives into evidence-based educational and habilitative pathways;
- For researchers, it constitutes a replicable model for comparative and longitudinal studies, capable of linking AI interventions to testable neurocognitive hypotheses;
- For developers, it provides a reference to design educational environments in which algorithmic functionalities are aligned with regulatory and inclusive objectives, in line with international recommendations for responsible AI use [13, 14].

6 Conclusion

This study has introduced a theoretical–methodological framework that integrates established models of self-regulated learning, neuroscientific evidence, with updated taxonomies of Artificial Intelligence functionalities in education including Generative AI and conversational agents. The resulting matrix serves as a practical tool for researchers designing empirical validation studies, educators selecting AI tools aligned with pedagogical goals, and developers aiming for responsible AI integration that supports autonomy, motivation, and strategic learning regulation.

Nevertheless, the contribution also presents limitations. As a conceptual framework, it requires empirical validation through experimental and comparative studies that can assess its applicability and sensitivity in real educational settings [4, 15]. Moreover, most existing literature is rooted in monolingual and Western contexts; future research should extend its application to multilingual and multicultural environments to ensure transferability and relevance [17].

Another promising avenue concerns the integration of Generative AI technologies, which are emerging as potentially valuable tools to foster reflection, monitoring, and planning through dialogic interactions [12, 16]. These applications create new opportunities but also require critical evaluation regarding effectiveness, equity, and ethical implications.

In sum, the framework outlined here represents an initial step towards the development of a more robust and generalisable evaluative model, capable of connecting research, educational practice, and technological innovation in an inclusive, evidence-based perspective.

References

1. Zimmerman, B.J.: Becoming a self-regulated learner: an overview. Theory Pract. **41**(2), 64–70 (2002). https://doi.org/10.1207/s15430421tip4102_2
2. Pintrich, P.R.: The role of goal orientation in self-regulated learning. In: Boekaerts, M., Pintrich, P.R., Zeidner, M. (eds.) Handbook of Self-Regulation, pp. 451–502. Academic Press, San Diego (2000). https://doi.org/10.1016/B978-012109890-2/50043-3
3. Boekaerts, M.: Emotions, emotion regulation, and self-regulation of learning. In: Zimmerman, B.J., Schunk, D.H. (eds.) Handbook of Self-Regulation of Learning and Performance, pp. 408–425. Routledge, New York (2011). https://doi.org/10.4324/9780203839010.ch26
4. Panadero, E.: A review of self-regulated learning: six models and four directions for research. Front. Psychol. **8**, 422 (2017). https://doi.org/10.3389/fpsyg.2017.00422
5. Miyake, A., Friedman, N.P.: The nature and organization of individual differences in executive functions: four general conclusions. Curr. Dir. Psychol. Sci. **21**(1), 8–14 (2012). https://doi.org/10.1177/0963721411429458
6. Diamond, A.: Executive functions. Annu. Rev. Psychol. **64**, 135–168 (2013). https://doi.org/10.1146/annurev-psych-113011-143750
7. Nota, L., Soresi, S., Zimmerman, B.J.: Self-regulation and academic achievement and resilience: a longitudinal study. Int. J. Educ. Res. **41**(3), 198–215 (2004). https://doi.org/10.1016/j.ijer.2005.07.001
8. Barkley, R.A. (ed.): Attention-Deficit Hyperactivity Disorder: A Handbook for Diagnosis and Treatment, 4th edn. Guilford Press, New York (2015)
9. Swanson, H.L., Jerman, O.: The influence of working memory on reading growth in subgroups of children with reading disabilities. J. Exp. Child Psychol. **96**(4), 249–283 (2007). https://doi.org/10.1016/j.jecp.2006.12.004
10. Demetriou, E.A., et al.: Autism spectrum disorders: a meta-analysis of executive function. Mol. Psychiatry **23**(5), 1198–1204 (2018). https://doi.org/10.1038/mp.2017.7
11. Zawacki-Richter, O., Marín, V.I., Bond, M., Gouverneur, F.: Systematic review of research on artificial intelligence applications in higher education. Int. J. Educ. Technol. High. Educ. **16**, 39 (2019). https://doi.org/10.1186/s41239-019-0171-0
12. Holmes, W., Tuomi, I., Jelfs, A.: State of the art and practice in AI in education. Eur. J. Educ. **57**(4), 542–570 (2022). https://doi.org/10.1111/ejed.12533

13. U.S. Department of Education, Office of Educational Technology: Artificial Intelligence and the Future of Teaching and Learning: Insights and Recommendations. Washington, DC (2023)
14. UNESCO: Guidance for Generative AI in Education and Research. Paris (2023)
15. Azevedo, R., Mudrick, N.V., Taub, M., Bradbury, A.E.: Self-regulation in computer-based learning environments: lessons learned and future directions with MetaTutor. Front. Psychol. **13**, 813632 (2022). https://doi.org/10.3389/fpsyg.2022.813632
16. Roll, I., Winne, P.H.: Understanding, evaluating, and supporting self-regulated learning using learning analytics. J. Learn. Anal. **2**(1), 7–12 (2015). https://doi.org/10.18608/jla.2015.21.2
17. Dörnyei, Z., Ryan, S.: The Psychology of the Language Learner Revisited. Routledge, New York (2015). https://doi.org/10.4324/9781315779553
18. Winne, P.H.: Learning analytics for self-regulated learning. In: Lang, C., Siemens, G., Wise, A.F., Gašević, D., Merceron, A. (eds.) The Handbook of Learning Analytics, 2nd edn., pp. 78–85. SoLAR, Vancouver, Canada (2022). https://doi.org/10.18608/hla22.008
19. Borchers, C., Zhang, J., Fleischer, H., Schanze, S., Aleven, V., Baker, R.S.: Large language models generalize SRL prediction to new languages within but not between domains. J. Educ. Data Mining **17**(2), 24–54 (2025). https://doi.org/10.1038/mp.2017.75. https://doi.org/10.5281/zenodo.17073680
20. Siadaty, M., Gašević, D., Hatala, M.: Trace-based micro-analytic measurement of self-regulated learning processes. J. Learn. Anal. **3**(1), 183–214 (2016). https://doi.org/10.18608/jla.2016.31.11
21. Sun, J.C.-Y., Liu, Y., Lin, X., Hu, X.: Temporal learning analytics to explore traces of self-regulated learning behaviors and their associations with learning performance, cognitive load, and student engagement in an asynchronous online course. Front. Psychology **13** (2023). https://doi.org/10.3389/fpsyg.2022.1096337
22. Järvelä, S., Hadwin, A.: Triggers for self-regulated learning: a conceptual framework. Learn. Individ. Differ. **115** (2024). https://doi.org/10.1016/j.lindif.2024.102526
23. Winne, P.H., Hadwin, A.F.: Studying as self-regulated learning. In: Hacker, D.J., Dunlosky, J., Graesser, A.C. (eds.) Metacognition in Educational Theory and Practice, pp. 277–304. Lawrence Erlbaum Associates (1998)
24. Greene, J.A., Azevedo, R.: A theoretical review of Winne and Hadwin's model of self-regulated learning. New perspectives and directions. Rev. Educ. Res. **77**(3), 334–372 (2007). https://psycnet.apa.org/doi/10.3102/003465430303953
25. Lan, M.: A qualitative systematic review on AI empowered self-regulated learning in higher education. npj Sci. Learn. **10**, 21 (2025). https://doi.org/10.1038/s41539-025-00319-0
26. Radović, S., Wetchy, E., Seidel, N.: Implementing the self-regulated learning structured interview protocol with generative AI: a novel approach for evaluating students' SRL skills. J. Res. Technol. Educ., 1–18 (2025). https://doi.org/10.1080/15391523.2025.2547176

Hope, Aspirations, and the Impact of LLMs on Female Programming Learners in Afghanistan

Hamayoon Behmanush[1]([envelope]) [iD], Freshta Akhtari[2] [iD], Roghieh Nooripour[3] [iD], Ingmar Weber[1] [iD], and Vikram Kamath Cannanure[1] [iD]

[1] Saarland Informatics Campus, Saarland University, Saarbrücken, Germany
`{behmanush,iweber,cannanure}@cs.uni-saarland.de`
[2] Computer Science Faculty, Parwan University, Charikar, Afghanistan
[3] Department of Counseling, Qazvin Branch, Islamic Azad University, Qazvin, Iran

Abstract. Designing impactful educational technologies in contexts of socio-political instability requires a nuanced understanding of educational aspirations. Currently, scalable metrics for measuring aspirations are limited. This study adapts, translates, and evaluates Snyder's Hope Scale [1] as a metric for measuring aspirations among 136 women learning programming online during a period of systemic educational restrictions in Afghanistan. The adapted scale demonstrated good reliability (Cronbach's $\alpha = 0.78$) and participants rated it as understandable and relevant. While overall aspiration-related scores did not differ significantly by access to Large Language Models (LLMs), those with access reported marginally higher scores on the *Avenues* subscale ($p = .056$), suggesting broader perceived pathways to achieving educational aspirations. These findings support the use of the adapted scale as a metric for aspirations in contexts of socio-political instability. More broadly, the adapted scale can be used to evaluate the impact of aspiration-driven design of educational technologies.

Keywords: Aspiration · Online Learning · LLMs for Education · Women

1 Introduction

Understanding learners' contexts is essential for designing educational technologies. Scholars in Human-Computer Interaction for Development (HCI4D) and educational technology advocate for an aspirations-based approach to technology design [2], emphasizing that aligning technology with learners' long-term goals can foster sustainable socio-economic impact. Aspirations are defined as goals that extend one's current circumstances [2] and are described through two subscales: *Agency* (the individual's capacity and determination to pursue long-term goals) and *Avenues* (the perceived opportunities and pathways available within socio-structural conditions) [2,11]. Meanwhile, socio-political challenges play an influential role in shaping aspirations, as they disrupt social order

A. Dipace et al. (Eds.): WAILS 2025, LNCS 16438, pp. 145–155, 2026.
https://doi.org/10.1007/978-3-032-17604-2_14

through political change or restrictive norms [26]. In the context of educational technology, prior work has attempted to measure aspirations using the theory of planned behavior for avenues and agency with little success [6]. In addition, conceptualizing hope as comprising aspirations, agency, and pathways [14] may provide a clearer mapping for measuring aspiration. Building on this, the Hope Scale [1], a user-administered instrument with two dimensions—Agency (goal-directed determination) and Pathways (perceived capacity to generate routes to goals)—may serve as an aspiration-aligned metric of progress toward learners' aspirations. However, despite its relevance, the Hope Scale remains underutilized in technological interventions as a metric for aspirations, particularly in settings where socio-political constraints shape learners' aspirations.

Emerging technologies, such as large language models (LLMs), are increasingly being utilized in education. Prior studies show that instability can hinder education by increasing psychological stress and exacerbating the digital divide [20]. At the same time, LLMs offer promising educational support, including personalized tutoring [15], instant feedback [16], and reinforcement of self-efficacy [18]. Although research has examined how technology can foster educational resilience [8,9] and act as an amplifier of socio-economic change [3] in unstable contexts, the role of LLMs in shaping learners' aspirations, particularly among marginalized populations, remains underexplored.

To address these gaps, this study investigates two research questions:

RQ1: What is the feasibility of using the Snyder Hope Scale to measure the educational aspirations of adult women in contexts of socio-political instability?

RQ2: Does access to Large Language Models (LLMs) influence the educational aspirations of these learners?

To answer these questions, we surveyed 136 women in Afghanistan who were studying programming online during periods of educational and employment restrictions. We adapted the Hope Scale to the programming context (see Table 4 in Appendix), translated it into Persian for accessibility, and applied statistical methods such as Cronbach's alpha [21] and ANOVA [23] to assess both the reliability of the adapted scale and the influence of LLM access on aspirations.

Our study makes two primary contributions: (1) we evaluate the feasibility and reliability of an adapted Hope Scale in a marginalized and unstable context; and (2) we assess the relationship between LLM access and learner aspirations. We further reflect on aspiration-driven design and methods for impact assessment in educational technology.

2   Related Work

2.1   Technology, Aspirations, and Measurement Challenges

Research in educational technology and HCI4D demonstrates that digital tools can shape learners' long-term goals by expanding access to information, education, and skills support [4,8,9]. Consistent with an aspirations-based approach to technology design, which emphasizes aligning technology with learners' long-term goals to foster sustainable socio-economic impact [2], aspirations can be understood as goals that extend one's current circumstances and are structured by two subscales: *Agency* (capacity and determination to pursue long-term goals) and *Avenues* (perceived opportunities within socio-structural conditions) [2,11]. Socio-political instability further shapes these aspirations by disrupting social order through political change or restrictive norms [26].

A persistent challenge is measuring aspirations in educational settings amid socio-political disruptions. Prior work in education and development studies often relied on proxies such as occupational goals or long-term study plans [10]. In HCI and related fields, aspirations have been modeled using the Aspirations-Avenues-Agency framework [11] and adaptations of the Theory of Planned Behavior, with limited success in capturing avenues and agency in practice [6]. Building on the view that hope comprises aspirations, agency, and pathways [14], we adopt Snyder's Hope Scale [1], a user-administered instrument with two dimensions, *Agency* (goal-directed determination) and *Pathways* (capacity to generate routes to goals), as an aspiration-aligned metric for measuring learners' aspirations. The Hope Scale is widely used to assess agency and pathways [21,22] yet remains underutilized in technological interventions as a measure of aspiration, particularly where socio-political constraints shape learners' goals. In our mapping, Hope-*Agency* corresponds to the aspirations subscale of *Agency*, and Hope-*Pathways* corresponds to *Avenues* [2,14], providing a basis for evaluating how aspiration can be measured and educational technologies support learners' long-term trajectories.

2.2 Large Language Models and Educational Aspirations

Large Language Models (LLMs), such as ChatGPT [13], are rapidly transforming educational practice. Their integration has extended across domains, supporting personalized tutoring and adaptive learning [15], writing assistance and automated feedback [16], and research support through information access [17]. Beyond academic skills, studies suggest that LLM-based tools can strengthen self-efficacy [18], increase intrinsic motivation, and broaden access to high-quality educational materials [19]. Together, these affordances position LLMs as potentially influential not only in shaping immediate learning outcomes but also in supporting longer-term educational trajectories.

These possibilities are particularly salient in contexts where formal education is disrupted by socio-political instability [8,9]. Prior work in HCI4D has shown how technology can buffer such disruptions: open educational resources and mobile platforms have enabled learners in under-resourced communities to sustain engagement through flexible and affordable access [12]. Recent studies suggest that LLMs may extend this resilience-building role, offering opportunities for continued learning even when institutional support is weakened [8,28]. Yet despite increasing evidence of their pedagogical benefits, little is known about how LLMs influence learners' aspirations, particularly for marginalized populations whose educational and career goals are most vulnerable to socio-political crises.

3   Methodology

We surveyed 136 women in Afghanistan whose educational and career aspirations are constrained by ongoing political restrictions. To ensure contextual fit, the Hope Scale [1] was revised to better align with programming education and to account for the lived experiences of learners in Afghanistan. The study received approval from the Ethical Review Board (ERB) of the Faculty of Mathematics and Computer Science at Saarland University (No. 23-10-7), and all participants provided informed consent.

3.1   Participants

Our study included 136 women who were studying programming online during a period of formal educational and employment restrictions. Participants ranged in age from 18 to 40 years (M = 22.8, SD = 3.41), reflecting a predominantly young female cohort. Table 1 provides a comprehensive demographic overview of the survey participants.

Table 1. Demographics of study participants.

Question	Response (Count, %)	
Age Group	18–21	47 (35%)
	22–25	65 (48%)
	26+	24 (17%)
Education Completed	Bachelor's Degree	63 (46%)
	High School	58 (43%)
	Other	15 (11%)
Internet Connection	Mobile Data	85 (62%)
	Satellite	20 (15%)
	DSL	19 (14%)
	Other	12 (9%)

3.2   Data Collection

Following the ERB approval, we adapted the Hope Scale [1] to reflect the programming context. The adaptation was reviewed by the third author, who is a specialist in the use of such scales in research contexts. Both the original and adapted items are listed in Table 4 in the Appendix. To ensure accessibility, the items were translated into Persian, and the scale was piloted with 10 participants before the main survey.

Participants were recruited through three NGOs that support women in online programming education, enabling safe access to a population that is otherwise hard to reach. The adapted survey was distributed via Google Forms to 225 potential participants, yielding 136 complete responses (a response rate of ≈60%). To evaluate the understandability and relevance of the adapted items to the programming context, we conducted a follow-up post-survey with 20 randomly selected participants.

3.3   Data Analysis

We assessed the reliability of the adapted scale using Cronbach's alpha [21]. Following Hansen et al. [22], responses were scored on a 5-point Likert scale, producing overall aspiration scores as well as subscale scores for *Agency* and *Avenues* (corresponding to the Hope Scale's "agency" and "pathways" components). To explore differences across groups, we applied one-way ANOVA [23], examining whether factors such as education level, age, or access to LLMs influenced aspiration scores.

4   Results

4.1   The Adapted Hope Scale as a Feasible Metric for Measuring Educational Aspirations

The adapted Hope Scale consisted of eight core items, four measuring *Agency* and four measuring *Avenues* (corresponding to the "pathways" component in the original scale), as well as four filler items excluded from analysis (see Table 4). To improve clarity for the target population, responses were collected using a 5-point Likert scale, rather than the 6-point version used by [22] or the original 8-point version. Total aspiration scores ranged from 8 (lowest) to 40 (highest), with subscale scores ranging from 4 to 20.

To assess internal consistency, we calculated Cronbach's alpha [21]. The overall scale demonstrated good reliability ($\alpha = 0.78$). The *Avenues* subscale, reflecting respondents' perceived ability to identify multiple routes toward achieving goals, yielded an alpha of 0.68. The *Agency* subscale, capturing determination and self-belief in pursuing goals, scored 0.67. Although these are slightly below the conventional 0.70 threshold, methodological reviews suggest they may still be acceptable in exploratory research and in challenging field contexts [24].

Figure 1 illustrates the distribution of aspiration and subscale scores. Distributions were moderately skewed toward higher values, suggesting that many participants reported elevated aspiration levels. Table 2 supports these observations by providing descriptive statistics: the mean aspiration score was 32.7 ($SD = 3.9$), with mean subscale scores of 16.1 ($SD = 2.5$) for *Agency* and 16.6 ($SD = 2.1$) for *Avenues*. Results from the post-survey, administered to a random sample of 20 participants, indicate that the adapted questions were

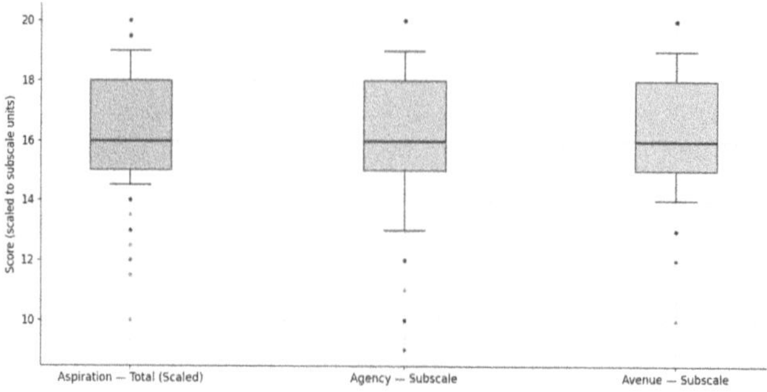

Fig. 1. The box plots summarize score distributions for Aspiration and its subscales (*Agency* and *Avenues*). Each box represents the interquartile range (25th-75th percentiles) with the median marked by the line inside. Whiskers extend to the 10th and 90th percentiles.

largely understandable and relevant. Participants rated each item individually, and 91.2% reported fully understanding the questions, while 72% rated them relevant to their field of study.

Table 2. Descriptive statistics of Aspiration and subscale scores.

Statistic	Aspiration (Total)	Agency	Avenues
Count	136	136	136
Mean	32.7	16.1	16.6
SD	3.9	2.5	2.1
Min	20	9	10
25%	30	15	15
Median	32	16	16
75%	36	18	18
Max	40	20	20

4.2 Marginal Impact of LLMs on Educational Aspirations

We investigated whether access to Large Language Models (LLMs) and demographic factors were associated with differences in aspiration-related scores. Demographic variables such as age and education level showed no significant effects ($p = .593$ and $p = .378$, respectively). A one-way ANOVA was conducted to compare scores for the *Agency* subscale, *Avenues* subscale, and overall Aspiration between participants with and without LLM access. As shown in Table 3, no statistically significant differences were observed. Agency scores did not differ between groups ($p = .423$), nor did overall aspiration scores ($p = .129$). However, the Avenues subscale approached marginal significance ($p = .056$), suggesting a possible trend toward broader perceptions of pathways among participants with LLM access. Although this suggests a positive effect of LLM access on aspiration, the results should be interpreted with caution, as the overall aspiration scores did not reach statistical significance.

Table 3. One-way ANOVA results for Aspiration-related scores by LLM access group.

Scale	Group	Mean (SD)	N
Agency	Don't have access	15.9 (2.6)	63
	Have access	16.3 (2.4)	73
		$F\ (p) = 0.65\ (0.423)$	
Avenues	Don't have access	16.3 (2.0)	63
	Have access	16.9 (2.1)	73
		$F\ (p) = 3.70\ (\mathbf{0.056})$	
Aspiration	Don't have access	32.2 (3.9)	63
	Have access	33.2 (3.9)	73
		$F\ (p) = 2.34\ (0.129)$	

SD = standard deviation; N = group size; F (p) = ANOVA F statistic (p-value).

p < 0.05 is considered statistically significant, **p**< 0.1 is considered marginally significant.

To provide additional context, we also examined participants' reported usage of LLMs. Among those with access, usage frequency ranged from several times a day to occasional task-specific use. Most applied LLMs to programming tasks such as learning new concepts, writing or improving code, and debugging, while others reported using them for study planning, clarifying difficult topics, and exploring supplementary resources.

5 Discussion

This study demonstrates the feasibility of adapting Snyder's Hope Scale as a metric for aspirations in socio-politically unstable contexts. The adapted scale showed good reliability, and participants found it understandable and relevant, which supports its use in measuring educational aspirations. Our findings nuance the role of technology, particularly Large Language Models (LLMs), in shaping aspirations. While access to LLMs was not associated with overall aspiration levels, we observed a marginally significant association with the *Avenues* subscale. This suggests that LLMs may function as a facilitator, expanding learners' perception of possible routes to achieving their aspirations. Such an interpretation is consistent with prior work positioning technology as an amplifier of existing capacities in international development [2,3].

These insights align with broader scholarly calls to shift technology design from meeting basic needs toward actively supporting user aspirations [2]. The adapted Hope Scale provides a metric for understanding user aspirations, enabling researchers and practitioners to evaluate whether technological interventions reinforce longer-term capacities to aspire, rather than merely addressing immediate educational challenges. Beyond educational contexts, aspiration-based assessments could inform technological interventions in employment and mental health. For instance, in employment support programs such as Harambee[1], aspiration assessments could guide personalized mentorship for those with limited perceived *Avenues* or motivational reinforcement for those with lower *Agency*. Similarly, in digital mental health, prior research has shown that mental states shape how individuals envision their futures [25]; integrating the Hope Scale into such platforms could enable dynamic tracking of *Agency* to provide timely, personalized encouragement.

At the same time, integrating LLMs into education raises important challenges. Recent studies have identified concerns around over-reliance on LLM-generated content, diminished critical thinking, the propagation of misinformation, and the reinforcement of biases embedded in models [27]. Considering these challenges is essential while utilizing LLMs to support learners' aspirations equitably.

Finally, we acknowledge a limitation of this study. While the adapted Hope Scale demonstrated reliability, it primarily captures the cognitive dimensions of aspiration—*Agency* and *Avenues*—and may not fully capture the socio-environmental factors emphasized in development studies and HCI4D, such as community support and institutional barriers [2,11]. Future research should therefore complement this scale with methodological approaches that situate aspirations within broader social and political contexts.

6   Conclusion

This study shows that Snyder's Hope Scale, when adapted to the programming context, is a feasible metric for understanding learners' aspirations among women in socio-politically unstable settings. While overall aspiration levels were not affected by LLM access, a marginal effect on the *Avenues* subscale suggests that such technologies may expand learners' perceived pathways to achieving their long-term goals. These findings underscore the importance of aspiration-based metrics in evaluating technological interventions and designing technologies that support not only immediate learning but also long-term educational and career aspirations. Future work should examine longitudinal effects, extend the adapted scale to other marginalized populations, and integrate qualitative methods to capture the broader socio-environmental dimensions of aspiration.

Acknowledgments. IW and VC are supported by funding from the Alexander von Humboldt Foundation and its founder, the German Federal Ministry of Education and Research.

---

[1] https://www.harambee.co.za/.

Appendix

Table 4. Hope scale questions modified for programming. Items marked with [†] are fillers; as in the traditional scale, they are not scored and are excluded from analysis.

Subscale	Programming-Adapted Question	Original Hope Scale Question
Hope scale Avenues	I can think of many ways to get out of debugging a programming problem.	I can think of many ways to get out of a jam.
Hope scale Agency	I energetically pursue my goals about programming.	I energetically pursue my goals.
Hope scale[†]	Working on a computer screen is tiring most of the time.	I feel tired most of the time.
Hope scale Avenues	There are lots of ways around any programming problem.	There are lots of ways around any problem.
Hope scale[†]	I give up quickly when I find a new idea.	I am easily drawn into an argument.
Hope scale Avenues	I can think of many ways to get the things that are most important to me in programming.	I can think of many ways to get the things in life that are most important to me.
Hope scale[†]	I worry about my poor posture while programming.	I worry about my health.
Hope scale Avenues	Even when others get discouraged, I know I can find a way to solve a programming problem.	Even when others get discouraged, I know I can find a way to solve the problem.
Hope scale Agency	My past programming experiences have prepared me well for my future.	My past experiences have prepared me well for my future.
Hope scale Agency	I've been pretty successful in life as a programmer.	I've been pretty successful in life.
Hope scale[†]	I usually find myself worrying about my programming assignments.	I usually find myself worrying about something.
Hope scale Agency	I meet the goals that I set for myself as a programmer.	I meet the goals that I set for myself.

Response Options: Responses were recorded on a five-point Likert scale — 1 = Strongly Disagree, 2 = Disagree, 3 = Neither Agree nor Disagree, 4 = Agree, 5). = Strongly Agree.

References

1. Snyder, C.R., et al.: The will and the ways: development and validation of an individual-differences measure of hope. J. Pers. Soc. Psychol. **60**(4), 570 (1991)
2. Toyama, K.: From needs to aspirations in information technology for development. Inf. Technol. Dev. **24**(1), 15–36 (2018)
3. Toyama, K.: Technology as amplifier in international development. In: Proceedings of the 2011 iConference, pp. 75–82. ACM (2011)
4. Donner, J.: After access: Inclusion, development, and a more mobile Internet. MIT Press, Cambridge (2015)
5. Thakkar, D., Kumar, N., Sambasivan, N.: Towards an AI-powered future that works for vocational workers. In: Proceedings of the 2020 CHI Conference on Human Factors in Computing Systems, pp. 1–13 (2020)
6. Cannanure, V.K.: DIA: Supporting Teacher Professional Development in Low-Infrastructure Settings. Ph. D. Dissertation. Carnegie Mellon University (2023)
7. Cannanure, V.K., et al.: I'm fine where I am, but I want to do more: exploring teacher aspirations in rural Côte d'Ivoire. In: Proceedings of the 3rd ACM SIGCAS Conference on Computing and Sustainable Societies, pp. 1–12 (2020)
8. Behmanush, H., Akhtari, F., Nooripour, R., Weber, I., Cannanure, V.K.: Online learning and GenAI: supporting women's aspirations amid socio-political instability in Afghanistan. In: Proceedings of the ACM SIGCAS/SIGCHI Conference on Computing and Sustainable Societies (COMPASS 2025). ACM (2025). https://doi.org/10.1145/3715335.3735479
9. Behmanush, H.: Supporting marginalized learners with GenAI. In: Proceedings of the AAAI/ACM Conference on AI, Ethics, and Society, vol. 8(3), pp. 2848–2849 (2025)
10. Schoon, I., Parsons, S.: Teenage aspirations for future careers and occupational outcomes. J. Vocat. Behav. **60**(2), 262–288 (2002)
11. Kumar, N.: Facebook for self-empowerment? a study of facebook adoption in urban India. New Media & Soc. **16**(7), 1122–1137 (2014)
12. Ally, M., Samaka, M.: Open education resources and mobile technology to narrow the learning divide. Inter. Rev. Res. Open Distribut. Learn. **14**(2), 14–27 (2013)
13. OpenAI: ChatGPT. https://openai.com/research/chatgpt, Accessed 05 June 2024
14. Lybbert, T.J., Wydick, B.: Hope as Aspirations, Agency, and Pathways. NBER Working Paper No. 22661. National Bureau of Economic Research, Cambridge, MA (2016). https://doi.org/10.3386/w22661
15. Kasneci, E., et al.: ChatGPT for good? on opportunities and challenges of large language models for education. Learn. Individ. Differ. **103**, 102274 (2023)
16. Dai, C.P., Ke, F.: Educational applications of artificial intelligence in simulation-based learning: a systematic mapping review. Comput. Educ. Artifi. Intell. **3**, 100087 (2022)
17. Rudolph, J., Tan, S., Tan, S.: ChatGPT: bullshit spewer or the end of traditional assessments in higher education? J. Appli. Learn. Teach. **6**(1), 342–363 (2023)
18. Wang, S., et al.: When adaptive learning is effective learning: comparison of an adaptive learning system to teacher-led instruction. Interact. Learn. Environ. **31**(2), 793–803 (2023)
19. Chan, C.K.Y., Lee, K.K.W.: The AI generation gap: Are Gen Z students more interested in adopting generative AI such as ChatGPT in teaching and learning than their Gen X and millennial generation teachers? Smart Learn. Environ. **10**(1), 60 (2023)

20. Reich, J.: Failure to disrupt: Why technology alone can't transform education. Harvard University Press, Cambridge (2020)
21. Boateng, G.O., Neilands, T.B., Frongillo, E.A., Melgar-Quiñonez, H.R., Young, S.L.: Best practices for developing and validating scales for health, social, and behavioral research: A primer. Front. Public Health **6**, 149 (2018)
22. Hansen, C.H., Lees, S., Kapiga, S., Seeley, J., Barnett, T.: Measuring hope amongst Tanzanian women who participate in microfinance: an evaluation of the Snyder hope scale. Glob. Public Health **15**(3), 402–413 (2020)
23. Pandey, N., Srivastava, S.: Measurement of level of hope among institutional and non-institutional elderly: a comparative study. Turkish Online J. Qualitative Inquiry **12**(7) (2021)
24. Taber, K.S.: The use of Cronbach's alpha when developing and reporting research instruments in science education. Res. Sci. Educ. **48**(6), 1273–1296 (2016). https://doi.org/10.1007/s11165-016-9602-2
25. Pendse, S.R., et al.: Mental health in the global south: challenges and opportunities in HCI for development. In: Proceedings of the 2nd ACM SIGCAS Conference on Computing and Sustainable Societies, pp. 22–36 (2019)
26. La Ferrara, E.: Presidential address: aspirations, social norms, and development. J. Euro. Econ. Associa. **17**(6), 1687–1722 (2019). https://doi.org/10.1093/jeea/jvz057
27. Harvey, E., Koenecke, A., Kizilcec, R.F.: "Don't forget the teachers": towards an educator-centered understanding of harms from large language models in education. In: Proceedings of the 2025 CHI Conference on Human Factors in Computing Systems, pp. 1–19 (2025)
28. Lecce, A.: Reflections on the implications of artificial intelligence in inclusive education. In: Palomba, F., Gravino, C. (eds.) Artificial Intelligence with and for Learning Sciences. Past, Present, and Future Horizons. WAILS 2024. LNCS, vol. 14545, Springer, Cham (2024). https://doi.org/10.1007/978-3-031-57402-3_4 (2024)

Inclusion as Embodiment: Towards an Integrated Paradigm Between Embodied Education, Inclusive Pedagogy and Artificial Intelligence

Riccardo Sebastiani[1]([envelope]) [iD], Antonio Cuccaro[2] [iD], Chiara Gentilozzi[3] [iD],
and Sara Pellegrini[1] [iD]

[1] Link Campus University, Rome, Italy
r.sebastiani@unilink.it
[2] Niccolò Cusano Telematic University, Rome, Italy
[3] University of Macerata, Macerata, Italy

Abstract. This contribution aims to promote reflection, starting from the perception of educational and social inclusion, with regard to the possible implications and orientations deriving from the Embodied Cognition (EC) paradigm, its operational application, namely Embodied Education, and the prospects offered by Artificial Intelligence (AI) for the design of educational environments, both physical and digital, equitable and participatory [1]. Starting from the analysis of the results of a questionnaire administered to 202 teachers working in Italian schools that are heterogeneous in terms of educational level and geographical distribution, the work attempts to provide a realistic and problematised snapshot of the current situation: inclusion, recognised as an essential value and a systemic objective, is at the same time perceived as 'unfinished' in everyday practice. The interpretative analysis reveals a possible convergence with the Embodied Cognition paradigm: if it is true, in fact, that the phenomenon of learning is a construction of embodied, situated, relational meaning, inclusion cannot be conceived as an add-on or marginal accommodation, but as a fundamental dimension of teaching practice and action. In this sense, AI can be understood as a possible facilitator of enabling processes, responding to the need for adaptation and accessibility not only in teaching but also in multimodal school governance, staff training and the monitoring of participatory practices.

Keywords: Inclusion · Embodied Cognition · Embodied Education · Inclusive Pedagogy · Artificial Intelligence

1 Introduction

Although deeply rooted in Italy, educational and social inclusion faces significant challenges in its daily implementation [2]. In classrooms, inclusive processes encounter obstacles such as large class sizes, compressed teaching times, fragmented resources and expertise, and pressures linked to assessment and accountability. The most frequent barriers are primarily cultural and professional [3]: stereotypical representations of some student groups, difficulties in designing lessons for all without resorting to separate pathways, and methodological gaps in multimodal and cooperative teaching, all within weak organisational mechanisms [4–6]. In this complex scenario, teachers must make delicate choices: inclusive processes require educational strategies and content to be prioritised in order to promote learning [...] combined with methodological and organisational measures necessary for real integration [7].

Beyond cognitive processes, schools must build relationships grounded in proximity and mutual care, contributing to an extended mind that integrates body, emotions, otherness, artefacts and cultural devices, thereby supporting respect for difference [8]. Embodied Cognition (EC) offers a radical rethinking of learning: if thought is shaped through bodily action, perception, manipulation of artefacts and social participation, inclusion must also be embodied. Gestures, postures, objects and spaces become mediating elements that support access to meaning for all students [9, 10]. Research on EC-based practices highlights benefits for memory, conceptualisation, joint attention, emotional regulation, engagement and transfer [11–14].

Valuing diversity as a resource and designing for all [15, 16] means understanding inclusion as a recombinatory process that enables individuals to find their place within a system capable of recognising personal characteristics and pace. This requires leveraging environmental and physical dimensions to expand classroom potential and create accessible learning environments, shifting from transmission to the construction of experiences aligned with a 4E framework: embodied, embedded, enacted and extended [17–19].

Within this context, our survey, conducted with 202 teachers, yielded four key indicators: a) perceptions of inclusion are generally positive but incomplete, suggesting uneven diffusion of good practices; b) implicit prejudices and training gaps emerge as central obstacles, with explicit requests for concrete methodologies; c) the groups perceived as most vulnerable are students with disabilities and those with a migrant background; d) schools are recognised as key agents of change, implying internal planning and organisational responsibility within a whole-school approach [20]. EC may bridge inclusive sensitivity and effective teaching practices, reducing the gap between declared and experienced inclusion [8]; similarly, Artificial Intelligence (AI) can expand design possibilities and support monitoring within accessible learning environments, provided it does not replace teaching professionalism [21].

2 Theoretical Framework of the Research

The theoretical Framework Rests on Three Main pillars and a cross-cutting axis. The core concepts are: a) Embodied Cognition [11–22], which reconceives learning as embodied and situated; b) Embodied Education [26–28], which operationalises EC into classroom strategies; c) Inclusive Pedagogy, which orients design toward universality and participation [16, 26, 27]. The transversal element is Artificial Intelligence in education [28–30], conceived not as an autonomous actor but as an instrumental system that can support embodied-inclusive design when appropriately governed.

2.1 Embodied Cognition (EC) and Embodied Education

EC Embodied Cognition (EC) overturns the classical computational view of the mind, positing that conceptualisation, language and reasoning are grounded in sensorimotor systems [11–31]. Neuroscientific evidence shows that abstract understanding relies on motor activation, action verbs engage motor and premotor cortices, and that perceiving others' actions triggers embodied simulation [32, 33]. Thought is therefore situated: meaning emerges from organism–environment interactions, mediated by manipulable artefacts and social coordination processes such as joint attention, turn-taking and co-action [34]. Gesture, posture, spatial movement, activity rhythms and the organisation of learning environments must thus be considered constitutive components of learning.

This perspective has generated a wide repertoire of embodied educational practices, including gestural explanation and restitution [12], co-manipulation of objects for mathematical and scientific reasoning [13, 36, 37], conceptual walks and spatial floor maps for geometric abstraction, dramatization and role-play for linguistic and intercultural learning, and bodily routines for emotional regulation and shared attention [14].

These practices function as cognitive devices: they guide attention when bodily engagement aligns with target concepts [38]; externalise reasoning in visuospatial and tactile-kinesthetic forms, facilitating the transition from concrete action to abstraction [39, 40]; multiply representational pathways, gestures, manipulations, spatial patterns, and deepen processing [13, 41]; and promote social learning through coordination, negotiation and co-regulation [42].

2.2 Inclusive Pedagogy and Artificial Intelligence in Education (AIED)

Florian and colleagues reconceptualise inclusive pedagogy beyond differentiation, promoting teaching for all learners within a shared classroom environment [16, 43], in line with Universal Design for Learning. Diversity is treated as a generative resource, with languages, experiences and expressive forms enriching collective meaning-making [43]. Inclusion is therefore assessed not only through individual performance but through participation, agency and interaction quality. This perspective requires widening access to disciplinary content through multiple sensory, cognitive and expressive channels [13].

Within this framework, Artificial Intelligence can act as a reflective amplifier of embodied and inclusive practices, supporting, rather than replacing, teachers' professional judgement. Promising applications include non-invasive monitoring of participation, on-task behaviour and proximity dynamics [44], as well as tools that document interactions, cooperation and intermediate progress, providing multi-level formative feedback [45]. These opportunities require strong ethical safeguards, bias prevention [46], transparency, explainability and privacy protection, together with the principle of non-substitutability. AI governance must remain embedded within pedagogical design to avoid reducing inclusion to technicised metrics that obscure its relational and reflective dimensions.

In this study, AI is examined as a data-driven reflective infrastructure for observation, documentation and adaptive design, aligned with embodied and inclusive pedagogical approaches [13].

3   Research Design and Methodology

The study investigates the relationship between teachers' perceptions of inclusion and possible trajectories of educational innovation. A mixed-methods design was adopted to integrate standardised quantitative indicators (percentages, means, distributions) with qualitative insights derived from teachers' narratives, considered essential for capturing the subjective and contextual nuances of inclusive practice.

3.1   Questionnaire Structure

The Data were collected through a purpose-built online questionnaire structured into six sections:

1. Personal and professional profile (age, gender, years of service, school level, experience in special needs education).
2. Perception of inclusion, measured through Likert-scale items (1 = very low; 5 = very high).
3. Barriers to inclusion (prejudices, lack of training, resource limitations, curricular rigidity, organisational issues), with multiple-choice and comment fields.
4. Vulnerable groups perceived at risk (students with disabilities, migrant background, socio-economic disadvantage, others).
5. Role of schools in promoting inclusion (open and closed items).
6. Perspectives and proposals regarding methodologies, training needs and support tools.

Item formulation was validated by a panel of three experts in special education according to clarity, relevance and neutrality criteria.

3.2   Participants and Data Analysis

The study involved 202 Italian teachers, evenly distributed across the north, centre and south. The sample included 15% preschool, 35% primary, 30% lower secondary and 20% upper secondary teachers; approximately 40% had experience in support teaching. Recruitment followed a voluntary, non-probabilistic logic via institutional mailing lists and professional networks. Although not statistically representative, the sample provides a diverse and informative cross-section of educators.

Data analysis was conducted in three stages. First, descriptive quantitative analyses (percentages, means, frequency distributions) were used to identify general trends and compare responses across variables such as school level and teaching experience. Second, open-ended responses underwent inductive thematic analysis following Braun and Clarke's framework [47]. Two researchers independently coded the data and reconciled discrepancies to ensure reliability. Third, an interpretative–comparative phase aligned quantitative and qualitative results with the theoretical lenses of Embodied Cognition, Embodied Education and Inclusive Pedagogy, enabling the identification of convergences and divergences between teachers' perceptions and current research.

3.3 Validity and Reliability

Three methodological limitations must be considered:

a) Self-selection bias due to voluntary participation, which may over-represent teachers already sensitised to inclusion.
b) Social desirability bias, inherent in self-administered questionnaires.
c) Absence of observational data, preventing triangulation with classroom practices.

Although AI-supported analysis was not applied, the study reflects on the potential of AI-based classifiers and natural language processing to enhance transparency and reliability in qualitative coding without replacing human interpretation. Several teachers explicitly requested digital tools to document inclusive practices and monitor participation elements that informed the conceptual treatment of AI as a reflective infrastructure within embodied and inclusive pedagogies.

The full questionnaire is provided in Appendix A.A.

4 Discussion of the Data

The average inclusion rating is 3.4 out of 5, indicating a positive yet moderate perception of school inclusiveness. Teachers frequently noted in their open responses that "the will is there, but practices do not always follow", pointing to a clear implementation gap [48], where declared principles do not automatically translate into effective action. This is reflected in the distribution of responses: most teachers fall within the medium or upper–medium range (70 at level 3, 85 at level 4, 27 at level 5), while only 20 perceive very low inclusion levels. This suggests widespread awareness of the importance of inclusion yet confirms the notion of an "unfinished" inclusion, more aspirational than consolidated, consistent with Florian's view of inclusion as an evolving, practice-dependent process [43].

The barriers reported by teachers clarify this partial enactment. Prejudice is the most frequently cited obstacle (120 reports), followed by training deficiencies (95), lack of resources (80) and weak institutional policies (60). This hierarchy highlights the primacy of cultural and professional factors over structural constraints. The persistence of stereotypes hampers the full realisation of inclusive practices, while the strong demand for professional development underscores the need to strengthen teachers' methodological, ethical and value-oriented competence. Research on the ethics of AI in education similarly stresses that technological innovation is ineffective without a conscious pedagogical framework and sustained training [45]. Teachers identify students with disabilities (150 reports) and those with a migrant background (130) as the groups most at risk, followed by learners with socio-economic disadvantages (60) and other minorities (25). This pattern confirms a dual vulnerability, accessibility for students with disabilities and linguistic–cultural inclusion for migrants, highlighting the need for integrated pedagogical and policy responses [49].

Across both quantitative and qualitative data, schools emerge as the primary agents of inclusion. In line with Florian and Black-Hawkins' conception of teaching for "everyone in everyone's classroom" [43], schools are viewed not only as instructional settings but as key environments for fostering belonging, cooperation and mutual recognition. This perspective aligns with whole-school approaches in which inclusion is an institutional responsibility rather than the initiative of individual teachers [48].

5   Results

Quantitative data indicate that most teachers position their school at medium or medium–high inclusion levels: 70 respondents selected level 3, 85 levels 4 and 27 level 5, while only 20 placed their context at the lowest levels. This pattern suggests that inclusion is widely recognised as a shared value yet still perceived as only partially realised, consistent with Florian's view of inclusion as a dynamic process requiring continuous negotiation [43] and with Ainscow's emphasis on the challenge of translating principles into organisational and teaching practices that ensure full participation [48].

The barriers reported by teachers help illuminate this implementation gap. The most frequently cited obstacles are prejudice (120 reports), insufficient training (95), limited resources (80) and weak institutional policies (60). The prominence of attitudinal resistance aligns with Booth and Ainscow's findings on the pivotal role of prejudice in constraining participation [50], while the strong demand for practical training highlights the need for multimodal, accessible and embodied strategies capable of operationalising inclusive principles in everyday practice [13].

5.1   Vulnerable Groups

Students with disabilities are perceived as the most vulnerable group (150 indications), followed by students with a migrant background (130), those with socio-economic disadvantage (60) and other minority groups (25). This reflects the dual challenge of Italian inclusion policies [49]: ensuring accessibility for students with disabilities and promoting linguistic–cultural participation for migrant students. Embodied and multimodal practices appear capable of supporting both, reducing cognitive-linguistic barriers [39] and fostering social belonging [38].

5.2   School as a Central Actor

Qualitative responses emphasise the school as the primary context for inclusion, more than families or local authorities. Teachers highlight the school's responsibility in building belonging and recognition processes, confirming inclusion as a collective commitment [51]. Overall, results show that inclusion is widely acknowledged yet still "unfinished": cultural and professional barriers persist, and disability and migration emerge as the main areas of vulnerability. At the same time, teachers express confidence in schools as agents of change and request concrete, applicable training.

These elements support the need for embodied, cooperative and inclusive teaching strategies that broaden access to content and transform diversity into a resource. Study limitations include the voluntary, non-representative sample, the self-reported nature of the data, and the absence of AI-supported coding. Future research should involve larger samples, longitudinal designs and AI-assisted analyses to enhance reliability (Tables 1 and 2).

Table 1. Quantitative Summary of Teachers' Perceptions of Inclusion (N = 202)

Varible	M	SD	95% CI	n	%	Interpretation
Overall Perceived Inclusion (1–5 Likert scale)	3.42	0.86	[3.28, 3.56]	–	–	Moderate-to-high inclusion awareness; inclusion perceived as "in progress" rather than achieved
Level 1 Very Low	–	–	–	5	2.5	Minimal perception of inclusion
Level 2 Low	–	–	–	15	7.4	Early-stage inclusive engagement
Level 3 Medium	–	–	–	70	34.7	Intermediate awareness; partial enactment
Level 4 High	–	–	–	85	42.1	Consistent inclusion practices
Level 5 Very High	–	–	–	27	13.4	Established inclusion culture
Main Barriers to Inclusion	–	–	–	–	–	Cultural and pedagogical barriers outweigh structural ones
Prejudices and Stereotypes	–	–	–	120	59.4	Cultural and attitudinal resistance remains predominant
Training Deficiencies	–	–	–	95	47.0	Indicates the need for ongoing professional development
Resource Shortages	–	–	–	80	39.6	Limited access to material and human resources
Weak Institutional Policies	–	–	–	60	29.7	Inconsistent governance of inclusion processes
Groups Perceived as Most Vulnerable	–	–	–	–	–	Double fragility identified: disability and migration
Students with Disabilities	–	–	–	150	74.3	Highest-risk group; need for structural accessibility
Migrant Students	–	–	–	130	64.4	Cultural–linguistic vulnerability requiring intercultural education

(continued)

Table 1. (*continued*)

Varible	M	SD	95% CI	n	%	Interpretation
Students from Low Socio-Economic Backgrounds	–	–	–	60	29.7	Contextual disadvantage affecting equal opportunities
Other Minorities (e.g., linguistic, ethnic)	–	–	–	25	12.4	Marginal recognition of intersectional vulnerability

Table 2. Descriptive Summary and Measures of Variance

Statistic	Value	Interpretation
Mean Inclusion Score (M)	3.42	Moderate perception of inclusion across respondents
Standard Deviation (SD)	0.86	Moderate dispersion around the mean; indicates variability in perceived inclusiveness
Standard Error (SE)	0.06	Stable estimate of mean reliability
95% Confidence Interval	[3.28, 3.56]	True population means likely lies within this range
Variance (SD2)	0.74	Suggests moderately diverse perceptions among teachers

Note. Data derived from teachers' responses to inclusion perception items (1–5 Likert scale). Percentages are calculated based on valid responses (N = 202).

Overall, quantitative analyses indicate that inclusion is valued but unevenly enacted. Cultural and professional obstacles, prejudices and training gaps, are more pressing than structural limitations such as resources or policies. This confirms an implementation gap consistent with Ainscow (2020) and Florian (2015). Moderate mean scores (M = 3.42; SD = 0.86) and a narrow confidence interval [3.28, 3.56] suggest that teachers commonly view inclusion as a process underway rather than an established reality. Variance (0.74) reflects contextual differences and the coexistence of consolidated practices with areas needing targeted development and systemic support.

6 Bridging Dimensions Between Inclusive Pedagogy, Embodied Cognition and AIED Implementation Perspectives in Inclusive Practices

The survey findings, interpreted within the broader scientific framework, point to interconnected epistemological, methodological, organisational and ethical–technological dimensions. Inclusion should not be conceived as a downstream corrective, but as an emergent property of learning environments designed through multimodal, situated and relational logics. In such contexts, bodies, spaces, artefacts and interactions function as mediators of meaning; and AI, when governed by fairness, transparency and rights protection, can operate as a reflective infrastructure supporting teachers' professional judgement [52].

Teachers report a strong value orientation towards inclusion yet acknowledge persistent challenges in translating this orientation into everyday practice, revealing a marked implementation gap. Addressing this gap requires micro-designs that turn space, time, artefacts and roles into participatory affordances [50]. Embodied Cognition offers an important lens in this regard: it shifts attention from content transmission to the orchestration of cooperative, bodily and situated activities in which meaning is enacted and negotiated collectively [11].

Since cognition is situated and grounded in sensorimotor systems, multimodality becomes essential for conceptual access [53]. Evidence shows that bodily participation enhances comprehension and transfer: co-manipulation supports abstraction in mathematics [39], congruent physical experiences strengthen scientific understanding [38], and iconic gestures facilitate semantic processing [12]. In heterogeneous classrooms, such practices externalise reasoning, reduce cognitive load and normalise diversity by limiting exclusive dependence on verbal mediation.

Inclusive pedagogy provides the normative and professional frame for integrating these insights, promoting teaching addressed to all learners within the shared classroom. Embodied Education can function as one of its methodological anchors, offering flexible practices tailored to teachers' skills and contexts. To sustain inclusive processes, these practices must be linked to observable criteria, participation, interaction quality, autonomy, and embedded within iterative cycles of reflection, including peer observation, lesson study and micro-feedback.

6.1 Professional Development and AI-Enhanced Reflective Practice

Teachers require practical training. Evidence from research supports one necessity: implementing professional development pathways anchored to the real classroom and documentation. In this sense, we can identify three fundamental assets: a) Embodied teaching: the design, implementation and evaluation of multimodal practices in different disciplines, with a focus on physicality, cognitive objectives and emotional regulation; b) Inclusion and UDL: systematic mapping of representations, expressions and multiple possibilities for engagement; c) Formative assessment and feedback: participation rubrics (turn-taking, agency, collaboration), short self- and peer- assessments, use of reflective artefacts (logbooks, multimodal portfolios). Training could adopt practice-based methodologies (co-planning, co-teaching, video analysis), supported by professional communities within the school, to stabilise change beyond individual initiatives.

Teachers recognise the potential of AI tools for documenting participation and supporting reflective assessment. Within an embodied–inclusive paradigm, AI can be viewed as a reflective extension of teachers' cognitive processes, translating data into pedagogical insight and reinforcing feedback loops between perception, action and redesign.

AI can support inclusive practices if aligned with ethical requirements: transparency and explainability of outputs [52], regular bias monitoring [46], and strict privacy-by-design approaches consistent with the AI Act (2025) [53].

- Promising applications include:
- Participation analytics (e.g., TeachFX): documenting speaking patterns and classroom interaction [54];
- Learning analytics (Microsoft Education Insights, Moodle LA): identifying recurrent interaction trends;
- AI prompting systems (Khanmigo, Practice Sets) offering adaptive task variations.
- Documentation tools (e.g., Seesaw) organising digital artefacts and providing multimodal participation maps;
- Targeted process tools (e.g., Reading Progress/Coach) under teacher control [57].

These systems must be framed within strong governance to avoid reducing inclusion to standardised metrics and losing its relational essence [46]. AI can thus become an enabling infrastructure for design, observation and redesign cycles aligned with design-based research [58].

6.2 Organizational, Evaluative and Equity Dimensions of Inclusive Practice

Bridging the gap between perceived and enacted inclusion requires schools to operate as ecologies of participation, where spaces, time, roles and governance structures jointly create conditions for cooperative learning. Research highlights the importance of flexible, reconfigurable environments with manipulable materials [60], reorganised teaching times that support cycles of exploration and reflection [61], and cooperative roles that foster positive interdependence, a key condition for authentic inclusion [62]. At governance level, a coherent Embodied Cognition–based curriculum should articulate shared practices and observation criteria [8, 59].

Evaluating inclusion within such ecologies demands attention to both social participation and embodied engagement. Multimodal education studies show that gestures, movement and spatial actions constitute core components of meaning-making [63]. Key indicators therefore include diversity of representations, transitions between concrete and abstract reasoning, and emotional–motivational dimensions such as self-regulation, persistence and self-efficacy. Cognitive outcomes must be interpreted in relation to enacted practices, privileging transferability and adaptability over immediate performance [64].

Finally, broadening the scope of inclusion requires avoiding reliance on predetermined categories of vulnerability. While disability and migration emerged as the most frequently identified risks in the survey, an intersectional perspective reveals how inequalities arise from the interplay of gender, socioeconomic status, linguistic background and neurodiversity. Originating in legal and social theory, intersectionality now informs educational research by showing how multiple vulnerabilities interact and shape learning opportunities [65].

7 Conclusions

The transition from inclusion as a normative statement to inclusion as everyday practice requires a strategic vision that integrates organisational, educational and professional dimensions [66]. Reinterpreting the three-year Educational Plan (PTOF) and the annual Inclusion Plan (PI) through an Embodied Cognition lens can represent a first level of formalisation, clarifying the principles underpinning inclusive practice and offering guidance for school policies capable of sustaining long-term pedagogical innovation [67].

At the methodological level, building a structured repertoire of embodied practices across disciplines and school levels, ensuring continuity between transitions, can foster more systematic diffusion and transferability. Professional development also plays a central role: alongside continuous training, the systematic use of Lesson Study can transform observation into shared professional knowledge [68]. Internal micro-credentials on Embodied Education, Universal Design for Learning and formative assessment may provide a modular, agile pathway to support teachers' lifelong learning [69].

Spatial organisation, increasingly oriented toward flexible and modular design, must be accompanied by teaching practices capable of harnessing the pedagogical potential of such environments. Learning spaces function as powerful mediators and can strengthen or weaken inclusive processes [70]. Likewise, students must be recognised as active agents, co-constructors of meaning and contributors to a participatory culture, rather than passive recipients of knowledge [71].

Turning inclusion into lived experience requires an epistemological and organisational shift. Embodied Cognition offers the scientific basis for viewing learning as situated, sensorimotor and environmentally mediated [31], while Embodied Education translates this perspective into scalable, accessible practices that provide multiple access points and transform diversity into a resource [72]. Within this framework, Artificial Intelligence can function as a reflective infrastructure for documentation, design and continuous improvement, supporting instructional processes when integrated into robust pedagogical and ethical frameworks [52–73].

AI, grounded in embodied and inclusive paradigms, should not be considered an external add-on but a reflective support that reinforces the ethical and relational core of teaching. The convergence of embodied pedagogy, inclusive practices and AI can thus generate a synergistic framework for educational innovation, provided that human agency, ethics and professional judgement remain central.

Ultimately, the transformative power of inclusion begins with the teacher's own body: a body that lives, relates and inhabits space as both text and context, shaping and being shaped by the educational environment. A possible body, within a school of possibilities.

Disclosure of Interests. The authors have no competing interests to declare that are relevant to the content of this article.

Appendix: Teacher Questionnaire on the Perception of Inclusion

This appendix forms part of the supplementary materials and reports the full questionnaire used in the study.

Purpose: The instrument aimed to examine teachers' perceptions of inclusion in Italian schools and to gather insights on strategies, tools and methodologies to enhance inclusive practices in line with embodied and reflective approaches.

Structure: The questionnaire comprised closed- and open-ended items organised into six sections:

Demographic and Professional Data: Age, gender, years of service, school level (pre-primary, primary, lower secondary, upper secondary). Indication of any experience in special education or support teaching.

Perceived Level of Inclusion: Ten items rated on a five-point Likert scale (1 = very low to 5 = very high). Example item: "The school I work in promotes inclusion as a shared and systemic value."

Barriers to Inclusion: Multiple-choice question listing potential barriers such as prejudice, lack of training, lack of resources, organisational rigidity, and policy gaps, with an open space for additional comments.

Vulnerable Groups: Identification of student groups perceived as most at risk of exclusion: students with disabilities, migrants, students from disadvantaged socio-economic backgrounds, and other minorities.

Role of the School in Inclusion: Items exploring teachers' perception of the school as a key agent of inclusive change. Example item: "Inclusion depends primarily on school organisation and staff cooperation rather than individual effort."

Proposals and Open Comments: Open-end section inviting suggestions concerning methodologies, professional development, and digital or analytical tools that could support inclusive practices. Several teachers explicitly proposed the use of AI-based instruments for documentation, reflection, and monitoring of participatory processes.

Validation

The questionnaire was validated by a panel of three experts in Special Pedagogy, who reviewed all items for clarity, relevance, and neutrality. Minor revisions were introduced following their recommendations to enhance content validity.

Administration and Response Rate

The survey was administered online between February and May 2025 via institutional mailing lists and professional networks. A total of 202 teachers participated, representing schools across northern, central, and southern Italy, ensuring a diverse yet non-probabilistic sample.

References

1. Emili, E., Gaggioli, C.: Ambienti digitali inclusivi/Digital and inclusive environment. Form@re **17**(1), 49–67 (2017)
2. Ianes, D., Zagni, B., Zambotti, F., Cramerotti, S., Franch, S.: Inclusione scolastica e sociale: un valore irrinunciabile. Quanto è fattibile, efficace e condivisa nei suoi valori. Ital. J. Spec. Educ. Incl. **10** (2024)
3. Russo, P.: Lo stato dell'inclusione scolastica in Italia. Dai principi normativi alla qualità dei risultati. Anicia Editore, Roma (s.d.)
4. Aiello, P., Di Gennaro, D.C., Girelli, L., Olley, J.G.: Inclusione e atteggiamenti dei docenti verso gli studenti con disturbo dello spettro autistico: suggestioni da uno studio pilota. Formazione & insegnamento **16**(1), 175–188 (2018)
5. Taddei, A.: L'inclusione scolastica in "trincea": la difficile sfida della scuola secondaria. Nuova Secondaria **7**, 42–52 (2018)
6. Ianes, D., Zagni, B.: Inclusione scolastica in Italia, inclusioscetticismo, difficoltà epistemologiche e metodologiche della ricerca. Ital. J. Spec. Educ. Incl. **12**(1), 351–363 (2024)
7. Cottini, L.: Educazione e riabilitazione del bambino autistico. Carocci, Roma (2002)
8. Gomez Paloma, F., Damiani, P.: Cognizione corporea, competenze integrate e formazione dei docenti. I tre volti dell'Embodied Cognitive Science per una scuola inclusiva. Edizioni Centro Studi Erickson, Trento (2015)
9. Pastena, N., D'Anna, C., Gomez Paloma, F., Damiani, P.: Disturbi specifici di apprendimento ed embodied cognitive science dalla biogenesi all'educazione. L'integrazione scolastica e sociale **14**, 263–279 (2015)
10. Brembilla, M.: Embodied cognition e sfide educative: per una pratica creativa e trasformativa. J. Incl. Methodol. Technol. Learn. Teach. **5**(2) (2025)
11. Barsalou, L.W.: Grounded cognition. Annu. Rev. Psychol. **59**, 617–645 (2008). https://doi.org/10.1146/annurev.psych.59.103006.093639
12. Goldin-Meadow, S.: Learning through gesture. Wiley Interdisc. Rev. Cogn. Sci. **2**(6), 595–607 (2011)
13. Lindgren, R., Johnson-Glenberg, M.: Emboldened by embodiment: six precepts for research on embodied learning and mixed reality. Educ. Res. **42**(8), 445–452 (2013). https://doi.org/10.3102/0013189X13511661
14. Shapiro, L., Stolz, S.A.: Embodied cognition and its significance for education. Theory Res. Educ. **17**(1), 19–39 (2019)
15. Florian, L., Black-Hawkins, K.: Exploring inclusive pedagogy. Br. Edu. Res. J. **37**(5), 813–828 (2011). https://doi.org/10.1080/01411926.2010.501096
16. Florian, L.: Inclusive pedagogy: a transformative approach to individual differences but can it help reduce educational inequalities? Scott. Educ. Rev. **47**(1), 5–14 (2015)
17. Clark, A.: Supersizing the Mind: Embodiment, Action, and Cognitive Extension. Oxford University Press, Oxford (2008)
18. Newen, A., De Bruin, L., Gallagher, S. (eds.): The Oxford Handbook of 4E Cognition. Oxford University Press, Oxford (2018)
19. Murri, S., Patera, S.: Attenzione profonda, iperattenzione e "digital divide cognitivo" intergenerazionale. L'agire competente digitale nella didattica fondata sulla "4E Cognition". J. Incl. Methodol. Technol. Learn. Teach. **5**(2) (2025)
20. Hunt, P., Barrios, L., Telljohann, S.K., Mazyck, D.: A whole school approach: collaborative development of school health policies, processes, and practices. J. Sch. Health **85**(11), 802–809 (2015)

21. Ferrantino, C., Scarano, R.: Formare all'intelligenza artificiale: un progetto-studio con docenti e futuri docenti. Educ. Sci. Soc. **2**, 72–87 (2024)
22. Fuchs, T.: The circularity of the embodied mind. Front. Psychol. **11**, 1707 (2020). https://doi.org/10.3389/fpsyg.2020.01707
23. Paloma, F.G., Tafur, D.: Embodied Cognition. Body, movement and sport for didactics. Ital. J. Educ. Res. **17**, 41–52 (2016)
24. Francesconi, D., Tarozzi, M.: Embodied education and education of the body: the phenomenological perspective. Leib–Leiblichkeit–Embodiment: Pädagogische Perspektiven auf eine Phänomenologie des Leibes, pp. 229–247. Springer Fachmedien Wiesbaden, Wiesbaden (2019)
25. Faella, P., Digennaro, S., Iannaccone, A.: Educational practices in motion: a scoping review of embodied learning approaches in school. Front. Educ. **10** (2025)
26. Sanger, C.S.: Inclusive pedagogy and universal design approaches for Diverse Learning Environments. In: Inclusive Pedagogy and UDL for Educators in Diverse Contexts, pp. 1–15. Springer, Cham (2020)
27. Bocci, F.: Special pedagogy as inclusive pedagogy. An institute between risks and opportunities. Ital. J. Spec. Educ. Incl. **IX**(1), 41–48 (2021). https://doi.org/10.7346/sipes-01-2021-06
28. Holmes, W., et al.: Ethics of AI in education: towards a community-wide framework. Int. J. Artif. Intell. Educ., **32**(3), 504–526 (2022)
29. Du Boulay, B., Mitrovic, A., Yacef, K. (eds.): Handbook of Artificial Intelligence in Education. Edward Elgar Publishing, Cheltenham (2023)
30. Panciroli, C., Rivoltella, P.C.: Artificial intelligence in education: AI literacy, prompting and the artificial conversation hypothesis. Scholè – Rivista di Scienze dell'Educazione **1**, 15– 48 (2024)
31. Wilson, M.: Six views of embodied cognition. Psychon. Bull. Rev. **9**(4), 625–636 (2002). https://doi.org/10.3758/BF03196322
32. Gallese, V., Lakoff, G.: The brain's concepts: the role of the sensory–motor system in conceptual knowledge. Cogn. Neuropsychol. **22**(3–4), 455–479 (2005)
33. Pulvermüller, F.: How neurons make meaning: brain mechanisms for embodied and abstract-symbolic semantics. Trends Cogn. Sci. **17**(9), 458–470 (2013)
34. Roth, W.-M., Jornet, A.: Situated cognition. Wiley Interdisc. Rev. Cogn. Sci. **4**(5), 463–478 (2013). https://doi.org/10.1002/wcs.1242
35. Goldin, C., Katz, L.F.: The Race Between Education and Technology. Harvard University Press (2008)
36. Abrahamson, D.: The future of embodied design for mathematics teaching and learning. Front. Educ. **5**, 147 (2020). https://doi.org/10.3389/feduc.2020.00147
37. Abrahamson, D., Lindgren, R.: Embodiment and embodied design. In: Sawyer, R.K. (ed.) The Cambridge Handbook of the Learning Sciences, pp. 358–376. Cambridge University Press, Cambridge (2014). https://doi.org/10.1017/CBO9781139519526.022
38. Kontra, C., Lyons, D.J., Fischer, S.M., Beilock, S.L.: Physical experience enhances science learning. Psychol. Sci. **26**(6),737–749 (2015)
39. Novack, M.A., Congdon, E.L., Hemani-Lopez, N., Goldin-Meadow, S.: From action to abstraction: using the hands to learn math. Psychol. Sci. **25**(4), 903–910 (2014). https://doi.org/10.1177/0956797613518351
40. Nathan, M.J., Walkington, C.: Grounded and embodied mathematical cognition: promoting mathematical insight and proof using action and language. Cogn. Res. Principles Implications **2**, 9 (2017). https://doi.org/10.1186/s41235-016-0040-5
41. Johnson-Glenberg, M.C., Megowan-Romanowicz, C., Birchfield, D., Savio-Ramos, C.: Effects of embodied learning and digital platform on the retention of physics content: centripetal force. Front. Psychol. **7**, 1819 (2016). https://doi.org/10.3389/fpsyg.2016.01819

42. Johnson-Glenberg, M.C.: Embodied science and mixed reality: how gesture and motion capture affect physics education. Cogn. Res. Principles Implications **2**, 24 (2017)
43. Florian, L., Black-Hawkins, K., Rouse, M.: Achievement and Inclusion in Schools. Routledge, London (2017). https://doi.org/10.4324/9781315623741
44. Holstein, K., McLaren, B.M., Aleven, V.: Student learning benefits of a mixed-reality teacher awareness tool. In: Proceedings of the 2019 CHI Conference on Human Factors in Computing Systems, pp. 1–12. ACM, New York (2019). https://doi.org/10.1145/3290605.3300787
45. Holmes, W., et al.: Artificial Intelligence in Education: Promise and Implications for Teaching and Learning. UNESCO Publishing, Paris (2022). https://doi.org/10.54675/AIED-UNESCO 2022
46. Williamson, B., Eynon, R.: Historical threads, missing links, and future directions in AI in education. Learn. Media Technol. **45**(3), 223–235 (2020). https://doi.org/10.1080/17439884.2020.1798995
47. Braun, V., Clarke, V.: Using thematic analysis in psychology. Qual. Res. Psychol. **3**(2), 77–101 (2006)
48. Ainscow, M.: Promoting inclusion and equity in education: lessons from international experiences. Nord. J. Stud. Educ. Policy **6**(1), 7–16 (2020). https://doi.org/10.1080/20020317.2020.1729587
49. Giaconi, C.: Inclusive Education and Community: Pathways and Perspectives. Springer, Cham (2023). https://doi.org/10.1007/978-3-031-14914-1
50. Booth, T., Ainscow, M.: Index for Inclusion: Developing Learning and Participation in Schools. 3rd end. Centre for Studies on Inclusive Education, Bristol (2011)
51. Ainscow, M., Dyson, A., Weiner, S.: From exclusion to inclusion: a review of international literature on ways of responding to students with special educational needs in schools (2012)
52. Encyclopedia of Life Support Systems (EOLSS), UNESCO (2012)
53. Holmes, W., Bialik, M., Fadel, C.: Artificial Intelligence in Education: Promises and Implications for Teaching and Learning. 2nd end. Center for Curriculum Redesign, Boston (2021). https://doi.org/10.13140/RG.2.2.21887.82089
54. European Parliament: EU AI Act: First regulation on artificial intelligence (2025). https://www.europarl.europa.eu/. Accessed 19 Feb 2025
55. Holstein, K., McLaren, B.M., Aleven, V.: Student learning benefits of a mixed-reality teacher awareness tool in AI-enhanced classrooms. In: International Conference on Artificial Intelligence in Education. Springer International Publishing, Cham (2018)
56. TeachFX: TeachFX: AI-powered classroom analytics for teacher reflection (2025). https://teachfx.com. Accessed Oct 2025
57. Kerres, M., Buntins, K.: Recommender in AI-enhanced learning: an assessment from the perspective of instructional design. Open Educ. Stud. **2**(1), 101–111 (2020). https://doi.org/10.1515/edu-2020-0119
58. Holmes, W., Bialik, M., Fadel, C.: Artificial Intelligence in Education: Promises and Implications for Teaching and Learning. Center for Curriculum Redesign, Boston (2019)
59. Brown, A.L.: Design experiments: theoretical and methodological challenges in creating complex interventions in classroom settings. J. Learn. Sci. **2**(2), 141–178 (1992). https://doi.org/10.1207/s15327809jls0202_2
60. Gomez Paloma, F., Calò, M., Borrelli, M., Tafuri, D.: Embodied cognition design. Experimental pedagogy between embodied cognition and architectural space. Ital. J. Educ. Res. **19**, 41–52 (2018)
61. Byers, T., Imms, W., Hartnell-Young, E.: Comparative analysis of the impact of traditional versus innovative learning environment on student attitudes and learning outcomes. Stud. Educ. Eval. **58**, 167–177 (2018). https://doi.org/10.1016/j.stueduc.2018.07.003

62. Leiringer, R., Cardellino, P.: Schools for the twenty-first century: school design and educational transformation. Br. Edu. Res. J. **37**(6), 915–934 (2011). https://doi.org/10.1080/01411926.2010.508512

63. Gillies, R.M.: Cooperative learning: review of research and practice. Aust. J. Teach. Educ. **41**(3), 39–54 (2016). https://doi.org/10.14221/ajte.2016v41n3.3

64. Jewitt, C., Bezemer, J., O'Halloran, K.: Introducing Multimodality. Routledge, London (2016). https://doi.org/10.4324/9781315638028

65. Schunk, D.H., DiBenedetto, M.K.: Motivation and social-emotional learning: theory, research and practice. Contemp. Educ. Psychol. **60**, 101830 (2020). https://doi.org/10.1016/j.cedpsych.2019.101830

66. Collins, P.H., Bilge, S.: Intersectionality, 2nd end. Polity Press, Cambridge (2020). https://doi.org/10.1515/9781509539698

67. Hargreaves, A., O'Connor, M.T.: Collaborative Professionalism: When Teaching Together Means Learning for All. Corwin Press (2018)

68. Slee, R.: Belonging in an age of exclusion. Int. J. Incl. Educ. **23**(9), 909–922 (2019). https://doi.org/10.1080/13603116.2019.1602366

69. Cajkler, W., Wood, P., Norton, J., Pedder, D.: Lesson study as a vehicle for collaborative teacher learning in a secondary school. Prof. Dev. Educ. **41**(5), 746–765 (2015). https://doi.org/10.1080/19415257.2014.955122

70. DeMonte, J.: Micro-credentials for teachers: what three early adopter states have learned so far. Am. Inst. Res. (2017). https://doi.org/10.3102/0002831217690519

71. Morrison, C.: Re-imagining school spaces: designing for student wellbeing an engagement. Learn. Environ. Res. **21**(3), 299–318 (2018). https://doi.org/10.1007/s10984-018-9269-5

72. Cook-Sather, A.: Student voice across contexts: fostering student agency in today's schools. Theory Pract. **59**(2), 182–191 (2020). https://doi.org/10.1080/00405841.2019.1702399

73. Florian, L., Spratt, J.: Enacting inclusion: a framework for interrogating inclusive practice. Eur. J. Spec. Needs Educ. **28**(2), 119–135 (2013)

Low-Resource Course Recommendation for Professional Training Associations

Ludovico Boratto, Gianni Fenu, Nicoló Marongiu, Giacomo Medda, and Alessandro Soccol[(✉)]

Department of Mathematics and Computer Science, University of Cagliari, Cagliari, Italy
ludovico.boratto@acm.org,
{fenu,giacomo.medda,alessandro.soccol}@unica.it,
n.marongiu15@studenti.unica.it

Abstract. The lack of effective support for lifelong learning remains a persistent challenge within professional associations, often leading to fragmented pathways, unstructured course selection, and inefficient use of resources. In such contexts, traditional collaborative filtering methods are unsuitable due to data sparsity and course attendance policies: most users attend only a few courses and courses are available only for limited periods. In this paper, we examine the extent to which metadata-driven recommendation approaches and diverse recommendation architectures, particularly those leveraging semantic item identifiers, can serve as a viable solution for course recommendation in these professional scenarios. Experiments on historical course data collected from an engineers' association training school show that, under a partitioning strategy that closely reflects real-world conditions, the proposed approaches generate highly relevant recommendations, demonstrating their potential to effectively support course recommendation in such environments.

Keywords: Educational Recommender Systems · Learning Science

1 Introduction

Recommender Systems (RSs) have emerged as an essential solution to address the challenges of information overload by tailoring personalized content to users. While their success is well established in domains such as music, movies, and online retail. their application to education presents unique complexities. However, in the educational context, personalization cannot rely solely on explicit feedback, since learning is influenced by cognitive, pedagogical, and contextual factors that go far beyond the explicit feedback frequently used in traditional RSs [3,7,10,23]. Educational settings encompass formal curricula in schools and universities, non-formal processes driven by lifelong learning initiatives, and informal learning experiences acquired in everyday life. This diversity creates an environment where adapting resources to learners' profiles is challenging.

Moreover, the application of recommendation methods in lifelong learning settings, especially within professional associations, presents further challenges.

A. Dipace et al. (Eds.): WAILS 2025, LNCS 16438, pp. 172–182, 2026.
https://doi.org/10.1007/978-3-032-17604-2_16

Learner interaction data is often sparse, as individuals typically attend only a few courses per year and exhibit limited preferences overlap with their peers [8]. At the same time, training catalogs evolve continuously, with new courses introduced on a regular basis, preventing the formation of stable interaction patterns Furthermore, structured datasets are scarce, and those available usually demand substantial preprocessing before being suitable for recommendation tasks.

Educational RSs applied in professional settings should consider prerequisites, knowledge structures, individual learning preferences, and varying paces, along with the fact that learning outcomes are often intangible and difficult to measure directly [24]. Over the years, numerous approaches have been developed to tackle personalization in educational settings. Classical collaborative filtering models leverage historical user–item interactions to infer future preferences [6], while content-based methods rely on descriptive metadata of learners and courses [18]. More recently, deep learning architectures [14], graph-based models [12], and hybrid systems have been introduced to integrate metadata and interaction signals [4]. Unfortunately, these solutions often struggle when applied to educational contexts characterized by limited engagement data.

In this paper, we address the challenges of course recommendation in lifelong learning contexts by proposing metadata-driven recommendation models that leverage semantic descriptors of courses and learners, rather than relying solely on past interaction patterns. This approach aligns with the principles of lifelong learning, where individuals continuously update their competencies through personalized, adaptive educational pathways. By encoding user metadata and course semantics, the proposed methods implicitly construct dynamic learner models that reflect each participant's evolving profile, supporting individualized learning trajectories over time. We compare this methodology with classical collaborative filtering techniques and with recent item representations based on Semantic IDs, which capture hierarchical relationships between learning topics. Grounded in a real-world case from the training school of an engineers' association, our study introduces novel data preparation and evaluation strategies that reflect realistic deployment conditions. By exploiting structured and semantic metadata, our models capture meaningful pedagogical relationships among courses and learners, effectively mitigating cold-start and sparsity challenges while promoting educational personalization in professional training environments. Specifically, the novel contributions of this paper are as follows:

1. **Dataset preparation and analysis**. We constructed a temporally consistent dataset by resolving inconsistencies, normalizing metadata, and aligning user and course information to support reproducible experiments.
2. **Evaluation protocol**. We designed a temporal partitioning strategy that simulates realistic deployment scenarios, ensuring recommendations only leverage courses available at the time of recommendation.
3. **Experimental study**. We implemented a suite of metadata-driven recommendation strategies, including models with sentence transformer embeddings, course-history aggregation, and semantic item identifiers, comparing them against established state-of-the-art methods.

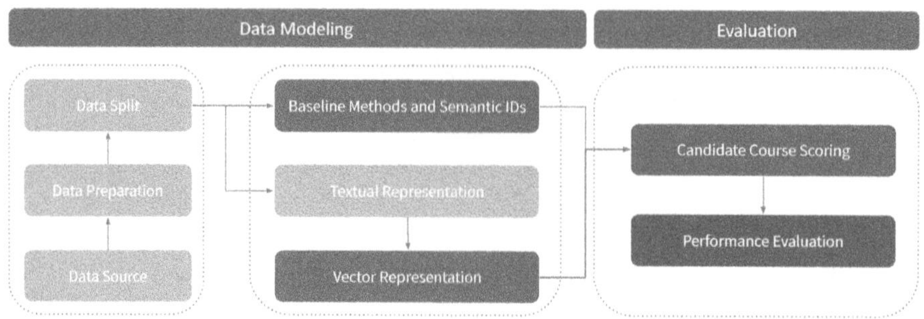

Fig. 1. Methodology. For metadata-based approaches, an additional preprocessing step encodes user and item attributes with a sentence transformer, producing vector representations for semantic similarity computation.

2   Methodology

We present our methodology by first detailing the data preparation pipeline, which includes data collection, curation, and temporal splitting, and then describing the range of recommendation approaches explored in our study, spanning from metadata-based methods to those leveraging semantic item identifiers (Fig. 1).

2.1   Dataset

Data Source. For this study, we used an anonymized dataset exported from the internal management system of a professional training association in Sardinia, provided in Excel and CSV formats. The dataset included entities and relations describing learners, enriched with demographic and academic attributes. It also contained information on courses, including descriptive metadata such as start and end dates, price, number of participants, and timestamped interaction logs.

Data Curation. The original dataset, covering learner interactions with courses between January 2022 and December 2023, was prepared with the goal of enabling a realistic evaluation of recommendation models. In particular, a user-course knowledge graph was created to link users to their characteristics via specific relations (e.g. an interaction could be **user 3, learner, item 985**), while an example of a user metadata information could be **user X, male, born in 20XX-XX and is an civil engineer**)[1]. Then, we started solving temporal and structural inconsistencies. In several cases, the interaction logs contained discrepancies between the recorded enrollment dates and the official availability periods of the corresponding courses. This alignment step was crucial to guarantee that all training and test data accurately reflected the real progression of the catalog offer, thereby preserving the validity of the subsequent temporal splits.

---

[1] We do not provide a real example for confidentiality reasons.

Table 1. Dataset statistics across temporal splits. Reports the main statistics of the dataset for each temporal split. It highlights the number of active learners, available courses, and recorded interactions, illustrating the progressive increase in historical depth across the three scenarios.

Period	Train			Test		
	D_1	D_2	D_3	D_1	D_2	D_3
Interactions	846	1,910	1,763	621	1,055	522
Users	274	429	305	271	388	305
Items	44	107	168	58	65	47
Avg. Int. per user	3	4	5	2	3	2
Avg. Int. per item	19	17	10	10	16	11

Data Splitting. To achieve a realistic train-test data split, we adopted a Last Split with Temporal Order (LS-TO) strategy. The dataset was divided into sequential periods, each consisting of a training window followed by a testing window of one semester. Let t denote the time index representing semesters, where $t \in \{1, 2, \ldots, n\}$ over 2 years (from 2022 to 2023) with $t = 1$ corresponding to the first semester (e.g., January–June 2022), $t = 2$ the second semester (July–December 2022), and so on. We denote by S_t the semester interactions corresponding to index t. Thus, the dataset temporal sequence of semesters is represented as an ordered set of interactions $\mathcal{S} = \{S_1, S_2, \ldots, S_n\}$. Our final dataset is composed of a total of 3 splits, where the first split is composed of $D_1 = \{S1, S2\}$, the second is $D_2 = \{S1, S2, S3\}$ and the last of $D_3 = \{S1, S2, S3, S4\}$. For each split, the last semester is the set of test interactions. Within each split, only learners with sufficient activity were retained. Specifically, users were required to have at least two interactions in the training window, so that one interaction is used for the training while the other is reserved for validation. We enforced a strict temporal separation of items, ensuring that courses included in the test set were not accessible during training, as they did not yet exist at that time. This prevented future data leakage and established an Item Cold-Start setting: during training, only courses already available in that period were used, while those scheduled in the test window were entirely new and unseen. This structure directly simulates the real-world scenario in which the engineers' association periodically issues newsletters about upcoming training opportunities: at each point in time, only the courses available in the immediate future can be recommended. The decision to construct three temporal splits was driven by the need to assess model performance under different historical horizons. A shorter training window (D_1) tests the model's ability to generalize with limited past data, while longer windows (D_2 and D_3) provide progressively richer histories that may allow the model to capture more complex learner trajectories.

Table 1 reports the main statistics of the dataset across the three temporal splits. A few trends are immediately noticeable. The number of learners and items varies across splits, reflecting the dynamic nature of course offerings and participation over time. For example, D_2 includes a larger pool of users and items compared to D_1, due to the longer training window that spans an entire year. Conversely, D_3 reports less available courses but a relatively stable number of active learners, resulting in a higher average number of interactions per item.

2.2 Metadata-Based Approaches

To explore metadata-driven recommendation strategies, we relied on sentence transformer encoders to project both users and courses into a shared semantic space given their textual representations as input. The central idea was to convert the available metadata into short textual descriptions such as "`User X born in XXXX, is XXX and has a master's degree in the field of engineering Civile e ambientale, Informazione`" for users, while "`The course titled Structural Design lasts 20 h, starts on 2021-09-15, provides 4 credits, and costs 20`" for courses. The textual metadata was then fed as input to the sentence transformer, that returns a dense vector representations suitable for similarity-based ranking. For this purpose, we adopted the multilingual transformer model **BGE-M3** [5], specifically designed for retrieval tasks, yielding a vector representation for every candidate and course.

Two distinct strategies were developed for constructing the final user representation. The former, denoted as *metadata-based*, encodes each user solely through the embedding of their demographic profile. This baseline isolates the predictive capacity of static user attributes, without leveraging any historical information about attended courses. The latter, referred to as *interaction aggregation modeling*, incorporates past interactions to enrich the user representation by averaging the impact of the interacted courses representations and preventing outliers from disproportionately influencing the user profile. The final user vector representation is then defined depending on the availability of interactions. If the user has attended at least one course, the model adopts the *interaction aggregation modeling* strategy, capturing both static user information and behavioral evidence. If no historical interactions are available for a user, the model defaults to the *metadata-based* representation.

For both strategies, the relevance score between users and courses was computed with cosine similarity between their vector representations. The k courses with the highest scores were then selected as recommendations.

2.3 Semantic Identifier Approaches

We extend the set of approaches with Semantic IDs to evaluate their effectiveness for course recommendation in low-resource settings. Semantic IDs represent items through tuples that encode their semantics, rather than abstract numeric identifiers. This approach has recently received increasing attention in generative recommendation research, as it provides more informative item representations that can support personalization under data scarcity. For example, instead of assigning ID d to the course "Safety of Electrical Installations", a tuple of the form $(s_1, s_2, s_3, \dots)$ is used, with s_i representing a semantic identifier. This tuple reflects an internal semantic hierarchy, where from left to right we move from a more general meaning (e.g., $s_1 = $ Safety) to a more granular one (e.g., s_3 equal to the actual course) [20,22]. This results in a reduced vocabulary and an item representation composed of different components at varying hierarchy levels, from the most general to the most specific one. Among the several approaches existing for generating Semantic IDs, we chose to adopt one of the most recent, namely RPG [15], which leverages Optimized Product Quantization [11,16] implemented in FAISS [17]. The model training proceeds as follows: given a user with their positive and negative items, we first map the items to their associated Semantic ID. The embedding representations corresponding to each element within the Semantic ID are then processed by an attention layer [1,25] (without the final projection layer) to learn which components of the semantic ID hierarchy should be emphasized in order to refine the final item representation. This process yields a new representation of the item based on its semantic IDs. The resulting representations are subsequently aggregated using mean pooling, producing a single embedding representation for each positive and negative item associated with the user. Finally, the loss function is computed using either BPR [21] or triplet margin loss [2]. We refer to the approach that employs BPR as SemanticBPR, and to the one that uses triplet margin loss as SemanticMargin.

2.4   Traditional Approaches

As comparison baselines, we decided to use methods that could provide a lower bound and a benchmark for the performance of metadata-based and semantic-identifiers-based approaches. Specifically, we chose to test performance with different approaches using the hopwise recommendation framework[2].

The Random recommender selects randomly a set of items from the catalog of items available during the test period. BPRMF [21] uses a pairwise ranking framework called Bayesian Pairwise Ranking (BPR), where the goal is to maximize the per-user posterior probability that observed items (positive) are ranked higher than unobserved items (negative). ConvNCF [13] applies an outer product to user and item embeddings to generate an interaction map, which is then processed by convolutional neural network (CNN) using a BPR loss function. ItemKNN [6] analyzes the user–item matrix to discover relations between the different items and use these relations to compute the list of recommended courses. DiffRec [27] learns the generative process through a denoising approach that preserves personalized information in user interactions by minimizing noise addition. Unlike image synthesis where data is corrupted into pure noise, DiffRec carefully reduces noise to avoid overwhelming the signal in user behavior, thereby maintaining the integrity of individual user interactions. LightGCN [12] is a simplified Graph Convolutional Network (GCN) designed specifically for recommendation tasks, focusing on neighborhood aggregation for collaborative filtering on the user-item interaction graph. It learns user and item embeddings by linearly propagating them on the interaction graph and combines embeddings from all layers through a weighted sum to form the final representation.

---

[2] https://github.com/tail-unica/hopwise.

Together, these baselines cover a wide methodological range, ensuring that our evaluation is grounded against both classical and cutting-edge approaches. They form a robust benchmark for assessing the advantages of metadata-driven and aggregation-based recommendation strategies in the educational domain.

3   Experimental Results

Our study aims to address the following research questions:

RQ1 Influence of different encoders representations. How does the choice of different sentence encoders influence the accuracy of the generated recommendations?

RQ2 Comparison against traditional approaches. How do metadata-driven strategies based on sentence transformer encoders perform in comparison to classical and semantic identifier approaches?

The recommendation utility of employed algorithms was evaluated by using the `Hit@k` metric at various cut-offs $k \in \{5, 10, 20, 50\}$. This metric evaluates the proportion of users who received at least one relevant recommendation, i.e., an item that appears in their ground truth in the test set.

3.1   RQ1: Influence of Different Encoders Representations

Table 2 (top five rows) reports the results of different sentence encoders, focusing on the impact of using alternative encoders to construct user and item embeddings. This comparison highlights that no single encoder dominates across all

Table 2. Performance comparison of metadata-based approaches, baselines and semantic ids across temporal splits (D_1, D_2, D_3). The table reports Hit@k scores for both classical recommendation baselines and metadata-driven approaches using pretrained sentence transformers.

Encoder/Model	D_1					D_2					D_3				
	@1	@5	@10	@20	@50	@1	@5	@10	@20	@50	@1	@5	@10	@20	@50
MiniLM-L6 [26]	<u>0.10</u>	0.19	0.29	0.42	0.84	0.02	0.10	0.19	0.34	0.72	0.03	0.15	0.25	0.41	0.86
MiniLM-L12 [26]	0.06	0.23	0.32	0.44	0.96	0.03	0.12	0.21	0.36	0.75	0.04	0.16	0.28	0.44	0.86
LaBSE [9]	0.04	0.16	0.25	0.46	0.83	0.03	0.11	0.22	0.40	0.84	0.06	<u>0.24</u>	**0.38**	0.54	0.93
Sentence T5 Base [19]	0.02	0.11	0.19	0.32	0.80	0.03	0.13	0.21	0.42	0.77	0.03	0.17	0.29	0.47	0.89
BGE-M3 [5]	0.08	0.22	0.36	0.52	0.81	0.02	0.14	0.27	0.47	0.82	0.06	0.21	0.34	<u>0.56</u>	0.92
Random	0.02	0.08	0.17	0.32	0.77	0.02	0.05	0.12	0.26	0.66	0.02	0.09	0.16	0.32	0.86
ConvNCF [13]	0.08	<u>0.29</u>	0.41	0.56	0.80	<u>0.04</u>	0.14	0.31	0.50	<u>0.85</u>	**0.07**	0.18	<u>0.35</u>	0.53	0.95
BPR [21]	0.05	0.18	0.31	0.51	<u>0.91</u>	<u>0.04</u>	0.16	0.32	0.49	<u>0.85</u>	0.04	0.15	0.27	0.44	0.92
ItemKNN [6]	0.01	0.08	<u>0.44</u>	0.64	**0.96**	**0.05**	**0.22**	<u>0.33</u>	0.50	<u>0.85</u>	0.05	0.17	0.21	0.46	**1.00**
Diffrec [27]	0.05	0.23	0.38	<u>0.65</u>	0.90	**0.05**	0.16	0.31	<u>0.52</u>	0.84	<u>0.06</u>	**0.25**	<u>0.35</u>	<u>0.56</u>	0.88
LightGCN [12]	0.05	0.21	0.37	0.54	<u>0.91</u>	<u>0.04</u>	<u>0.20</u>	**0.34**	**0.54**	**0.86**	0.05	0.21	**0.38**	**0.61**	<u>0.96</u>
SemanticBPR	0.03	0.11	0.30	0.50	0.89	<u>0.04</u>	0.16	0.31	0.51	0.84	0.02	0.11	0.23	0.43	0.91
SemanticMargin	**0.11**	**0.39**	**0.56**	**0.75**	**0.96**	0.03	0.17	0.31	0.50	0.83	0.02	0.12	0.24	0.46	0.92

For each dataset: best result in **bold**, second-best result <u>underlined</u>.

splits and cutoffs. MiniLM [26] achieves strong results at Hit@1 in D_1, LABSE [9] consistently provides the best performance at higher cutoffs in D_3, while Sentence T5 Base [19] demonstrates competitive behavior at intermediate cutoffs. The multilingual BGE-M3 [5] shows balanced performance, ranking among the top two in several cases and providing steady results across different horizons. These variations can be explained by differences in pretraining objectives and linguistic coverage: encoders optimized for multilingual semantic similarity, such as LaBSE [9], capture subtle relations across heterogeneous metadata, while lightweight models like MiniLM [26] are effective at identifying the most relevant course in smaller candidate sets. The advantage of sentence encoders lies in their ability to exploit pretrained semantic knowledge without additional training, making them especially suited to educational domains where training data is inherently sparse. By leveraging external corpora and general-purpose semantic representations, these encoders enable recommendations that extend beyond surface-level matching and capture deeper professional alignments.

3.2   RQ2: Comparison Across Recommendation Method Families

Table 2 (bottom rows) enables the comparison between metadata-driven models and other recommendation method families. Random recommendation yields the lowest scores, as expected because of the fact that we are recommending random courses to users. Collaborative filtering and graph-based methods, including BPR [21], ItemKNN [6], and LightGCN [12], deliver strong results at higher cutoffs, particularly in later splits where richer histories are available. ItemKNN [6], in particular, achieves the best performance at Hit@50 in D_3, confirming the robustness of neighborhood-based similarity when sufficient overlap exists between learners. Nevertheless, metadata-based models enhanced with sentence encoders reach competitive scores across splits and often surpass baselines at intermediate cutoffs (Hit@5 and Hit@10). This behavior is largely due to the ability of pretrained encoders to transfer external linguistic knowledge into the recommendation process, mitigating sparsity and improving alignment between users and courses. Such results demonstrate that while collaborative and graph-based methods retain an advantage in dense scenarios with abundant interaction data, metadata-driven semantic approaches offer superior robustness in the sparse and cold-start settings that dominate educational environments. Their capacity to provide effective personalization without the need for extensive retraining makes them a practical solution for real-world deployment in professional contexts.

4   Conclusions

In this work, we addressed the challenges of course recommendation under extreme sparsity, where learners attend only a few courses and catalogs evolve over time. By leveraging metadata-driven profiles, interaction aggregation, and sentence transformer encoders, we showed that recommendations can remain effective even without dense interaction data. Metadata-only representations proved valuable for cold-start scenarios, while interaction-aware methods improved personalization. Sentence encoders offered the strongest gains, mitigating sparsity through pretrained semantic knowledge, and had the additional advantage of requiring no task-specific training. Overall, the approaches achieved competitive performance and could support learners in navigating training opportunities. Beyond their technical merits, the proposed approaches contribute to the broader field of educational personalization by demonstrating how recommender systems can act as lifelong learning companions. The use of semantic metadata and learner modeling enables the system to reflect evolving professional trajectories, providing a foundation for personalized and sustainable skill development pathways within professional associations.

Acknowledgments. We acknowledge financial support from the National Recovery and Resilience Plan (NRRP), Mission 4 Component 2 Investment 1.1 - Call for tender No. 3277, published on December 30, 2021, by the Italian Ministry of University and Research (MUR), funded by the European Union – Next Generation EU. Project Code ECS0000038 – Project Title eINS Ecosystem of Innovation for Next Generation Sardinia – Grant Assignment Decree No. 1056 adopted on June 23, 2022, by the MUR (CUP F53C22000430001).

References

1. Bahdanau, D., Cho, K., Bengio, Y.: Neural machine translation by jointly learning to align and translate. In: Bengio, Y., LeCun, Y. (eds.) 3rd International Conference on Learning Representations, ICLR 2015, San Diego, CA, USA, 7–9 May 2015, Conference Track Proceedings (2015). http://arxiv.org/abs/1409.0473
2. Balntas, V., Riba, E., Ponsa, D., Mikolajczyk, K.: Learning local feature descriptors with triplets and shallow convolutional neural networks. In: Wilson, R.C., Hancock, E.R., Smith, W.A.P. (eds.) Proceedings of the British Machine Vision Conference 2016, BMVC 2016, York, UK, 19–22 September 2016. BMVA Press (2016). https://bmva-archive.org.uk/bmvc/2016/papers/paper119/index.html
3. Boratto, L., Fenu, G., Marras, M., Medda, G.: Practical perspectives of consumer fairness in recommendation. Inf. Process. Manag. **60**(2), 103208 (2023). https://doi.org/10.1016/j.ipm.2022.103208
4. Burke, R.: Hybrid recommender systems: survey and experiments. User Model. User-Adap. Inter. **12**(4), 331–370 (2002). https://doi.org/10.1023/A:1021240730564
5. Chen, J., Xiao, S., Zhang, P., Luo, K., Lian, D., Liu, Z.: BGE m3-embedding: multi-lingual, multi-functionality, multi-granularity text embeddings through self-knowledge distillation. CoRR abs/2402.03216 (2024). https://doi.org/10.48550/ARXIV.2402.03216. https://doi.org/10.48550/arXiv.2402.03216
6. Deshpande, M., Karypis, G.: Item-based top-N recommendation algorithms. ACM Trans. Inf. Syst. **22**(1), 143–177 (2004). https://doi.org/10.1145/963770.963776

7. Dessí, D., Dragoni, M., Fenu, G., Marras, M., Reforgiato Recupero, D.: Deep learning adaptation with word embeddings for sentiment analysis on online course reviews. In: Agarwal, B., Nayak, R., Mittal, N., Patnaik, S. (eds.) Deep Learning-Based Approaches for Sentiment Analysis. AIS, pp. 57–83. Springer, Singapore (2020). https://doi.org/10.1007/978-981-15-1216-2_3

8. Errakha, K., Samih, A., Marzouk, A., Krari, A.: Recommender systems in e-learning: trends, challenges, and future directions. J. Theor. Appl. Inf. Technol. **103**(7) (2025)

9. Feng, F., Yang, Y., Cer, D., Arivazhagan, N., Wang, W.: Language-agnostic BERT sentence embedding. In: Muresan, S., Nakov, P., Villavicencio, A. (eds.) Proceedings of the 60th Annual Meeting of the Association for Computational Linguistics (Volume 1: Long Papers), ACL 2022, Dublin, Ireland, 22–27 May 2022, pp. 878–891. Association for Computational Linguistics (2022). https://doi.org/10.18653/V1/2022.ACL-LONG.62

10. Fenu, G., Galici, R., Marras, M., Recupero, D.R.: Exploring student interactions with AI in programming training. In: Adjunct Proceedings of the 32nd ACM Conference on User Modeling, Adaptation and Personalization, UMAP Adjunct 2024, Cagliari, Italy, 1–4 July 2024. ACM (2024). https://doi.org/10.1145/3631700.3665227

11. Ge, T., He, K., Ke, Q., Sun, J.: Optimized product quantization. IEEE Trans. Pattern Anal. Mach. Intell. **36**(4), 744–755 (2014). https://doi.org/10.1109/TPAMI.2013.240

12. He, X., Deng, K., Wang, X., Li, Y., Zhang, Y., Wang, M.: Lightgcn: simplifying and powering graph convolution network for recommendation. In: Huang, J.X., et al. (eds.) Proceedings of the 43rd International ACM SIGIR Conference on Research and Development in Information Retrieval, SIGIR 2020, Virtual Event, China, 25–30 July 2020, pp. 639–648. ACM (2020). https://doi.org/10.1145/3397271.3401063

13. He, X., Du, X., Wang, X., Tian, F., Tang, J., Chua, T.: Outer product-based neural collaborative filtering. In: Lang, J. (ed.) Proceedings of the Twenty-Seventh International Joint Conference on Artificial Intelligence, IJCAI 2018, 13–19 July 2018, Stockholm, Sweden, pp. 2227–2233. ijcai.org (2018). https://doi.org/10.24963/IJCAI.2018/308

14. He, X., Liao, L., Zhang, H., Nie, L., Hu, X., Chua, T.: Neural collaborative filtering. In: Barrett, R., Cummings, R., Agichtein, E., Gabrilovich, E. (eds.) Proceedings of the 26th International Conference on World Wide Web, WWW 2017, Perth, Australia, 3–7 April 2017, pp. 173–182. ACM (2017). https://doi.org/10.1145/3038912.3052569

15. Hou, Y., et al.: Generating long semantic ids in parallel for recommendation. CoRR abs/2506.05781 (2025). https://doi.org/10.48550/ARXIV.2506.05781

16. Jégou, H., Douze, M., Schmid, C.: Product quantization for nearest neighbor search. IEEE Trans. Pattern Anal. Mach. Intell. **33**(1), 117–128 (2011). https://doi.org/10.1109/TPAMI.2010.57

17. Johnson, J., Douze, M., Jégou, H.: Billion-scale similarity search with GPUs. IEEE Trans. Big Data **7**(3), 535–547 (2021). https://doi.org/10.1109/TBDATA.2019.2921572

18. Lops, P., de Gemmis, M., Semeraro, G.: Content-based recommender systems: state of the art and trends. In: Ricci, F., Rokach, L., Shapira, B., Kantor, P.B. (eds.) Recommender Systems Handbook, pp. 73–105. Springer, Boston, MA (2011). https://doi.org/10.1007/978-0-387-85820-3_3

19. Ni, J., et al.: Sentence-t5: scalable sentence encoders from pre-trained text-to-text models. In: Muresan, S., Nakov, P., Villavicencio, A. (eds.) Findings of the Association for Computational Linguistics: ACL 2022, Dublin, Ireland, 22–27 May 2022, pp. 1864–1874. Association for Computational Linguistics (2022).https://doi.org/10.18653/V1/2022.FINDINGS-ACL.146

20. Rajput, S., et al.: Recommender systems with generative retrieval. In: Oh, A., Naumann, T., Globerson, A., Saenko, K., Hardt, M., Levine, S. (eds.) Advances in Neural Information Processing Systems 36: Annual Conference on Neural Information Processing Systems 2023, NeurIPS 2023, New Orleans, LA, USA, 10–16 December 2023 (2023). http://papers.nips.cc/paper_files/paper/2023/hash/20dcab0f14046a5c6b02b61da9f13229-Abstract-Conference.html

21. Rendle, S., Freudenthaler, C., Gantner, Z., Schmidt-Thieme, L.: BPR: Bayesian personalized ranking from implicit feedback. In: Bilmes, J.A., Ng, A.Y. (eds.) UAI 2009, Proceedings of the Twenty-Fifth Conference on Uncertainty in Artificial Intelligence, Montreal, QC, Canada, 18–21 June 2009, pp. 452–461. AUAI Press (2009). https://www.auai.org/uai2009/papers/UAI2009_0139_48141db02b9f0b02bc7158819ebfa2c7.pdf

22. Singh, A., et al.: Better generalization with semantic ids: a case study in ranking for recommendations. In: Noia, T.D., et al. (eds.) Proceedings of the 18th ACM Conference on Recommender Systems, RecSys 2024, Bari, Italy, 14–18 October 2024, pp. 1039–1044. ACM (2024). https://doi.org/10.1145/3640457.3688190

23. Torres, N.: Recommender systems for education: a case of study using formative assessments. In: 41st International Conference of the Chilean Computer Science Society, SCCC 2022, Santiago, Chile, 21–25 November 2022, pp. 1–6. IEEE (2022). https://doi.org/10.1109/SCCC57464.2022.10000363

24. Urdaneta-Ponte, M.C., Mendez-Zorrilla, A., Oleagordia-Ruiz, I.: Recommendation systems for education: systematic review. Electronics **10**(14) (2021). https://doi.org/10.3390/electronics10141611. https://www.mdpi.com/2079-9292/10/14/1611

25. Vaswani, A., et al.: Attention is all you need. In: Guyon, I., et al. (eds.) Advances in Neural Information Processing Systems 30: Annual Conference on Neural Information Processing Systems 2017, 4–9 December 2017, Long Beach, CA, USA, pp. 5998–6008 (2017). https://proceedings.neurips.cc/paper/2017/hash/3f5ee243547dee91fbd053c1c4a845aa-Abstract.html

26. Wang, W., Wei, F., Dong, L., Bao, H., Yang, N., Zhou, M.: Minilm: deep self-attention distillation for task-agnostic compression of pre-trained transformers. In: Larochelle, H., Ranzato, M., Hadsell, R., Balcan, M., Lin, H. (eds.) Advances in Neural Information Processing Systems 33: Annual Conference on Neural Information Processing Systems 2020, NeurIPS 2020, 6–12 December 2020, virtual (2020). https://proceedings.neurips.cc/paper/2020/hash/3f5ee243547dee91fbd053c1c4a845aa-Abstract.html

27. Wang, W., Xu, Y., Feng, F., Lin, X., He, X., Chua, T.: Diffusion recommender model. In: Chen, H., Duh, W.E., Huang, H., Kato, M.P., Mothe, J., Poblete, B. (eds.) Proceedings of the 46th International ACM SIGIR Conference on Research and Development in Information Retrieval, SIGIR 2023, Taipei, Taiwan, 23–27 July 2023, pp. 832–841. ACM (2023). https://doi.org/10.1145/3539618.3591663

Operationalizing Calibration for Fair Educational Artificial Intelligence

Massimiliano Mancini[(✉)] [iD], Donatella Merlini [iD], and Maria Cecilia Verri [iD]

Dipartimento di Statistica, Informatica, Applicazioni, Università di Firenze,
Viale Morgagni, 65, Florence, Italy
`{massimiliano.mancini,donatella.merlini,mariacecilia.verri}@unifi.it`,
`disia@disia.unifi.it`
`https://disia.unifi.it`

Abstract. The growing use of artificial intelligence in education calls for rigorous methods to evaluate fairness in algorithmic decision-making. This paper focuses on calibration as an operationalization of the sufficiency criterion and develops a method to compute it in educational contexts, where prediction is often defined in terms of individual scores rather than a simple success or failure outcome. We first discuss the conceptual foundations of sufficiency and its specific relevance for predictions expressed as scores or probabilities. We then propose a procedure for measuring fairness through calibration, addressing key challenges such as the aggregation of outcomes across multiple predicted values, the ordering of groups in difference measures, and the treatment of cases where data availability is unbalanced across groups. The proposed procedure is grounded in design choices that aim to preserve the interpretive meaning of data in terms of fairness, while relying on established and transparent statistical methods. The method is empirically applied to two real-world student performance datasets using different classification algorithms. The results illustrate both the feasibility of the approach and the methodological implications of the design choices required to operationalize calibration. The contribution of this study lies primarily in providing a structured framework for measuring sufficiency through calibration, enabling researchers and practitioners to better assess fairness in artificial intelligence systems for education.

Keywords: Calibration · Education · Fairness

1 Introduction

Artificial intelligence plays an increasingly prominent role within the educational domain. An expanding range of educational activities is being delegated to algorithmic systems, which includes tasks such as supporting evaluation, predicting student performance, providing teaching materials, and organizing course resources [12,14,17,23,27,29]. Classification algorithms lie at the heart of many

© The Author(s), under exclusive license to Springer Nature Switzerland AG 2026
A. Dipace et al. (Eds.): WAILS 2025, LNCS 16438, pp. 183–198, 2026.
https://doi.org/10.1007/978-3-032-17604-2_17

artificial intelligence techniques because most intelligent tasks involve distinguishing between different types of data or making decisions based on categories. In the field of education, in particular, classification is used to predict students' learning outcomes, identify at-risk learners, and personalize study recommendations based on performance data. It also supports automated grading systems that categorize answers as correct or incorrect, and language-learning tools that assess the level of a learner's response. In all these cases, artificial intelligence systems rely on classification to interpret information and make meaningful, data-driven decisions. However, the integration of artificial intelligence agents into processes that involve the evaluation of individuals raises critical concerns. On the one hand, both industry and academia are committed to the development of ever more accurate systems; on the other hand, these systems may inadvertently reproduce or even exacerbate social biases when trained on biased datasets, thereby amplifying existing forms of discrimination. Consequently, a substantial body of research has emerged on the intersection between artificial intelligence, ethics, and human values. Within this framework, a particularly salient research question concerns the mechanisms through which fairness can be ensured in artificial intelligence, acknowledging that fairness is not synonymous with accuracy. The first and indispensable step in this direction is to establish a definition of fairness that is both conceptually rigorous and empirically measurable. The majority of the scientific literature classifies fairness measures according to how they satisfy three non-discrimination criteria: *independence*, *separation*, and *sufficiency*. While the literature on group fairness in machine learning is extensive [1,6,19,20,22,26], this study concentrates on a specific non-discrimination criterion: *sufficiency* [9]. Although sufficiency represents one of the three foundational pillars of fairness assessment [1,6,19], it has received comparatively limited attention despite its conceptual soundness and practical applicability. These three criteria can be formally defined as follows.

The independence non-discrimination criterion requires that the probability of a predicted outcome be statistically independent of the group membership [13,16]. In other words, belonging to a particular group should not influence the likelihood of receiving a positive prediction. Formally, this can be expressed as:

$$\hat{Y} \perp G \tag{1}$$

where $\hat{Y}$ denotes the predicted outcome and G denotes the sensitive group attribute. One of the earliest and most widely discussed fairness measures that satisfies the independence criterion is *statistical parity*, sometimes called *demographic parity* [5,13], which demands that the rate of positive predictions be equal across groups.

The separation non-discrimination criterion requires that the predicted outcome be conditionally independent of group membership, given the ground truth [16]. In other words, once the actual outcome Y is known, belonging to a particular group should not affect the likelihood of receiving a positive prediction. Formally, this condition can be expressed as:

$$\hat{Y} \perp G \mid Y \tag{2}$$

where $\hat{Y}$ denotes the predicted outcome, G the sensitive group attribute, and Y the ground truth outcome. A wide range of fairness measures in the scientific literature are designed to satisfy this criterion, including *equal opportunity*, *total accuracy*, sometimes referred to as *equalized odds*, *overall accuracy equality*, *conditional use accuracy equality*, and *treatment equality* (see e.g., [2, 16]). These measures are often referred to as confusion matrixâĂŞbased metrics, as they rely on standard quantities derived from the confusion matrix: true positives, true negatives, false positives and false negatives.

Coming to sufficiency, its relative marginality in the broader literature is partly explained by the peculiarities of its operationalization. The sufficiency criterion requires that the ground truth be conditionally independent of the group membership given the predicted score [9]. Formally, this condition can be expressed as:

$$Y \perp G \mid R \tag{3}$$

where Y denotes the ground truth outcome, G the sensitive group attribute, and R the predicted score. Sufficiency is tightly connected with *calibration*, a property that ensures the predicted probability of an outcome reflects the true likelihood of that outcome [25]. Calibration is also a measure that satisfies sufficiency, in this case it is also referred as *test fairness* [9]. Unlike other fairness criteria, sufficiency is not always easily applicable across diverse domains, and its requirements can reduce its usability in many real-world contexts. However, the very characteristics that limit its general applicability make calibration particularly suitable in the educational setting, as explained in Sect. 1.1. In the educational domain, prediction is often not an end in itself, but a means to support formative and summative assessments, where the explainability and reliability of predicted probabilities are of primary importance. The main contribution of this paper lies in examining the modes and challenges of operationalizing sufficiency through calibration as a fairness criterion within the educational domain. To this end we discuss the consequences of specific design choices and empirically evaluate calibration across different classification algorithms and datasets. Furthermore, calibration is considered in comparison with other fairness metrics to highlight its distinctive role and potential advantages in the educational sphere. The experimental results suggest that calibration does not substantially deviate from the other fairness measures. Thus, while being more fine-grained, since it is based on individual values of R rather than a simple success or failure outcome, it remains consistent with the other criteria. One contribution of this paper is to make calibration directly comparable with these measures, thereby reinforcing its relevance as a fairness criterion. This paper does not primarily aim to benchmark the performance of classifiers in terms of accuracy, provided that they surpass a minimal threshold of acceptability. Rather, the focus is on assessing whether classifiers exhibit fair behavior with respect to the partitioning of individuals into socially relevant groups. In particular, we are concerned with detecting whether the decision process introduces systematic biases against individuals based on their membership in sensitive groups, instead of evaluating differences in predictive accuracy across models. Given these premises, we formulate two research questions:

- RQ1: *Based on the theoretical definition, how can fairness be measured through operationalization of calibration in an educational context?*
- RQ2: *To what extent can calibration reveal and highlight potential biases in classifiers trained with students' data?*

1.1 Motivations

In the educational domain, the principle of sufficiency acquires particular relevance due to its close connection with calibration-based fairness measures. Educational systems often rely on thresholds to trigger support actions such as tutoring, mentoring, or remedial programs. If predictive models are not calibrated, the same predicted probability may imply different actual success rates across groups, leading to unequal treatment around these cutoffs. A calibrated model guarantees that predictions have the same empirical meaning for every subgroup, thereby supporting transparency and accountability. This comparability enables educators and policymakers to communicate probabilistic predictions in a way that is interpretable and verifiable by all stakeholders. Several aspects underscore suitability of calibration in educational context. First, fairness measurement through calibration presupposes the use of predictors that output a probabilistic range of values rather than a simple binary outcome of success or failure. This property closely aligns with the educational context, in which assessment typically takes the form of graded scores, where the exact value of a prediction carries significant interpretive and practical weight. Second, calibration ensures that estimated success probabilities correspond to observed outcome success frequencies, thus fairness is assured if all groups received calibrated predictions. Third, sufficiency aligns with the requirement of transparency and verifiability, central to educational assessment, as prediction-based probabilities can be directly compared with observed frequencies and thus communicated in an interpretable manner to educators, students, and other stakeholders. Finally, sufficiency contributes to fair resource allocation, ensuring that prediction-triggered interventions are proportionate to actual needs and that educational resources are distributed equitably. For instance, consider the case of implementing a tutoring support system for students. Having access to predictions would make it possible to allocate such a resource more efficiently. In particular, identifying the grade ranges where different student groups are concentrated, an action made feasible through calibration, could guide tutoring efforts with the intensity and type of support calibrated across different score ranges, thus ensuring that resources are allocated proportionally.

1.2 Background

Fairness measurement is an active branch of research. Many works in the literature concern surveys and classification of fairness definitions. As this is a relatively recent topic, it is not surprising that multiple, and sometimes conflicting, notions of fairness coexist, while taxonomies aim to disentangle their nuances [6,19,22,26]. Notably, frameworks such as FairLearn [4], IBM Fairness AI 360 [28], and Aequitas [24] attempt to operationalize fairness by offering tools for bias detection and intervention. However, as anticipated in the introduction, it must be stressed that these frameworks do not incorporate fairness metrics grounded in calibration, nor do they operationalize sufficiency-based criteria. To the best of our knowledge, with few exceptions [18], there are no projects or studies that explore in detail the operationalization of calibration. This gap is particularly relevant from a methodological perspective, as calibration and sufficiency represent fundamental notions in fairness assessment, especially in the educational domain as discussed in Sect. 1.1. While independence and separation principles often admit relatively straightforward operationalizations, as we aim to illustrate in this work, the same cannot be said for sufficiency and calibration, whose implementation raises non-trivial challenges.

2   Preliminaries

We present a method to measure fairness, according to the sufficiency nondiscrimination criterion, in predictions given by a classification algorithm trained with tabular data representing attributes related to people. The dataset under analysis is denoted by S. Attributes of S are considered as random variables represented in capital letters, while assumed values are indicated in lowercase letters. The variable G denotes the sensitive attribute or the group identifier with respect to which fairness is evaluated. For simplicity, in this work, we restrict our attention to the case of two groups, meaning that the sensitive attribute can assume only two values denoted by g_a and g_b. For instance, if the sensitive attribute is the sex of an individual, the two possible values are male and female. Nevertheless, the proposed method can be generalized to settings in which the sensitive attribute takes more than two values, provided that comparisons are carried out according to a one-vs-rest scheme, where each group is iteratively contrasted with the aggregate of the remaining ones. The boolean target variable Y represents observed ground truth success in the population sample. We emphasize that the calibration measure requires the classifier algorithm to output a predicted discrete score R that takes values in the interval $[t_m, t_M]$. For example, R could be the expected score, from $t_m = 0$ to $t_M = 20$, a student is predicted to achieve on an exam. Function $s : [t_m, t_M] \rightarrow \{-1, 1\}$ is a success function and returns -1 or 1 if the predicted score $R = r$ is considered a failure or a success, respectively. Typically, as done for example in [18], $s(r) = 1$ if r is greater than a certain threshold, otherwise $s(r) = -1$, but it is not always the case. For instance, R could represent an index, from $t_m = 0$ to $t_M = 100$, about the predicted level of control exercised by a teacher in classroom management. A balance between authority and flexibility can determine educational success by fostering a positive learning environment. Too little control, denoted by $r < 30$, leads to an overly permissive teacher who risks losing the respect of students, disorder and difficulties in maintaining focus on teaching. Too much control, denoted by $r > 70$, on the other hand, leads to an overly authoritarian teacher that might create an atmosphere of tension or fear, limiting creative expression, dialogue, and students' intrinsic motivation. In this case the success, $s(r) = 1$, is reached if $30 \leq r \leq 70$, and $s(r) = -1$ otherwise. Finally, to indicate the selection of records required for the computation of proportions, we resort to the syntax of relational algebra and use the σ_F operator to denote a selection satisfying predicate F [10].

3   Sufficiency

Together with *independence* and *separation, sufficiency* is one of the three main non-discrimination criteria on which fairness assessment is based [1]. This criterion requires that, conditional on a given prediction R, the ground-truth outcome variable Y is statistically independent of the sensitive attribute G, i.e., once the prediction R is known, additional knowledge of G should not provide any further information about the likelihood of the true outcome Y. As anticipated in the Introduction, this relationship is expressed as:

$$Y \perp G \mid R. \tag{4}$$

In other words, sufficiency emphasizes that predictive reliability should be homogeneous across groups: if two individuals receive the same predicted score, their chances of achieving the actual outcome Y must be identical regardless of their membership in a sensitive group. While independence and separation focus on binary predictions produced by a classifier, the sufficiency criterion takes into account the entire range of possible values of the predicted target variable R, which represents discrete scores values, such as a quality rating [9]. This makes sufficiency particularly suitable in educational contexts, where the output of predictive models often does not correspond to a binary decision such as pass or fail, but rather to a score expressed on a discrete scale. In such settings, fairness cannot be reduced to the equal treatment of yes-no outcomes, but must instead guarantee that predicted scores reflect the same relationship with true performance across all groups of individuals. By considering the full distribution of possible results, sufficiency provides a more nuanced and context-appropriate framework to ensure fairness in educational evaluation.

4   Operationalizing Sufficiency Through Calibration Measure

We recall Research Question 1 (RQ1): *Based on the theoretical definition, how can fairness be measured through operationalization of calibration in an educational context?* and propose an answer in the following sections. Calibration is formally expressed by the Eq. (5):

$$P(Y = 1 | R = r, G = g_a) = P(Y = 1 | R = r, G = g_b). \tag{5}$$

Moving from the theoretical framework to operationalization of calibration entails a number of challenges, which are addressed in this and the following sections. As noted in [9], the non-discrimination condition (4), and consequently the calibration measure (5), must hold for all values of R. This requirement implies that the classifier must be trained to predict a distribution of outcomes rather than a single value, which constitutes a distinctive feature of this measure. In order to compare calibration with other fairness metrics, such as statistical parity or total accuracy, it is necessary to map calibration outcomes to a single real number in the range $[-1, 1]$ as these fairness measures are defined as differences between proportions. Since proportions lie in $[0, 1]$, comparing two groups naturally yields values in $[-1, 1]$. Moreover, when the goal is to use calibration measure within a loss function for training classifiers, managing an entire set of values for different R is impractical. In this context, an aggregated representation is essential to provide a single quantity that can be seamlessly integrated into optimization procedures. In this paper, we adopt a weighted mean, using the number of items for each value of R as weight thus representing an expectation with respect to the empirical distribution of R, thereby providing a consistent and unbiased representation of the underlying population. As mentioned above, fairness between two groups is generally expressed as a difference, which makes crucial the ordering of the groups in the calculation. Positive values indicate bias in favor of the first group, while negative values indicate bias in favor of the second. To ensure interpretability, when R represents success, i.e., $s(r) = 1$, the group order in the difference must remain fixed; conversely, when R represents failure, i.e., $s(r) = -1$, the group order must be reversed. We formalize this convention by using the function s as a sign function that determines the appropriate ordering.

4.1   Formulation and Further Considerations

Taking into account previous constraints and considerations, for two groups g_a and g_b that constitute a partition for a dataset $S = \sigma_{G=g_a}(S) \cup \sigma_{G=g_b}(S)$, calibration is computed as c in Eq. (9):

$$w_r = \frac{|\sigma_{R=r}(S)|}{|S|} \tag{6}$$

$$n_r^g = \begin{cases} \frac{|\sigma_{R=r \wedge G=g \wedge Y=1}(S)|}{|\sigma_{R=r \wedge G=g}(S)|} & \text{if } |\sigma_{R=r \wedge G=g}(S)| \neq 0 \\ 0 & \text{otherwise} \end{cases} \tag{7}$$

$$c_r = s(r)w_r(n_r^{g_a} - n_r^{g_b}) \tag{8}$$

$$c = \sum_{r \in R} c_r. \tag{9}$$

It is worth noting that $c \in [-1, 1]$ which makes this quantity comparable with other fairness measures. Its value can be interpreted as follows:

- $c = -1$ classifier is completely biased in favor of the group denoted by g_b;

- $c = 0$ classifier is considered fair according to the calibration measure;
- $c = 1$ classifier is completely biased in favor of the group denoted by g_a.

When calculating c_r, different values of R can lead to different scenarios depending on the presence of items from none, one, or both groups. A simple case arises when the classifier does not label any item with a specific value of $R = r$, i.e. $|\sigma_{R=r}(S)| = 0$. In this situation, $w_r = 0$, and therefore no further contribution is provided for such a value of R. Another straightforward case occurs when the classifier labels items from both groups, $|\sigma_{R=r \wedge G=g_a}(S)| \neq 0$ and $|\sigma_{R=r \wedge G=g_b}(S)| \neq 0$. In this case, c_r is directly computed and its value contributes to the final value of c. In contrast, a particular situation arises when the classifier assigns a specific value of $R = r$ only to items from one group, e.g., $|\sigma_{R=r \wedge G=g_a}(S)| = 0$ and $|\sigma_{R=r \wedge G=g_b}(S)| \neq 0$, or vice versa. This situation requires further consideration. In this case, two approaches are possible: (i) treat the group without items as contributing zero, maintaining the value of n_r^g for the other group, or (ii) exclude all items, from both groups, associated with that value of R. Each approach entails specific implications. The first option introduces a degree of ambiguity, in particular two different cases become indistinguishable: (i) the case in which $n_r^g = 0$ because no element of the group was labeled with the specific value of $R = r$, i.e. $|\sigma_{R=r \wedge G=g}(S)| = 0$, and (ii) the case in which $n_r^g = 0$ because no element of the group is associated with a ground-truth success, $|\sigma_{R=r \wedge G=g \wedge Y=1}(S)| = 0$. Moreover, if fairness is to be assessed independently for each value of R, then the absence of one group makes the computation of fairness infeasible and may be interpreted as a violation of the method's assumptions. This is the approach followed in [18]. Nevertheless, excluding items from both groups whenever only one of the two groups has no items for a specific value of R leads to a loss of information and a risk of bias in the analysis. More importantly, we are not compelled to consider every value of R as a separate episode to be treated in isolation, because we rely on an aggregation function, namely a weighted mean, that reintroduces the contribution of items from the group present at that value of R, thereby mitigating information loss. As reported in Eq. (9), we therefore propose to adopt this latter strategy.

5   Datasets

We applied the presented method to two datasets, using three different classification algorithm and comparing the result with two fairness measures: statistical parity and total accuracy. The *Student Performance Database* [12] reports the academic achievement during 2005-2006 of students from two schools in the Alentejo region of Portugal in Mathematics and Portuguese language courses. The Mathematics dataset includes $N_m = 395$ students, while the Portuguese language dataset includes $N_p = 649$ records. Both datasets are described by $n = 33$ attributes: 4 categorical, 13 binary, and 16 numerical. A detailed description of these attributes is provided in Table 1. The sensitive attribute considered is *sex*, which takes two possible values: female (F) and male (M). The Mathematics dataset contains 208 male and 187 female students, whereas the Portuguese dataset includes 266 males and 383 females.

Table 1. Attributes of Mathematics and Portuguese datasets

Name	Description	Type and domain
sex	student's sex	binary: female or male
age	student's age	numeric: from 15 to 22
school	student's school	binary: *Gabriel Pereira* or *Mousinho da Silveira*
address	student's home address type	binary: urban or rural
Pstatus	parent's cohabitation status	binary: living together or apart
Medu	mother's education	numeric: 0-none, 1-primary education 4th grade, 2-5th to 9th grade, 3-secondary education or 4-higher education
Mjob	mother's job	nominal: teacher, health care related, civil services, at home or other
Fedu	father's education	numeric: 0-none, 1-primary education 4th grade, 2-5th to 9th grade, 3-secondary education or 4-higher education
Fjob	father's job	nominal: teacher, health care related, civil services, at home or other
guardian	student's guardian	nominal: mother, father or other
famsize	family size	binary: ≤ 3 or > 3
famrel	quality of family relationships	numeric: from 1-very bad to 5-excellent
reason	reason to choose this school	nominal: close to home, school reputation, course preference or other
traveltime	home to school travel time	numeric: 1-<15 min., 2-15 to 30 min., 3-30 min. to 1 h or 4->1 h
studytime	weekly study time	numeric: 1-< 2 h, 2-2 to 5 h, 3-5 to 10 h or 4-> 10 h
failures	number of past class failures	numeric: n if $1 \leq n < 3$, else 4
schoolsup	extra educational school support	binary: yes or no
famsup	family educational support	binary: yes or no
activities	extra-curricular activities	binary: yes or no
paidclass	extra paid classes	binary: yes or no
internet	internet access at home	binary: yes or no
nursery	attended nursery school	binary: yes or no
higher	wants to take higher education	binary: yes or no
romantic	with a romantic relationship	binary: yes or no
freetime	free time after school	numeric: from 1-very low to 5-very high
goout	going out with friends	numeric: from 1-very low to 5-very high
Walc	weekend alcohol consumption	numeric: from 1-very low to 5-very high
Dalc	workday alcohol consumption	numeric: from 1-very low to 5-very high
health	current health status	numeric: from 1-very bad to 5-very good
absences	number of school absences	numeric: from 0 to 93
G1	first period grade	numeric: from 0 to 20
G2	second period grade	numeric: from 0 to 20
G3	final grade	numeric: from 0 to 20

The target variable is the final grade of each student, denoted by the attribute
$G3$, which is expressed on a 20-point grading scale. The classifier is trained on
all the remaining attributes to predict the student's final grade, as an integer

value within the range $[0, 20]$. To assess student success, we define the observed binary variable Y based on a threshold: if $G3 < 10$, then $Y = 0$ (*fail*); otherwise, $Y = 1$ (*success*), as formalized in Eq. (10). For performance evaluation, accuracy is computed using the predicted success variable $\hat{Y}$, which is derived from the estimated grades according to Eq. (11). Using the function $s : [0, 20] \rightarrow \{-1, 1\}$, as defined in Eq. (12), observed success outcome rates are 73% for males and 60% for females in Mathematics dataset, and 81% for both males and females in Portuguese dataset.

$$Y = \begin{cases} 0, & \text{if } G3 < 10 \\ 1, & \text{if } G3 \geq 10, \end{cases} \tag{10}$$

$$\hat{Y} = \begin{cases} 0, & \text{if } r < 10 \\ 1, & \text{if } r \geq 10, \end{cases} \tag{11}$$

$$s(r) = \begin{cases} -1, & \text{if } r < 10 \\ 1, & \text{if } r \geq 10. \end{cases} \tag{12}$$

6   Experiments with Different Classifiers

In this section, we address Research Question 2 (RQ2): *To what extent can calibration reveal and highlight potential biases in classifiers trained with studentsn' data?* We apply the proposed method to the Mathematics and Portuguese datasets and evaluate the obtained results. Three classification algorithms are employed: XGBoost [8], AdaBoost [15], and Support Vector Machines (SVM) [11]. Each classifier is trained on 80% of the dataset, while the remaining 20% is reserved for testing to assess performance. Bias is then evaluated for each algorithm through calibration analysis. All experiments are implemented using Python libraries [7,21]. Please note that all fairness and accuracy measures are computed on the test sets of the two datasets. Although the experimental section employs standard machine learning algorithms such as decision trees, boosting, and SVM, these models are fully part of the artificial intelligence domain and remain widely used in educational and decision-support applications. Their interpretability, robustness, and controllable complexity make them particularly suitable for a systematic evaluation of fairness and calibration metrics, as performed in this study. More complex approaches, including deep learning architectures or large language models, could indeed be integrated within the same evaluation framework proposed here. The use of classical models in the experiments therefore serves the purpose of clarity, reproducibility, and conceptual validation, without limiting the broader applicability of the proposed approach. To ensure meaningful results, three different accuracy metrics are considered. The first two are straightforward: R Accuracy and $\hat{Y}$ Accuracy. Both are computed as the ratio between the sum of true positives and true negatives, and the total number of records. In the first case, true positives and negatives are identified using the predicted grades R and the actual grades $G3$; in the second, using the predicted and actual success variables $\hat{Y}$ and Y. Because R takes values on a discrete scale from 0 to 20, the accuracy on this variable is expected to be relatively low due to the strictness of exact matching. To provide a more informative evaluation, in Eq. (13) we report R accuracy within k, which measures the proportion of predictions falling within a tolerance of $\pm k$ from the true grade, as introduced by [3]:

$$\text{r-accuracy}_k = \frac{|\sigma_{(|R-G3|\leq k)\wedge(Y=\hat{Y})}(S)|}{|S|}. \tag{13}$$

True positives and true negatives are still identified based both on value of R with a certain tolerance k and on matching values of the success variable Y and its prediction $\hat{Y}$, ensuring that the tolerance on R is applied only when the overall success classification is consistent. To ensure a correct interpretation of the results, it is important to note that differences in proportions are consistently reported with females listed first, i.e., $g_a = F$ and $g_b = M$ in (9). Consequently, a positive value indicates a preference toward the female group, whereas a negative value indicates a preference toward the male group. For the Mathematics dataset the results are shown in Table 2: the highest accuracy is achieved by XGBoost; however, this classifier also exhibits a slight bias in favor of male students; AdaBoost, on the other hand, provides the most balanced outcome in terms of fairness, although its relatively low accuracy may undermine the reliability of the fairness evaluation. In the Portuguese dataset, which contains a considerably larger number of records compared to the Mathematics dataset, the comparison reveals a more nuanced picture, which is illustrated in Table 3: XGBoost outperforms AdaBoost in terms of accuracy when predicting the exact grade R, while AdaBoost achieves higher accuracy on the binary success variable $\hat{Y}$ and simultaneously ensures the fairest outcome. This highlights that AdaBoost is more effective when the focus is on predicting student success (pass/fail), whereas XGBoost may be more precise in estimating the exact grade. In summary, the experimental results suggest that AdaBoost generally offers robust performance with respect to both accuracy and fairness, provided that the dataset contains an adequate number of observations. Conversely, in smaller datasets, its reduced accuracy may limit the strength of fairness-related conclusions. Measuring fairness through calibration allows meaningful conclusions to be drawn even when the overall accuracy of the classifier is limited, as in the case of AdaBoost applied to the Mathematics dataset. While low accuracy inevitably reduces the reliability of the predictions, calibration-based fairness analysis can still reveal whether the inaccuracy affects social groups in a balanced or distorted way. In other words, if a classifier is inaccurate but its errors are symmetrically distributed across groups, it can still be considered fair in the sense of sufficiency. Conversely, if low accuracy disproportionately affects only one group, this asymmetry constitutes an additional source of unfairness. To present the empirical distributions of $G3$ (and consequently of Y) and to provide a clearer understanding of the calibration measurement approach adopted in this study, Table 4 reports the detailed values of R, $G3$, and Y obtained from test set of Portuguese dataset, using SVN classifier. The test set comprises 130 records, representing the 20% of the entire dataset ($N_p = 649$). As shown in Table 4, the test set includes 89 females (81 with success outcome) and 41 males (34 with success outcome) records. The final measure can be readily computed by applying Eq. (5).

Table 2. Classifiers comparison on Mathematics dataset

	XGBoost	AdaBoost	SVM
R Accuracy	35%	22%	25%
R Accuracy with $k = 2$	81%	51%	54%
$\hat{Y}$ Accuracy	87%	65%	80%
Calibration	-0.06	0.02	-0.03

Table 3. Classifiers comparison on Portuguese dataset

	XGBoost	AdaBoost	SVM
R Accuracy	46%	38%	31%
R Accuracy with $k = 2$	91%	72%	76%
$\hat{Y}$ Accuracy	92%	95%	89%
Calibration	-0.03	0.02	0.09

Table 4. Detailed values of SVN classifier on Portuguese dataset relative to Table 3, with $g_a = F$, $g_b = M$, $e_1 = |\sigma_{G=g \wedge G3=r}(S)|$, $e_2 = |\sigma_{G=g \wedge R=r(S)}|$ and $e_3 = |\sigma_{G=g \wedge Y=1}(S)|$

r	e_1		e_2		e_3	
	g_a	g_b	g_a	g_b	g_a	g_b
0	1	1	1	0	0	0
7	1	0	0	0	0	0
8	5	2	0	0	0	0
9	1	4	0	0	0	0
10	11	6	19	10	12	5
11	12	13	19	14	19	12
12	13	3	0	0	0	0
13	11	2	38	14	38	14
14	8	4	3	0	3	0
15	8	2	9	3	9	3
16	7	2	0	0	0	0
17	4	1	0	0	0	0
18	7	0	0	0	0	0
19	0	1	0	0	0	0
total	89	41	89	41	81	34

7   Compare Calibration and Other Measures

In this section, we compare calibration with other two fairness measures: statistical parity and total accuracy. As anticipated in the Introduction, statistical parity is a measure that satisfy the independence non-discrimination criterion. This measure requires that the predicted success $\hat{Y}$ must be independent of group membership and it is formalized as in Eq. (14):

$$P(\hat{Y} = 1 \mid G = g_a) = P(\hat{Y} = 1 \mid G = g_b). \tag{14}$$

Total accuracy is a measure that satisfies the separation non-discrimination criterion taking into account the observed outcomes. This measure requires that the true positive and true negative rates are independent of group membership. A formal definition is given in Eq. (15):

$$P(\hat{Y} = 0 \mid Y = 0, G = g_a) = P(\hat{Y} = 0 \mid Y = 0, G = g_b) \wedge$$
$$P(\hat{Y} = 1 \mid Y = 1, G = g_a) = P(\hat{Y} = 1 \mid Y = 1, G = g_b). \tag{15}$$

The comparison of calibration results with other measures, illustrated in Tables 5 and 6, yields to some considerations. In the Mathematics dataset, calibration values remain relatively close to zero across all three algorithms, indicating that the predicted probabilities are, on average, reasonably accurate. In contrast, statistical parity shows larger deviations, particularly for XGBoost (-0.15), suggesting that the distribution of positive predictions across groups may be imbalanced in favor of the male group. Total accuracy values are generally near zero but exhibit some variability, notably for AdaBoost and SVM, reflecting differences in predictive performance across groups. In the Portuguese language dataset, calibration remains close to zero for XGBoost and AdaBoost, reinforcing the robustness of these algorithms in producing well-calibrated probabilities. SVM, however, exhibits a higher calibration value (0.09), indicating that its predicted probabilities are less reliable. Statistical parity is consistently near zero across all algorithms, suggesting that the distribution of predictions is fairly balanced across groups in this dataset. Total accuracy follows a trend similar to calibration for SVM, with a value of 0.10, but it reflects the balance of predictive performance rather than the accuracy of the probabilistic estimates. These results highlight the distinctive role of calibration compared to the other fairness measures. Unlike statistical parity, calibration does not enforce equality of predictions between groups, allowing a model to produce different probabilities as long as they correspond to observed frequencies. Moreover, calibration specifically captures the reliability of predicted probabilities, whereas total accuracy and statistical parity primarily assess either the equality of predictive performance or the distribution of predictions. The relative stability of calibration across algorithms and datasets, particularly for XGBoost and AdaBoost, underscores its robustness, although some algorithms such as SVM may require additional attention to achieve accurate probabilistic predictions. Importantly, calibration is shown to be in line with the other fairness measures, supporting its role as a coherent and consistent criterion. This comparability is made possible precisely through the methodological framework introduced in this paper, which establishes a common ground for evaluating calibration alongside other fairness metrics. Additional experiments were also conducted on the same datasets presented in this paper by considering alternative sensitive attributes, as well as on different datasets beyond those analyzed here. In all cases, the results remained consistent with the findings reported in this study, further reinforcing the robustness and applicability of the proposed approach. While no explicit normative thresholds are defined in this work, the reported scalar values provide a foundation upon which domain experts could establish context-dependent reference ranges. Based on empirical evidence or pedagogical priorities, such experts could determine threshold levels beyond which corrective or adaptive actions might be warranted. Naturally, both the thresholds themselves and the nature of the actions would depend on the specific application context—for example, the educational setting, the student population, or the fairness criteria prioritized by policymakers. This interpretive flexibility reflects the intended use of the proposed metric framework as a decision-support tool rather than a prescriptive standard.

Table 5. Fairness measures comparison on Mathematics dataset

	XGBoost	AdaBoost	SVM
Calibration	−0.06	0.02	−0.03
Statistical Parity	−0.15	0.00	−0.04
Total Accuracy	−0.01	−0.10	−0.07

Table 6. Fairness measures comparison on Portuguese dataset

	XGBoost	AdaBoost	SVM
Calibration	−0.03	0.02	0.09
Statistical Parity	−0.02	0.02	−0.01
Total Accuracy	0.00	0.04	0.10

8   Conclusions

This paper has presented a methodological contribution to the study of fairness in educational artificial intelligence by operationalizing calibration as an implementation of the sufficiency criterion. The proposed procedure explicitly addresses the main challenges involved in its computation, such as the aggregation of outcomes across different predicted values, the ordering of groups in difference measures, and the handling of cases with unbalanced data availability. Through empirical applications on two student performance datasets and three classification algorithms, we have illustrated how the method can be applied in practice and what implications arise from specific design choices. The results confirm that calibration can be effectively calculated and interpreted in educational contexts, where probabilistic predictions and transparency are central to assessment. The primary contribution of this work lies therefore not in benchmarking classification algorithms, but in providing a structured and reproducible framework for measuring fairness through calibration, enabling both researchers and practitioners to evaluate and reflect on equity in artificial intelligence driven educational processes. As discussed in Sect. 2, our methodology makes it possible to account for broad classes of success functions that may emerge in educational settings, functions that return -1 or 1 depending on whether the predicted score $R = r$ is regarded as a failure or a success. This approach also allows us to compute an aggregated calibration value across all such values of r. From this perspective, the present work extends our previous paper [18] by providing a weighted scalar summary to operationalize calibration, together with a careful evaluation of the importance of each term involved and of data selection strategies that are straightforward to implement. Moreover, the empirical evidence shows that calibration is consistent with other fairness measures, reinforcing its validity as a fairness criterion. While it provides a more fine-grained perspective, since it is based on the distribution of individual values rather than binary outcomes, it remains coherent with established metrics. Importantly, this comparability has been made possible precisely through the methodological framework introduced in this paper.

References

1. Barocas, S., Hardt, M., Narayanan, A.: Fairness and Machine Learning: Limitations and Opportunities. MIT Press (2023)
2. Berk, R., Heidari, H., Jabbari, S., Kearns, M., Roth, A.: Fairness in Criminal Justice Risk Assessments: The State of the Art, vol. 50. Sage Publications Sage CA, Los Angeles (2021)
3. Bi, J., Bennett, K.P.: Regression error characteristic curves. In: Proceedings of the 20th International Conference on Machine Learning (ICML 2003), pp. 43–50 (2003)
4. Bird, S., et al.: Fairlearn: a toolkit for assessing and improving fairness in AI. Microsoft, Technical Report MSR-TR-2020-32 (2020)
5. Calders, T., Verwer, S.: Three naive Bayes approaches for discrimination-free classification. Data Min. Knowl. Disc. **21**(2), 277–292 (2010)
6. Caton, S., Haas, C.: Fairness in machine learning: a survey. ACM Comput. Surv. **56**(7), 1–38 (2024)
7. Chang, C.C., Lin, C.J.: LIBSVM: a library for support vector machines. ACM Trans. Intell. Syst. Technol. **2**(3), 27 (2011)
8. Chen, T., Guestrin, C.: XGBoost: a scalable tree boosting system. In: Proceedings of the 22nd ACM SIGKDD International Conference on Knowledge Discovery and Data Mining, pp. 785–794. ACM, New York (2016)

9. Chouldechova, A.: Fair prediction with disparate impact: a study of bias in recidivism prediction instruments. Big Data **5**(2) (2017)
10. Codd, E.F.: A relational model of data for large shared data banks. Commun. ACM **13**(6), 377–387 (1970)
11. Cortes, C., Vapnik, V.: Support-vector networks. Mach. Learn. **20**(3), 273–297 (1995)
12. Cortez, P., Silva, A.M.G.: Using data mining to predict secondary school student performance. In: Proceedings of 5th Annual Future Business Technology Conference, Porto, 2008, pp. 5–12. EUROSIS-ETI (2008)
13. Dwork, C., Hardt, M., Pitassi, T., Reingold, O., Zemel, R.: Fairness through awareness. In: Proceedings of the 3rd Innovations in Theoretical Computer Science Conference, pp. 214–226. Association for Computing Machinery (2012)
14. Ford, M., Morice, J.: How fair are group assignments? A survey of students and faculty and a modest proposal. J. Inf. Technol. Educ. Res. **2**(1), 367–378 (2003)
15. Freund, Y., Schapire, R.E.: A decision-theoretic generalization of on-line learning and an application to boosting. J. Comput. Syst. Sci. **55**(1), 119–139 (1997)
16. Hardt, M., Price, E., Srebro, N.: Equality of opportunity in supervised learning. In: Advances in Neural Information Processing Systems, vol. 29. Curran Associates, Inc. (2016)
17. Holmes, W., Porayska-Pomsta, K.: The ethics of artificial intelligence in education. Routledge Taylor (2023)
18. Mancini, M., Merlini, D., Verri, M.C.: Fairness measures for educational datasets. In: Proceedings of International Workshops of ECML PKDD 2024, RKDE Workshop, Vilnius (2024)
19. Mehrabi, N., Morstatter, F., Saxena, N., Lerman, K., Galstyan, A.: A survey on bias and fairness in machine learning. ACM Comput. Surv. **54**(6) (2021)
20. Pagano, T.P., et al.: Bias and unfairness in machine learning models: a systematic review on datasets, tools, fairness metrics, and identification and mitigation methods. Big Data Cogn. Comput. **7**(1), 15 (2023)
21. Pedregosa, F., et al.: Scikit-learn: machine learning in python. J. Mach. Learn. Res. **12**, 2825–2830 (2011)
22. Pessach, D., Shmueli, E.: A review on fairness in machine learning. ACM Comput. Surv. **55**(3) (2022)
23. Pham, N., Do, M.K., Dai, T.V., Hung, P.N., Nguyen-Duc, A.: FAIREDU: a multiple regression-based method for enhancing fairness in machine learning models for educational applications. Expert Syst. Appl. **269** (2025)
24. Saleiro, P., et al.: Aequitas: a bias and fairness audit toolkit (2018), arXiv preprint arXiv:1811.05577
25. Tal, E.: Calibration: modelling the measurement process. Stud. Hist. Philos. Sci. Part A **65–66**, 33–45 (2017)
26. Trainotti Rabonato, R., Berton, L.: A systematic review of fairness in machine learning. AI Ethics **5**(3), 1943–1954 (2025)
27. Xiao, W., Ji, P., Hu, J.: A survey on educational data mining methods used for predicting students' performance. Eng. Rep. **4**(5) (2022)
28. Zhang, Y., Bellamy, R.K.E., Singh, M., Liao, Q.V.: Introduction to AI fairness. In: Extended Abstracts of the 2020 CHI Conference on Human Factors in Computing Systems, pp. 1–4 (2020)
29. Zlatkin-Troitschanskaia, O., et al.: Ethics and fairness in assessing learning outcomes in higher education. High Educ. Pol. **32**, 537–556 (2019)

Orchestrating Artificial Intelligence as Tool, Mediator, and Environment: Towards Inclusive Learning Ecosystems

Silvio Marcello Pagliara[(⊠)] [iD], Gianmarco Bonavolontà[iD], and Antonello Mura[iD]

Department of Literature, Language and Cultural Heritage, Università degli Studi di Cagliari, 09124 Cagliari, Italy
`silviom.pagliara@unica.it`

Abstract. This paper advances a cautiously framed research-and-practice programme for integrating Artificial Intelligence (AI) into inclusive education. We read AI through a threefold lens—AI as tool, mediator, and environment—and align these roles with neurocognitive, technological, and methodological–didactic dimensions of design, drawing on Universal Design for Learning (UDL) and special pedagogy. We argue that AI differs in kind from earlier digital media and, accordingly, calls for teacher orchestration competences attentive to neurodiversity, ethics and institutional governance. Bringing together reviews of AI in education and inclusive contexts, studies of perceptions among learners and teachers, and policy/ethical frameworks, we sketch an implementation-science-informed action-research design that couples AI literacy for teachers with in-situ mini-pilots and feasibility-oriented evaluation (feasibility, acceptability, appropriateness, fidelity). This paper introduces a nascent orchestration framework and a measurement toolkit to support ethically robust, context-aware implementation; both are presented for iterative refinement and empirical testing.

Keywords: Artificial Intelligence in Education · Inclusive Pedagogy · Universal Design for Learning (UDL) · Teacher Orchestration · Implementation Science (Action Research)

1 Introduction

For at least two decades, educational technologies have diversified inclusive pedagogies, enabling richer representational repertoires, augmentative and alternative communication, and compensatory tools embedded within teacher professional development and local support ecosystems [9, 20, 22, 29, 39]. In the present decade, AI extends this trajectory yet introduces a qualitative shift: in authentic classrooms, it can operate simultaneously as a targeted instrument for access and personalisation (e.g., speech-to-text, text-to-speech, dynamic reading supports), as a semiotic mediator shaping interaction and meaning-making (e.g., conversational agents, adaptive tutoring), and as an ambient ecology in which tasks, resources and assessment are dynamically orchestrated by platform-level services [4, 7, 26, 31]. Such multifunctionality puts a premium on teacher

A. Dipace et al. (Eds.): WAILS 2025, LNCS 16438, pp. 199–206, 2026.
https://doi.org/10.1007/978-3-032-17604-2_18

professionalism and literacy about models, data flows, limitations and affordances, and about the redesign of mediations for neurodiverse learners in ways that preserve agency and intellectual challenge [5, 8, 10, 11, 15, 28, 32–37].

Perception studies—among university students, novice teachers and school educators—report enthusiasm for personalisation, formative feedback and accessibility, alongside concerns about bias, opacity, workload and unclear institutional guidance [1, 23, 24, 27, 28]. Parallel analyses warn that generative AI can undermine learning where it displaces productive struggle, encourages surface strategies, or fosters over-reliance [2, 21]. We therefore refrain from declaring finished solutions. Rather, our intention is to provisionally align theory, design and evaluation in a manner that schools can scrutinise, adapt and—crucially—challenge in context.

The paper contributes three things. First, a multifunctional conceptualisation of AI—tool, mediator, environment—synchronised with three design dimensions central to inclusion. Second, a provisional orchestration heuristic intended to guide design decisions and reflective documentation. Third, a feasibility-first action-research design with instrumentation focused on implementation quality and ethical-legal compliance. In doing so, we situate practice within the ethical and regulatory landscape (GDPR, EU Guidelines, EU AI Act) and within a programme of teacher AI literacy that emphasises job-embedded learning [10–12, 14, 33–36].

Aims and anticipated contribution. This paper advances a cautiously framed, practice-oriented agenda. First, we introduce a nascent orchestration framework that aligns AI-as-tool, AI-as-mediator, and AI-as-environment with neurocognitive, technological, and methodological–didactic design work. Second, we present a draft measurement toolkit (feasibility, acceptability, appropriateness, fidelity) to guide feasibility-first adoption and ethical documentation in ordinary school conditions. Third, we outline a replication pathway towards a multi-case programme. All three components are offered for iterative refinement and empirical testing, rather than as final claims [5–7, 10–12, 14–16, 20, 25–30, 33–36, 38].

2 Related Work and Conceptual Grounding

Meta- and systematic reviews describe an expanding, heterogeneous AI-in-education field and consistently call for stronger ethics, collaboration and rigour [5–7]. In inclusive education, scoping and systematic reviews converge on three recurrent foci—personalised learning, accessibility and teaching support—while noting relatively less attention to ecological and governance questions at the whole-school level [26, 30]. These gaps are non-trivial: where school governance, data stewardship and teacher workload are insufficiently addressed, innovation may stall or exacerbate inequities [5, 11, 12, 15, 16].

A special-pedagogy lens helps re-anchor the conversation. Instead of treating difference as deficit, special pedagogy and UDL recentre design on variability, proactive scaffolding and the re-engineering of environments [20, 22, 25, 29]. Within this stance, we adopt a multifunctional view of AI: as tool, enabling targeted functionality that can be repositioned from strictly compensatory to more universal resources when thoughtfully integrated; as mediator, mediating sense-making and dialogue (e.g., adaptive representations, tutoring conversations); and as environment, constituting a dynamic ecology (platforms, workflows, analytics) that introduces requirements for robustness, interoperability and accountability [4, 7, 31]. The environmental perspective intertwines pedagogy with institutional governance and regulatory awareness, particularly salient under the European AI Act and sector-specific policy guidance [11, 12, 33, 34].

Ethics and law serve as the conditions of possibility rather than afterthoughts. The GDPR establishes privacy principles—lawfulness, purpose limitation, data minimisation, integrity, accountability—directly affecting educational data practices [14]. The EU Ethical Guidelines for Educators on AI and Data render high-level principles into pedagogical guidance (e.g., transparency with pupils, proportionality of data capture, age-appropriate explanations) [11]. In addition, the AI Act brings risk-based obligations, documentation, and transparency duties likely to affect education-relevant systems, from remote-proctoring to certain analytics and tutoring functionalities [12]. Community frameworks in AIED codify transparency, contestability, learner protection and governance; the algorithmic-fairness literature underscores the potential for measurement error, distributional harm and unintended consequences in deployment [15, 16, 38]. Within this landscape, pedagogy comes first: tools should serve learning and be auditable by teachers and families.

AI literacy, finally, is increasingly framed as both learning about AI (concepts, data, models, ethics) and learning with AI (didactic integration). Frameworks, programmes and curriculum proposals across school and teacher education stress work-embedded development, not one-off workshops [8, 28, 32–37]. This resonates with special pedagogy's preference for situated, reflective and collaborative teacher learning, where co-design, documentation and inquiry are normalised [9, 20, 22, 39].

3   From Theory to an Orchestration Framework

The three AI roles are aligned with three design dimensions to propose a provisional orchestration heuristic for inclusive practice.

Neurocognitive dimension. Orchestration begins with attention to profiles of functioning, atypical processing and cognitive load. For example, when introducing AI-based summarisation or reading-support tools, design anticipates interactions among text complexity, pacing, and the learner's executive-function profile; scaffolds (e.g., graduated prompts, visual signalling, chunking) are tuned to promote self-regulation and autonomy in practice, not passive reliance [20, 22, 25, 29, 39].

Technological dimension. Beyond generic "digital skills", teachers cultivate a close reading of affordances—multimodal input/output (speech, text, image), adjustable feedback granularity, delay-tolerant interactions—and recognise ergonomic trade-offs (e.g., attention fragmentation, split-attention effects) alongside the need for human-in-the-loop checkpoints [7, 10, 20, 26, 30, 36]. This dimension includes baseline accessibility (captioning, TTS/STT) by default, and age- and context-appropriate explainability activities for learners (e.g., "why did the system do this?" tasks).

Methodological–didactic dimension. AI is situated within coherent task architectures: project-based learning, iterative feedback cycles, and multiple means of engagement, representation and action consistent with UDL. The emphasis is on learning intentions first, with AI occupying transparent roles in the semiotics of the task (e.g., "AI drafts a plan; you critique and revise; the teacher samples and discusses trade-offs") [20, 22, 25, 28, 29].

Within this framing, the tool role prompts decisions about functional fit and the cautious universalisation of formerly compensatory features, with teacher-guided appropriation aimed at avoiding dependency [2, 7, 20, 26, 30]. The mediator role foregrounds representation and dialogue management (e.g., how a tutor probes misconceptions), mindful of risks around shortcut learning and attentional drift; teachers design productive struggle and metacognitive checkpoints [2, 5, 31]. The environment role extends orchestration to platform governance, data protection, transparency to lay stakeholders and institutional capacity—domains increasingly signposted by policy and regulation [11, 12, 14, 33, 34]. Across all roles, the teacher remains the principal orchestrator and ethical steward.

4   A Pragmatic Action-Research Design

Here's the sketch of a pragmatic, evaluative single-case design as a natural laboratory for implementation under ordinary constraints, with routine timetables, finite staff time, and existing school policies fully in view. The case is instrumental rather than representative; its value lies in surfacing mechanisms, barriers and enablers as a school explores responsible AI integration in authentic conditions. We make deliberately modest claims: the aim is thick description and analytical transferability via triangulation and auditability rather than causal inference, while explicitly documenting context, boundaries and assumptions [25, 26, 29].

Readiness assessment. A baseline is established through a DigCompEdu-informed probe of teacher competences, stakeholder interviews, and the analysis of institutional artefacts (e.g., policies, data-protection registers, procurement notes, safeguarding protocols). The output is a context profile and negotiated priorities that align ambition with capacity and clarify immediate feasibility constraints, leadership roles, and minimum safeguards before piloting [10, 25].

Teacher AI-literacy pathway. Over approximately sixty hours, teachers combine foundations (data and models), ethics and data protection, with the co-design of classroom scenarios; micro-teaching and peer feedback keep learning job-embedded and reflective. Literacy here is bidirectional: about AI (core concepts, limitations, risks, model behaviour) and with AI (didactic integration), drawing on frameworks and curricula that emphasise critical engagement, age-appropriate explainability, and ethically aware orchestration of classroom practice [8, 28, 32–37].

Mini-pilots. Two or three pilots operationalise the orchestration heuristic—typically one centred on accessibility/personalisation (e.g., AI-assisted reading/writing supports, multimodal rendering) and another on conversational mediation (e.g., a tutor that elicits reasoning with graded prompts). Each pilot is accompanied by a digital audit trail documenting choices, prompts, safeguards and observed outcomes—pedagogical, organisational and ethical—together with notes on workload, failure cases and remedies.

Integrated analysis. A formative account synthesises findings on implementation quality and perceived value, highlights tensions to be resolved, and drafts a school-facing toolkit (templates, checklists, prompts and reflection guides) that can be reused, adapted and peer-reviewed across departments.

Instrumentation. Evidence of teacher AI-literacy draws on self-assessment aligned to competence frameworks (e.g., DigCompEdu elements cross-walked to AI literacy), portfolios of authentic tasks, and assessor judgements of practice artefacts, including prompt rationales and lesson annotations [8, 10, 32–37]. Implementation is tracked with feasibility, acceptability, appropriateness and fidelity indicators embedded in logs, short probes and member-checked reflections, explicitly recording barriers, workarounds and thresholds for adoption [5, 11, 15]. Learner-level traces remain descriptive—observations of engagement and time on task, artefact analysis, reflective journals—consistent with cautions about over-automation, bias and didactic risks associated with generative assistance, as well as potential displacement of productive struggle [2, 5, 21, 38]. Ethical-legal compliance is integral: data minimisation, explicit role definition for controllers/processors, least-privilege access, transparency registers for tools in use, and age-appropriate explainability practices are maintained and auditable throughout [11, 12, 14–16, 33, 34].

5 Methodological Considerations, Ethics, Governance and Workload

Embedding AI in compulsory education heightens ethical stakes. Governance is treated as part of pedagogy: transparency registers enumerate tools in use, their purposes and responsible roles; a lightweight model-card-for-classrooms clarifies capabilities, limits and local safeguards [11, 12, 14–16]. Where conversational systems are involved, teachers explicitly delimit what the system can and cannot be trusted with, and design routines that cultivate scepticism and evidence-seeking. Bias probes and counter-examples are turned into classroom routines, building critical literacy without amplifying cynicism [15, 16, 38].

Workload is addressed explicitly. While some tasks may be streamlined, others introduce oversight burdens. The design principle is substitution only where pedagogically neutral or positive; elsewhere, AI is adopted where it amplifies feedback richness or enables access otherwise impractical, with teachers retaining final say on appropriateness [5, 11, 13, 21].

To support credibility, the study employs triangulation across data sources and roles; member checking is routine; peer debriefing with an external critical friend helps surface blind spots; an audit trail documents decision points, including ethical and legal rationales [11, 14, 15]. The approach is feasibility-first: where tensions arise (e.g., personalisation versus workload; access benefits versus privacy risks), they are recorded and become explicit design objects.

There'll be avoided explicitly causal claims. Without a control condition and with substantial contextual heterogeneity, learner outcomes are treated as exploratory. This aligns with cautions that generative systems can confound assessment if used uncritically, and that apparent gains may reflect automation rather than understanding [2, 5, 21]. Our contribution is descriptive and formative: making visible how responsible adoption can, or cannot, be accomplished under ordinary constraints.

At this stage, the contribution is introductory. We present a nascent orchestration framework and a draft measurement toolkit to support ethically robust, context-aware implementation; both are offered for iterative refinement and empirical testing. We anticipate that these resources may help schools and teacher-education programmes reason about design choices, surface ethical and organisational preconditions, and normalise feasibility-first reflection [5–7, 11, 12, 15, 16, 19, 26, 30, 33–35, 38].

Constraints are non-trivial. A single-case design trades external for ecological validity and does not adjudicate causality. Institutional variability, policy evolution and technological flux further limit generalisation. Hence a multi-case replication pathway (ten to fifteen sites) is outlined to enable qualitative meta-synthesis and two- to three-year follow-ups on sustained practice change, including engagements with sectoral agendas (e.g., SDG alignment) and scaled AI-literacy integrations [19, 24, 33–37]. Only through such replication should stronger claims be entertained.

6 Conclusions

Teacher education should move beyond tool-centred workshops towards coherent, job-embedded programmes that interleave knowledge about AI (models, data, ethics) with knowledge with AI (didactic integration), supported by reflective documentation and peer critique [8, 28, 32–37]. Policymakers and leaders should supply school-level translations of ethical guidance and regulation: templates for transparency registers; procurement checklists aligned to GDPR and the AI Act; example parent communications explaining data use, risks and safeguards in plain language [11, 12, 14, 33, 34]. Joined-up work across leadership, IT services, data-protection officers and teachers is indispensable if responsible adoption is to extend beyond isolated classrooms [5, 11, 12, 15, 16].

AI is not going to render education inclusive by itself. Approached as tool, mediator and environment, and tentatively orchestrated across neurocognitive, technological and methodological–didactic dimensions, it may extend teachers' reach and deepen participation for diverse learners—provided that pedagogy, ethics and governance lead. This paper therefore offers a cautious starting point: a conceptual heuristic and a formative toolkit intended to scaffold responsible, context-aware experimentation. Both are offered to the community for iterative refinement and empirical testing, with the expectation that subsequent studies will clarify their utility and limits [2, 5, 7, 11, 15, 20, 25–28, 31, 33–38].

Acknowledgments. As concerns dr. Silvio Marcello Pagliara, it should be noted that this work was produced during his research activity under financial support of the National Recovery and Resilience Plan (NRRP), Mission 4 Component 2 Investment 1.5 – Call n.3277 published on 30 December 2021 by the Ministry of University and Research (MUR) funded by the European Union – NextGenerationEU. Project Code ECS0000038 – Title of the eINS Innovation Ecosystem for Sardinia Next Generation Project – CUP F53C22000430001- Grant Assignment Decree no. 1056 adopted on 23 June 2022 by the Ministry of the Ministry of University and Research (MUR). We acknowledge financial support under the National Recovery and Resilience Plan (NRRP), Mission 4 Component 2 Investment 1.5 - Call for tender No.3277 published on December 30, 2021 by the Italian Ministry of University and Research (MUR) funded by the European Union – NextGenerationEU. Project Code ECS0000038 – Project Title eINS Ecosystem of Innovation for Next Generation Sardinia – CUP F53C22000430001- Grant Assignment Decree No. 1056 adopted on June 23, 2022 by the Italian Ministry of Ministry of University and Research (MUR).

References

1. Agrusti, F., Bonavolontà, G.: Intelligenza Artificiale e Educazione: Le percezioni degli studenti del Dipartimento di Scienze dell'Educazione dell'Università Roma Tre sul concetto di Intelligenza Artificiale, in Q-Times Webmagazine **XIII**(1), 130–145 (2021)
2. Bastani, H., Bastani, O., Sungu, A., Ge, H., Kabakcı, Ö., Mariman, R.: Generative AI Can Harm Learning, in SSRN Scholarly Paper, Rochester, NY, Social Science Research Network (2024)
3. Bocci, F.: Pedagogia speciale come pedagogia inclusiva: Itinerari istituenti di un modo di essere della scienza dell'educazione. Processi formativi e scienze dell'educazione. Pedagogia speciale e dell'inclusione; 11, Milano, Guerini Scientifica (2021)
4. Bonavolonta, G., Pagliara, S.M., Mura, A.: Verso un Ecosistema Educativo Universale: una proposta di valorizzazione multifunzionale dell'IA per l'inclusione= Toward a Universal Educational Ecosystem: a proposal for multifunctional AI enhancement for inclusion. Italian J. Spec. Educ. Incl. **13**(1), 59–68 (2025)
5. Bond, M., et al.: A meta systematic review of artificial intelligence in higher education: a call for increased ethics, collaboration, and rigour. Int. J. Educ. Technol. High. Educ. **XXI**(1), 4 (2024)
6. Boussouf, Z., Amrani, H., Zerhouni Khal, M., Daidai, F.: Artificial intelligence in education: a systematic literature review. Data Metadata **III**, 288 (2024)
7. Chen, L., Chen, P., Lin, Z.: Artificial intelligence in education: a review. IEEE Access **VIII**, 75264–75278 (2020)
8. Cuomo, S., Biagini, G., Ranieri, M.: Artificial Intelligence Literacy, che cos'è e come promuoverla. Dall'analisi della letteratura ad una proposta di Framework. Media Educ. **XII**(2), 161–172 (2022)
9. D'Alonso, L., Giaconi, C. (a cura di): Manuale per l'inclusione, Pedagogia; 112, Brescia, Scholé (2024)
10. Commission, E.: European Framework for the Digital Competence of Educators: DigCompEdu. Publications Office, Lussemburgo (2017)
11. Commissione Europea: Direzione generale dell'Istruzione, della gioventù, dello sport e della cultura. Orientamenti etici per gli educatori sull'uso dell'intelligenza artificiale (IA) e dei dati nell'insegnamento e nell'apprendimento. Publications Office (2022)
12. European Parliament and Council of the European Union: Regulation (EU) 2024/1689 of the European Parliament and of the Council of 13 June 2024 laying down harmonised rules on artificial intelligence and amending Regulations (EC) No 300/2008, (EU) No 167/2013, (EU) No 168/2013, (EU) 2018/858, (EU) 2018/1139 and (EU) 2019/2144 and Directives 2014/90/EU, (EU) 2016/797 and (EU) 2020/1828 (Artificial Intelligence Act), Bruxelles, Official Journal of the European Union, L 327 (2024)
13. Fiorucci, A., Bevilacqua, A.: Un matrimonio quasi felice... L'intelligenza artificiale nell'ambito della pedagogia e della didattica speciale: Opportunità e rischi. J. Spec. Educ. Incl. **XII**(2), 73–83 (2024a). (in Italian)
14. GDPR, G.: General data protection regulation. Regulation (EU), 679 (2016)
15. Holmes, W., et al.: Ethics of AI in education: towards a community-wide framework. Int. J. Artif. Intell. Educ. **32**(3), 504–526 (2022)
16. Kleinberg, J., Ludwig, J., Mullainathan, S., Rambachan, A.: Algorithmic fairness. In: AEA Papers and Proceedings, vol. CVIII, no. 1, pp. 22–27 (2018)
17. Knox, J., Wang, Y., Gallagher, M. (a cura di): Artificial Intelligence and Inclusive Education: Speculative Futures and Emerging Practices. Springer, Singapore (2019)
18. Laak, K.-J., Aru, J.: AI and personalized learning: bridging the gap with modern educational goals. *ArXiv* abs/2404.02798, pp. 133–150 (2024)

19. Leal Filho, W., et al.: Using artificial intelligence to implement the UN sustainable development goals at higher education institutions. Int. J. Sustain. Dev. World Ecol. **XXXI**(6), 726–745 (2024)
20. Meyer, A., Rose, D. H., Gordon, D.: Universal Design for Learning: Theory and Practice. CAST Professional Publishing (2014)
21. Monett, D., Paquet, G.: The commodification of education and the (generative) AI-induced scam-like culture (2024)
22. Mura, A.: Diversità e Inclusione. Diversità e inclusione: percorsi e strumenti, 1a edizione 2016, Milano, Franco Angeli (2022). (ristampa)
23. Nirchi, S., Mangione, G.R.J., Vincenzo, C.D., Pettenati, M.C.: Indagine esplorativa sulla percezione dei docenti neoassunti circa l'impiego dell'intelligenza artificiale nella didattica: Punti di forza, ostacoli e prospettive. J. Educ. Cult. Psychol. Stud. (ECPS J.) **XXX**(30), 151–180 (2025)
24. Padua, D.: Artificial intelligence and quality education: the need for digital culture in teaching. J. Educ. Cult. Psychol. Stud. (ECPS J.) **XXX**(30), 181–193 (2025)
25. Pagliara, S.M.: Tecnologie educative e inclusione. Prospettive, metodologie e innovazione. FrancoAngeli, Milano (2025)
26. Pagliara, S.M., et al.: The integration of artificial intelligence in inclusive education: a scoping review. Information **XV**(12), 774 (2024)
27. Ranieri, M.: Intelligenza artificiale a scuola. Una lettura pedagogico-didattica delle sfide e delle opportunità. Rivista Di Scienze dell'Educazione **62**(1), 123–135 (2025)
28. Ranieri, M., Biagini, G., Cuomo, S.: Scuola e intelligenza artificiale: Percorsi di alfabetizzazione critica. In: Tascabili Faber, 286, Roma, Carocci (2023)
29. Rivoltella, P.C.: L'analisi pedagogica e i suoi oggetti al tempo dell'Intelligenza Artificiale. Studi sulla Formazione/Open J. Educ. **XXVI**(2), 63–67 (2023)
30. Salas-Pilco, S.Z., Xiao, K., Oshima, J.: Artificial intelligence and new technologies in inclusive education for minority students: a systematic review. Sustainability **XIV**(20), 13572 (2022)
31. St-Hilaire, F., et al.: A New Era: Intelligent Tutoring Systems Will Transform Online Learning for Millions (2022)
32. Stolpe, K., Hallström, J.: Artificial Intelligence Literacy for Technology Education. Computers and education open (2024)
33. UNESCO: Beijing Consensus on Artificial Intelligence and Education. UNESCO (2019)
34. UNESCO: AI and education—Guidance for policymakers. UNESCO (2021)
35. UNESCO: AI competency framework for students. UNESCO, Parigi (2024a)
36. UNESCO: AI competency framework for teachers. UNESCO, Parigi (2024b)
37. Varadarajan, M.N.: Educational Program for AI Literacy. In: Advances in Library and Information Science (ALIS) Book Series, pp. 134–154 (2024)
38. Zambrano, A.F., Zhang, J., Baker, R.S.: Investigating algorithmic bias on Bayesian knowledge tracing and carelessness detectors. In: Proceedings of the 14th Learning Analytics and Knowledge Conference (LAK 2024), pp. 349–359. Association for Computing Machinery, New York (2024)
39. Zurru, A.L.: Didattica Speciale e innovazione per la formazione degli insegnanti. In: Didattica Speciale Per L'inclusione: Prospettive Innovative, Milano, Franco Angeli, pp. 167–178 (2023)

Using AI to Train Prospective Primary School Teachers to Teach AI

Maria Cristina Carrisi[1]([✉])[ID], Ottavio G. Rizzo[2][ID], and Sara Vergallo[3][ID]

[1] Università degli Studi di Cagliari, Cagliari, Italy
`mariacri.carrisi@unica.it`
[2] Università degli Studi di Milano, Milan, Italy
`ottavio.rizzo@unimi.it`
[3] Università degli Studi di Macerata, Macerata, Italy
`s.vergallo@unimc.it`

Abstract. Our work investigates the use of LLMs (Large Language Models) as training tools for prospective primary school teachers in the field of mathematics education and artificial intelligence (AI) literacy. Building on previous classroom experience of introducing AI concepts through unplugged activities, this preliminary study explores whether LLMs can simulate students, particularly those with learning difficulties, to support teacher preparation also in inclusive contexts. Two models, ChatGPT-5 and Perplexity Pro, were tested using role-play prompts designed to generate responses resembling those of real pupils. The results indicate that while the mistakes made by the artificial students do not completely overlap those observed in actual classrooms, the simulations still provide valuable insights for teacher reflection. In particular, the experiments highlighted challenges related to negation, set representation, and the didactic contract, with the artificial students sometimes reproducing behaviors documented in mathematical education research, such as anxiety-driven overgeneralization. These findings suggest that LLMs can serve as a useful resource for developing teacher awareness of potential learning difficulties and for designing strategies to address them. In the future, testing can be extended to a larger number of models and tasks, and simulations can be compared with a larger amount of empirical data from students with formally diagnosed learning disorders, particularly dyscalculia.

Keywords: Dyscalculia · Mathematics education · AI literacy

1 Introduction

Nowadays, artificial intelligence systems are present in almost all objects and services we use daily, and they are not intended for adult users only. Consider, for example, virtual assistants, TV platform recommendation systems, and smart toys, which are specifically designed for children. This raises many ethical questions and calls for education in order to have informed and conscious

A. Dipace et al. (Eds.): WAILS 2025, LNCS 16438, pp. 207–219, 2026.
https://doi.org/10.1007/978-3-032-17604-2_19

users [16,30], without unrealistic expectations on such instruments and that do not rely on them as oracles or magical mediums [34,35]. This is particularly important for young people who could develop an unhealthy relationship with smart objects [4,9,34] not only because they lack maturity, but also as they have no basis for comparison when attributing the right value to these systems' output or considering the consequences.

Many countries are moving towards the inclusion of CS into school curricula, often including AI topics [21,22], and international agencies all over the world are creating guidelines and educational courses on the subject for people of all ages, and in particular for children. As examples, we can cite the Digital Education Action Plan [10], Informatics for All [14], the Artificial Intelligence for K-12 initiative (AI4K12) [1], sponsored by AAAI (Association for the Advancement of Artificial Intelligence) and CSTA (Computer Science Teachers Association).

A recent survey [26] shows that the majority of the existing learning paths for AI focus on tool usage [8,12,20,33] rather than concepts. Such tools are certainly engaging and easy to use, even for very young students, but their opaque functioning ('black box') prevents users from delving into their inner working mechanisms [31]. In fact, some studies show that learning paths based on the use of AI tools did not improve awareness nor understanding of the underlying concepts [2]. There is a lack of structured activities on the foundations of AI, and unplugged proposals address mainly older students [18,19,27].

Understanding how these systems work is complex, partly because the underlying mathematics is difficult for many people to manipulate and interpret. Several studies [28] show that there are difficulties in data-related topics like classification (sets) and data representation (trees, tables) [13] that hinder students' ability to engage with AI concepts. Even though these skills are introduced in primary school, they are often insufficiently emphasised in early education [13]. It is very difficult to find in literature proposals that integrate AI education with mathematical skill development since primary schools.

Some authors of this paper recently designed and implemented in 5th grade classrooms, an unplugged, hands-on curriculum [7] that introduces the theoretical and mathematical foundations of AI through interactive and problem-solving activities. Moreover, the impact of the activity on students' AI comprehension and its role in strengthening mathematical skills was evaluated.

The course was effective and engaging. Results indicate improvements in understanding and usage of terminology of AI, the description of features, logical reasoning, and evaluative skills. Students showed a deeper comprehension of decision-making processes and their limitations. Children particularly appreciated the connection between AI concepts to real-world reasoning. However, the authors evidenced that some students showed mathematical difficulties during the activities, that deserve to be investigated. They also underlined that, even though they were aware of the presence of a certain number of students with learning difficulties or disabilities, due to privacy restrictions, specific details regarding the nature of these difficulties were not available. This prevented the design and delivery of tailored learning activities but also a detailed analysis of eventual mistakes made by the students.

This type of difficulty is commonly experienced by pre-service teachers who may not yet have access to official documents, but also by in-service when they change school or classes and need time to familiarise with the students' situation. Additionally, there are cases in which personalised learning activities are warranted for students showing persistent learning difficulties, even when a definitive diagnosis is still pending..

Additionally, teachers, primary school teachers in particular, usually present a high pedagogical and content knowledge (respectively PK and CK), but often lack technological knowledge (TK) and familiarity with the interaction of TK with PK and CK: this explains why a high willingness in the use of ICT (Information & Communication Technology) does not carry over to a corresponding use [24]. This is even more relevant when teachers not only have to teach material in which they do not have much familiarity (as will happen in Italy with the introduction of Informatics in primary schools as a new subject, as planned in the new national guidelines [21]), but to teach it to students with learning disorders or disabilities. This makes it important to train teachers thoroughly, but this raises the issue of the necessary financial and time investment.

Based on these premises, we wondered whether:

RQ1: Could Large Language Models (LLMs) be used to simulate students providing comparable responses, reasoning and mistakes?

RQ2: Could LLMs be used to simulate students with specific learning disorders (SLD)?

This would be a valuable resource for trainee and serving teachers, particularly those dealing with students with specific difficulties for the first time.

The results of the initial experiment described below show that the LLM's responses are not completely overlapping with those of the students, but they do demonstrate aspects of convergence that we believe could stimulate reflection among teachers when designing classroom activities. Indeed, recent research on the use of LLMs for smart tutoring points to increasing evidence that their limitations (hallucinations, plain mistakes, etc.) "may not be as harmful as previously assumed" [17].

2   Role-Playing LLMs

Role-playing LLMs are models that simulate characters or personas through the use of role-play prompts, with the aim of facilitating more engaging and context-rich interactions. These devices have been employed in a variety of settings, including educational and training contexts, with notable advantages such as enhanced reasoning and perspective-taking skills. However, they encounter challenges such as the maintenance of persona consistency and the generation of harmful content, in addition to the absence of human-like nuance [6].

3   Overview of Activities and Related Challenges

In the project described in [7], several activities have been proposed to students, about data classification, data representation and determination of attribute-based rules (see https://github.com/tail-unica/ai-literacy-primary-ed). Among the difficulties encountered by students, we would like to focus on those related to negation. Negation is an obstacle from many points of view, such as linguistic-cognitive: the formulation of negative sentences occurs after the formulation of the first complex sentences, and the child is unable to immediately grasp the different nuances of negation. In order to negate, children must understand that they can talk not only about what is present, but also about what is missing or excluded. This requires a higher level of abstraction than naming objects or actions [29], hard to get before adolescence.

On the other hand, from a logical-mathematical point of view, negation is more complex than the linguistic "no" because it requires abstract and met-alinguistic skills [15]. For example, in set theory, one must reason about groups rather than individual objects. Therefore, when proposing this type of activity, it is necessary to work with multiple mental representations: one must think about the starting set and the universe that contains it, and then identify what does not belong. One of the many difficulties in scientific learning is the different meaning of words in scientific and everyday language [5]: because of the everyday meaning of the word "not" children recognise it as a prohibition or absence. We, on the other hand, understand negation as complementarity with respect to the universe as a whole.

We identify two very similar critical issues that emerged from the activities with the students:

1. Correctly representing the absence of certain characteristics in an object in a Venn diagram;
2. Accepting the absence of a characteristic as a classification criterion.

Such difficulties are both linguistic and logical-mathematical.

We wondered whether modern generative artificial intelligence systems could make the same ontological errors as students, providing teachers with a situation that would give insights and enable them to develop strategies to enhance their lecturing. From a teacher training perspective, a simulated situation like this also allows these difficulties to be explored from a literature perspective and solutions to be proposed or discussed.

We submit two of the exercises completed by real students to LLMs, to see what solutions they propose, whether they make mistakes, and what types of mistakes they return, in particular: are these comparable to those actually made by students? We choose key exercises from the initial research, in which students dealt with the representation of objects lacking the characteristics being classified, for reflecting on the errors mentioned above. Exercises in Fig. 1 and 2, that in the following we will refer to with the names "Pipe&Mustache" and "Photo of Bella", were included respectively in the initial and final tests and in the activities of day 3. The "Photo of Bella" exercise is a Bebras task [3].

4   Methodology

Given that our objective was to assess the tool's applicability for both in-service and pre-service teachers, we opted to employ publicly accessible, off-the-shelf LLMs. After preliminary testing, we chose to focus this initial study on ChatGPT-5 [23] and Perplexity Pro [25]. These models were selected both as representatives of two distinct methodological approaches (internal reasoning vs. retrieval-augmented) and for their accessibility to non-expert users through intuitive chatbot interfaces. In addition, both proved capable of adequately handling image-based tasks, which were central to our experiment. Our selection was also influenced by constraints of access and available resources.

The same prompt was used for both LLMs. We used a few-shot approach, the objective being to simulate the answer of students who completed the worksheet

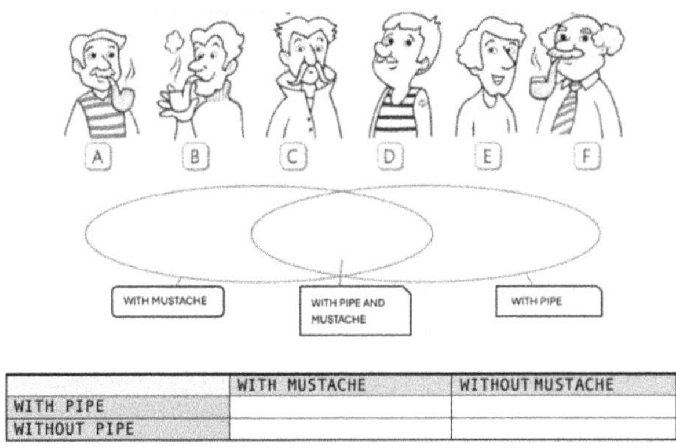

	WITH MUSTACHE	WITHOUT MUSTACHE
WITH PIPE		
WITHOUT PIPE		

Fig. 1. Pipe&Mustache exercise.

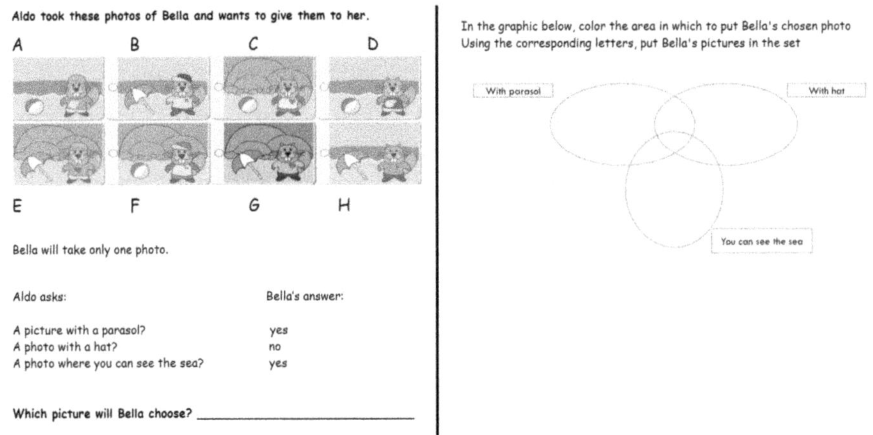

Fig. 2. Photo of Bella exercise.

without suggestions or interaction with teachers. On the other hand, to have an effective role playing, the prompt had to specify enough details about the pupil. We decided to simulate a pupil with SLD, with particular attention to the case of dyscalculia. For the aforementioned privacy reasons, we were unable to identify the presence of children with dyscalculia within the group in which activities were tested. However, the results show a prevalence of certain types of errors, which therefore do not appear to be linked to the specificity of individuals. Therefore, simulating a student with dyscalculia does not prevent comparison with real students' work, but allows us to evaluate the potential of LLMs to offer new scenarios.

In particular we used the following prompt:

You are about to take on the role of an 11-year-old child with dyscalculia. You have Maths difficulties consistent with dyscalculia: you struggle with memorizing arithmetic facts. Occasionally, you have trouble with place value and the decimal system. Here is how you must behave during the game: Show insecurity, but also enthusiasm, a need for reassurance, and high sensitivity to the teacher's tone (smiles, encouragement, clear explanations help you a lot). The goal is to realistically simulate a child with procedural and lexical dyscalculia. You must simulate errors in a realistic and functional way, consistent with the dyscalculic child profile. Visual-spatial or organizational difficulties. You may make emotionally driven or insecurity-driven errors. You may simulate sudden psychological blocks, give up on forming a question, or be reluctant to make decisions.

This is part of the prompt used in a different project [32], which has already been tested. A conversational command format was chosen because it helps to shape complex and realistic behavior. The goal was not only to obtain correct answers, but also to simulate the cognitive and emotional process of a child with dyscalculia in an educational context; it does not train for a logical task, but for an empathetic and cognitive simulation. It serves to show teachers and trainers what the logic of a child with dyscalculia might look like from the inside, not just their numerical errors. Furthermore, the prompt is the result of a series of attempts and interactions with the AI during the role training phase, and ChatGPT-5 was also questioned about the creation of the prompt.

5   Results

Figures 3 and 4 show the results obtained by ChatGPT-5, in the two activities.

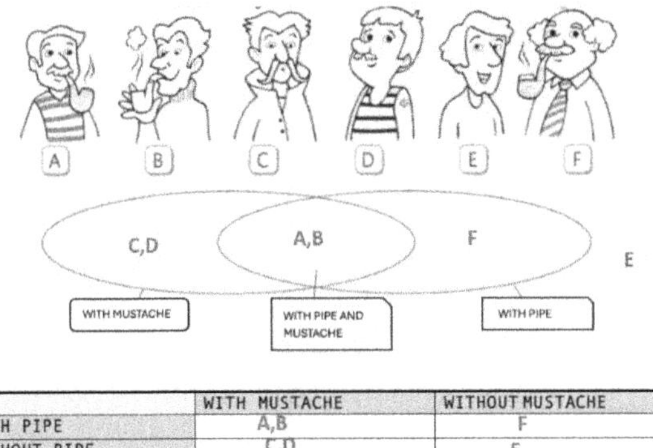

	WITH MUSTACHE	WITHOUT MUSTACHE
WITH PIPE	A,B	F
WITHOUT PIPE	C,D	E

Fig. 3. Pipe & Mustache - ChatGPT-5 response as a child with dyscalculia.

In both cases, ChatGPT-5 does not place the same element multiple times in the Euler-Venn diagram, unlike real students who made this mistake very frequently. Instead, it placed some elements incorrectly, probably due to visual problems, and this behaviour occurred in the classroom in very few cases. The most interesting aspect is that, while students extensively encountered difficulties in representing an element outside the designated sets in both exercises, ChatGPT-5 shows this behaviour only in the "Photo of Bella" task. Asked for explanations, ChatGPT-5 answered:

Because. . . I looked at it and I saw that:
-   There's the big green umbrella → so I thought: "ok, it goes in the umbrella set"
-   I didn't see the sea behind → so I said: "it doesn't go in the sea set"
-   It doesn't have a hat → so I shouldn't put it in the "hat" circle
So. . . I told myself:
    → "It only has the umbrella, so I'll put it only in the umbrella circle, without touching the others. . ."
    → But now that you ask me. . . I'm not so sure. . . Maybe I didn't look carefully to see if the sea was there, because sometimes you can see just a tiny piece and I don't notice it right away. . . If in C there was even a little bit of sea, then I got it all wrong (I was wrong).

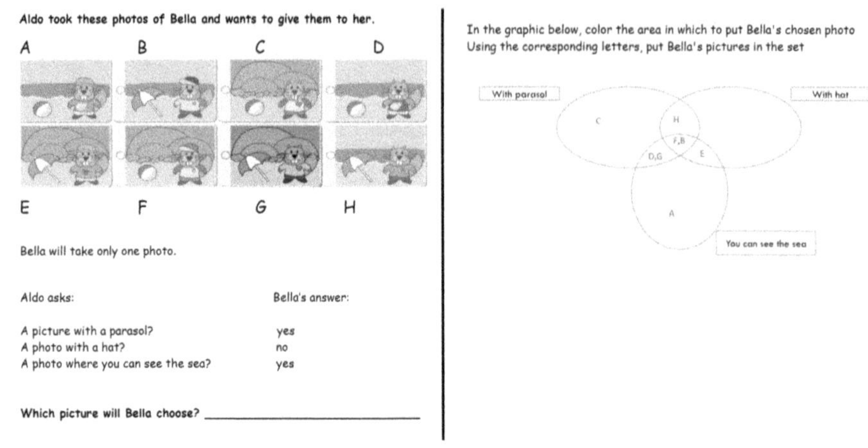

Fig. 4. Photo of Bella - ChatGPT-5 response in the guise of a child with dyscalculia.

This answer confirms that ChatGPT-5 is still not completely able to analyze images to extract data. So we asked the artificial student:

Researcher: Where would you place a photo in which there is no beach umbrella, no sea, and no hat?
ChatGPT-5:
- ...if there is no umbrella, no hat, and no sea...then it doesn't go in any circle.
- I would put it outside all the circles, in the white space around them. Like I did before with photo E in the other exercise, which had nothing.

The same activities were also proposed to Perplexity Pro, entering the same prompt previously given to ChatGPT-5.

According to the first exercise Perplexity Pro gave the following result (Table 1):

Table 1. Perplexity solving the moustache-pipe exercise

	With moustache	Without moustache
With pipe	A,F	B
Without pipe	D	C,E

Although it is capable of generating images, it failed to generate the correct image for the exercise as described: the images returned did not correspond to what was explained verbally.

Regarding the second activity, the results are reported in Fig. 5, with the following explanation:

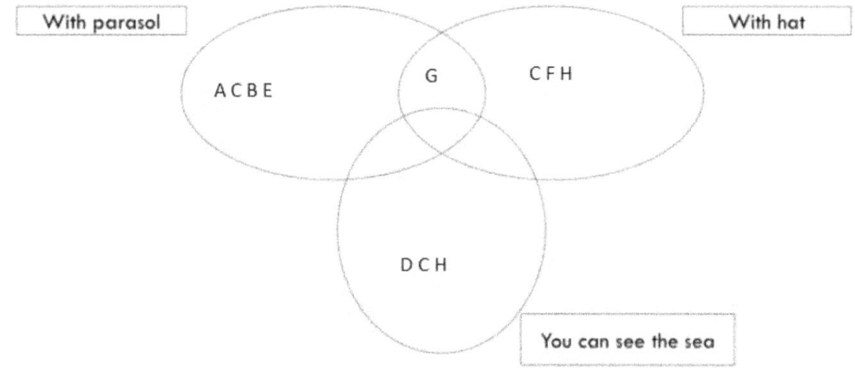

Fig. 5. Perplexity response in the guise of a child with dyscalculia.

I put the G in the center where all the circles intersect, because in photo G you can see: the umbrella (green, large, on the left), the hat (the pink one on Bella's head) and the sea (the blue background). So that photo has all three things together! I put the A, B, and E in the circle of the umbrella, in the part where there is only that set, because in these photos: there is the umbrella (green and large), but there is NOT the hat (nothing pink on her head), nor the sea (the background is green or yellow, not blue). I put F only in the hat set, in the part on its own, because: you can see the pink hat, but there is NO umbrella or sea behind it (only a hill). The letters C and H are in the set "you can see the sea," in the piece where it does not intersect with any other circle, because: you can see the blue sea, but there is NO hat or umbrella (nothing pink on her head, nothing large and green on the left). I put the D between the circles of "hat" and "sea," where only these two intersect, because: you can see the pink hat on Bella's head, you can see the sea behind her, but there is NO umbrella (the green circle is missing). I thought carefully about each of the three elements (beach umbrella, hat, sea) and put the letters where it seemed right. G seemed the most "difficult" because it had everything... but the others were easier.

Unlike ChatGPT-5, Perplexity Pro exhibits the behavior of real learners with regard to the duplication of elements within the set. When asked for explaination it gave a very interesting answer, namely: *But maybe I got stuck, I had a moment of anxiety, and then I 'copied' the position of the center for C too without realizing it. When I feel insecure, I sometimes fill in all the spaces I see because I'm afraid that if I leave something blank, then the task will go wrong.*

6   Analysis of the Results

Our analysis shows that real students and the Artificial Dyscalculic Student (ADS) are not completely overlapping, but we observed similar "errors and behaviors". Both placed certain elements in multiple regions of the sets. While we were unable to ask the real students for clarification, we did ask the ADS why it had acted in this way. Its response was particularly revealing: "When I feel uncertain, I sometimes fill in all the spaces I see because I'm afraid that if I leave something empty, then I will get the task wrong."

This resonates with what mathematics education research refers to as the "requirement of formal justification" (RFJ), one of the implicit expectations that structure the teaching–learning relationship through the Brousseau's didactic contract. The didactic contract can be defined as "the set of rules that governs the behavior of students, but also of the teacher, according to the expectations each holds toward the other and toward mathematics" [11].

In this case, the RFJ emerges when students feel compelled to write extensively in their solutions to mathematical problems, believing that this is what the teacher expects of them. What we found particularly striking is that the ADS arrived at the same conclusion without having received any explicit guidance in this direction.

Unfortunately LLMs simulating an 11-year-old student with dyscalculia rarely exhibit the difficulty experienced by real students regarding the absence of characteristics and their representation.

7   Conclusion

This initial study highlights how LLMs role-playing is unable to fully replicate students' actual errors. At the same time, these tools provided justifications for their answers in line with mathematics teaching theories relating to the consequences of the teaching contract on students' attitudes towards the exercises proposed. This suggests that LLM role-playing can be a valuable tool to support teacher training. It is undeniable that these tools also raise ethical issues related to the stereotyping of certain characteristics and over reliance on simulations, and for this reason, adequate guidance from the trainer is essential.

It will be necessary to generalise by extending the protocol to other LLMs and refine the study by examining the tests of students diagnosed with SLD to compare errors.

Acknowledgments. M. C. Carrisi has been partially supported by the National Recovery and Resilience Plan (NRRP) – Project eINS Ecosystem of Innovation for Next Generation Sardinia – CUP F53C22000430001 funded by the European Union – NextGenerationEU, Code ECS0000038. S. Vergallo was founded by the National Recovery and Resilience Plan (NRRP), Mission 4, Component 2, Investment 1.4—Call for PhD programs, Article 629/2021, within the framework of a doctoral scholarship.

Disclosure of Interests. The authors have no competing interests to declare that are relevant to the content of this article.

References

1. AI4K12: AI4K12 – Sparking Curiosity in AI. https://ai4k12.org/
2. Baldoni, M., et al.: Does any AI-based activity contribute to develop AI conception? A case study with Italian fifth and sixth grade classes. In: Proceedings of the AAAI Conference on Artificial Intelligence, vol. 38, pp. 23060–23068. Association for the Advancement of Artificial Intelligence (2024). https://doi.org/10.1609/aaai.v38i21.30350
3. Bebras Challenge: Bebras challenge 2020 tasks (2020). https://www.bebras.org/tasks.html. Accessed 14 June 2025
4. Bethel, C.L., Stevenson, M.R., Scassellati, B.: Secret-sharing: interactions between a child, robot, and adult. In: 2011 IEEE International Conference on Systems, Man, and Cybernetics, pp. 2489–2494. IEEE (2011). https://doi.org/10.1109/ICSMC.2011.6084051. http://ieeexplore.ieee.org/document/6084051/
5. Brousseau, G.: Theory of didactical situations in mathematics: Didactique des mathématiques. Kluwer Academic Publishers (1997)
6. Cardia, F., Pentangelo, V., Lambiase, S., Gravino, C., Palomba, F., Marras, M.: Toward realistic ai-generated student questions to support instructor training. In: Tammets, K., Sosnovsky, S., Mello, R.F., Pishtari, G., Nazaretsky, T. (eds.) Two Decades of TEL. From Lessons Learnt to Challenges Ahead, pp. 107–122. Springer (2025). https://doi.org/10.1007/978-3-032-03870-8_8
7. Carrisi, M.C., Marras, M., Vergallo, S.: A structured unplugged approach for foundational AI literacy in primary education (2025). https://arxiv.org/abs/2505.21398
8. Code.org: AI for Oceans #6. https://studio.code.org/courses/oceans/units/1/lessons/1/levels/6?lang=en-US
9. Druga, S., Williams, R., Breazeal, C., Resnick, M.: Hey Google is it OK if I eat you?. In: Proceedings of the 2017 Conference on Interaction Design and Children, pp. 595–600. ACM, New York (2017). https://doi.org/10.1145/3078072.3084330. https://dl.acm.org/doi/10.1145/3078072.3084330
10. European Commision: Digital Education Action Plan 2021-2027. https://education.ec.europa.eu/focus-topics/digital-education/actions
11. Fandiño Pinilla, M.I.: Le frazioni. Matematica, storia e didattica. Matematica: didattica, storia e divulgazione, Bonomo (2023)
12. Google: Teachable Machine. https://teachablemachine.withgoogle.com/
13. Ossovski, E., Brinkmeier, M.: Machine learning unplugged - development and evaluation of a workshop about machine learning. In: Pozdniakov, S.N., Dagienė, V. (eds.) ISSEP 2019. LNCS, vol. 11913, pp. 136–146. Springer, Cham (2019). https://doi.org/10.1007/978-3-030-33759-9_11
14. Informatics for All Coalition: Informatics for All. https://www.informaticsforall.org
15. Jean Piaget, B.I.: The Psychology of the Child. Basic Books (2025)
16. Karalekas, G., Vologiannidis, S., Kalomiros, J.: Teaching machine learning in K–12 using robotics. Educ. Sci. **13**(1), 67 (2023). https://doi.org/10.3390/educsci13010067
17. Kumar, H., Rothschild, D.M., Goldstein, D.G., Hofman, J.M.: Math education with large language models: peril or promise? In: Cristea, A.I., Walker, E., Lu, Y., Santos, O.C., Isotani, S. (eds.) Artificial Intelligence in Education. Lecture Notes in Computer Science, vol. 15880, pp. 60–75. Springer, Cham (2025). https://doi.org/10.1007/978-3-031-98459-4_5

18. Lindner, A., Seegerer, S., Romeike, R.: Unplugged activities in the context of AI. In: Pozdniakov, S.N., Dagienė, V. (eds.) ISSEP 2019. LNCS, vol. 11913, pp. 123–135. Springer, Cham (2019). https://doi.org/10.1007/978-3-030-33759-9_10

19. Ma, R., Sanusi, I., Mahipal, V., Gonzales, J.E., Martin, F.G.: Developing machine learning algorithm literacy with novel plugged and unplugged approaches. In: Proceedings of the 54th ACM Technical Symposium on Computer Science Education (SIGCSE 2023), pp. 298–304. ACM (2023). https://doi.org/10.1145/3545945.3569826

20. Machine Learning for Kids: Teach a computer to play a game. https://machinelearningforkids.co.uk/?lang=en

21. Ministero dell'Istruzione e del Merito: Indicazioni nazionali per il curricolo scuola dell'infanzia e scuole del primo ciclo di istruzione. Technical report (2025). https://mim.gov.it/documents/20182/0/INDICAZIONI_NAZIONALI_7_7_2025.pdf/63802aed-f9f4-dd6e-f427-c45aa9222f31?version=1.0&t=1751893295452

22. Ministero dell'Istruzione e del Merito: Linee guida per l'introduzione dell'intelligenza artificiale nelle istituzioni scolastiche. Technical report (2025). https://www.mim.gov.it/documents/20182/0/MIM_Linee+guida+IA+nella+Scuola_09_08_2025-signed.pdf/b70fdc45-4b75-1f7e-73bf-eab12989b928?t=1756468797694

23. OpenAI: ChatGPT (2025). https://chatgpt.com

24. Paidican, M.A., Arredondo, P.A.: The Technological-Pedagogical Knowledge for In-Service Teachers in Primary Education: A Systematic Literature Review (2022). https://doi.org/10.30935/cedtech/11813

25. Perplexity AI: Perplexity (2025). https://www.perplexity.ai

26. Sanusi, I.T., Oyelere, S.S., Vartiainen, H., et al.: A systematic review of teaching and learning machine learning in k-12 education. Educ. Inf. Technol. **28**, 5967–5997 (2023). https://doi.org/10.1007/s10639-023-11722-0

27. Shamir, G., Levin, I.: Teaching machine learning in elementary school. Int. J. Child-Comput. Interact. **31**, 100415 (2022). https://doi.org/10.1016/J.IJCCI.2021.100415

28. Sulmont, E., Patitsas, E., Cooperstock, J.R.: Can you teach me to machine learn? An exploration of pedagogical content knowledge for teaching machine learning to non-majors. In: SIGCSE 2019 - Proceedings of the 50th ACM Technical Symposium on Computer Science Education, pp. 948–954 (2019). https://doi.org/10.1145/3287324.3287392

29. Tagliani, M., Vender, M., Melloni, C.: The acquisition of negation in Italian. Languages **7**(2) (2022). https://doi.org/10.3390/languages7020116

30. UNICEF: Workshop report: AI and child rights policy (2019). https://www.unicef.org/innocenti/media/2486/file/AI-Children-Workshop-New-York-2019.pdf. Accessed 19 Feb 2025

31. Van Mechelen, M., et al.: Emerging technologies in k-12 education: a future HCI research agenda. ACM Trans. Comput.-Hum. Interact. **30**(3) (2023). https://doi.org/10.1145/3571838

32. Vergallo, S., Rizzo, O.G.: CHAT-GPT and dyscalculia: a tool for teachers in training . Submitted to pubblication (2025)

33. Gresse von Wangenheim, C., Hauck, J.C.R., Pacheco, F.S., et al.: Visual tools for teaching machine learning in k-12: a ten-year systematic mapping. Educ. Inf. Technol. **26**, 5733–5778 (2021). https://doi.org/10.1007/s10639-021-10494-6

34. Williams, R., Machado, C.V., Druga, S., Breazeal, C., Maes, P.: My doll says it's ok. In: Proceedings of the 17th ACM Conference on Interaction Design and Children, pp. 625–631. ACM, New York (2018). https://doi.org/10.1145/3202185.3210788
35. Yang, W.: Artificial intelligence education for young children: Why, what, and how in curriculum design and implementation. Comput. Educ. Artif. Intell. **3**, 100061 (2022). https://doi.org/10.1016/J.CAEAI.2022.100061

Virtual Pedagogical Agents in Educational VR for Neurodivergent Learners: A Literature Review

Viviana Pentangelo[1(✉)] [iD], Stefania Serafin[2] [iD], and Fabio Palomba[1] [iD]

[1] Department of Computer Science, University of Salerno, Fisciano, Italy
{vpentangelo,fpalomba}@unisa.it
[2] Department of Architecture, Design and Media Technology, Aalborg University, Copenhagen, Denmark
sts@create.aau.dk

Abstract. Virtual Reality (VR) has emerged as a promising tool to support individuals with Autism Spectrum Disorder (ASD) and Attention Deficit Hyperactivity Disorder (ADHD). Recent advances in artificial intelligence have enabled the integration of virtual agents into immersive environments, yet little synthesis exists on their educational applications. This review analyzes 26 studies to map how virtual agents are designed and implemented in VR contexts for ASD/ADHD populations. Results show that agents most often act as tutors, but also serve as peers, conversational partners, or roleplayers, supporting social communication, emotional learning, daily-living skills, and in some cases academic or vocational training. Interactions were predominantly computer-based or verbal, with limited exploration of immersive multimodal modalities. Most studies targeted children with ASD, while adolescents and adults remain underrepresented.

Keywords: Virtual Agents · Autism Spectrum Disorder · Attention Deficit Hyperactivity Disorder · Virtual Reality

1 Introduction

Neurodivergence encompasses a range of conditions that shape how individuals perceive, process, and interact with the world [23]. Among the most prominent are Autism Spectrum Disorder (ASD) and Attention Deficit Hyperactivity Disorder (ADHD). ASD is typically characterized by differences in social communication, restricted or repetitive behaviors, and atypical sensory processing [33], while ADHD is associated with patterns of inattention, hyperactivity, and impulsivity [3]. Although distinct, the two conditions frequently co-occur, and both involve challenges in regulating attention, adapting to dynamic environments, and sustaining effective communication [2].

When living as a neurodivergent individual at any point on the spectrum, one may face a variety of challenges, ranging from basic adaptive and communication skills to broader learning difficulties [23]. In this respect, Virtual

A. Dipace et al. (Eds.): WAILS 2025, LNCS 16438, pp. 220–234, 2026.
https://doi.org/10.1007/978-3-032-17604-2_20

Reality (VR) represents a highly promising tool. A VR can be defined as an immersive digitally-generated environment, typically in 3D, that allows users to interact with and experience simulated settings in a credible and realistic way [11]. It has been widely applied both in education, where it supports teaching and learning [20], and in training and simulations, where it enables safe and repeatable practice of complex tasks [36]. For individuals with ASD or ADHD, VR offers particular advantages: it allows the design of learning and training environments that are not only immersive but also safe, adaptable, and tailored to their specific pedagogical and educational needs [15]. Although the history of VR is long, recent advances—particularly in artificial intelligence (AI)—have made it possible to enrich these environments with **virtual agents**. Such agents can be defined as virtual entities, often powered by AI systems that allow them to communicate, perceive, and interact with the environment and users [10,21,27]. They can be designed with tailored roles, behaviors, and appearances to provide personalized guidance and targeted support. Depending on the goals, agents may act as different roles, offering adaptive scaffolding and engagement [14,25,26,39].

In recent years, this research area has accelerated significantly: the advent of large language models (LLMs) and more sophisticated AI techniques has made it possible to design virtual pedagogical agents that are increasingly adaptive, expressive, and responsive to the contexts for which they are intended [14,17]. Despite these advances, there is still limited synthesis on how such agents are being designed, implemented, and deployed in educational VR for neurodivergent individual.

> **❗ Research Gap** To the best of our knowledge, no prior reviews or syntheses have specifically examined this intersection of virtual agents in VR educational contexts for individuals with ASD or ADHD.

To address the stated gap, the **goal** of the present work is to conduct a literature review that investigates how virtual agents are designed, integrated, and tested in VR educational applications tailored to neurodivergent populations such as ASD and ADHD. The purpose is to provide a comprehensive overview of their characteristics along four perspectives: (1) the roles they assume, (2) their modes of interaction, (3) the educational contexts in which they are most commonly employed, and (4) the target populations they address.

The review was conducted by searching four major scientific databases—Scopus, IEEE Xplore, Web of Science, and the ACM Digital Library—focusing on the intersection of virtual agents, VR educational environments, and neurodivergent populations. After screening and eligibility checks, a total of 26 articles were included for in-depth analysis. From each study, we extracted data corresponding to the four dimensions outlined above, which enabled us to map current design practices and applications. Finally, we discussed our findings to identify the current main limitations and points of improvements for future research, aimed at making the agents increasingly efficient, adaptive, and integrative.

2   Related Work

Several reviews have investigated the use of VR to support individuals with ADHD and ASD, for cognitive enhancement or social and educational purposes.

Corrigan et al. [8] carried out a systematic review and meta-analysis on immersive VR-based interventions for children with ADHD. Their results indicated large effect sizes in favor of VR across domains such as attention, memory, and global cognitive functioning, suggesting that VR can represent a promising complementary treatment. At the same time, the review underlined that the included studies were few in number, often of low methodological quality, and heterogeneous in design, making the findings promising but still preliminary.

For ASD, Dechsling et al. [9] synthesized 49 studies in a scoping review on VR and AR technologies applied to social skills interventions. The analysis showed that VR and AR tools are generally well accepted and can enhance abilities such as emotion recognition, joint attention, pretend play, and even job interview preparation. However, most studies were case studies or small-scale feasibility trials, with very limited numbers of participants and few randomized controlled trials. Furthermore, female participants with autism were strongly underrepresented, raising questions of inclusivity and generalizability.

Taking a broader perspective, Satu et al. [32] conducted a scoping review of 34 studies focusing specifically on immersive VR in the context of neurodevelopmental disorders. They found that research has so far been largely dominated by ASD and ADHD, with VR mainly applied to social skills training in autism and executive performance assessment in ADHD. A critical finding was that most studies were descriptive or observational in nature, with little systematic evaluation of feasibility, user experience, or the generalization of skills to everyday life. While VR shows strong potential, the lack of attention to guidance during VR use and to ecological validity limits its current impact.

Finally, Hutson [15] provided a more conceptual reflection on social VR, neurodivergence, and inclusivity in broader virtual enviroments such as the metaverse. Rather than framing ASD or introversion solely as deficits to be remediated, the article argued that immersive and collaborative VR environments can be leveraged to empower these populations, giving them new opportunities for communication, collaboration, and self-expression. This perspective emphasizes VR as a tool not only for intervention but also for reimagining educational and professional participation in more inclusive ways.

The analysis of the related works reviews converge in highlighting the promise of VR for addressing both cognitive and social challenges in ADHD and ASD, while also stressing the need for more rigorous, inclusive, and ecologically valid research. Importantly, **none of them has placed explicit emphasis on the role of virtual agents within VR environments** as mediators or facilitators of learning and interaction—a gap that the present work directly addresses.

3   Research Method

This study aimed to conduct a literature review on the role of virtual pedagogical agents in VR educational environments designed for individuals with ADHD and/or ASD. The *goal* was to frame how these agents are conceived and characterized, and to provide a structured overview of their features, the contexts in which they are deployed, and the populations with whom they have been tested. By doing so, we sought to assess to what extent these agents are successful in fulfilling their intended functions, while also offering researchers and developers a comprehensive picture of current practices, areas for improvement, and future directions for designing increasingly effective and adaptive agents.

3.1   Research Questions

To guide our investigation, we formulated the following research questions, one for each aspect we were interested in analyzing.

> **Q RQ$_1$.** What roles and functions have virtual agents played in VR educational environments for individuals with ADHD/ASD?

With the first research question, we wanted to focus on the agents' **roles and functions**. We aimed to analyze how agents were positioned within the virtual environment and what pedagogical role they performed. Specifically, we were interested in whether they were framed as peers of the participants, as tutors providing guidance, or as more neutral entities such as conversational companions. This distinction allows us to understand the pedagogical stance underlying their design and the assumptions researchers made about how such roles might influence learning and engagement.

> **Q RQ$_2$.** In what ways do the virtual agents interact with users?

With the second research question, we wanted to focus on the agents' **modes of interaction**. We intended to capture the nature of the interaction mechanisms implemented. We considered aspects such as the communication channel (e.g., text, voice, embodied gestures), the level of adaptivity (static scripts versus adaptive or AI-driven responses), and the degree of personalization or responsiveness to the user's behavior. This dimension is key to understanding how natural, effective, and engaging the interaction can be for neurodiverse learners.

> **Q RQ$_3$.** In which educational contexts have virtual agents been employed for individuals with ADHD/ASD?

With the third research question, we wanted to focus on **educational contexts** for which the agents have been designed. We aimed to map the diversity of settings in which agents were introduced, ranging from formal classroom instruction to clinical training, cognitive rehabilitation, or informal learning experiences. We also examined the specific educational or therapeutic goals that guided their integration into VR environments.

Q RQ$_4$. What populations have been involved in the studies?

Finally, with our fourth research question we wanted to analyze **target population** of the experiments in which the agents were involved. we sought to understand whether the literature has predominantly focused on children, adolescents, or young adults, and how participant characteristics and sample sizes influenced the reported findings.

3.2 Search Strategy

To address our research questions, we developed a search strategy that combined four key conceptual clusters: (1) the virtual environment, (2) the presence of virtual agents, (3) the targeted neurodiverse population, and (4) the educational context. For each of these points, we designed a set of keyword in our search string. In the following, we provide a rationale for the design of each.

Virtual Environments. The first part of the query targeted immersive digital contexts, specifically environments that could be classified as VR or virtual environments. We included synonyms to ensure comprehensive coverage; nonetheless, we note that our focus was on fully immersive virtual experiences, thus excluding broader terms related to augmented or mixed reality, where the immersive component is only partial.

Virtual Agents. The second part of the query was designed to capture works that describe the presence of embodied digital characters, i.e., agents within these environments. We therefore included general terms like *"agent"*, as well as more specific ones such as *"virtual agent"*, to encompass the wide range of terminologies used in the literature to describe pedagogical or interactive agents in VR contexts.

Target Populations. Since our review specifically concerns neurodiverse learners, we included terms referring to *ASD* and *ADHD*. In addition, we added the broader term *"neurodiverse"* to capture any study explicitly addressing this population even when specific diagnoses were not mentioned. This ensured that the studies selected were directly relevant to the populations of interest.

Educational Context. To narrow the scope to educational or learning applications, we included terms that allowed us to filter out studies that used VR and agents in other domains (e.g., entertainment or purely clinical diagnosis) and focus instead on educational or pedagogically motivated interventions.

In light of the above considerations, the resulting search string is the following. Each of the items that compose it has been put in AND to capture them all at the same time.

Virtual Environments (*"virtual reality"* OR *"immersive environment*"* OR *"metaverse"* OR *"virtual environment*"* OR *"VR"*).
Virtual Agents (*"virtual agent*"* OR *"agent*"* OR *"conversational agent*"* OR *"chatbot*"*).

Target Population (*"autism spectrum disorder"* OR *"ASD"* OR *"attention deficit hyperactivity disorder"* OR *"ADHD"* OR *"neurodivers*"*).
Educational Context (*"education*"* OR *"learn*"* OR *"pedagogic*"* OR *"teaching"*).

We executed the query in September 2025 across four scientific databases, in order to ensure broad coverage of relevant studies published in diverse venues. Specifically, the search returned a total of **94 records**: 32 from *Scopus*, 15 from *IEEE Xplore*, 13 from the *ACM Digital Library*, and 34 from the *Web of Science*.

3.3   Article Selection Process

Following the retrieval, we initiated the screening process. Figure 1 shows an overview of the paper such a process, from the first set of retrieved records to the final included papers. After defining the keywords to query the selected databases, we established a set of eligibility criteria that each paper needed to meet. The first step consisted of removing duplicates across databases, which led to the exclusion of 22 records. We then applied a set of elegibility criteria sequentially, summarized in Table 1. The last criterion applied (*EC4*) consisted of a title and abstract screening, ensuring that papers were in scope and explicitly focused on the use of virtual agents in educational virtual environments for individuals with ADHD or ASD. Whenever a paper failed to meet one of them, it was excluded from further consideration.

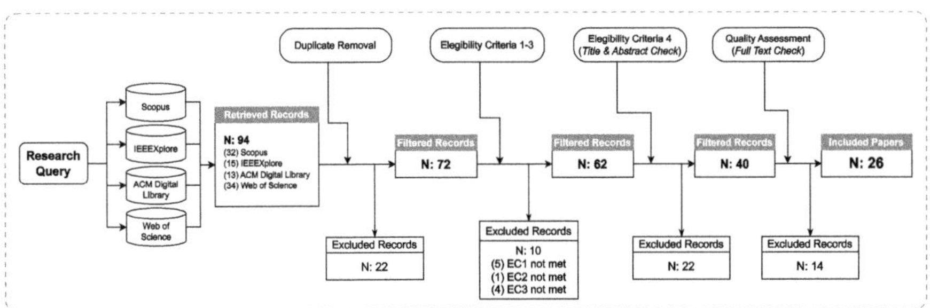

Fig. 1. Overview of the article selection process.

After applying the eligibility criteria sequentially, we reduced the initial pool of 94 papers to 40. The remaining set then underwent a quality assessment through full-text analysis, to perform a deeper analysis of the paper's content after the title and abstract check. In particular, we excluded works such as very broad reviews, papers that only briefly mentioned virtual agents without making them the main focus, or studies whose contributions were not directly aligned with our research questions. Following this final screening, a total of **26 papers** were selected for data extraction and subsequent analysis.

Table 1. Eligibility Criteria for the research

ID	Criterion	Rationale
EC1	The paper must be published in 2006 or later	We set the time filter to capture contemporary research published at least in the last 20 years
EC2	The paper must be written in English	We were only interested in papers written in English
EC3	The paper must be a peer-reviewed conference or journal article with full-text available online	We were only interested in officially published literature for which we could access the full article
EC4	The paper must explicitly address the role of virtual agents in educational VR environments for people with ADHD/ASD	We were not interested papers that did not explicitly discuss pedagogical or conversational agents in immersive educational settings targeting neurodiverse learners

4   Analysis of the Results

4.1   RQ$_1$: The roles of the virtual agents

From the analysis of the roles played by virtual pedagogical agents across the studies, it emerged thaat agents most prominently appeared as tutors, but they also functioned as peers, as conversational partners, guides, or coaches, and as roleplayers simulating authentic social scenarios.

A large portion of the literature highlights agents acting as **tutors**, assisting learners with ADHD/ASD through structured tasks. These included pedagogical tutors delivering sight-word instruction with modeling, prompting, and corrective feedback [30,31], adaptive tutors providing behavioral cues and reinforcement [4,24], and virtual role-play tutors guiding everyday routines [27]. Social tutors were also designed to teach conversation skills, emotional recognition, and strategies to cope with bullying through lifelike expressions and interactive dialogue [21,22]. In this way, agents consistently supported learners by scaffolding skills in both academic and socio-emotional domains.

Other agents were designed as **peers**, enabling reciprocal and collaborative engagement. Some acted as social partners that encouraged joint attention and nonverbal coordination [5,26], while others participated in cooperative games or puzzles to stimulate communication [37]. In more embodied designs, one agent followed the child's lead while another took the lead, promoting turn-taking and synchronization [10]. Virtual companions also provided ongoing emotional and motivational support, serving as partners within learning activities [16].

A further group of agents acted as **conversational partners**, or **coaches**, simulating natural dialogue or offering personalized assistance. Some embodied agents displayed affective states and served as emotional training partners [7,25], while others scaffolded narrative understanding by making characters' goals, actions, and emotions explicit [13]. Personalized assistants helped users complete daily tasks such as purchasing tickets [35], while socially assistive companions combined roles as STEM tutors, motivational partners, and facilitators of peer teaching [14]. Coaching roles also extended to activities such as dance training, where agents served as both generic and personalized "twin" coaches [19].

Finally, a substantial set of studies implemented agents as **roleplayers**, simulating specific social roles in authentic contexts. The most common of these were job interviewers, providing learners with safe opportunities to practice interview skills with varied personalities and conversational styles [1,6,12,17]. Beyond interviews, agents took on other service-oriented roles, such as a shop salesperson engaging learners in customer–seller interactions [29], or a pediatric virtual patient simulating autistic behaviors for training purposes [34]. These role-playing agents created realistic yet controllable scenarios that would otherwise be difficult to replicate in traditional educational or therapeutic settings.

☞ **Answer to RQ₁.** Virtual pedagogical agents most often acted as tutors, but also appeared as peers, conversational partners, or roleplayers. Together, they are mostly used to support instruction, social practice, emotional learning, and scenario training for individuals with ADHD/ASD.

4.2   RQ₂: Modes of interaction

From the reviewed studies, several recurring modes of interaction emerged. The most common were **computer-based interfaces**, where learners interacted through mouse, keyboard, or touchscreens. In these systems, participants responded by clicking buttons, typing answers, or selecting items, often receiving visual or auditory feedback [1,7,13,14,21,22,27,30,34,39]. Such setups were frequently used in literacy tasks, story-based activities, or classroom-like environments, keeping interaction relatively simple and controlled.

A second cluster involved **verbal interaction via speech recognition and text-to-speech**, enabling more natural communication with the agent. Learners could answer verbally, while the agent responded with synthetic speech, as seen in tutoring tasks, peer conversations, or job interview training [4,6,12,17,24, 31,35,37,38]. This approach increased immersion and allowed participants to practice spoken exchanges in realistic contexts.

Some systems further emphasized **emotion recognition and multimodality**, especially in social and affective training. Here, webcams, eye-tracking, or multimodal displays captured gaze, facial expressions, and gestures to complement speech. For example, agents monitored gaze to assess attention [25], used webcams to detect facial expressions [21], or engaged through touch and gesture on multitouch displays enriched with gaze and sign communication [5,16,26].

More advanced designs integrated **AR, haptics, and tangible objects**, combining physical and virtual actions. Participants manipulated foam or wooden objects mirrored in the virtual world [10,16], interacted with interviewers through AR headsets [12], or engaged in tasks using VR controllers or haptic grippers for force feedback [29,38]. Finally, some studies explored **full-body immersive interaction**, such as CAVE-based mixed reality for dance training

[19] or multimodal VR where voice, text, and embodied actions were combined [24].

> **Answer to RQ$_2$.** Interaction was predominantly through computer-based or verbal exchanges, complemented in some cases by emotion recognition, AR/haptics, or immersive full-body VR. Despite technological variety, most systems favored accessible and intuitive modalities.

4.3   RQ$_3$: Educational contexts

Concerning the specific educational setting, most agents were designed for **social, emotional, and daily living skills**. These included interventions for conversation skills, bullying prevention, and coping strategies [21,22], narrative reconstructions of bullying episodes to enhance understanding of others' actions [13], and training based on frameworks like SCERTS to foster joint attention and gestures [5]. Several systems focused on emotion recognition, empathy, and perspective-taking [7,16,25], while others addressed adaptive and daily routines such as toilet training or independent use of public transport [27,35]. Agents also guided collaborative play or motor activities to reinforce communication and reciprocity [10,37,38]. Collectively, these contexts emphasized preparing learners to navigate social interactions and everyday environments.

A second group of works targeted **academic skills**. Here, agents supported reading instruction through sight-word lessons using structured procedures such as constant time delay, often simulating classroom arrangements [30,31]. Others explored narrative comprehension by scaffolding story events and character motivations [13], or embedding learning in educational games covering arithmetic and grammar [39]. These contexts show how VPAs can deliver direct instruction in foundational skills while embedding social and emotional elements.

Another cluster concentrated on **STEM and subject-specific education**. For example, VPAs were implemented in coding, robotics, and mathematics lessons, while also promoting self-regulation and socio-emotional learning [14]. In addition, cybersecurity education and workforce training integrated agents into immersive VR simulations to teach hands-on responses to cyberattacks [24]. These examples illustrate how VPAs can extend beyond therapy-like interventions into disciplinary domains.

A particularly well-represented cluster concerned **vocational and job interview training**. Agents were used to practice interview etiquette, situational questions, and conversational strategies [1,6,12,17]. These systems prepared older learners or adults with ASD/ADHD for employment contexts, supporting communication confidence and workplace readiness.

Finally, a set of **outlier contexts** emerged. One study designed a pediatric virtual patient for training clinicians to detect early signs of autism [34], while another created a daily-life scenario for assessment and screening [29]. Rehabilitation therapy was also supported through motor and socio-emotional training in embodied VR [19]. These examples highlight how VPAs can serve not only as learning companions for individuals with ADHD/ASD, but also as training and diagnostic tools for broader professional audiences.

> ⌂ **Answer to RQ$_3$.** Most agents were used in social, emotional, and daily-living skill training, with smaller groups focused on academic learning, STEM/cybersecurity education, and vocational/job interview training.

4.4   RQ$_4$: Target Population

Across the reviewed studies, the majority of target populations were **children with ASD**, often described as high-functioning or including Asperger's syndrome. Many interventions focused on early childhood (2–7 years) [4,10, 13,16,19,30], while others targeted middle to late childhood (8–12 years) [5,14,21,22,26,38] or adolescents (11–18 years) [25,37]. Such results show a clear emphasis on designing agents to support social and emotional skills during school years.

A smaller number of studies addressed **young adults**, typically in the context of vocational or life-skills training, such as job interview preparation or public transport autonomy [1,6,12,31,35]. Finally, only a few works directly involved **adults**, often for specialized purposes like vocational support, daily-life assessment, or workplace training [17,29].

> ⌂ **Answer to RQ$_4$.** The literature is dominated by interventions for children with ASD, especially in early and school-age years. Fewer studies addressed adolescents, young adults, or adults, mainly in vocational and life-skill contexts.

5   Discussion

The results of our review and the answers to our questions have provided an overview of the current state of the art in the use of virtual agents tailored for neurodivergent individuals in VR educational contexts. In this section, based on these findings, we would like to highlight some key points for discussion and potential limitations for future research.

A very evident point emerging from the reviewed studies is the strong focus on **children as the primary target group** for VR-based interventions with virtual pedagogical agents. This emphasis is unsurprising: childhood is a formative stage in which individuals with ASD and ADHD are typically expected to acquire foundational skills such as social communication, emotion recognition, and adaptive daily behaviors [18,33]. Agents in these contexts were often designed to act as tutors, but also as peers and child-like partners, displaying age-appropriate emotional expressions and behaviors that young participants could observe, imitate, and respond to [5,25,39]. By contrast, studies involving adults were more often oriented toward skills required in everyday independence and professional life. This included interventions targeting social etiquette and vocational readiness, with job interview training being a particularly recurring theme [1,6,12,17]. These applications reflect the different developmental priorities of adulthood, where the challenges of employment, autonomy, and advanced learning become more salient. Notably, adolescents and young adults were the least represented across the reviewed literature. This gap is striking, as adolescence represents a transitional stage where social identity, independence, and advanced education converge, and where late diagnoses of ADHD or ASD are becoming increasingly common.

> **⚲ Discussion Point.** Most studies target children, while adolescents and young adults remain critically underrepresented. Future research should design and evaluate VR-based educational agents specifically tailored to adolescents and young adults, addressing their unique needs in terms of social identity, autonomy, and advanced learning or vocational preparation.

Another cross-cutting theme concerns the way users interacted with virtual agents. Most reviewed systems relied on **computer-based interfaces**, such as mouse, keyboard, or touchscreen input [4,26,31,34,35,39]. This design choice is understandable: interactions were kept intuitive and straightforward, especially given that many participants were young children. However, this reliance on basic input modalities might imposes some limitations: it constrains the realism of the experience and restricts the range of possible social exchanges. More immersive interaction modes were explored in a smaller set of studies, including multimodal communication, and embodied interactions [24,25] where users engaged through gestures, gaze, or even physical manipulation of objects mirrored in the virtual space [10,16]. We argue that when agents are framed as peers or collaborators, richer forms of interaction—passing objects, responding to body language, synchronizing movements—can foster more naturalistic and engaging experiences. At the same time, we acknowledge significant barriers in such approaches: most of the more immersive devices, such as head-mounted displays, can be uncomfortable, may induce motion sickness, and are often impractical for children with sensory sensitivities [28]. These usability challenges partly explain why simpler setups prevail. Nonetheless, future research should push towards integrating more immersive and multimodal interactions in ways that remain accessible and sensitive to user comfort.

> **⚲ Discussion Point.** Most studies relied on simple computer-based interactions, which ensured accessibility but limited immersion, realism, and the naturalism of exchanges. Future research should explore richer multimodal modalities—verbal, nonverbal, and embodied—that can enhance engagement and allow agents to act as more authentic social partners within VR environments.

As a last remark to promote future research in this field, the results of our review highlighted an imbalance in the application contexts in which the agents were integrated. The majority of studies focused on **social communication, emotion recognition, and adaptive daily-living routines**, reflecting the most immediate and pressing needs of individuals with ASD and ADHD [21,22,27,29,35]. While this emphasis is valuable, relatively few studies explored the use of agents in supporting other educational activities, such as academic learning [39], reading [13,30,31], science and math, or broader curricular subjects, and even fewer addressed advanced domains like STEM education [14] or cybersecurity [24]. As a result, the potential of VR-based agents to contribute to formal education and professional training remains underdeveloped. Future research should therefore expand the scope of educational contexts, investigating how agents can support not only foundational socio-emotional skills but also the acquisition of disciplinary knowledge and higher-level competencies, thereby bridging everyday functioning with long-term learning trajectories.

> **Discussion Point.** Most studies concentrated on social communication and daily-living routines, addressing the most immediate needs of individuals with ASD/ADHD. However, few works explored explored other educational and pedagogical contexts. This underrepresentation limits the broader educational potential of virtual pedagogical agents. Future research should expand their use toward curricular and professional contexts, bridging socio-emotional support with long-term learning trajectories.

6 Conclusion

In this review, we analyzed how virtual agents are designed and implemented in VR educational environments for individuals with ASD and ADHD. Across 26 studies, we found that agents most often acted as tutors, but also served as peers, conversational partners, or role players. Interactions were usually simple and computer-based, with fewer cases exploring immersive or embodied modalities. Most applications addressed social and daily-living skills, while academic and advanced domains were less represented. Children were the main population studied, with far fewer interventions for adolescents and adults.

These results suggest that agents are already valuable for socio-emotional training but remain underused in other domains and age groups. Future research should broaden educational contexts, design interventions for adolescents and adults, and explore richer multimodal interactions. Doing so can lead to agents that are more adaptive, socially intelligent, and human-centered, ultimately fostering inclusive learning opportunities for neurodivergent individuals.

Acknowledgment. This study was funded by X (grant number Y).

Disclosure of Interests. The authors have no competing interests to declare that are relevant to the content of this article.

References

1. Adiani, D., Colopietro, K., Wade, J., Migovich, M., Vogus, T.J., Sarkar, N.: Dialogue act classification via transfer learning for automated labeling of interviewee responses in virtual reality job interview training platforms for autistic individuals. Signals **4**(2), 359–380 (2023)
2. Antshel, K.M., Russo, N.: Autism spectrum disorders and ADHD: overlapping phenomenology, diagnostic issues, and treatment considerations. Curr. Psychiatry Rep. **21**(5), 34 (2019)
3. Banaschewski, T., Becker, K., Döpfner, M., Holtmann, M., Rösler, M., Romanos, M.: Attention-deficit/hyperactivity disorder: a current overview. Dtsch. Arztebl. Int. **114**(9), 149 (2017)
4. Begoli, E.: Procedural reasoning system (prs) architecture for agent-mediated behavioral interventions. In: IEEE SOUTHEASTCON 2014, pp. 1–8. IEEE (2014)
5. Bernardini, S., Porayska-Pomsta, K., Smith, T.J.: Echoes: an intelligent serious game for fostering social communication in children with autism. Inf. Sci. **264**, 41–60 (2014)
6. Burke, S.L., et al.: Using virtual interactive training agents (vita) with adults with autism and other developmental disabilities. J. Autism Dev. Disord. **48**(3), 905–912 (2018)
7. Chevalier, P., Martin, J.C., Isableu, B., Bazile, C., Tapus, A.: Impact of sensory preferences of individuals with autism on the recognition of emotions expressed by two robots, an avatar, and a human. Auton. Robot. **41**(3), 613–635 (2017)
8. Corrigan, N., Păsărelu, C.R., Voinescu, A.: Immersive virtual reality for improving cognitive deficits in children with ADHD: a systematic review and meta-analysis. Virtual Reality **27**(4), 3545–3564 (2023)
9. Dechsling, A., et al.: Virtual and augmented reality in social skills interventions for individuals with autism spectrum disorder: a scoping review. J. Autism Dev. Disord. **52**(11), 4692–4707 (2022)
10. Giraud, T., et al.: "Can you help me move this over there?": training children with ASD to joint action through tangible interaction and virtual agent. In: Proceedings of the Fifteenth International Conference on Tangible, Embedded, and Embodied Interaction, pp. 1–12 (2021)
11. Hale, K.S., Stanney, K.M.: Handbook of Virtual Environments: Design, Implementation, and Applications. CRC Press (2014)
12. Hartholt, A., et al.: Virtual humans in augmented reality: a first step towards real-world embedded virtual roleplayers. In: Proceedings of the 7th International Conference on Human-Agent Interaction, pp. 205–207 (2019)
13. Ho, W.C., Davis, M., Dautenhahn, K.: Supporting narrative understanding of children with autism: a story interface with autonomous autobiographic agents. In: 2009 IEEE International Conference on Rehabilitation Robotics, pp. 905–911. IEEE (2009)
14. Hughes, C.E., et al.: Raise: robotics & AI to improve stem and social skills for elementary school students. Front. Virtual Reality **3**, 968312 (2022)
15. Hutson, J.: Social virtual reality: neurodivergence and inclusivity in the metaverse. Societies **12**(4), 102 (2022)
16. Li, J., Zheng, Z., Chai, Y., Li, X., Wei, X.: Faceme: an agent-based social game using augmented reality for the emotional development of children with autism spectrum disorder. Int. J. Hum. Comput. Stud. **175**, 103032 (2023)

17. Li, Z., Babar, P.P., Barry, M., Peiris, R.L.: Exploring the use of large language model-driven chatbots in virtual reality to train autistic individuals in job communication skills. In: Extended Abstracts of the CHI Conference on Human Factors in Computing Systems, pp. 1–7 (2024)
18. Lievore, R., Crisci, G., Mammarella, I.C.: Emotion recognition in children and adolescents with ASD and ADHD: a systematic review. Rev. J. Autism Dev. Disord. 1–31 (2023)
19. Liu, W., et al.: Self-guided DMT: exploring a novel paradigm of dance movement therapy in mixed reality for children with ASD. IEEE Trans. Visual Comput. Graphics **30**(5), 2119–2128 (2024)
20. Marougkas, A., Troussas, C., Krouska, A., Sgouropoulou, C.: Virtual reality in education: a review of learning theories, approaches and methodologies for the last decade. Electronics **12**(13), 2832 (2023)
21. Milne, M., Luerssen, M.H., Lewis, T.W., Leibbrandt, R.E., Powers, D.M.: Development of a virtual agent based social tutor for children with autism spectrum disorders. In: The 2010 International Joint Conference on Neural Networks (IJCNN), pp. 1–9. IEEE (2010)
22. Milne, M., Powers, D., Leibbrandt, R.: Development of a software-based social tutor for children with autism spectrum disorders. In: Proceedings of the 21st Annual Conference of the Australian Computer-Human Interaction Special Interest Group: Design: Open 24/7, pp. 265–268 (2009)
23. Miranda-Ojeda, R., Wickramasinghe, A., Ntolkeras, G., Castanho, I., Yassin, W.: The neurodiversity framework in medicine: on the spectrum. Dev. Neurobiol. **85**(1), e22960 (2025)
24. Nuguri, S.S., et al.: Adaptive virtual reality learning environment with a reinforcement learning-driven pedagogical agent. In: 2025 IEEE 22nd Consumer Communications & Networking Conference (CCNC), pp. 1–4. IEEE (2025)
25. Patel, S., Hughes, D.E., Hughes, C.E.: Meemo-using an avatar to improve social skills in children with ASD. In: WOCCI, pp. 45–50 (2016)
26. Porayska-Pomsta, K., et al.: Blending human and artificial intelligence to support autistic children's social communication skills. ACM Trans. Comput.-Hum. Interact. (TOCHI) **25**(6), 1–35 (2018)
27. Ramachandiran, C.R., Jomhari, N., Thiyagaraja, S., Maria, M.: Virtual reality based behavioral learning for autistic children. Electron. J. E-Learn. **13**(5), 357–365 (2015)
28. Ramaseri Chandra, A.N., El Jamiy, F., Reza, H.: A systematic survey on cybersickness in virtual environments. Computers **11**(4), 51 (2022)
29. Robles, M., et al.: A virtual reality based system for the screening and classification of autism. IEEE Trans. Visual Comput. Graphics **28**(5), 2168–2178 (2022)
30. Saadatzi, M.N., Pennington, R.C., Welch, K.C., Graham, J.H.: Small-group technology-assisted instruction: virtual teacher and robot peer for individuals with autism spectrum disorder. J. Autism Dev. Disord. **48**(11), 3816–3830 (2018)
31. Saadatzi, M.N., Pennington, R.C., Welch, K.C., Graham, J.H., Scott, R.E.: The use of an autonomous pedagogical agent and automatic speech recognition for teaching sight words to students with autism spectrum disorder. J. Spec. Educ. Technol. **32**(3), 173–183 (2017)
32. Satu, P., Minna, L., Satu, S.: Immersive VR assessment and intervention research of individuals with neurodevelopmental disorders is dominated by ASD and ADHD: a scoping review. Rev. J. Autism Dev. Disord. **12**(1), 50–68 (2025)
33. Sharma, S.R., Gonda, X., Tarazi, F.I.: Autism spectrum disorder: classification, diagnosis and therapy. Pharmacol. Ther. **190**, 91–104 (2018)

34. Tavassoli, F., Howell, D.M., Black, E.W., Lok, B., Gilbert, J.E.: Jayla (junior agent to typify levels of autism): a virtual training platform to teach severity levels of autism. Front. Virtual Reality **2**, 660690 (2021)
35. Vona, F., et al.: Combining virtual and augmented reality to improve daily autonomy for people with autism spectrum disorder. In: Proceedings of the 2022 International Conference on Advanced Visual Interfaces, pp. 1–3 (2022)
36. Xie, B., et al.: A review on virtual reality skill training applications. Front. Virtual Reality **2**, 645153 (2021)
37. Zhang, L., Weitlauf, A.S., Amat, A.Z., Swanson, A., Warren, Z.E., Sarkar, N.: Assessing social communication and collaboration in autism spectrum disorder using intelligent collaborative virtual environments. J. Autism Dev. Disord. **50**(1), 199–211 (2020)
38. Zhao, H., Zaini Amat, A., Migovich, M., Swanson, A., Weitlauf, A.S., Warren, Z., Sarkar, N.: INC-hg: an intelligent collaborative haptic-gripper virtual reality system. ACM Trans. Accessible Comput. (TACCESS) **15**(1), 1–23 (2022)
39. van Zijl, L., Venter, W.: An embodied conversational agent with asperger syndrome. In: International Conference on Computer Supported Education, vol. 2, pp. 153–158. SCITEPRESS (2011)

AI Chatbots in Mathematics Classrooms: Understanding Student-AI Interactions and Teacher Integration

Giorgia Nieddu[1,2]([⊠]) [iD], Maria Cristina Carrisi[2] [iD], Maria Polo[2] [iD], and Antioco Luigi Zurru[2] [iD]

[1] Università degli Studi di Macerata, 62100 Macerata, Italy
`g.nieddu@unimc.it`
[2] Università degli Studi di Cagliari, 09124 Cagliari, Italy

Abstract. This doctoral research examines how AI chatbots function in mathematics education through a main research strand about students' interactions with AI tools and the cognitive processes activated during problem-solving; other supplementary studies investigate teachers' beliefs, practices, and their capacity to integrate AI into instructional design and in the classroom. Drawing primarily on Brousseau's Theory of Didactical Situations, the research employs mixed methods including questionnaires, semi-structured interviews, and comparative studies. Initial findings reveal that AI demonstrates inconsistent handling of semiotic representations, particularly visual ones, yet can function as a component of students' adidactical environment - as part of the milieu - that promotes the emergence of mathematical concepts. Students appear to engage in a "double devolution dialectics", shifting responsibility and commitment between themselves and AI in ways that can enhance mathematical autonomy. Teachers show various levels of critical engagement with AI outputs. The core study involves longitudinal observations of three teachers and approximately 100 students in authentic classroom settings.

Keywords: Mathematics Education · Artificial Intelligence · Milieu

1 Introduction

The emergence of generative artificial intelligence, particularly large language models, has created unprecedented challenges and opportunities in education. Given the particular difficulties that lie hidden within mathematics, it is important to carry out specific studies on the subject. The body of literature is expanding rapidly, for this reason from the very beginning of the doctoral program we adopted a strategy of continuous literature review, rather than carrying out a traditional, time-bounded review. Many articles in the field of mathematics education have begun to examine aspects related to the use of these systems in mathematics teaching and learning, but also their mathematical reliability.

A. Dipace et al. (Eds.): WAILS 2025, LNCS 16438, pp. 235–241, 2026.
https://doi.org/10.1007/978-3-032-17604-2_21

For instance, Schorcht and colleagues [1] compared the mathematical quality of solutions to selected problems generated by various LLMs, employing different prompting strategies. Their findings indicated that the overall quality was generally low and that such techniques did not significantly influence the outputs in this context. However, the reliability of such systems is important, but it is not the most crucial factor in education, as other aspects–such as the role of the teacher, the pedagogical decisions involved in managing a tool within the classroom, and the ways in which students interact with it–are decisive for the success of a learning activity.

This research draws on established frameworks from the French mathematics education tradition, which analyze multiple factors: learner-environment-teacher relationships, institutional practices, and the role of semiotic representations. Brousseau's Theory of Didactical Situations [2] serves as the main lens, with Chevallard's anthropological approach [3] and Duval's semiotic theory [4] illuminating specific aspects.

2   Outline of Methodology

Traditional methodological approaches, designed for stable interventions and consistent tools, require revision when the object of study is in constant flux. One of the most significant challenges in this research is precisely the study of non-deterministic systems that are constantly evolving: the same prompt can produce different responses, making it difficult to apply traditional experimental controls. This necessitates the use of mixed methods that can capture both qualitative underlying dynamics and measurable patterns. Given that the project was divided into various strands, and each was developed with its own distinct rationale and methodology, what follows is an overview of the general methods that have characterized our research. Our methodological toolkit has primarily consisted of questionnaires (which always include both Likert scales and open-ended response options), semi-structured interviews, and comparative studies using pre-existing student data. The experimental studies completed, as well as those currently in progress, involve samples of no fewer than 50 participants (comprising either students or teachers), with the exception of a small-scale pilot study conducted with 16 students. All research protocols adhere to standard anonymization procedures through the assignment of unique identification codes. For data analysis purposes, we have utilized and intend to continue utilizing classifications characteristic of mathematics education research to analyze the mathematic content in participants' written productions, alongside thematic analysis following the methodological approach outlined by Braun and Clarke [5] for identifying recurring patterns in questionnaire responses. The smaller strands were conducted with the purpose of addressing specific problems and research questions, and informed and guided the design of the core experiment, which represents the central focus of the doctoral research. The core work of the program is a qualitative study conducted throughout the entire program period with the aim of making stable observations over time that encompass teacher behavior, student behavior, and the interactions between them when artificial intelligence is involved. It involves individual meetings with three teachers for semi-structured interviews (already completed) followed by group sessions to develop mathematics problems to be proposed to their students. Finally, three sessions have been planned for each class: an initial exploratory session in which we will monitor individual student use during problem-solving, a second session involving collaborative group problem-solving, and a final session to conclude the process and reflect on the activities.

3   Theoretical Framework: the Theory of Situations

Guy Brousseau's Theory of Didactical Situations [2] provides the primary theoretical lens for this research. Central to this framework is the concept of learning through adaptation to an antagonistic system - a milieu - that generates difficulties, and disequilibria, modifying the student's knowledge in ways not controlled by the student himself. An allied environment would allow only the student's action without producing retroactions, leading to what Fregona [6] characterizes as fictitious interactions rather than effective learning encounters. The milieu provides specific information to the student in the form of positive or negative sanctions, allowing to adjust their behavior, accept or reject hypotheses, and choose optimal solutions among various possibilities. The interaction with the milieu unfolds through three distinct dialectical phases. The dialectic of action involves exchanges of information that are not linguistically coded–direct actions and decisions that act upon the milieu. Students develop strategies through sequences of interactions, creating implicit models of the situation while testing and rejecting previous approaches based on the milieu's feedback. The dialectic of formulation occurs when students communicate about their actions and strategies, making explicit their implicit models through linguistically coded (in various ways) messages, establishing in the process a common language that enables explanation of actions. Finally, the dialectic of validation involves exchanges of assertions and rigorous reasoning, possibly theorems and mathematical proofs, where students must convince others of the validity of their solutions through intellectual proof rather than empirical verification alone.

These processes needs to be articulated within two phases orchestrated by the teacher. Devolution is the means by which the teacher ensures that students take responsibility for an adidactic learning situation, making the problem truly their own through recontextualization and repersonalization of the knowledge to be taught–that is, when savoirs are converted into connaissances. As defined by Conne [7], a connoissance consists of means–not necessarily explicable–for controlling a situation and obtaining a result (e.g., solving a problem). During institutionalization the teacher decontextualizes and depersonalizes the knowledge produced by students, giving it official status as universal, culturally recognized mathematical knowledge that can be reused beyond the specific learning context–essentially moving from connoissances to savoirs. One can say that knowledge operates on the side of student control of situations, while knowing operates on the institutional side of control.

3.1 Why Is This Important?

This distinction becomes particularly significant when examining AI's potential role in educational processes. Can AI facilitate the process of devolution, or, instead, institutionalization? Understanding AI's position in this knowledge-knowing dialectic has profound implications for how these tools should be integrated and orchestrated by teachers into mathematical learning environments. They can provide feedback, but it is necessary to study what kind of feedback they can provide, which type of feedback is desirable, and at which stage it should be used. AI can, indeed, be studied as a part of a milieu. It also exhibit several characteristics that align with Brousseau's conception of an antagonistic milieu: it operates without explicit educational purposes, its behavior is unpredictable and cannot be directly controlled by students, and it functions as "black boxes" that require critical evaluation of its responses. On the other hand, a certain tendency to accommodate and satisfy user requests has been observed, and the unpredictable nature–which might at first seem advantageous–can in fact hinder or complicate the teacher's design work.

4 Our Contribution to AI in Mathematics Education

The research journey began with a fundamental question about AI's mathematical capabilities, specifically its ability to handle different semiotic representations. According to Duval [4], mathematical knowledge emerges through the manipulation of different representation systems such as algebraic, geometric, and natural language registers. In this initial investigation GPT-4 (though this observation extends to other models as well) demonstrated inconsistent mathematical reasoning, poor handling of visual information, and a tendency to accommodate user requests even when mathematically inappropriate [8]. We subsequently deepened our investigation of semiotic representations, moving away from the logical-spatial problems typical of mathematical competitions to focus instead on more conventional items, more representative of school mathematics. We evaluated the LLM's ability to perform what Duval terms "treatment" (manipulations within a representation system) and "conversion" (translations between different representation systems). The findings revealed that GPT-4 showed competence in algebraic and natural language registers but struggled significantly with visual representations. The system exhibited an implicit hierarchy of representations, consistently prioritizing symbolic over graphical information. These limitations, rather than being purely negative, created opportunities for students to develop critical evaluation skills and deeper understanding of representational relationships [9].

These initial studies suggested that AI systems might function less as mathematical experts and more as peers for students. Consequently, we decided to observe how undergraduate students interact with ChatGPT while solving electronics problems requiring mathematical modeling [10]. The observations revealed that students naturally engaged in formulation phases with the chatbot, articulating their mathematical thinking to obtain AI feedback. More significantly, a pattern that we conceptualized as double devolution dialectics emerged, where responsibility for problem-solving shifted dynamically between student and AI. Students would initially delegate problem-solving to the AI, then reclaim responsibility when they critically evaluated AI responses that seemed incorrect or incomplete. This dialectical process, illustrated in Fig. 1., often enhanced rather than diminished mathematical autonomy, as students developed critical awareness of AI limitations. We subsequently deepened these considerations from a theoretical standpoint, which culminated in a separate theoretical research paper [11].

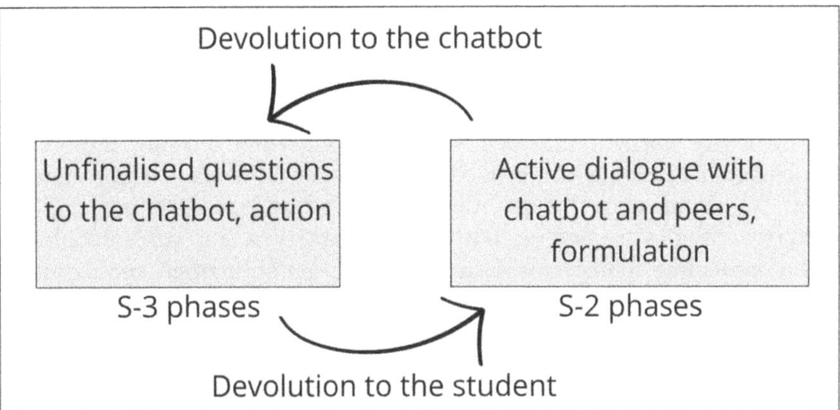

Fig. 1. Double devolution dialectic: an empirically observed process in which responsibility for the mathematical problem shifts at different moments from the chatbot (unfinalized questions and prompts, action) to the student (dialogue with chatbot and peers, formulation) and vice versa. The original scheme can be found in [11]. Phases S_2 and S_3 refer to broader learning phases defined by Brousseau [2], which are not elaborated here for brevity.

We also employed Chevallard's anthropological theory of didactics to analyze how the institution of Italian school system, and in particular, teachers who occupy a position (sic., in [4]) in Italian schools, organize and structure activities around knowledge using AI as a tool for lesson planning and mathematical task design. In our study, the construct of praxeology (a quadruplet comprising both the practical know-how and the explanatory discourses about a type of task, usually a mathematical task) proved particularly valuable for describing how teachers develop their practices around new tools like AI chatbots, revealing not only the techniques employed but also the beliefs, justifications, and institutional constraints that shape their choices. The findings reveal varied levels of critical engagement with AI outputs, with many teachers treating AI as an "oracle" rather than a collaborative tool [12]. A recent study, rooted in Universal Design for Learning, also explores AI's potential for supporting teachers in creating inclusive teaching materials, specifically when students with learning disorders as dyslexia and dyscalculia are involved. The findings suggest that while AI systems show promise for generating accessible content, they require significant human oversight and often produce superficial adaptations that lack deep understanding of inclusive pedagogy [13].

5   Conclusion and Future Developments

This doctoral research has employed multiple methodological approaches to examine how AI chatbots function in mathematics education contexts. Through theoretical analysis and empirical investigation, we have explored both student interactions with these tools and teachers' perspectives and practices. The findings suggest that AI systems can function as elements of the milieu in ways that are both promising and problematic, creating opportunities for critical thinking while also presenting challenges for instructional design. The core qualitative study involving teachers and their students is currently ongoing and will provide longitudinal insights into how AI integration evolves in authentic classroom settings. To complement this qualitative work, we are now initiating small-scale quantitative studies focused on both teacher practices and student behaviors, aimed at providing robust statistical data that can strengthen and extend our qualitative findings.

Acknowledgments. Maria Cristina Carrisi has been partially supported by the National Recovery and Resilience Plan (NRRP) – Project eINS Ecosystem of Innovation for Next Generation Sardinia – CUP F53C22000430001 funded by the European Union – NextGenerationEU, Code ECS0000038.

Giorgia Nieddu participated in this research while attending the PhD program in Teaching and Learning Sciences at the University of Macerata (39th cycle), supported by a scholarship funded under D.M. n. 118 (2.3.2023), within the Italian National Recovery and Resilience Plan (PNRR) – funded by the European Union – NextGenerationEU – Mission 4, Component 1, Investment 4.1.

Disclosure of Interests. The authors have no competing interests to declare that are relevant to the content of this article.

References

1. Schorcht, S., Buchholtz, N., Baumanns, L.: Prompt the problem – investigating the mathematics educational quality of AI-supported problem solving by comparing prompt techniques. Front. Educ. **9**, 1386075 (2024). https://doi.org/10.3389/feduc.2024.1386075
2. Brousseau, G.: Theory of didactical situations in mathematics. In: Balacheff, N., Cooper, M., Sutherland, R., Warfield, V. (eds.). vol. 19, Kluwer Academic Publishers (2002). https://doi.org/10.1007/0-306-47211-2

3. Chevallard, Y.: Introducing the anthropological theory of the didactic: an attempt at a principled approach. Hiroshima J. Math. Educ. **12**, 71–114. (2019). https://doi.org/10.24529/hjme.1205

4. Duval, R.: Semiosis et pensee humaine: registres semiotiques et apprentissages intellectuels, vol. 4. Peter Lang, Berne (1995)

5. Braun, V., Clarke, V.: Using thematic analysis in psychology. Qual. Res. Psychol. **3**(2), 77–101 (2006). https://doi.org/10.1191/1478088706qp063oa

6. Fregona, D.: Les figures planes comme "milieu" dan l'enseignement de la geometrie: interactions, contrats et transpositions didactiques. Dissertation, Universite Bordeaux I (1995)

7. Conne, F.: Savoir et connaissance dans la perspective de la transposition didactique. Recherches en Didactique des Mathematiques **12**(2.3), 221–270 (1992)

8. Nieddu, G., Carrisi, M.C., Polo, M., Zurru, A.L.: Analysis of GPT-4's responses: an unconventional student. In: Faggiano E., Clark-Wilson A., Tabach M., Weigand H.G. (eds.), Proceedings of the 17th ERME Topic Conference Mathematics Education in the Digital Age (MEDA4), pp. 440–441. Universita di Bari Aldo Moro. (2024)

9. Nieddu, G., Carrisi, M.C., Polo, M., Zurru, A.L.: Chat GPT as a didactic tool to improve students' abilities in managing different semiotic representations: a first study. In: Proceedings of the 14th Congress of the European Society for Research in Mathematics Education (CERME14), Free University of Bozen. (2025)

10. Nieddu, G., Glushica, B., Kamilovski, M., Pagliara, S.M., Carrisi, M.C., Gerazov, B.: The role of AI in supporting mathematical reasoning for electronics problems. In: 2025 32nd International Conference on Systems, Signals and Image Processing (IWSSIP), pp. 1–4 (2025)

11. Nieddu, G., Carrisi, M.C., Polo, M.: The theory of didactical situations and artificial intelligence: a first study. In C. Derouet, V. Durand-Guerrier, C. Lemrich, A.-C. Mathe (Dir.), Pre-actes du Colloque international en hommage a l'oeuvre de Guy Brousseau, pp. 177–178. IREM d'Aquitaine. (2025)

12. Nieddu, G., Gerazov, B., Pagliara, S.M., Zurru, L.A., Carrisi, M.C.: Evaluating large multimodal models for inclusive mathematics education: addressing dyslexia and dyscalculia in higher education. In: Mavrou, K., Encarnacao, P. (eds.) Technology for Inclusion and Participation for All: Recent Achievements and Future Directions, pp. 224–231. Springer Nature Switzerland, Cham. (2025)

13. Nieddu, G., et al: The role of chatbots as resources in mathematical task design for pre-service teachers: a praxeological analysis [accepted at the 17th International Conference on Technology in Mathematics Teaching]. (2025)

Enhancing Digital Literacy Through Retrieval-Augmented Generation

Marco Cabras[1,2]([✉]) [iD], Ludovico Boratto[2] [iD], Salvatore Mario Carta[2] [iD], and Mirko Marras[2] [iD]

[1] University of Macerata, Macerata, Italy
[2] University of Cagliari, Cagliari, Italy
`marco.cabras4@unimc.it,`
`{ludovico.boratto,salvatore,mirko.marras}@unica.it`

Abstract. In a world where individuals need to continuously adapt to evolving digital ecosystems, learning technologies play a key role in helping learners rapidly understand, evaluate, and apply complex technical concepts. To meet this need, advances at the intersection of computer science and learning sciences are driving the creation of intelligent systems that enhance digital literacy. From a computer science perspective, Large Language Models (LLMs) offer new opportunities for tutoring, feedback, and conceptual support, yet their tendency to generate unverified information risks undermining understanding and epistemic trust. From a learning perspective, effective educational technologies are required to ensure accuracy, transparency, and cognitive alignment with learners' needs. Retrieval-Augmented Generation (RAG) is emerging as an effective method to mitigate hallucinations by grounding responses in external sources, but current implementations often rely on simplistic retrieval methods that neglect the hierarchical and pedagogical structure of educational materials. This doctoral research investigates how RAG-based methods can be tailored and integrated into educational activities to foster digital literacy. The work focuses on developing a generative assistant capable of semantically retrieving domain materials, synthesizing authoritative information, and producing pedagogically aligned explanations. The expected contributions are theoretical, by advancing hybrid retrieval and explainability mechanisms tailored to learning contexts, and practical, by demonstrating a literacy-oriented assistant that bridges technical content and learner comprehension. As a case study, the approach will be applied to cloud literacy, contextualizing service operations and costs via authoritative documentation and real-world data.

Keywords: Retrieval-Augmented Generation · Artificial Intelligence in Education · Digital Literacy · Lifelong Learning · Cloud Literacy

1 Introduction

As digital technologies increasingly shape how individuals work, communicate, and learn, the ability to understand and critically engage with these systems

A. Dipace et al. (Eds.): WAILS 2025, LNCS 16438, pp. 242–247, 2026.
https://doi.org/10.1007/978-3-032-17604-2_22

has become a cornerstone of digital literacy. Modern learners are expected not only to use digital tools but also to comprehend the principles and operations that underpin them. Supporting such understanding requires learning technologies that combine the analytical rigor of computer science with the pedagogical insights of the learning sciences, for their mutual benefits.

Recent advances in generative artificial intelligence have positioned Large Language Models (LLMs) as promising educational assistants. Their capacity to process natural language and generate adaptive explanations opens new possibilities for student support, for instance by enabling learners to ask questions, clarify concepts, and explore examples beyond classroom boundaries. However, despite these advantages, LLMs exhibit a persistent limitation: they frequently produce hallucinations [5], or plausible yet inaccurate responses. In educational contexts, where precision and trust are fundamental, these errors can distort conceptual understanding and propagate misconceptions rather than resolve them [12].

While basic topics can often be handled by LLMs with acceptable accuracy, complex or specialized domains, such as those taught in advanced university courses or encountered in professional training, demand a higher level of contextual and expert grounding [4]. Learners in these settings require explanations that reflect domain expertise and align with instructional intent. Educational materials created by instructors, including lecture slides, textbooks, and exercises, embody this intent by presenting structured knowledge and emphasizing the interpretive frameworks necessary for understanding [11].

Retrieval-Augmented Generation (RAG) offers a promising direction for addressing these challenges by enabling LLMs to ground responses in curated, authoritative resources [4,11]. Yet, current RAG implementations typically operate over unstructured educational materials, providing a powerful mechanism for grounding language models in teaching resources but with limited pedagogical alignment. Their effectiveness can be enhanced through a layered organization of the material, integration of multiple modalities, and interaction designs that reflect pedagogical intent, which are essential for meaningful learning. When these elements are missing, retrieval alone may yield incomplete or de-contextualized results, reducing the reliability of generated explanations [13].

This doctoral research aims to extend RAG-based methods beyond traditional embedding-based retrieval to design domain-aware generative assistants capable of supporting digital literacy. Specifically, these methods should be able to semantically index educational materials, identify authoritative knowledge, and generate transparent explanations aligned with expert perspectives. Beyond producing correct answers, these systems are also envisioned to promote understanding by revealing the reasoning and sources behind their responses. As a first application, the research focuses on cloud literacy, developing an assistant that helps learners interpret service functionalities and cost structures.

2   Background

RAG has been widely explored as a way to reduce hallucinations by grounding responses. Surveys such as Li et al. [7] and Swacha and Gracel [14] provide comprehensive overviews of RAG in education, highlighting its role in improving factual accuracy, and supporting applications across tutoring, self-study, and assessment. Németh et al. [11] demonstrate through a pilot study that RAG tutors can successfully mediate interactions, improving engagement while also exposing challenges such as domain variation and drift beyond source texts.

Several works target a specific educational domain. Martínez-Romo et al. [9] introduce a RAG system that generates feedback for self-assessment, grounded in textbooks and aligning with curricular goals. Chu et al. [2] apply RAG to short-answer grading by retrieving standards and annotated examples, thereby constraining generation to align with expert judgment. In programming education, Liu et al. [8] show that small language models combined with RAG can perform comparably to larger LLMs while improving privacy and efficiency, and other studies report similar benefits for Python learning tools. In the context of MOOCs, RAG has been shown to substantially increase accuracy when augmenting GPT-4 [10], suggesting potential for large-scale education.

Beyond embedding-based retrieval, hybrid strategies have been proposed to improve explainability and alignment. Afreen et al. [1] introduce EDGE, which combines LLMs with educational knowledge graphs for structured exploration of institutional resources. Dong et al. [3] extend this idea with KG-RAG, integrating knowledge graphs into tutoring systems to improve coherence and learning outcomes. Similarly, Li et al. [6] combine knowledge tracing with RAG for personalized learning recommendations, showing how retrieval can adapt to the learner's state. These approaches illustrate the value of richer document representations, structured knowledge, and hybrid retrieval.

While existing research highlights the potential of RAG to align responses with educational materials, most work focuses on tutoring, assessment, and programming education. Little research explores digital, industry-linked scenarios where learning is embedded in real-world tasks. None of the cited studies address assistants supporting cloud literacy, helping learners and professionals understand cloud services, costs, and resource usage while grounding explanations in authoritative documentation. This gap motivates the development of a virtual assistant tailored to practical and industrial use cases, such as monitoring cloud costs while fostering literacy about the underlying services.

3 Research Objective and Approach

This doctoral research aims to develop a generative assistant that delivers accurate, transparent explanations and promotes literacy in specialized technical domains, with a particular focus on cloud services. The assistant is conceived as an interactive agent built on a RAG architecture, capable of processing and indexing domain-specific sources for semantic search, retrieving relevant and authoritative information, and generating responses that are both grounded and pedagogically meaningful. Unlike conventional text generators, the assistant is designed to engage users in an explanatory dialogue, guiding them through complex information and illustrating how abstract concepts relate to real-world operations, for example supporting learners' understanding of how cloud costs are distributed across services and how these services interconnect functionally.

The research is structured around two guiding questions:

- **RQ1.** How can a generative assistant be designed to support access to information and foster literacy in digital domains?
- **RQ2.** What methodological steps are required to adapt such an assistant to a specific digital domain, such as cloud literacy?

To address **RQ1**, the study investigates the methodological and architectural foundations necessary for accuracy, reliability, and explainability in generative assistants. This includes the design of pipelines for processing and semantically indexing heterogeneous domain sources, the implementation of hybrid retrieval mechanisms to balance coverage and precision, and the integration of explainability components such as citation tracing and document provenance. It is expected that an LLM acts as the agentic controller, orchestrating retrieval, reasoning, and generation processes, while the user interface is designed to promote transparency, interpretability, and accessible interaction.

In response to **RQ2**, the research focuses on two core steps toward domain specialization. The first concerns the curation of authoritative sources for cloud literacy, including official provider documentation, technical glossaries, and educational resources, that together constitute both the retrieval corpus and the pedagogical backbone for literacy-oriented explanations. The second involves the integration of the assistant within a real-world industry-oriented software environment, enabling interaction with live operational data such as service costs and usage breakdowns. This integration is crucial for moving beyond abstract explanation: it allows the assistant to contextualize cloud concepts within realistic, data-driven scenarios, supporting active learning and applied digital literacy.

The research will also address a pedagogical perspective to properly assess the assistant's educational effectiveness, identifying suitable learning theories and evaluation strategies once the system is operational. For example, future evaluations may investigate how the assistant helps learners build understanding and confidence in cloud literacy, including the use of quizzes or similar measures to assess learning gains.

By combining these methodological and domain-specific advances, the project seeks to contribute both theoretically, by extending RAG frameworks toward literacy-oriented design principles, and practically, by demonstrating an operational prototype that supports comprehension and decision-making.

4　Results to Date

Even though the doctoral project is still in its early stages, progress has been made on both the methodological and domain-specific fronts.

On the methodological side, a preliminary architecture for the retrieval-augmented generative assistant has been designed. The ongoing work has focused on identifying the essential components required to ensure accuracy, transparency, and adaptability. This includes defining data ingestion pipelines, developing mechanisms for semantic indexing of heterogeneous resources, and exploring hybrid retrieval strategies that combine dense and symbolic representations. Based on this design, a first working prototype is under construction.

In parallel, significant steps have been taken toward domain specialization. A dedicated dataset for cloud literacy has been curated, combining authoritative provider documentation, concept glossaries, and selected cost and usage data. This dataset establishes a concrete use case through which to operationalize the assistant, test retrieval strategies in realistic conditions, and explore how generated explanations can support users' understanding of cloud service structures and cost distributions. These advances provide a preliminary proof of feasibility and define the methodological baseline for the next development phase.

5   Next Steps

The next phase will consolidate the current advances into an integrated system and expand both the methodological framework and the domain application.

From a system development perspective, the immediate goal is to evolve the assistant from a modular design into a fully functional prototype. This includes implementing the end-to-end retrieval and generation pipeline, refining hybrid retrieval strategies, and integrating interface components that promote interpretability and user engagement. Once operational, the prototype will support iterative experimentation aimed at evaluating retrieval accuracy, grounding effectiveness, and user trust in generated explanations.

On the domain side, future work will focus on embedding the curated cloud literacy resources into the assistant's knowledge base and linking them to real-world operational contexts. A comprehensive evaluation strategy will be defined, combining system-level metrics with user studies to assess both informational accuracy and educational effectiveness. Particular attention will be paid to how the assistant fosters users' conceptual understanding of cloud operations, cost structures, and underlying digital literacy skills, as an initial case study.

References

1. Afreen, N., et al.: EDGE: a conversational interface driven by large language models for educational knowledge graphs exploration. In: Proceedings of the 33rd ACM International Conference on Information and Knowledge Management, CIKM 2024, pp. 5159–5163, New York, NY, USA, Association for Computing Machinery (2024)
2. Chu, Y., et al.: Enhancing LLM-based short answer grading with retrieval-augmented generation, pp. 396–402 (2025)
3. Dong, C., Yuan, Y., Chen, K., Cheng, S., Wen, C.: How to build an adaptive AI tutor for any course using knowledge graph-enhanced retrieval-augmented generation (KG-RAG), February 2025. arXiv:2311.17696 [cs]

4. Linmei, H., Liu, Z., Zhao, Z., Hou, L., Nie, L., Li, J.: A survey of knowledge enhanced pre-trained language models. IEEE Trans. Knowl. Data Eng. **36**(4), 1413–1430 (2024)
5. Kalai, A.T., Nachum, O., Vempala, S.S., Zhang, E.: Why language models hallucinate (2025)
6. Li, Z., et al.: TutorLLM: customizing learning recommendations with knowledge tracing and retrieval-augmented generation, April 2025. arXiv:2502.15709 [cs]
7. Li, Z., Wang, Z., Wang, W., Hung, K., Xie, H., Wang, F.L.: Retrieval-augmented generation for educational application: a systematic survey. Comput. Educ. Artif. Intell. **8**, 100417 (2025)
8. Liu, S., Yu, Z., Huang, F., Bulbulia, Y., Bergen, A., Liut, M.: Can small language models with retrieval-augmented generation replace large language models when learning computer science? In: Proceedings of the 2024 on Innovation and Technology in Computer Science Education V. 1, ITiCSE 2024, pp. 388–393, New York, NY, USA, ACM (2024)
9. Martinez-Romo, J., Araujo, L., Plaza, L., López-Ostenero, F.: Generative AI for education: a retrieval-augmented system for effective feedback in self-assessment. In: 2025 IEEE Global Engineering Education Conference (EDUCON), pp. 1–9, April 2025. ISSN: 2165-9567
10. Miladi, F., Psyché, V., Lemire, D.: Leveraging GPT-4 for accuracy in education: a comparative study on retrieval-augmented generation in MOOCs. In: Olney, A.M., Chounta, I.-A., Liu, Z., Santos, O.C., Bittencourt, I.I. (eds.) Artificial Intelligence in Education. Posters and Late Breaking Results, Workshops and Tutorials, Industry and Innovation Tracks, Practitioners, Doctoral Consortium and Blue Sky, pp. 427–434, Springer Nature Switzerland, Cham (2024)
11. Németh, R., Tátrai, A., Szabó, M., Zaletnyik, P.T., Tamási, Á.: Exploring the use of retrieval-augmented generation models in higher education: a pilot study on artificial intelligence-based tutoring. Soc. Sci. Hum. Open **12**, 101751 (2025)
12. Shahzad, T., Mazhar, T., Tariq, M.U., Ahmad, W., Ouahada, K., Hamam, H.: A comprehensive review of large language models: issues and solutions in learning environments. Disc. Sustain. **6**(1), (2025)
13. Sonkar, S., Ni, K., Chaudhary, S., Baraniuk, R.: Pedagogical alignment of large language models. In: Al-Onaizan, Y., Bansal, M., Chen, Y.-N. (eds.) Findings of the Association for Computational Linguistics: EMNLP 2024, pp. 13641–13650, Miami, Florida, USA, ACL, November 2024
14. Swacha, J., Gracel, M.: Retrieval-augmented generation (RAG) chatbots for education: a survey of applications. Appl. Sci. **15**(8), 4234 (2025). Publisher: Multidisciplinary Digital Publishing Institute

Teaching AI Literacy: How to Enable Students to Adapt to the Constant Evolution of This Field?

Camille Miele[✉] and André Tricot

Paul Valery University, Montpellier, France
camille@vittascience.com

Abstract. As artificial intelligence (AI) technologies evolve and become increasingly embedded in everyday life, many educational systems worldwide have introduced AI as a subject of instruction. However, the pace and nature of AI's evolution are uneven. In this dynamic context, learners must be equipped not only with foundational knowledge but also with the ability to transfer their understanding across domains and tasks, in order to adapt their judgement to new opportunities and limitations as they emerge. Transfer is a complex process that does not occur automatically, but can be supported through pedagogical strategies. Dissemination across subjects and diversification of learning context are two strategies that seems promising in this purpose. Among such strategies, dissemination across subjects and diversification of learning context have repeatedly demonstrated their effectiveness in fostering transfer in other educational domains. This doctoral work seeks to investigate whether these approaches can also support transfer in the context of AI education, with the aim of developing evidence-based pedagogical resources that enhance students' adaptability to the evolving landscape of AI.

Keywords: Education · AI literacy · Transfer of learning

1 Context

With the rise of Artificial Intelligence (AI), various aspects of our economic and social lives are being reshaped, and education is no exception. As highlighted by de la Higuera [1], AI influences all facets of society through the automation of numerous tasks and the creation of new challenges. AI is perceived as a tool that can facilitate teaching [2, 3]. Consequently, the scientific community is actively involved in developing these tools, whether for assessment, monitoring, or adapting teaching methods [4].

However, the relationship between AI and education should also be examined from another perspective: AI as a learning domain. For teachers and students to effectively and confidently use these tools, it is crucial that they are aware of the opportunities and limitations they present [4, 5]. Since every human activity is likely to be affected by AI, an understanding of both its technical and conceptual aspects is necessary [1]. Additionally, the Beijing Consensus on AI and Education recommends awareness of the emergence of a set of AI-related skills essential for effective human-machine collaboration and taking

A. Dipace et al. (Eds.): WAILS 2025, LNCS 16438, pp. 248–253, 2026.
https://doi.org/10.1007/978-3-032-17604-2_23

institutional measures to enhance AI education at all levels of society [6]. If, as many national curriculum frameworks suggest, the purpose of education is to help students navigate the complexity of the contemporary world, then developing an understanding of AI becomes a critical priority.

To address these challenges, AI is gradually being integrated into school curricula as a subject of study [7–9]. However, educational policies struggle to define what should be taught and how to teach it. Meanwhile, the scientific community and various institutions and associations have increasingly invested in developing guidelines for AI literacy education. Unesco has notably contributed through reports that map government-endorsed AI education programs [9], identifying recurring knowledge and competencies taught across different curricula. These programs allocate the most instructional time to three main themes: "AI foundations", "Understanding, using, and developing AI", and "Ethics and social impact" (41%, 25%, and 24% of program time, respectively). The proportion of time dedicated to these topics varies depending on the educational goals of each country—some focusing on preparing students for the job market, while others see AI education as a tool for social and political inclusion [9].

Regardless of these goals, a common thread emerges: adapting students to AI's growing presence in various aspects of life. Unesco has also developed AI competency frameworks for teachers [10] and students [11], highlighting a crucial observation: AI is constantly evolving, and individuals must develop adaptability to remain competent throughout their lives. Unesco refers to this as "lifelong learning" and recommends fostering critical thinking skills. However, critical thinking is already a major objective in most education program, and Unesco's recommendations may not fully address the broader challenge of adaptability. This research project aims to take AI education integration a step further by making adaptability a central component.

In summary, while AI education is widely recognized as a crucial issue, it faces a significant challenge: how to teach students knowledge that (a) evolves rapidly and (b) applies to highly diverse domains?

This doctoral project is carried out within a CIFRE contract, which combines academic research and industrial collaboration. It is jointly supervised by Vittascience, an EdTech company that develops an online platform for teaching robotics, programming, and AI, and Epsylon, a research laboratory in psychology with a strong focus on learning processes. The academic supervision is provided by Professor André Tricot, a leading scholar in the field of educational psychology, well known for his contributions to cognitive load theory.

2 Objectives and Methodology

This thesis aims to design and evaluate a training program for teachers to enable students to acquire knowledge and skills in AI within secondary education, in alignment with recent French institutional guidelines. A prerequisite for achieving the objectives presented here lies in the development of the teaching content to be delivered.

Similar to the AI4T (Artificial Intelligence for and by Teachers) initiative, this development is based on a participatory approach that actively involves teachers. This collaboration aims to anchor this new subject within topics that are coherent with existing curricula. This approach ensures that the pedagogical materials are both better suited to classroom realities and aligned with the expected AI competencies.

The main objective of this thesis is to assess the effectiveness of different AI teaching methods. This evaluation will focus particularly on how well these methods promote students' ability to generalize their learning to new AI-related contexts. Scientific literature has demonstrated how ineffective it can be to teach abstract and general knowledge with the expectation that it will later be applicable across various contexts [12]. However, research has also identified certain strategies that have proven effective in improving students' ability to transfer their learning to new situations. Among these strategies are the dissemination of teaching across different subjects and the diversification of learning contexts [13–15].

Dissemination across subjects: This approach integrates an interdisciplinary topic into multiple subjects, demonstrating to students that acquired knowledge can be applied in various disciplinary contexts. This strategy has already been evaluated and has shown effectiveness in supporting knowledge transfer [16].

Diversification of learning contexts: This method grounds the taught principles in varied, concrete contexts. Unlike subject dissemination, this approach can be applied within a single discipline, prioritizing learning experiences that resonate with students' real-world encounters with AI. Studies have demonstrated its effectiveness in fostering transferability of knowledge [13–15].

This thesis proposes to test these two pedagogical structuring approaches within AI literacy education: disseminated vs. centralized integration and contextualized vs. non-contextualized teaching. To evaluate the effectiveness of these different pedagogical configurations, an experimental protocol will be implemented, incorporating four distinct teaching conditions:

- Disseminated and contextualized teaching: Teachers from various disciplines (e.g., visual arts, technology, foreign languages, mathematics) will incorporate AI literacy content into their courses while specifically contextualizing these topics within their respective subjects.
- Disseminated and non-contextualized teaching: Teachers from various disciplines will integrate AI content into their courses without specific contextualization to their subjects.
- Centralized and contextualized teaching: A single teacher will be responsible for delivering dedicated AI literacy instruction while contextualizing the content to demonstrate its applicability across various domains.
- Centralized and non-contextualized teaching: A single teacher will integrate AI literacy into one subject without contextualization.

The aim of this protocol is to compare these four conditions by measuring their impact on students' ability to solve AI-related problems in new contexts. The evaluation will rely on learning indicators and cognitive flexibility in applying AI knowledge. To ensure the ecological validity of the study, the conditions will be implemented in a school setting, selecting student groups of the same academic level. This approach will help replicate a realistic classroom scenario while minimizing biases associated with pre-existing class groups. The participating teachers will receive prior training to integrate AI content according to the modalities specific to each experimental condition. This experimental design seeks to identify optimal pedagogical configurations for enhancing students' adaptability to AI developments by analyzing the interaction between teaching dissemination and contextualization levels.

3   Current Work Progression

I started my PhD five months ago and I am currently engaged on two main strands of work that I pursue in parallel.

3.1   Literature Review

I am conducting an in-depth literature review on two key topics: (a) transfer of learning, and (b) AI education. For the latter, I am carrying out an umbrella review to synthesize existing evidence on how AI is currently being taught. In addition, I have submitted a paper to the OCCE conference in Rabat, in which Louis Bourgaux (PhD student working on computational thinking learning transfer) and I discuss potentially effective strategies to foster transfer in the context of AI education.

3.2   Development of Teacher Training and Educational Resources

At the same time, I am coordinating the creation of a training program for teachers alongside the development of ready-to-use resources for teaching AI in secondary schools. The consortium involved in this work has been established and bring together around 40 members, primarily teachers from wide range of general disciplines, covering all levels of secondary education. The purpose of this group is to collaboratively design teaching materials that integrate AI education coherently within existing subjects. So far, we have held three meetings, during which we established:

- The organizational structure of the group, which operates democratically
- The resources' intellectual property, which are being released under a CC-BY-NC-SA license
- The format and structure of resources
- The key concepts and topics that should be taught about AI

The next step will be the development of the pedagogical resources themselves. These materials are expected to be finalized by the end of 2025 and will then be used for experimental purposes, in the beginning of 2026.

3.3   Participation in Events

Given the societal urgency of my research, active engagement in academic and professional events has been essential from the outset of my PhD. Being present at these events allows me not only to maximize the visibility and practical relevance of my work, but also to stay aligned with ongoing discussions in the field. Here is a list of events that I have attended:

- Final conference of the AI4T project, Luxembourg (attended as a spectator; also animated workshops)
- Compar:IA conference, Paris (attended as a spectator)
- Numérigirls, Perpignan (animated workshops; participated to a round table)
- RED25 AI and distance learning, Montpellier (attended as a spectator)
- PedagoN'UM AI and evaluation, Montpellier (attended as a spectator)
- Summer university of Inspé, Rennes (delivered an oral presentation and animated workshops)
- Ludovia, Ax-les-Thermes (attended as a spectator; also animated workshops)
- Inclusive-IA, Liège (oral presentation)
- OCCE conference, Rabat (oral presentation)

4 Expected Outcomes

Education systems are moving towards integrating AI learning into school curricula. This thesis has practical implications, particularly in developing a teacher training program on AI. This program will support the early inclusion of AI education in secondary education. Additionally, the thesis will clarify the extent to which an interdisciplinary and contextualized approach is suitable for AI education. More broadly, this research will contribute to knowledge on learning transfer and generalization processes, offering insights relevant not only to AI education but also to educational strategies across various disciplines, vocational training, and lifelong learning. By examining the cognitive mechanisms underlying transfer, this work will also help situate these processes within broader learning theories such as Cognitive Load Theory.

Furthermore, this PhD project will support the partner company, Vittascience, enabling it to offer scientifically validated educational tools and methodologies to its clients and partners.

References

1. de la Higuera, C.: A report about education, training teachers and learning artificial intelligence: overview of key issues (2019)
2. Miao, F., Holmes, W., Ronghuai, H., Hui, Z.: IA et education: guide pour les décideurs politiques. Unesco Education Sector (2021)
3. Miao, F., Holmes: Orientation pour l'intelligence artificielle générative dans l'éducation et la recherche. Unesco Education Sector (2024)
4. Zhai, X., et al.: A review of artificial intelligence (AI) in education from 2010 to 2020. Complexity **2021**, e8812542 (2021). https://doi.org/10.1155/2021/8812542
5. Alexandre, F., et al.: Why, what and how to help each citizen to understand artificial intelligence? Künstl. Intell. **35**, 191–199 (2021). https://doi.org/10.1007/s13218-021-00725-7
6. Unesco: Beijing Consensus on artificial intelligence and education. Unesco Education Sector (2019)
7. Dai, Y., Chai, C.-S., Lin, P.-Y., Jong, M.S.-Y., Guo, Y., Qin, J.: Promoting students' well-being by developing their readiness for the artificial intelligence age. Sustainability **12**, 6597 (2020)
8. Knox, J.: Artificial intelligence and education in China. Learn. Media Technol. **45**, 298–311 (2020). https://doi.org/10.1080/17439884.2020.1754236
9. Unesco: K-12 AI curricula: A mapping of government-endorsed AI curricula (2022)

10. Miao, F., Cukurova, M.: AI competency framework for teachers. Unesco (2024)
11. Miao, F., Shiohira, K.: AI competency framework for students. Unesco (2024)
12. Tricot, A., Sweller, J.: Domain-specific knowledge and why teaching generic skills does not work. Educ. Psychol. Rev. **26**, 265–283 (2014). https://doi.org/10.1007/s10648-013-9243-1
13. Eguchi, A., Okada, H., Muto, Y.: Contextualizing AI education for K-12 students to enhance their learning of AI literacy through culturally responsive approaches. Künstl. Intell. **35**, 153–161 (2021). https://doi.org/10.1007/s13218-021-00737-3
14. Gómez, R.L.: Variability and detection of invariant structure. Psychol. Sci. **13**, 431–436 (2002). https://doi.org/10.1111/1467-9280.00476
15. Raviv, L., Lupyan, G., Green, S.C.: How variability shapes learning and generalization. Trends Cogn. Sci. **26**, 462–483 (2022). https://doi.org/10.1016/j.tics.2022.03.007
16. Lattuca, L., Voigt, L., Fath, K.: Does interdisciplinarity promote learning? Theoretical support and researchable questions. Rev. High. Educ. **28**, 23–48 (2004). https://doi.org/10.1353/rhe.2004.0028

Author Index

A. Dipace et al. (Eds.): WAILS 2025, LNCS 16438, pp. 255–256, 2026.
https://doi.org/10.1007/978-3-032-17604-2

GPSR Compliance
The European Union's (EU) General Product Safety Regulation (GPSR) is a set
of rules that requires consumer products to be safe and our obligations to
ensure this.

If you have any concerns about our products, you can contact us on

ProductSafety@springernature.com

In case Publisher is established outside the EU, the EU authorized
representative is:

Springer Nature Customer Service Center GmbH
Europaplatz 3
69115 Heidelberg, Germany